1984
GUN DIGEST
HUNTING ANNUAL

**EDITED BY
ROBERT S. L. ANDERSON**

DBI BOOKS, INC., NORTHFIELD, ILL.

ABOUT OUR COVERS

It is one thing to simply say a firearm is "well designed." It's quite another to state that a particular firearm shows touches of genius. The latter example is, I'm sure, indicative of the product that graces the front and back covers of this, the First Edition of the Gun Digest Hunting Annual. *The product we are talking about is the new Ruger 22 Rimfire Bolt-Action rifle.*

This rifle is unique in that it outwardly encompasses Model 77 styling, while internally possessing features found in other Ruger products, i.e., the 10-shot, 10/22 rotary magazine and the unique hex-screw barrel/action mating system, also found in the 10/22. (More detailed information on the new Ruger rimfire can be found in the **New Products '84** *section of this book.) Engineering aside, this new Ruger offering will become a classic based on the aesthetics alone. It's that good.*

Our inside front cover features products from the "Good Old Boys" at Outers. You'll find Outers' new, portable target holder. It's well designed, and, well made—perfect for the hunting camp. Also seen is a traditional Outers Cleaning Kit (available in all popular calibers/gauges), that contains oil, rod, patches, solvent—everything you need to get the job done easily.

Near that cleaning kit you'll see Outers new portable, collapsible rifle cleaning rod that's available in popular calibers. This unit, called the Field Pocket Pack, is ideally suited to the hunter who has to travel light.

Our inside back cover features the latest offering from RCBS—the Reloader Special II reloading press. The new RS II is light, yet possesses great strength via the offset O-frame design. It will handle all popular handgun and rifle calibers. (See our **Loads and Reloads '84** *section for more info.) Also new on the inside back cover is a set of RCBS loading dies, CCI primers, and Speer's Grand Slam hunting bullets that are designed for optimum performance on big game.*

GUN DIGEST HUNTING ANNUAL STAFF

EDITOR
Robert S. L. Anderson
ASSISTANT TO THE EDITOR
Lilo Anderson
SENIOR STAFF EDITOR
Harold A. Murtz
CONTRIBUTING EDITOR
Edward A. Matunas
PRODUCTION MANAGER
Pamela J. Johnson
COVER PHOTOGRAPHY
John Hanusin
GRAPHIC DESIGNS
Mary MacDonald
PUBLISHER
Sheldon L. Factor

DBI BOOKS INC.

PRESIDENT
Charles T. Hartigan
VICE PRESIDENT & PUBLISHER
Sheldon L. Factor
VICE PRESIDENT — SALES
John G. Strauss
TREASURER
Frank R. Serpone

ISBN 0-910676-68-2   ISSN 0739-4403

Charles Stanhope Adams, Jr.
1940 — 1983

This, the First Edition of the GUN DIGEST HUNTING ANNUAL, is dedicated to Charles S. Adams, Jr., a man who lived his hunting life to the fullest. Charlie was, to all who knew him, a man who put his love of guns, and his friends, above all else. You could not ask more.

CONTENTS

CONTENTS

With years of experience to draw from, Jack Lott pulls no punches in relating the dangers and realities of hunting . . .

Africa's Dangerous Big Five

by JACK LOTT

AFRICA is the archtypical habitat of dangerous game, despite India's start as the classic jungle hunting ground of tigers, gaur, water buffalo, elephant, leopard and rhino. Now, India's once great big game hunting is a glorious epic era of the colonial and early post-colonial past, and rarely discussed or written about other than by elderly veterans. Despite Kenya's closure of hunting, ditto for Zaire, Uganda's horrors, continuing violence in Zimbabwe, Chad, and unfriendly dictatorships in Angola, Mozambique and Ethiopia, Africa's wilds remain comparitively vast and under-populated. South Africa, South West (Namibia), Botswana, Tanzania, the Sudan, Central African Republic and Zambia remain fine safari areas, thanks to political stability, conservation and game control.

A prime appeal of African safaris is the spice of danger — vicarious or actual. Few sportsmen choose an African safari, however, hoping to be charged and savaged by a lion's claws and jaws, trampled or gored by buffalo, spitted by a rhino's horn or an elephant's tusk.

Let us define the term "dangerous game" in the context of Africa. A dangerous species is anatomically and instinctively equipped for inflicting death or injury on humans. Individual African antelope have all killed and injured hunters, especially sable, roan, oryx, water buck and wildebeeste, but none are *dangerous species*. But when such an individual of a non-dangerous species actually wounds or kills somebody, that *individual* animal is truly dangerous, as opposed to a member of a dangerous species which, even when wounded, avoids confrontation. Visiting hunters normally have little to fear from dangerous African species when guided by a professional hunter armed with a powerful rifle. In most cases the client will hunt antelope, zebra or wart hog before dangerous game is tackled, to provide preliminary practice while securing non-dangerous trophies. This also gives the guide an opportunity to assess the client's shooting ability, temperament and fitness.

Some guides encourage their clients to use their heavy rifles on non-dangerous game at close range to gain proficiency with that seldom-fired rifle. Some hunters use "solids" (Full Jacketed) for all game, but usually they are men who have had bad experiences with poorly constructed soft-nosed bullets. Solids are designed for pachyderms (thick-skinned game) such as elephant, buffalo and rhino. With such superb "super bullets" available as the Nosler Partition and Bitterroots, there is no reason to use solids for thin-skinned game. On rib cage shots delivered broadside, solids frequently exit and wound adjacent animals unknowingly. This risk was tragically illustrated in 1971 when Kenya professional Douglas Collins shot a buffalo which charged and gored him, the solid exiting and killing his brother. Collins was, however, blameless since he was under attack and didn't know his brother was opposite the line of fire.

Few hunters seek mortal combat with dangerous game, but some seek the razor's edge of thrills produced by the knowledge that the lion, leopard, buffalo, elephant or rhino they hunt is capable of making a trophy out of them. It is the guide's job to insure that such a contretemps does not occur, especially by preventing or avoiding charges. An injured or dead client is not only the worst that can happen — and it does happen — it can cost an otherwise good hunter's license and career. The sight of a dangerous beast charging resolutely down on us is certainly exciting, especially when a cool-shooting professional with a powerful "stopper" stands beside us. Every professional hunter knows that once a charge starts, he can lose control of the situation with no time left to prevent it from ending on the beast's terms! This is every professional hunter's nightmare — the escalation of horror when the odds of one-in-10,000 are reversed and 500 grains of bullet and 5,000 pounds of muzzle energy are useless once the lion's jaws get past the front sight!

The Razor's Edge
Case No. 1

Here's the case of one young American who had saved for years in order to realize his childhood dream of a safari in Africa. He had read the better books on African hunting, exploration and natural history, from Selous, Baker to Roosevelt and Martin Johnson, but neither books nor motion pictures could slake his thirst "to drink Africa's waters." Long a shooter and collector of rifles, upon reaching his 30s he had finally acquired enough income to make an African safari, but not a "champagne safari" with a posh Nairobi outfitter.

For the hunter who could put up with rough camps and the Spartan shoestring outfits of a pioneer professional hunter instead of a guide, Mozambique in 1959 was unique in East Africa — a land where Portuguese disinterest in "progress" had left the hinterland in an 18th century time frame. Correspondence with a Portuguese agent in the port city of Beira led to a decision to ship a crate of camping gear, ammo, field gunsmithing tools, and all other necessities to the agent. He would set aside 3 months for ample time to learn the ropes of African hunting from professional teachers.

After an Air France flight to Eu-

This black rhino is in full charge, having been shot just behind the right shoulder (note the patch of blood). While the black rhino is the least intelligent of Africa's "Big Five," it is the quickest to charge.

The great white hunter Leonard E. Vaughan with a huge buffalo-killing lion he took in Zambia. The measure of such a lion's power and lethality is, here, dramatically illustrated by its ability to quickly dispatch the formidable Cape buffalo, the toughest African species to kill.

Lions at rest are deceptively peaceful, but when wounded or pushed out of cover, this demeanor can change, instantly turning a lion into a diabolical and deadly killing machine. More than any other African animal, the lion combines great strength with superior weaponry and speed, making him the most dangerous of the "Big Five."

rope, then a BOAC flight to Salisbury, Rhodesia, he arrived on a rickety Portuguese DETA DC-3 in Beira, Mozambique. After clearing customs it was a short taxi ride to the "agencia" where the genial agent verified that the pre-shipped kit was in his warehouse. Standing nearby was an un-Portuguese looking stocky red-faced man with piercing blue eyes, wearing a faded bush jacket and shorts from which protruded a pair of muscular legs, a pipe clamped in bulldog jaws. The look of him registered with total imagery as type-casting for a white hunter. The agent introduced the man as Wally Johnson — the very man who the American had been told, in Salisbury, was Mozambique's top professional hunter. Wally relaxed his death grip on the pipe long enough to say, "I heard you were coming, but I expected you 3 days ago. I can spare you a few weeks before I take out a

party from South Africa." The American accepted on the spot, elated at the sudden opportunity.

After a day in Beira securing licenses and supplies, they headed for Wally's mountainside farm near Vila de Manica on the Rhodesian border. After purchasing more supplies and loading up a big Chevrolet surplus Army truck, the American, Wally, his cook "Ticky" and his personal tracker and second hunter Luis, a Shangaan tribesman, climbed aboard the truck and headed north for the Pungwe river and the Makossa District. Wally sought zebra skins and meat and Lichtenstein's hartebeeste meat for *biltong* (jerky). Barue tribesmen along the Pungwe begged Wally to shoot some hippo which were devastating their vegetable gardens nightly, and the American obliged by braining a hippo with his 458. Later, in Makossa they hit the elephant

trail, but despite abundant spoor *N'zo* proved elusive.

After filling the lorry with meat, the group left Makossa and returned to the farm where the meat was cut into strips for drying into *biltong*. Supplies were replenished and once more the lorry headed into the wild bushveld, this time south. After a long ride through primeval forest the Revui river was reached and forded at a drift (crossing) where a camp was made on a bluff on the south bank. Along the river grew dense jungle — perfect cover for the Cape buffalo bulls which frequented the area. There they could find green grass throughout the dry season, while native mealies (corn) and sugar cane and other crops could be raided at night. A pair of local Shangaan trackers were engaged who knew the area intimately.

Next morning at 5:00 AM, Wally

and the American arose, grabbed a quick breakfast of bacon, eggs, toast and jam, a fast cup of coffee, then set off with the Shangaans downstream along a native footpath. Around 6:30 AM, fresh buffalo spoor was crossed where three bulls had drunk a few minutes before then headed into the jungle. The American checked his 458. It was fully loaded with a soft-nose in the chamber, then a solid, a soft, and a solid. Wally carried the Yank's 375 Holland-Mauser loaded with 300-grain Kynoch steel jacketed solids and Westley Richards capped bullets. The jungle was wet with dew as the little party threaded its way through the cover, and the cloven spoor was sharp in the soft soil. Tick birds heralded the presence of the buffalo who were on the alert for anything approaching along their backspoor. Soon three *inyati* (buffalo) bulls burst into view at 30 yards in a small clearing — all staring with contempt at the intruders. The American threw up the 458 and aimed at the lead bull's throat. He double-checked the sights — they were on — but this reassurance used up all the time the buffalo could spare.

The Winchester roared, but in the slight delay from the second check of the sights to the brain's decision to fire plus reaction time to the trigger finger, was enough for the buff to turn left as the striker fell. The buffalo

dashed off together, but the American fired a second shot at the bull's shoulder before all disappeared in thick bush. The lead bull didn't flinch at either shot and Wally called both shots misses, but the American was an experienced shot and called both shots as solid hits. Rushing ahead on the spoor, the trackers found where the bull had separated from his companions. One Shangaan working ahead, returned silently with a big leaf, holding it up to display a big red drop of blood — wounded buffalo! Wally's blue eyes were grim as he whispered "We'll just have to go in and get him!" The blood spoor twisted and turned as the buff sought a place of ambush, and soon the right front hoof's spoor revealed a drag mark indicating a solid bone hit. Soon more blood appeared and spooring was easier. At times Wally signaled a pause to listen for telltale rustling and the cry of the tick birds. After more stop and go spooring, Wally and the Shangaans froze into an alert. "He's near — moving to the right!"; Wally told the American to stay on the spoor and to shoot if the buff came, then disappeared into the jungle.

All fell silent, the American with his 458 ready, safety off, the trackers beside him listening. In seconds, the nearest Shangaan tugged at the American's sleeve, gestured with his head at the left rear then both track-

ers vanished into a thicket. Now alone, the American turned to the left as the buffalo burst through the bush with a maddened roar, head lowered, exposing the massive central horn boss, driving into the hunter, knocking the rifle aside, tossing him up and into a tree! As he fell upside down, his right hand skidded off the buff's upraised nose which was covered with blood-flecked foam. The hunter arose and tried to dodge behind a tree, but the buff was too quick, and he was tossed again, this time slamming his right ribs with a "crack" against a tree.

Unable to rise before being caught by the horns the American rolled erratically on the sandy ground as the *inyati* worked to hook and trample him. Somehow he managed to roll into a shallow dry stream bed, avoiding the horns and hooves, thanks mainly to the buff's right leg lameness. For an instant which seemed hours, the Yank crouched on all fours as the buff loomed black and monstrous at 10 yards. The suspended action was shattered by four rapid shots from an invisible shooter — a pause — then three more. The buff moved out of view, then Wally rushed to the Yank's side and urgently gasped "Where's your four-five-eight?" The dazed hunter stood up unsteadily as it dawned on him that it was Wally who had fired. "Isn't the buff dead?" the

This hunter, a professional, examines the ivory of this average size bull. Such tusks would weigh between 65 and 75 pounds. Note the broken tip of the left tusk.

The author took this big Rhodesian buffalo bull with his 577 H&H double-hammer rifle using 750-grain solids. Nothing the hunter can fire with adequate placement is too big in caliber when it comes to killing a buffalo.

American gasped. "Hell no — he's over there (gesturing), and he'll charge again!" The American un-buckled his cartridge belt handing it to Wally. Wally left the empty 375 with the American and then un-armed, disappeared again. After a seemingly long pause came two roars from the Winchester — then an envel-oping silence of death!

Wally and the two Shangaans rushed to the hunter who was upright but unsteady. The Shangaans felt un-der his bush jacket for protruding en-trails but miraculously there were none. Wally could only sputter, "Man, I thought you were buggered!" They ex-amined the buffalo, who even in death was formidable — 11 bullet holes — four from the 458 and seven from the 375 bore stark witness to his fighting last stand! The American forgot his painful injuries as this registered and awe and admiration flooded in. The su-premely brave *inyati* had not dropped until shot number 11 tore through his brain at three paces! Photos were tak-en, then the hunter sat down at the base of a tree accompanied by one Shangaan while Wally and the second tracker fetched the lorry.

The American had suffered broken ribs, many cuts, scratches and contu-sions, including a bad rupture of the left thigh fascia (muscle sheath), but

the worst was an injured right eye. A rapid journey to Wally's farm was made where his wife Lilly, a German ex-nurse applied medicines and seda-tives, but the American was so wound up that he paced the floor and talked all night in a delayed hyper-reaction. The next morning he was driven across the Rhodesian border to the farm of Wally's daughter Erika, then to Umtali Hospital where his infected right eye was treated by Dr. Sy Cor-ner, a semi-retired London opthalmo-logist. Dr. Corner, despite his 80 plus years, skillfully revealed a corneal scar and stopped the spreading infec-tion. He was the only opthalmologist within hundreds of miles!

The American had been lucky — first to survive the tossing and pound-ing of the enraged buffalo and then to have had his eye treated in time to save it. After 2 weeks of treatment and rest he returned to Wally for more hunting, then Wally introduced him to Willi Rehder, a German Farm-er-hunter in Mozambique who took him to his favorite water holes for more hunting. Hunting with a heavy limp and taped up ribs wasn't easy go-ing, but it was sweet to survive and return to the bush. The American felt wiser and stronger for the encounter, ready for the next round but deter-mined not to delay his aim again but

to fire just as the sights and aiming point line up.

I can vouch for the authenticity of this story, for the American was me and I still carry the scars of that great fight in the Mozambique bush.

My experience with Cape buffalo isn't typical, but such incidents can and do happen. A client injury or fa-tality is unlikely to happen when one is accompanied by a guide armed with a powerful "stopper." But my experi-ence does prove that the unpredict-able can occur. The professional is more apt to be the victim of a danger-ous animal than is the client. Wally Johnson himself was charged by a buffalo in 1969 while guiding my friend Jerry Knight, retail manager of the Pachmayr Gun Works. The wounded buff charged Wally from a few paces, and despite the 300-grain solids from Wally's 375, the buff knocked the Winchester from his hands, breaking the stock at the grip and injuring his hand. Then Wally was pinned to the ground by the buff's horns and one horn drove through Wally's thigh, missing the femoral ar-tery by a fraction of an inch! As the buff worked Wally over, Jerry killed the buff with his 458. Ironically, Wal-ly was using his old pre-war 375 Mod-el 70, but had left the 458 Winchester I had built for him on a 264 Model 70 action, in camp. Jerry himself used an especially fine Winchester 458 which I had sold him.

How do I rate Cape buffalo within the "big five" in order of dangerousness? To be objective, I rate them third, after lion and elephant. The psychological risk faced after such an experience as I had is that one can develop a paralyzing fear of the species involved. This can persist and become a permanent trauma with effects going beyond the subject of hunting. This fear of fear when facing buffalo grew more ominous in the near aftermath of the events of the morning of September 18, 1959. I resolved to return to the bushveld as soon as possible. After a few weeks of hunting with Willi Rehder and his fellow German farmer-hunter, Hein Arndt, they placed me in a wilderness area with a cook and two trackers. There, with no vehicle, we hunted on foot in the 19th century style. I did this for a month, the Germans coming each Saturday with groceries and beer, to pick up the fresh meat and biltong I provided. Both needed meat for their native labor and were busy managing the planting of crops on their farms, giving me the no-cost chance to live off of my rifles, thereby learning how to hunt unguided and to track. I make no claim to being a top tracker, but such an experience has made me a better hunter and has saved me from much unpleasantness. This primitive interlude over, I returned to Moribane with Wally and Luis for more hunting from a water hole camp where hundreds of buffalo, elephant and antelope drank nightly.

Cape buffalo can take more lead than any other African species, and nothing one can carry and shoot accurately is too powerful. Consensus is that steel-jacketed solids are the correct bullets for buff, to break down their heavy bones and reach their vitals from any angle. Expanding bullets should only be used on buff for heart and lung shots. Once wounded, buff are vindictive, but unwounded are simply placid bovines. Sometimes individual buffalo develop a hatred of man, usually after recovering from a native poacher's muzzle-loader, snare, spear or arrow wounds. Such rogues are endemic in thick riverine bush near native villages and farms. They often charge on sighting man, usually meaning that they can see you, but you only see them when they are charging. Buff don't charge en masse, such "charges" being stampedes when a herd winds a hunter who happens to be upwind and buff,

like most game, escape upwind. Famous is the buffalo's tactic of circling to one side of his spoor to await the hunter. When the hunter is adjacent to the buff's hide or just past, a charge is launched. Unwounded, the slightest human scent will send a herd off rapidly, but let one poorly placed bullet be received and the phlegmatic bovine is transformed into a single-minded diabolical fury. A buff charges with coughing grunts and sometimes a series of roars as did mine. I believe, as happened to me, that a wounded buff will often ignore others of a hunting party to attack whoever fired and wounded it — an aspect of simple justice which further enobles these beasts.

A consensus exists among African hunters that the lion is the most dangerous species based on sheer numbers of victims. This leaves out man-eaters and includes victims engaged in hunting lion or companions, trackers, etc. Elephant easily take second place, based on the same numbers of hunters killed. Add those killed by rogues, cows with calves, etc., and ele-

phant score high in producing carnage. Buffalo come third, based on hunters killed by buffalo they were hunting, but again, the score for buff zooms when the toll of rogues and poacher-wounded buff is tallied.

Rhinoceros are the least intelligent of dangerous game, but their unstable truculence makes black rhino the species most likely to charge with little or no provocation. Rhino are also the easiest charging game to turn with a frontally placed heavy bullet. Fortunately the number of hunters and others killed or injured by rhino is small, and few professionals rate rhino above the bottom rung. Leopard rate high in courage and quickness to charge when wounded, but with today's antibiotics, the former casualties from infection mainly, are rare among sportsmen and guides. Then of course, leopard have been killed in unarmed combat by men such as Carl Akeley and Charles Cottar, but such a thing is almost impossible with a much larger lion. However, many native women and children fall victim to man eaters, especially in areas with

The author's biggest buffalo was taken on his first Mozambique safari when he was tossed and injured by another buffalo that took eleven shots to bring down. The author is carrying his Holland-Mauser 375 Magnum while Luis, left, a Shangaan hunter, carries the author's 458 Winchester.

a decided paucity of game.

Hippopotami are a truly dangerous species, but are left out of the big five. In my view, hippo should be included in a "big six" based on their score of victims and their willingness to charge small boats or a man who comes between them and water. Based on sheer numbers of humans killed, it is the crocodile which takes the palm. It is an axiom that any croc from 9 to 10 feet to a maximum of 15 to 18 feet invariably has bracelets and bangles in its stomach from women who were taken while drawing water or bathing. Few croc hunters however, have fallen victims to their quarry. Crocodile are not regarded as a game species and in any case are protected in most of their range.

In what ways are the various "big five" members dangerous? What are the most common form of incidents and how to avoid them? It must be remembered that it isn't a *potentially* dangerous animal which inflicts death or injury, but a specific *individual*. A wounded wildebeeste which disembowels a hunter is truly dangerous, but a wounded lion which refuses fight and hides no matter how hard it is hunted is not dangerous. Animals, like humans, have group characteristics, but each are individuals, some quicker tempered than others. Herd species like buffalo or elephant became self-reliant when driven out of the herd or wounded. Once wounded and adrenalized the once placid herd member becomes more or less "paranoid" to use a favorite "psychobabble" term.

The lion isn't hard to kill, being thin-skinned and weighing from 400 to 500 pounds with relatively light bones but with massive shoulder and chest muscles. A rifle suited to larger antelope such as a 338 or 375 Magnum is ample for unwounded lion, but once wounded, a lion is apt to charge when it realizes it cannot escape. When it charges, it is in low bounds and speeds up to 50 miles per hour — or 50 yards in a bit over 2 seconds! This makes it difficult for a standing man to center the chest since the angle increases the closer it gets, often the lion running under the shot. For those who enjoy this sort of thing, the surest way to a stop a charging lion is with a 450 and up elephant rifle and soft-nosed bullets weighing a minimal 500 grains, while sitting, so the shot is delivered parallel to the ground! The massive and formidable Cape buffalo is a favorite prey of lion, and it is easy to see why the lion takes first place in the "big five".

The Razor's Edge Case No. 2

Despite a lion's potential for inflicting injury or death, it is rare for a sportsman to be injured or killed by a lion. However, there are certainly exceptions.

One such exception was the late Joe Shaw, an engineer from San Francisco who went to Angola in 1963 to secure a trophy lion. His white hunter was Cornelis Prinsloo, an Afrikaner whose grandparents were among the trekboers who trekked from South Africa to Angola in 1880. The late Jack O'Connor preceeded Shaw and was leaving when Shaw arrived. Shaw asked Jack about the lion hunting of the Mucusso area, and Jack told him it was the best and that both he and his wife Eleanor had secured full-maned trophy lions.

Prinsloo had a zebra hung from a tree for bait, and next morning he and Shaw left camp in a Land Rover to check the bait. The country is semi-desert and on the way they crossed fresh lion spoor but Prinsloo suggested they check the bait, and if no lion was on it, they would return and follow the spoor. No lion were on the bait so they returned to the spoor and followed it up — an easy job on sandy soil.

Near midday they came upon the lion where it was lying up in a patch of thornbush. Seeing the approaching humans, the lion slipped away by crossing an open area to a second thicket. It soon was located and again driven out and to another thicket. The lion was beginning to growl, and Prinsloo warned Shaw that the lion was tiring of the game and would charge if given an opportunity, suggesting that the thicket be fired and for Shaw to shoot the lion as it ran out. Shaw accused Prinsloo of being over-cautious and, ignoring his guide's advice, approached the thicket with his 300 Weatherby rifle. With a roar the lion charged out and reared up to pull Shaw down and under him as it worked with its teeth and claws. It was over in seconds, the lion dying of buckshot charges from a Browning 12. Shaw's right arm was torn from its socket and hung down held by the muscles stripped off by the lion's paw blow. Despite first aid and the best care he could be given in camp, Shaw died within hours.

Shaw's tragedy was more the result of his own headstrong-impatience with his white hunter's correct caution, than a result of the lion's purely defensive counter-attack.

The Razor's Edge Case No. 3

Typical of lion hunting incidents involving death or injury to the hunter is the case of Lt.-Commander A.B. Combe, Royal Navy, retired, a Rhodesian farmer who one pre-war July was hunting on the edge of the vast Okavango swamp, Bechuanaland. Combe stalked up to a zebra bait and found an entire pride of lions on it. He killed a fine male and the rest except a female made off — it approaching Combe in an ugly mood so he killed it. The largest of the group looked back after going 50 yards and Combe fired with his 7mm Mauser, but the lion ran into cover. Combe decided to let it stiffen up and meanwhile recover his first lion. After taking up the second lion's spoor and following a faint blood spoor for half an hour, Combe noted thick reeds where he guessed the lion had hidden. He told his tracker and gunbearers it was probably hopeless and that they should return to camp. At that precise moment the lion charged with a roar from 25 yards. Combe fired his 7mm Mauser, but there was no time for a second shot before the lion was upon him.

Combe jammed the empty rifle in the lion's mouth but the lion knocked it aside and pulled Combe down as he cried out for his gunbearer to shoot the lion, but the bearer had run off with Combe's 450 double and another with his shotgun. Meanwhile the lion worked on Combe's left knee and shin bone. He then thrust his right leg into the lion's face and the lion grabbed it. Combe tried to put his fingers into the lion's eyes but the looseness of the skin and the violent movements made this ineffective. Combe then got hold of the tongue, but it was too slippery.

When all seemed hopeless and as he was losing his strength, Combe heard the voice of his farmboy Chimoyra behind him, and there he was with Combe's 450 double. He had chased the panicked gunbearer, retrieved the rifle and returned to save his master — but he had never fired a rifle! As the lion chewed him, Combe instructed the boy how to disengage the safety and fire the rifle, fearful that the boy would shoot him instead of the lion! The 450 roared and the lion rolled over dead from a shoulder shot! Having only cotton and bandages with him, Combe had the natives bandage him and carry him back to camp on an improvised stretcher. At camp, Combe removed the bandages, washed his wounds and poured iodine into the fang punctures then injected anti-tetanus serum.

The original stretcher didn't last long so Combe directed the boys to make a strong one from woven reeds. After 3 days and nights of travel through the savage wilderness on stretcher, Combe and his men arrived at the dirt track from Maun to Victoria Falls, Rhodesia. Once a week there was a lorry service between

At the hospital, Dr. Harmer amputated Combe's left leg at the knee. His badly mangled right hand and leg were saved. Thanks to fine treatment and nursing, Combe was able to return to his farm in 3½ months. Three weeks later he sailed for England where he was fitted by the doctors for an artificial leg. In his own words: "Personally, I defy superstition, but for those who are superstitious it might be interesting to record the fact

tary, Sir Edward Grey, was killed by a Kenya lion in 1911 while using a 280 Ross. Though hit in the chest and mouth at 15, then 5 yards, the lion's charge was not stopped by the disintegrating 145-grain copper capped bullets. Another Kenya tragedy occurred when a game warden named Goldfinch and a farmer named Lucas were "galloping" lions, a dangerous sport of chasing a lion on horseback until it turns and charges. The hunter then

This big Kenya leopard, from around Mt. Kenya, weighed around 150 lbs. Size is no indication of the great strength of these great predators. Such a leopard can easily place an antelope (weighing more than twice its weight) in the branches of a tree. While rated No. 5 by the author, the leopard should never be underestimated.

Maun and Victoria Falls where it was a short crossing of the Zambesi bridge to the Livingstone Hospital. One native said the lorry had already passed but the other said it had not. Fortunately, the two lorries passed within 2 hours on the way to Maun — opposite the direction to Livingstone. One lorry rushed to summon a doctor, and 20 miles outside Maun, Dr. Gerber applied first aid and with a missionary, drove Combe to Livingstone over 270 miles non-stop through rough terrain.

that the lion was my thirteenth!"

In honor of Chimoyra's courage and initiative, Combe renamed his farm "Chimoyra Farm." Combe learned to walk almost perfectly with his artifical leg, even continuing his annual elephant hunting. He was a Member of Parliament in Rhodesia from Matabeleland for many years and a leader in conservation and hunting organizations.

Captain George Grey, brother of Britain's World War I Foreign Secre-

dismounts and tries to stop the charge. Before he could dismount, the lion pulled Goldfinch off his pony, then Lucas dismounted, but before he could shoot, the lion dropped Goldfinch and seized Lucas. Though painfully injured, Goldfinch killed the lion with a brain shot and both men rode to Lucas' farm to dress their wounds. Lucas died a week later but Goldfinch recovered.

Fritz Schindler, an Austrian white hunter in Nairobi, was pulled from

The former Mozambique professional hunter Harry Manners took this record elephant in the 1950s with a 10.75x68 Mauser. The tusks weigh over 150 lbs. each.

This 100-plus pounder was taken in Kenya in the 1960s by an American sportsman. Kenya was, until the closure of hunting, the prime habitat for trophy ivory bulls. Today it has been replaced by the Central African Republic.

the saddle by a lion as he tried to get it to charge so American pioneer cinematographer Paul Rainey could film it. He died 2 days later. The Swiss big game hunter Bernard de Watteville was attacked by a wounded lion — his 19th, on the Rutshuru Plains. Though terribly wounded, de Watteville managed to blow out the lion's brains. Staggering back to camp, de Watteville appeared covered with blood, his clothes in shreds and his right arm, head and both legs deeply mangled.

As he neared camp his daughter heard him faintly ask for water and called out: "Is something wrong?" Something indeed was wrong, and de Watteville answered: "The lion has got me this time!" Though his daughter strove heroically to save her father, he died by the following sunset.

One of Africa's greatest white hunters, Marcel Vincent, a much decorated French war hero, was trying to shoot a lion for the cinematographer of producer Alfred Mahuzier in Chad.

Vincent had his 375 H&H Magnum rifle, but he could not stop the lion when it charged. Mahuzier drove the lion from Vincent's prostrate body then killed it, but Vincent was so badly injured he died while Mahuzier bandaged him. In 1930, Bruneau de Laborie, the Chief Game Warden of French Equatorial Africa hunted a lion which one of his natives had wounded. He found out where the lion lay in wait, but before he could shoot, the lion was upon him. It was 4 days to Ft. Archambault and another 3 days wait for transport to Bangui where an operation was performed. After three operations and an amputation de Laborie died.

African hunters with a score of from 200 to 1,000 buffalo and from 100 to 500 elephant without incurring injuries are not rare, but a hunter who has killed 25 lions without experiencing a charge or injury is a lucky man and a fine shot. The man who has killed 50 lions unsupported and without serious injury is not only lucky but also distinguished. Fortunately for today's

lions, believed that any lion truly determined to press home a charge was unlikely to be stopped by anything short of a brain shot.

Elephant

Despite the lion's merited place as the "King of Beasts" of legendry and heraldry, the elephant takes a close second place. The elephant's formidable defensive and offensive capabilities are not based solely on size and strength, since these are hardly proof against modern steel solids. Unlike buffalo, elephant can be turned or

proach in the densest cover, thanks to the construction of its feet. Elephant walk on their toes which are surrounded by a spongy mass of tissue which muffles any sounds of dry vegetation or stones.

The elephant's trunk is one of nature's most wonderful sensory organs, like an olfactory periscope which can be raised and turned in all directions. Huge ears detect the slightest sound and combine with the trunk's sensitivity to pinpoint a hunter's position in thick cover.

Elephant however, are normally

Understandably happy is the late Truman Fowler, posing with this fine collection of ivory taken just before Kenya was closed to hunting. The largest tusks weigh 98 lbs. All were taken with Fowler's 577 Lancaster "best-quality" sidelock, ejector double.

sportsmen who are backed up by a guide with a powerful rifle, lion hunting is no longer so dangerous. Deaths on safari from infection are rare today with light aircraft and antibiotics available. But the spice of hunting the "King of Beasts" remains a supreme thrill, if only because of the knowledge that what the lion has done to others he can also do to you! The late great hunter and first warden of the Kruger National Park, Col. Stevenson-Hamilton, who killed over 200

stopped by a heavy bullet in the frontal skull, and in proportion to overall size and elephant's skin is much thinner than a buffalo's.

The elephant's ability to inflict death and injury to a hunter results from a combination of size and strength with superior intelligence, matchless scenting ability and hearing. An elephant's eyesight is poor but any movement can be seen at hunting ranges. Then there is the silence with which an elephant can depart or ap-

not steady-nerved like lion or buffalo and sometimes panic and flee from the hunter, wounded or not. Cows with calves or as herd leaders are more apt to charge without provocation. Usually a "demonstration charge" is tried so as to scare off a human before the real thing is launched. Rogue males, especially those who recover from wounds, can be very quick tempered and quick to charge. When an elephant charges home, it usually draws back or "cocks" the ears and doubles the trunk under the tusks and comes with a menacing throaty growl.

Individual elephant adopt peculiar methods of killing men including pulling them over a tusk, crushing the head with a trunk or first stepping on the feet and then grabbing the hunter by the body thereby pulling off the feet. Sometimes elephant grab a man by the torso and beat him against a tree or the ground as was done to the late Captain Hurst. Sometimes they kneel on a man and grind him into the ground or sit on him and rock back and forth until he is merely a bloody paste mixed with soil!

The great professional Will Judd was killed by an elephant as he and his sons hunted in thick bush. It was to have been Judd's final go at an ivory bull before retirement. His son wounded a bull, firing both barrels, and as he dodged the charging bull, trying to reload, he tripped over a vine. Judd fired to save his son's life but was caught by the bull's trunk, slammed to the ground and his head crushed.

The Rhodesian professional and wildlife expert, Johnny Uys (pronounced "ace") was guiding some tourists when they approached a water hole to photograph elephants. I was told Uys approached the elephants and tossed a stone to make them look up and then a cow charged. He tried to turn the cow by firing through her ear but she came on and his second barrel was fired too late— the cow grabbed Uys and crushed him. Such incidents are relatively common with elephant and it is hard to know which incidents to relate.

Rhino
Rhino are the least respected of the big five by professionals, but despite their stupidity and erratic antics, the black rhino is more apt to charge unprovoked than any dangerous African animal. The death of the great Kenya white hunter, the American, Charles "Bwana" Cottar in 1940, is a stark reminder that black rhino should always be treated with respect, and that one must be prepared to stop or kill them when, as is often the case, they charge without provocation. On the other hand they are easily turned by a heavy solid placed frontally and nonvitally.

Cottar, ex-Oklahoma frontiersman who emigrated to Kenya around the turn of the century became a famous and successful guide. His heavy rifle was a 470 Rigby double but his favorite was his Winchester Model '95 in 405. He conducted lectures in the United States, illustrated by motion pictures, and in 1940 he needed a rhino charge sequence. He had recently recovered from a stroke and was out in Tanganyika's thornbush rhino country with his sons Bud and Mike. The sons had gone after a rhino and left their father beside the Dodge truck with his 405, he being too infirm to do much walking. After a few minutes the sons heard shots and returned to find their father spitted by a dead rhino's horn. The old man had killed the rhino after being unable to stop it with his 405.

The sons tenderly extricated their father from the rhino, applied a tourniquet and placed him on his bedroll under a canopy. Cottar said to remove the canopy so he could take his last look at the African sky. His femoral artery was pierced, and he had lost much blood. Thus died Charles Cottar, one of the last of a great breed of 19th century frontiersmen.

Rules of the Hunt
I have tried to describe the dangers of hunting Africa's "big five," but it may seem that I overemphasize the dangers. It is undoubtedly more fun to experience the dangers of the "big five" vicariously than first-hand, as I can confirm. But I will have failed in my primary motive if future African hunters do not receive sound advice which could save their lives. The following rules for hunting dangerous game were gleaned by me from personal experience and from "picking the brains" of many top professional hunters around many campfires:

1. Respect the offensive and defensive capabilities of all game and take no unnecessary chances.
2. Carefully sight in your rifle and do not mix loads or bullet weights. Use only one bullet weight — the heaviest — for dangerous game, and sight the rifle to print these *dead on* at 50 yards.
3. Learn the anatomy of the game hunted and always aim for a vital spot *inside* the animal, not a spot on the outside.
4. Use only "solids" (Full Steel Jacketed) bullets on pachyderms, i.e. buffalo, elephant, rhino and hippo. Use expanding bullets on lion and leopard.
5. At close range and in thick cover and for charging game use 450- and over caliber rifles providing 5,000 pounds or more muzzle energy. Use the same caliber with soft-nosed bullets or heavy loads of buckshot for wounded lion and leopard.
6. Never shoot until certain of the shot and always take the steadiest position; brace your side opposite the rifle against a tree.
7. Reload immediately after firing without moving from the spot. Do not take your eyes off the game while doing so.
8. Never take low lung shots which allow the blood to flow out. Take high lung shots which fills the lungs with blood causing rapid death.
9. On charging game avoid head shots, except on elephant. A shot at the base of the throat usually cuts the arteries leading to the brain. Attempted brain shots at buffalo, lion, leopard or rhino are apt to miss—the target is small.
10. When closing with buffalo or elephant move off the spoor before shooting.
11. Never enter cover to pursue a wounded dangerous animal without first pinpointing its exact position if at all possible. Always move upwind. Don't talk — signal.
12. Never approach any downed beast from the front or the belly. Always apply a finisher to downed dangerous game despite apparent death. This means a brain or neck shot, but on cats a heart or shoulder shot can be used to avoid damaging a trophy. Toss stones at cats to see if they are dead.
13. Do not try to outrun game— only a bullet can do that!
14. Avoid coming between females and young, or hippo and the water.
15. If seized by a lion or leopard concentrate on keeping the abdomen on the ground and give the beast the weaker arm to work on, keeping the head away from the jaws. If you have a knife and can reach it, stab the cat low and behind the forelegs. If you have a powerful revolver and metal-piercing loads try for the brain.
16. Get as close as you can and make sure of the first shot and all following shots. Don't waste critical time dawdling over aim, thereby giving the beast the time you wasted to wipe you out.
17. No automatic safeties on double rifles. Disconnect these or you could open the breech to reload as the beast charges, then close it, forgetting the safety went on automatically. In such a case you won't forget to press the trigger, but you *could* die without knowing why the trigger pull was so heavy! ●

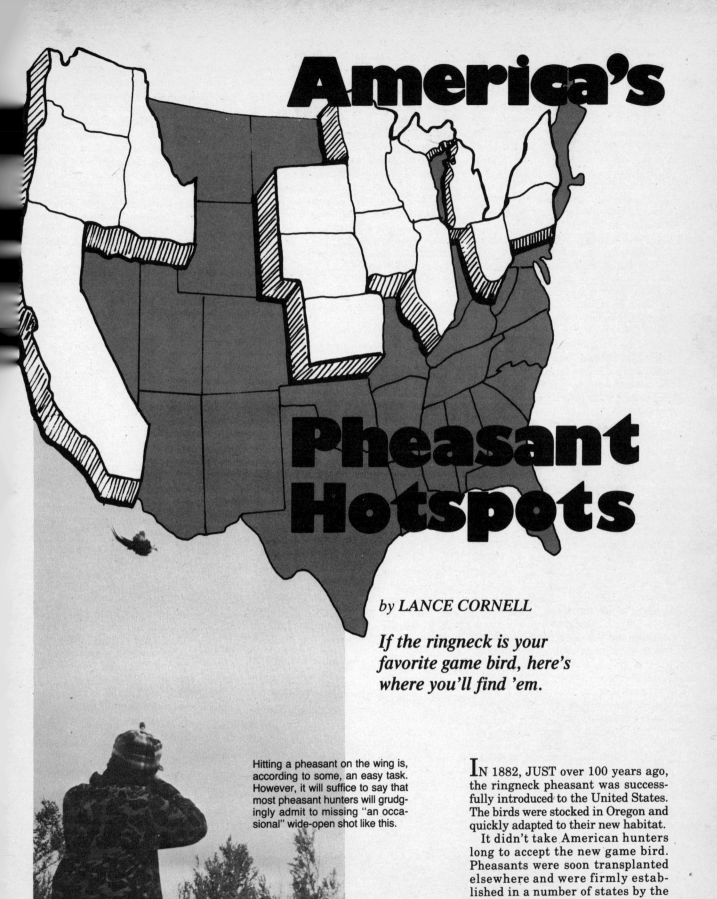

America's Pheasant Hotspots

by *LANCE CORNELL*

If the ringneck is your favorite game bird, here's where you'll find 'em.

Hitting a pheasant on the wing is, according to some, an easy task. However, it will suffice to say that most pheasant hunters will grudgingly admit to missing "an occasional" wide-open shot like this.

IN 1882, JUST over 100 years ago, the ringneck pheasant was successfully introduced to the United States. The birds were stocked in Oregon and quickly adapted to their new habitat.

It didn't take American hunters long to accept the new game bird. Pheasants were soon transplanted elsewhere and were firmly established in a number of states by the turn of the century. Just 11 years after the initial Oregon transplant, 50,000 birds were killed by hunters during the first hunting season in the

pheasants are almost entirely dependent on agricultural crops for feed. Various grains are required for survival, though birds have been known to live on weed seeds as well. Their reliance on farmers means they basically exist on private land. Hunting access is often difficult in some regions, especially near urban areas.

The best pheasant hunting in America occurs in the northern tier of the country. Efforts to stock birds in the South have been failures, though there are a few exceptions.

In marginal habitat, pheasants are often stocked on a put-and-take basis. Birds are released shortly before or during the hunting season, and hens or roosters are legal game. In good pheasant country, wild birds reproduce successfully, with roosters being fair game. Luckily, it's easy to quickly identify roosters and hens as they flush because of the color difference.

The following choice pheasant hunting areas identify the heaviest concentrations of birds in the top states. If you decide to hunt an area, be sure you've made arrangements to hunt on private land before you go, or leave early enough so you can have an extra day or two to seek permission. Don't overlook state wildlife areas or waterfowl refuges. Many have good public hunting, but competition could be keen from other hunters.

Introduced 100 years ago, the ringneck pheasant ranks first in the eyes of many upland bird shooters. A good gun, good dog, and, perhaps, one good hunting buddy is all it takes.

(Above right) In many areas where pheasant hunting is on a put-and-take basis, hens are legal fare.

(Right) One sure way to insure a full game bag is to hunt over a well-trained dog. Blessed with great running legs, wounded pheasants can cover a lot of ground, in a hurry. A good dog solves the problem.

area. Other regions echoed similar results, and pheasants were quickly on their way to becoming a top game bird in America.

It's easy to understand why pheasants are so popular. They have all the necessary qualities that endear a species to hunters. They're strong fliers; they're delicious on the table; they're gorgeous to look at; and they're big. Furthermore, they're a challenge in the field and are among the most intelligent of all our birds. Pheasants are superb hiders and sneakers; they sit unbelievably still when threatened and often flush well out of range.

Unlike many other game birds,

Northeast

This region has high pheasant hunting interest, but stocked birds are the norm in many areas due to poor habitat. However, some locations offer outstanding hunting where farmlands are extensive and birds are able to survive northern winters. New York, Pennsylvania and Ohio have good hunting. New England has marginal habitat for the most part, with most hunting on a put-and-take basis.

New York

The northwest region is by far the best in the state. Large agricultural areas are here, with good populations of self-sustaining pheasants. The top counties include Niagara, Orleans, Monroe, Wayne, Genesee, Erie, Livingston, Ontario and Seneca. Other counties rated almost as good are Yates and Wyoming. Rochester is the key city in this region, with good hunting in every direction outward.

Pennsylvania

This state offers very good pheasant hunting in several areas, with the southeast generally considered tops. The proximity to Philadelphia and surrounding urban area makes for competitive hunting, however. Key spots are the southern parts of Delaware, York, Chester and Lancaster counties. Further west, other good counties are Perry, Cumberland, Juniata, Adams, Snyder, and Franklin. In the east, try Lehigh, Bucks, and Northampton. In the northwest area near the New York and Ohio borders, Erie county is best. Pennsylvania has an excellent pheasant hunting program on state-administered game tract lands, many of which are in superb pheasant country.

Ohio

The northwest lake plain region offers the best pheasant hunting in Ohio. Toledo is the key city, with good bird populations down through Wood county. Paulding county also ranks among one of the best. In the northeast region, good hunting can be found in Mahoning county and the southern part of Trumbull county. Fayette county in the south-central area has good pheasant populations. Ohio has an abundance of state wildlife areas scattered throughout, many of them in good pheasant spots.

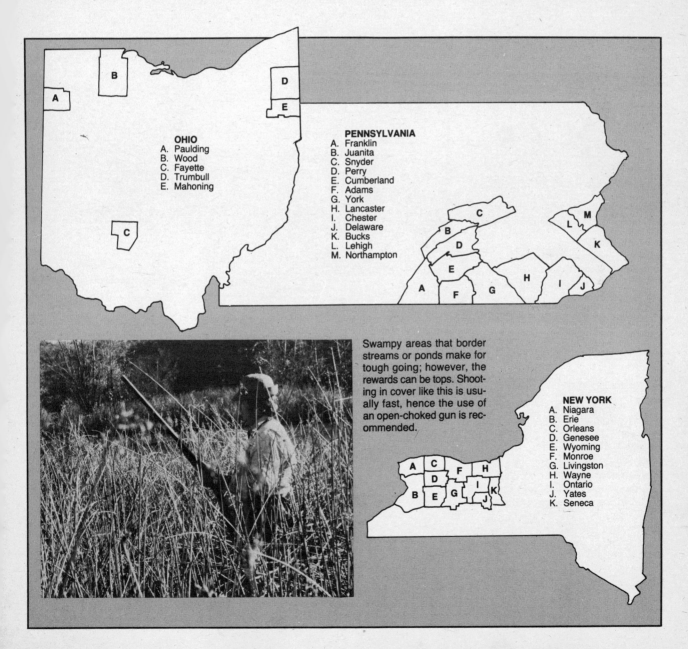

OHIO
A. Paulding
B. Wood
C. Fayette
D. Trumbull
E. Mahoning

PENNSYLVANIA
A. Franklin
B. Juanita
C. Snyder
D. Perry
E. Cumberland
F. Adams
G. York
H. Lancaster
I. Chester
J. Delaware
K. Bucks
L. Lehigh
M. Northampton

NEW YORK
A. Niagara
B. Erie
C. Orleans
D. Genesee
E. Wyoming
F. Monroe
G. Livingston
H. Wayne
I. Ontario
J. Yates
K. Seneca

Swampy areas that border streams or ponds make for tough going; however, the rewards can be tops. Shooting in cover like this is usually fast, hence the use of an open-choked gun is recommended.

Lake States

The three lake states, Michigan, Wisconsin, and Minnesota, all have good pheasant hunting, especially in the southern areas. Decreasing habitat, particularly in urban areas, has caused a reduction of birds from years past, but pheasants still are a big attraction.

Michigan

By far the best hunting is in the "Thumb" region, and the southeast area in general. Flint is generally in the center of much of the best pheasant range. Several State Game Areas (SGA) have good public hunting. One of the best is the Port Huron State Game Area. Others worth trying are the Dansville, Gourdneck, Oak Grove and the Pointe Mouille SGA's.

Wisconsin

The southern region of Wisconsin is tops for ringnecks, with a good share of the total state kill coming from that area. Good southern counties are Columbia, Crawford, Dane, Grant, Green, Iowa, Jefferson, Kenosha, Lafayette, Milwaukee, Racine, Richland, Rock, Sauk, Walworth and Waukesha. These are essentially the bottom tiers of counties bordering Illinois. Racine, Kenosha, Jefferson, and Dane are usually rated among the top counties, however, several counties in the east-central region are very good, with Manitowoc county as one of the best. Elsewhere, ringnecks are found in fair to good numbers, depending on local conditions.

Minnesota

More than half of Minnesota is considered to be good pheasant range, with top spots in the south-central, west-central, and southwest areas. Top counties in the south are Martin, Jackson, Watonwan, Cottonwood, Nicollet, and Brown. Numerous state Wildlife Management Areas are available for public hunting.

Midwest

This is considered to be the pheasant hunting capitol of the nation. Vast farmlands of various grains commonly stretch from one horizon to the other. Some fields are more than 1-mile square and are full of ringnecks during good years. Pheasant populations have declined drastically in the top states because of habitat alterations, but hunting is still outstanding in many places. Bird numbers are also locally affected by the severity of the winter. Hunting often depends on

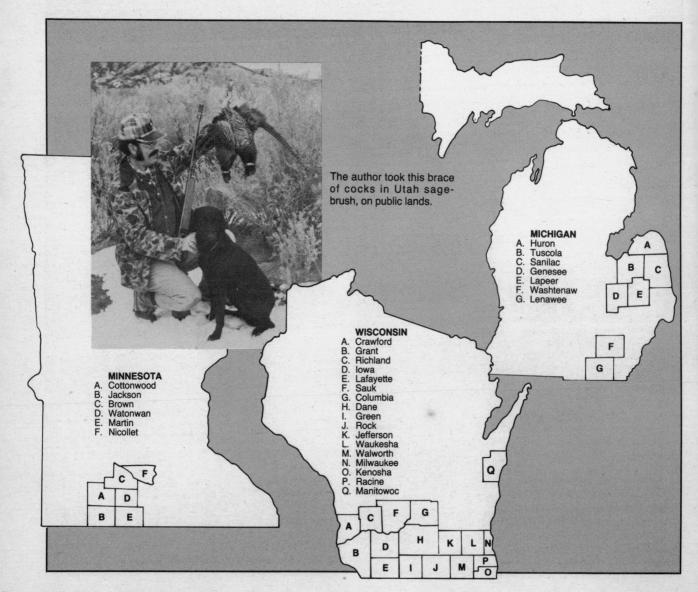

The author took this brace of cocks in Utah sagebrush, on public lands.

MICHIGAN
A. Huron
B. Tuscola
C. Sanilac
D. Genesee
E. Lapeer
F. Washtenaw
G. Lenawee

WISCONSIN
A. Crawford
B. Grant
C. Richland
D. Iowa
E. Lafayette
F. Sauk
G. Columbia
H. Dane
I. Green
J. Rock
K. Jefferson
L. Waukesha
M. Walworth
N. Milwaukee
O. Kenosha
P. Racine
Q. Manitowoc

MINNESOTA
A. Cottonwood
B. Jackson
C. Brown
D. Watonwan
E. Martin
F. Nicollet

mild winters in order to be at its very best.

South Dakota

Often thought to be the top state in the nation, South Dakota experienced a severe reduction in birds over the decades, but populations are now at excellent levels. The East River region is the top area in the state, though there are heavy concentrations of ringnecks in other places. Key cities in this area are Aberdeen, Watertown, Redfield, Brookings, Huron, Sioux Falls and Mitchell. In general terms the far eastern part of the East River region has the most birds. There is also very good hunting in the huge milo fields near Pierre, which is in the central part of the state. It's tough to hunt the prime spots in South Dakota and not have a good hunt. There are numerous Public Shooting areas in very good pheasant country.

Nebraska

Nebraska is one of the best pheasant hunting states in this region and is sometimes considered better than ever-popular South Dakota for pheasants. Top spots include Box Butte county near the city of Alliance, southeast portion of Dawes County, and most of Sheridan county. Look to these cities for good pheasant hunting around them: Norfolk, Fremont, Lincoln, and Columbus in the east; Grand Island in the central region, Alliance and Rushville in the northwest, Sidney in the southwest; and North Platte, McCook, and Broken Bow in the southern-central. There are several dozen state-run special use areas that offer public hunting, as well as federal waterfowl areas. Be sure to check out these state run, public shooting opportunities.

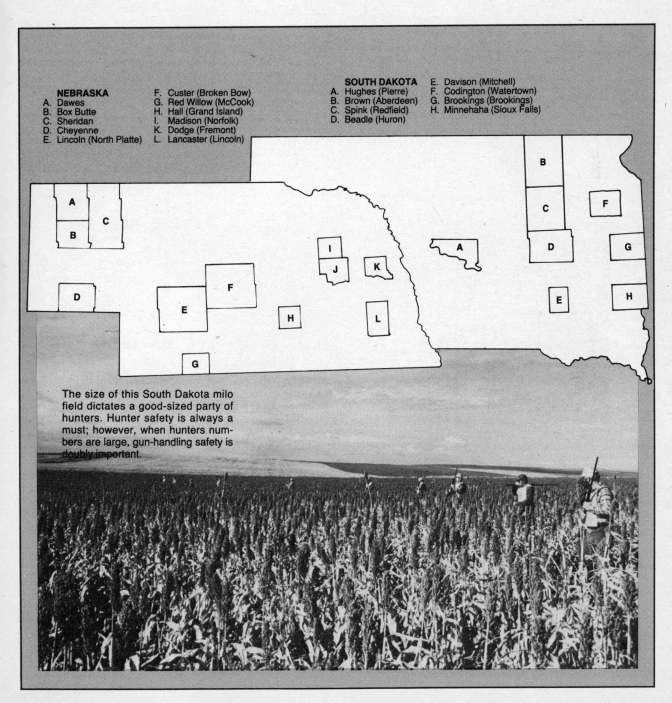

NEBRASKA
A. Dawes
B. Box Butte
C. Sheridan
D. Cheyenne
E. Lincoln (North Platte)
F. Custer (Broken Bow)
G. Red Willow (McCook)
H. Hall (Grand Island)
I. Madison (Norfolk)
K. Dodge (Fremont)
L. Lancaster (Lincoln)

SOUTH DAKOTA
A. Hughes (Pierre)
B. Brown (Aberdeen)
C. Spink (Redfield)
D. Beadle (Huron)
E. Davison (Mitchell)
F. Codington (Watertown)
G. Brookings (Brookings)
H. Minnehaha (Sioux Falls)

The size of this South Dakota milo field dictates a good-sized party of hunters. Hunter safety is always a must; however, when hunters numbers are large, gun-handling safety is doubly important.

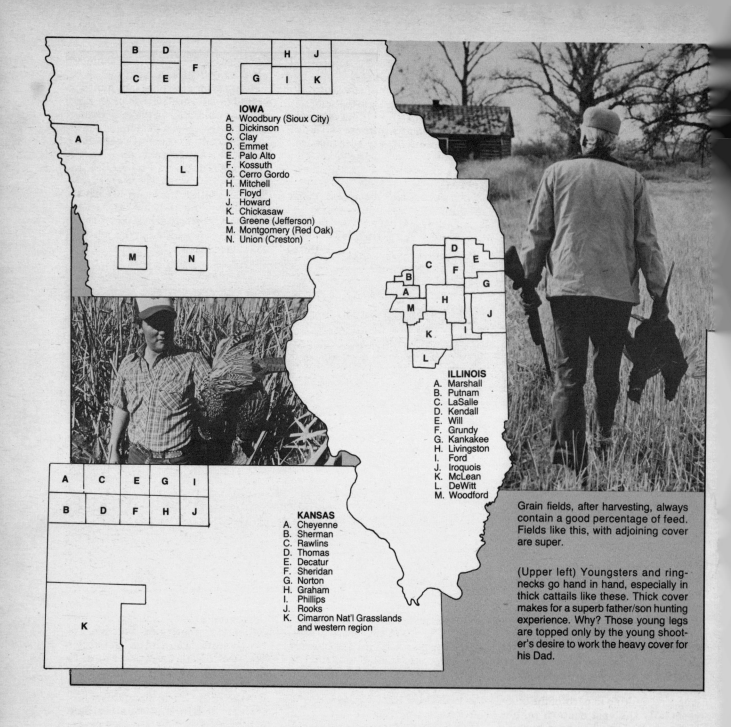

IOWA
A. Woodbury (Sioux City)
B. Dickinson
C. Clay
D. Emmet
E. Palo Alto
F. Kossuth
G. Cerro Gordo
H. Mitchell
I. Floyd
J. Howard
K. Chickasaw
L. Greene (Jefferson)
M. Montgomery (Red Oak)
N. Union (Creston)

ILLINOIS
A. Marshall
B. Putnam
C. LaSalle
D. Kendall
E. Will
F. Grundy
G. Kankakee
H. Livingston
I. Ford
J. Iroquois
K. McLean
L. DeWitt
M. Woodford

KANSAS
A. Cheyenne
B. Sherman
C. Rawlins
D. Thomas
E. Decatur
F. Sheridan
G. Norton
H. Graham
I. Phillips
J. Rooks
K. Cimarron Nat'l Grasslands
   and western region

Grain fields, after harvesting, always contain a good percentage of feed. Fields like this, with adjoining cover are super.

(Upper left) Youngsters and ring-necks go hand in hand, especially in thick cattails like these. Thick cover makes for a superb father/son hunting experience. Why? Those young legs are topped only by the young shooter's desire to work the heavy cover for his Dad.

Iowa

This is one of the finest pheasant states in the nation, with excellent hunting in various areas. Two separate localities stand out as best: the east-central area and in the southwest, north and east of Council Bluffs. In the north-central region, look to these counties for great action: Floyd, Chickasaw, Cerro Gordo, Mitchell and Howard. In the western area, these towns are in prime pheasant range: Sioux City, Smithland, Red Oak, Creston and Jefferson. There are many Public Hunting Areas in top pheasant range. Look for them espe-cially in the counties of Clay, Dickinson, Palo Alto, and Kossuth, among others.

Kansas

Pheasants are rated as a top game bird in this agricultural state. The high plains region in the northwest corner is tops, especially in the counties bordering Nebraska and Colorado. They include Cheyenne, Rawlins, Decatur, Norton and Phillips. In the next tier south, look for good hunting in Sherman, Thomas, Sheridan, Graham, and Rooks counties. The rest of the western region south along the Oklahoma border offers good hunting. The Cimarron National Grasslands has more than 100,000 acres of land open to public hunting.

Illinois

The best pheasant country in Illinois is generally regarded as being the northern and east-central regions. The very best counties are usually Livingston, McLean, and Ford. Other good counties are LaSalle, Kendall, Will, Marshall, Putnam, Grundy, Kankakee, Iroquois, Woodford and DeWitt. Several SGAs around the state offer very good bird hunting.

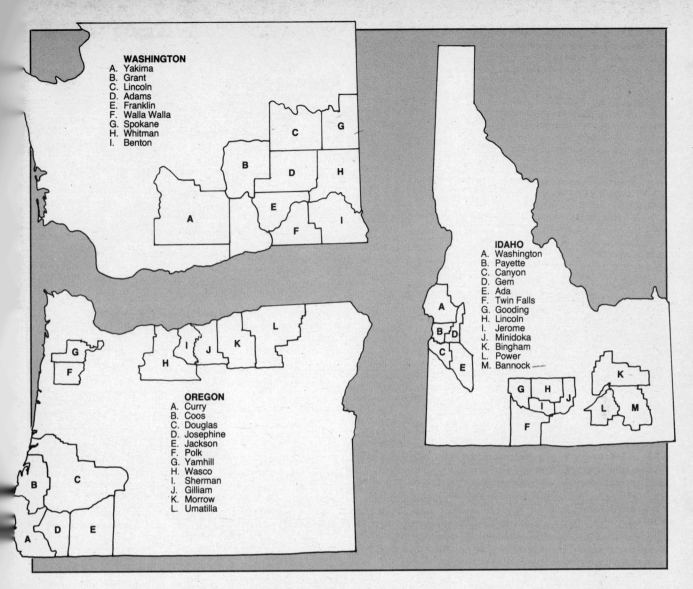

WASHINGTON
A. Yakima
B. Grant
C. Lincoln
D. Adams
E. Franklin
F. Walla Walla
G. Spokane
H. Whitman
I. Benton

IDAHO
A. Washington
B. Payette
C. Canyon
D. Gem
E. Ada
F. Twin Falls
G. Gooding
H. Lincoln
I. Jerome
J. Minidoka
K. Bingham
L. Power
M. Bannock

OREGON
A. Curry
B. Coos
C. Douglas
D. Josephine
E. Jackson
F. Polk
G. Yamhill
H. Wasco
I. Sherman
J. Gilliam
K. Morrow
L. Umatilla

West

The West is generally known for big game hunting, but excellent pheasant hunting is available in many areas. Montana, for example, has superb ringneck hunting in parts of the state, especially the vast eastern region. Colorado likewise has good hunting in the farming areas east of the Rockies. The southwest states of New Mexico and Arizona have marginal hunting in irrigated farmlands. The best western pheasant hunting occurs in Idaho and the three west coast states: Washington, Oregon, and California.

Idaho

The southern part of Idaho is the best in the state. In the western region, try Payette, Ada, Gem, Washington, and Canyon. In the Magic Valley region, there is good pheasant hunting in Gooding, Twin Falls, Lincoln and Minidoka. In the eastern re-

gion, the best counties are Bannock, Power, and Bingham. There is much BLM (Bureau of Land Management) land surrounding agricultural regions that offer quality public hunting. Pheasants often take shelter in the sagebrush on these federal lands after the season opens. Don't overlook these public hunting spots for excellent shooting.

Washington

There are two prime pheasant areas in Washington: the Columbia Basin and the Yakima Valley. Grant and Yakima counties are usually best, with Franklin, Adams and Whitman counties also good. Lincoln, Spokane, Benton, and Walla Walla are also very good. Numerous Game Ranges are good for pheasant hunting, as well as several waterfowl refuges.

Oregon

In this state where pheasants were

first introduced to America, hunters still enjoy superb gunning. West of the Cascade Mountains, the upper Willamette Valley is rated as tops. To the south there is good hunting in the Umpqua Basin of Douglas County, and the Rogue Basin along Curry, Josephine, and Jackson counties. East of the Cascades there are good pheasant concentrations in the counties close to the Columbia River. The upper Deschutes River area is also a good location. The city of Pendleton is in the midst of some of the best pheasant hunting in the area.

California

Top spot for pheasants in our most populous state is the Sacramento Valley, generally around the city of Sacramento. Look for good hunting in these counties: San Joaquin, Sacramento, Glenn, Yolo, Sutter, Butte, Colusa, Stanislaus, Merced, and Solano. Fresno County to the south is good, as well as Modoc, Siskiyou,

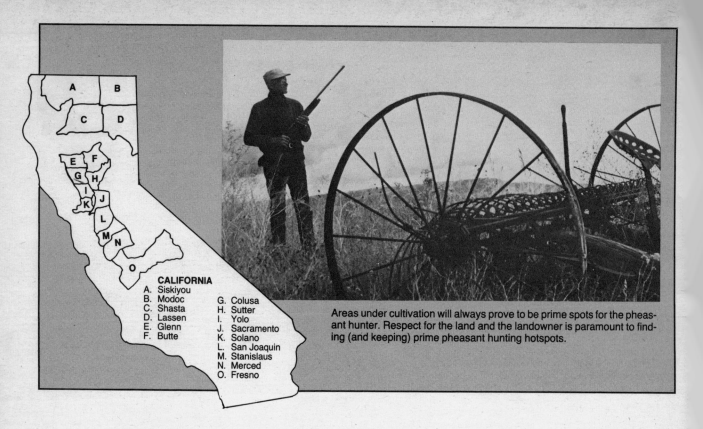

CALIFORNIA

A. Siskiyou
B. Modoc
C. Shasta
D. Lassen
E. Glenn
F. Butte
G. Colusa
H. Sutter
I. Yolo
J. Sacramento
K. Solano
L. San Joaquin
M. Stanislaus
N. Merced
O. Fresno

Areas under cultivation will always prove to be prime spots for the pheasant hunter. Respect for the land and the landowner is paramount to finding (and keeping) prime pheasant hunting hotspots.

Shasta, and Lassen. Much of the best hunting is on private lands, though there is much public hunting on state and federal grounds. Many preserves and private clubs offer put-and-take hunting to members.

While this completes our own pheasant hotspot roundup, it doesn't mean your search is over. The locations outlined here only serve as starting points for the serious hunter.

As you and your partner(s) move through these areas you will narrow down your selection to specific towns, and even farms, with the help of local landowners.

This brings us to the ultimate goal, if you will, of all pheasant hunters: to find a spot rife with prime birds and an open invitation on the part of the landowner to hunt his land. Pheasants hang around grain, the cover that surrounds the grain and the farmers who grow that grain. Of course, this means the hunter must be sincere, honest and respectful in his requests to hunt a farmer's lands. Without the farmer, the would-be hunter will find himself dead in the water. As a result, it must be said that the ultimate pheasant hunting hotspot is to be found in the warm handshake of the man who owns the land.●

Uncut strips of grain are usually quite productive. Open areas like this oftentimes mean running, far-rising birds. In this instance, tighter choked (modified or full) guns are a good choice..

4 STEPS TO RINGNECK SUCCESS

by DON ZUTZ

If you're looking for more birds in the bag, here's how to do it, the easy way.

I WAS JUST A KID then, trying every sport I could find, and for a moment I thought I was a cross between a hunter and a football player. We were working a grass-grown drainage ditch, my father on one side and I on the other, when my foot swung forward into a tangled clump and my toe actually nudged the pheasant skyward. A long-handled landing net would have done me more good than a Purdey just then.

"Hen!" my dad shouted, and we lowered our nearly-mounted guns.

Relaxing after the excitement of the moment, I bragged that, "If it had been a rooster, I'd have had him sure!" And then we paused for a couple minutes, discussing how we'd hunt once the ditch ran out.

When we resumed our hunt, I didn't take more than four steps before I kicked another field goal. Only this ball was brilliant and brassy. Its resentful cackle jolted me like a linebacker's tackle, and I never did get my act together. I didn't swing. I poked the gun, yanked the trigger, and missed by a yard.

"Just like that hen you'd have had *for sure!*" my father observed critically. My 12-year-old heart sank in despair. I was the original Charlie Brown.

But I learned something about ringnecks and hunting that morning, and those four steps between the hen and the cock have come to symbolize the four steps to improved pheasant hunting success:

Step One: Learn the habitat preferred by local birds.

Step Two: Study the habits of those birds within their covers, especially their reactions to dog and hunter pressure.

Step Three: Select equipment that will solidly anchor these heavy-boned, tough-as-a-boot roosters.

Step Four: Develop a wingshooting technique that will be smooth and uniformly coordinated at the peak of excitement.

1 *Learn the habitat.*

Here's a hunter who has stopped in a likely cover. This tactic often plays on a ringneck's nerves, producing a flush when the hunter really has no idea that a bird is nearby.

The first step is probably the easiest. Practically everyone knows that game birds require food, water, and shelter, and that this trio of essentials isn't always in the same spot. Pheasants will normally roost in one place and travel to feed in another. Depending upon the weather or the time of day they may be found in still other areas. In drizzly weather, for example, I've found them hunkered in relatively light cover, generally high grassy fields where the drainage is good, while casual thinking would suggest they'd be in the thickest covers. Thus, if tramping normal terrain doesn't pay off in soggy weather, a savvy pheasant hunter might try the shorter grasses above the swales, places where you generally don't find birds on dry, bright days.

Corn is the classic pheasant fare throughout much of the East and Midwest, and hunters aren't wrong in gravitating to standing or stubble fields. But pheasants aren't nearly as obsessed with corn as are many hunters and magazine illustrators; pheasants frequent corn fields mainly because the living is easy. However, they can exist perfectly on other diets,

and wildlife biologists tend to believe that weed seeds are a healthier food for pheasants than corn because it contains more protein and fat than do common cereals. Along with corn, some favored pheasant foods are sunflower seeds, ragweed, foxtail, bayberry, skunk cabbage fruits and snapweed, the latter two of which are considered especially nutritional. The colorful berries and grapes that lend their beauty to the glory of autumn are considered low in nutritive value. When corn isn't abundant, hunt for these types of food, and you'll be back in the ball game.

Some hunters are totally lost in the absence of corn. And many make mistakes by believing the ringneck is a bird of open fields. But cut the corn or the grain, and a ringneck will head for the grassy edges of farm woodlots and brush-cluttered thickets like a ruffed grouse. Indeed, the bird is a survivalist *par excellance*; it doesn't read books on what it ought to do — it does what's needed to save its tail feathers. And that brings us to our next step, step two, namely, learning to handle its actions within its weed-filled world.

Roosters often get nervous and head for thicker cover, when they're pushed. Too many hunters overlook the edges and interior of thick cover.

Study the birds' habits.

2

Thick cover, as found in open-field situations, is usually the pheasant's domain. That cover serves to confuse the hunter, even his dog, on occasion. This bird almost had to be stepped on before he flushed.

(Left) Until man's sense of smell improves, a retrieving dog, such as this Brittany, is an essential part of successful pheasant hunting.

During the autumn, a pheasant's daily schedule reads much like this: He'll break roost about a half hour before sunrise, often announcing himself robustly with a cackle that wakes the nearby barnyard rooster! The morning cackle may be dropped under hunting pressure, but serious hunters who want to do some pre-season scouting can spend some mornings up and afield, listening.

The birds will either walk or fly directly to feeding grounds. While sitting in goose blinds in farming country, I've seen pheasants vault from their roosts and then glide more than a ½-mile over a cattail swamp to their favorite corn or grain field. I've also heard others cackle without vaulting,

and minutes later, saw them walk leisurely to their breakfast. In either case, pheasants are up early and very businesslike about feeding. The only exception is during dirty weather, when feeding may be delayed if the bird is comfortable on its roost.

After feeding adequately, the pheasant may range a bit, depending on hunting pressure, weather, and the individual bird's inclinations. Those that take casual strolls along fence rows to gawk at passing cars are few and far between these days; poachers and those who have little respect for this regal bird have, unfortunately, taken to blasting them from the road. Poor sportsmanship aside, the sight of pheasants along a road can be misleading to hunters, because it tends to mark as a pheasant area a location that isn't even remotely so. The bird was just out, pecking at the gravel, walking at random, and wouldn't have been there had it wanted to do some important eating or sleeping.

When the corn is still high, most birds will stay in it or very near to it all day. This is especially true when weeds are heavy throughout the corn, which affords them additional protection as well as a varied diet of seeds.

Corn and grain stubble is still very attractive to ringnecks. Modern machinery leaves waste, and birds of all species pick it up. But stubble isn't adequate cover for birds that are spooky, and they'll seldom hold as hunters approach. One sweep through stubble will send the birds scampering well ahead, after which the serious hunting must be done in adjacent patches.

When food and protection are closely connected, pheasants will live their entire lives within a square mile. However, they won't hesitate to travel for food and/or cover. They feed indifferently during the afternoon hours, and the supposed evening feeding can be very short. Then the birds will glide or walk back into the marshy low lands to roost deep in the marsh grasses.In the main, American pheasants are ground-roosting types, whereas European strains will be found to roost in vines or trees, thus

This hunter found success in some thicker, woodlot cover that adjoined a field of swale. As can be seen, this particular patch of woodlot is similar to what many gunners would call "good woodcock cover."

minimizing the impact of nocturnal predators.

The second aspect to step two is studying the reactions of pheasant to different hunting pressures. Perhaps the most productive approach to pheasant hunting is driving. A line of hunters is posted at the far end of a corn field or other cover, while a second wave of hunters starts at the opposite end and advances like an army. With a few dogs added to slam-bang their way through, the birds will be ushered along and, generally, flushed at the end of the field. Shooting can then be fast and furious, even downright dangerous, given the wrong set of circumstances. Driving is a common method in Europe and the United Kingdom, but the drivers there don't carry guns. Stateside, however, it remains the most popular method used to shag pheasants from huge stands of corn.

But much American pheasant hunting is done solo or in very small groups, and that's when it gets tricky. For the ringneck is a sneak who runs like a thief. When he can't use straight-away speed, he'll zigzag and sit tight to let the threat pass. And the hunter working solo is at a tremendous disadvantage unless he knows his terrain like a pro or has snow to help him or can generate the confidence and patience of a saint. Snow's benefits need no explanation; the birds can simply be tracked. But the

value of confidence and patience can stand some elaboration. . . .

Hunters working solo or in tandem put little pressure on a cock to fly. The bird merely lowers his head and finds an opening off to the side or straight ahead. This tremendous escape potential puts a premium on the hunter's knowledge of the bird's tactics and psychology so that he can use tactics designed to counteract those of the wily rooster. Indeed, the best way to get skunked is by walking straight lines at steady paces! Such hunting produces good results only when foolhardy luck enters the picture.

Hunters make their own luck when they vary their course and pace. This is easily done when hunting solo or even in tandem or trio. Each man zigzags, thereby covering more area and pressuring birds that may have slid off to the side. But don't expect zigzagging alone to put birds up. Pheasants are past masters at sitting tight, as I learned along that drainage ditch as a kid. If you aren't lucky enough to nudge them with your boot, the next best move is — no move at all! Stand still frequently. This plays on a pheasants nerves, and it'll often move birds that would have sat out a steadily walking hunter.

Interestingly enough, I've met lots of hunters who know this zigzag/stop-and-start technique, but they don't use it! They continue to hunt covers in a straight line and a steady pace. At

fault is their own mental game plan: their offense isn't plotted to offset the pheasants' defense. To develop the proper state of mind, the hunter must assume there are birds in his cover and that they are evading him by running and sitting tight. He must junk the idea that birds are so dumb as to sit stupidly in his path, waiting. As I stated before, they are survivors. Even pen-raised birds have the instincts to sneak away and sit tight rather than to fly. And the only way a single hunter, or small groups of hunters, will flush birds is to make moves that counteract the birds' evasiveness *even though the hunter doesn't see anything!* If in his mind he knows that pheasants frequent the area, the hunter must proceed with confidence and assume there's a rooster nearby. He must zigzag and stand to pressure a flush. When the hunter stops concentrating on the possibility of a pheasant being near and reverts to a casual straight line stride, he's opening the door for Mr. Ringneck's escape. This type of mental game should be ideal for the person who is trying to get away from the everyday rat race, as the concentration redirects his mind for hours.

It is obvious that, without snow or the help of a dog, a single hunter doesn't know where a bird is or where it's going. But walking zigzag routes — or even circling small patches of cover and then spiraling to the center in ever-tightening rings — can put one very close to birds that have tried to slip off. Nearing them is somewhat accidental, of course, but it's the lone hunter's only chance. He must cover as much ground as possible, because a tight-sitting pheasant can ball up like a hunkered cottontail and let the rest of the world go by. Just last week, about the same time this was being written, a friend and I walked right past a rooster we had seen running in corn stubble. It had pushed under a bent stalk and a few corn leaves where I couldn't have hidden my hunting cap! We'd probably have lost that cock bird entirely if we hadn't stopped in its vicinity, which unnerved it.

If snow overlaps the latter part of a pheasant season, the dogless hunter is lucky. He can pick up and follow tracks. Shelter belts, standing corn, low swamps and thickets now become favorite haunts. When available, alder swales and willow patches attract the major concentration, especially if there is a dense matting of marsh grass. But don't believe that snow makes it any easier! It only lets you know when birds are around. For ringnecks will still sneak around, sprinting ahead as the hunter claws his way through the thicket or swale. When caught feeding in stubble or weed fields, the birds will push under the matted grasses and sit tight. Despite the greater visibility, it is still mainly a high wind that will cause long-range flushes.

An interesting method is calling pheasants. This practice isn't used widely, but it can sometimes pay dividends for dogless hunters going solo. Cock birds can become protective of their domain, and they will threaten any interloper. The call simulates a challenge to established cocks, and they will respond pugnaciously. This tells a hunter if there are birds around, and it sometimes stirs the cock into a fighting mood so that he isn't as likely to run off. Don't expect roosters to come running at you for a fight; merely use their replies to pinpoint them.

The use of a dog can put a new perspective on things. Here the dog does the hunting, the sportsman merely follows. But there is a *caveat*: beware the poorly trained dog, because it can race after birds and bust them well out of range. Few typical hunters spend enough time with their dogs to keep them within effective shooting range; hence, dogs can spoil hunts as well as improve them, depending on their training.

When I was young, the flushing breeds (springers, mainly) had much more popularity than they do now. The pointing breeds are currently in vogue, with the Brittany and German shorthair apparently dominant, trailed by setters. An important part of their training is teaching them to hold point. This is the average hunter's failure. Rampaging dogs that break point quickly and bust the birds make pheasant hunting seem more difficult than it is. If the dog can be trained to range reasonably close and to hold point, the shooting will be within effective range. Too, ringnecks will hold because sitting tight is part of their instinct. Without undue dog pressure they may sneak around a bit, but they won't flush wildly. Many times the hunter must get in the heavy cover and roust birds nailed by pointers.

One of the most productive hunts is in the low, marshy areas or heavy grasses where birds roost. Hunters with limited time would do well to schedule their free hours for the tag end of the day when birds move back into these sites. While they couldn't be flushed from standing corn during the midday, they'll now be easier for a pointer to handle. A thrust through such areas in the fading minutes of legal hunting time can produce birds.

Select the right equipment.

Perhaps the best all-around pheasant gun is a double bored IC&M fed the right loads.

But learning pheasant habitat and antics is only part of the game. A third step — having the right equipment and some wing-gunning skill — is just as important. For the pheasant is a big, strong bird that isn't easily anchored for a positive retrieve. Unfortunately, many birds are dropped each season and lost because of light loads and/or fringe hits.

Although pheasants are ofttimes boomed as wild-running, far-flushing birds, improved hunting techniques and well-trained dogs negate that popular myth. Heavy hunting pressure in open areas and bungling dog work can present long-range shooting, of course, and for those situations a full-choked barrel and 1¼ ounces of No. 5 shot is suggested.

But overall, most pheasants are taken at close or moderate ranges. My experience has been that even in heavily hunted areas the birds breaking well are out too far for sensible shooting, and that careful, patient, zigzag hunting interspersed with stop-and-go tactics will give the best sure-kill opportunities. Thus, why outfit for dicey long-range shots when the law of averages is on your side at moderate distances? If you could hit and drop cleanly every bird flushing inside 35 yards, you wouldn't have to think about those 50-60 yard chances! Your birds-to-shells ratio would be much higher.

A typical hunter would do far better with improved cylinder or modified choke than with full choke. As the seasons go by, I can't help but believe that a double bored IC&M is the best bet, be it in 12-gauge or 3-inch 20. In a pump or autoloader, I believe I'd opt for IC with at least 1¼ ounces of shot. The longest string of clean kills I ever had was with a 12-gauge gas-operated Skeet gun using 1½ ounces of No. 6 shot. Certainly, an improved-cylinder choke would do as well, perhaps even a mite better because an IC choke is made to throw a slightly tighter center density than a Skeet choke. In short, the IC boring gives you a bit more range.

Some writers push fine shot, such as 7½'s, for pheasants, claiming the tiny pellets are more likely to find the head and neck while also adding to the overall shocking power by multiple hits. I can't buy that! My experience with 7½'s on pheasants has been

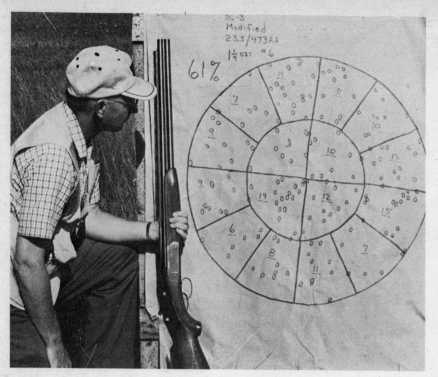

This 40-yard pattern of No. 6 shot shows about what a modified-choked barrel will do with 1¼-ounce loads. The pattern is about as evenly distributed as you'll get and is reaching the extent of its positive-performance ranges. The pheasant, however, has a big body and will probably absorb enough pellets from this pattern for a knockdown. Beyond 40 yards, however, No. 5 shot is suggested for these tough-as-a-boot game birds.

disastrous, resulting in feathered and lost birds. The reason is that many, if not most, Yankee ringnecks offer outgoing shots that put the bird's heavily feathered tail and strong body between the muzzle and the vital head-/neck region. Moreover, even on crossing shots or flushes that present a side view, the bird's broad wings can act as a shield to fend off fine shot from light loads. Indeed, the only way to anchor a game bird of this size, strength, and spirit is by breaking bones and driving pellets deeply. In my experience, that means 6's up to 40 yards and 5's thereafter.

(Right) A 12-gauge, short (24") barreled, autoloader with an adjustable choke can be very effective for all-round pheasant hunting.

(Below) A lightweight over-under is a thing of beauty and a perfect companion in the uplands. This gun is a Beretta 12-gauge.

Sixes and 5's may seem a bit coarse for American upland hunting (the writers are always promoting 7½'s and 8's), but that'll be forgotten when you find the ol' cock right where he dropped from a pattern of something heftier. For ringnecks, you've got to ignore the fancy stuff and get rough!

The 3-inch Magnum 20 can be deadly with 1¼-ounce 3-inch loads of 5's or 6's. Being light, easy to carry and generally responsive, the 20-gauge shotgun gets to the shoulder quickly — if the hunter has good gun-handling technique, that is — and can cleanly drop birds out to 45 yards. Here, again, IC&M is adequate for such hunting, and modified is a good all-around choice in repeaters. Remington has contributed in this direction, announcing modified-choked barrels

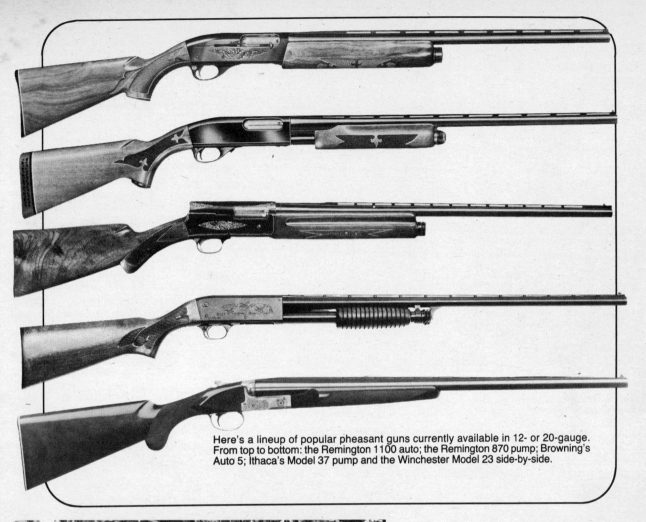

Here's a lineup of popular pheasant guns currently available in 12- or 20-gauge. From top to bottom: the Remington 1100 auto; the Remington 870 pump; Browning's Auto 5; Ithaca's Model 37 pump and the Winchester Model 23 side-by-side.

(Left) This pair of early season ringnecks was taken at close range, over a pointer, with a European-made smallbore. When the roosters get old and smart, the 12-gauge with 1¼-ounce loads is highly recommended. Smallbores can be sporty when the shooter is disciplined, but how much sport is there in wounding and losing crippled birds?

for the 3-inch, 20-gauge M1100 and M870.

I have no respect for the hunter who uses the 410 on pheasants. It's a crippler. The 28 is somewhat better, but it also has a light shot charge that doesn't fill the pattern well with 5's or 6's. In my opinion the 28 shouldn't be stretched beyond 30 yards.

The ideal pheasant gun, especially in the eastern half of the U.S., may prove to be a 12-, 16-, or 20-gauge double bored IC&M. Models with screw-in chokes are great; in the case of changing conditions, they can be switched to IC&F or M&F. If you have a pointer that can pin and hold birds, Remington's new "Special Field" M1100 with straight grip, shortened fore-end, and 21-inch barrel might just be the ticket.

4 Develop a wingshooting technique.

Note that the hunter's gun is in the lowered position much like that of the Skeet shooter discussed in the text. This photo dramatically proves the author's point that practice on the Skeet field, with a lowered gun, duplicates the reality of the hunt.

Practicing on Skeet with the gun held at a lowered starting position will greatly improve your shooting effectiveness on ringnecks.

But we could discuss guns forever. The fourth and final point is that the best dogs, guns and loads won't produce any pheasants by themselves. The hunter must develop a reasonably good technique, and the typical hunter who doesn't touch a gun between seasons is only fooling himself when he says, "I won't shoot unless I can *eat* the birds!" A well broken series of clay birds can spell the difference between an excellent field shot and a loser who's constantly running off alibis. Wingshooting, is an athletic event. Surely, you wouldn't expect a halfback to run for touchdowns without conditioning, would you?

The key to success afield is practice during the summer and early autumn, and the best place is on the Skeet field. Only *don't* follow the lead of tournament Skeetmen and shoot with a premounted gun! That approach won't help you kill cocks. Hold the gun in a lowered, field-carry position when calling "Pull!" and mount the gun only after the clay emerges. The value of Skeet lies in the fact you'll be working on gun handling with targets flying—all the basic angles encountered afield. When you begin to average 85-90 percent on "low-gun" Skeet, you've come a long way and have about completed the fourth step toward more ringnecks.

You're still going to walk past a few — and miss a couple easy shots. Love it! That's what makes pheasant hunting such a challenging sport! ●

IT WAS mid-afternoon when I parked the 4-wheel drive and headed for a patch of white oak timber that swept in close to the old dirt road. At the edge of the woods, I put a round in the chamber, closed the bolt and shoved a full clip of 22 target ammo into the belly of the rifle. The spot I had chosen earlier was more than 300 yards back in the woods. A long dry spell made the leaf carpet brittle and noisy. Instead of trying to ease over the long distance, I hit a steady stride and didn't stop until I was between two large white oaks that were surrounded by squirrel nests and several den trees.

I spent another minute pushing the leaves back from the base of each tree until I had a complete circle of bare

the Small Game Challenge SQUIRRELS

They're fast, elusive and provide the hunter with some of the finest small game hunting he can find.

by DON LEWIS

ground. There's no question my entrance and digging in had been anything close to quiet; in fact, some dyed-in-the-wool squirrel hunters would have classed me as insane or a sheer beginner or both. However, I had learned from years of matching wits with the wily tree climbers that this type of approach when conditions are extremely dry is just as successful as the attempted silent one. It's possi-

ble the "get-in-fast-and-dig-in-quick" method has a distinct advantage.

With all the ruckus I had made, I still knew it would only be a matter of time until things would be back to normal. I was right, too. Before 10 minutes had passed, a black-phased gray squirrel darted out of a snag and raced to the top of a large oak over 40 yards away. It was an ideal shot for the rifleman squirrel hunter. I rested the Kimber 82 rimfire against one of the oaks, allowed the dot reticle in the T-6 Weaver silhouette scope to settle between the head and shoulder and touched off the 3-pound trigger. The squirrel dangled for several seconds and fell with a distinct thud; it was a clean kill.

While congratulating myself on making a good shot, a second gray sped up a scrub oak not 30 yards distant. The squirrel came to a quick stop, providing me with a wide open chest shot. This would be like shooting fish in a barrel, or so I thought. When the dot reticle seemed to imbed itself on the squirrel's chest, I moved in against the trigger taking great pains to make a full-hand squeeze—like squeezing an orange or shaking hands. When the rifle cracked, the gray remained motionless for a second or so, and then with a whisk of the tail churned up through the maze of limbs and disappeared. I stared in dis-

belief! In squirrel hunting with the 22 rimfire, there are no absolutes.

For some strange reason, squirrel hunting does not rank high on the hunter's priority list. There are no hard statistics to show the exact number of hunters across the nation who take this tantalizing sport seriously, but it has to be a distinct minority. For the vast majority, squirrel hunting is a secondary hunting activity;

success. Making a precise shot at 60 yards with a rimfire outfit isn't a cakewalk by any means. Insignificant as squirrel hunting may seem, the dedicated buff derives satisfaction from understanding his target, enjoys the tranquility of a squirrel woods and is engulfed with inner satisfaction when his knowledge and shooting skill puts meat on the table.

Sciurus carolinensis, or the gray squirrel, is primarily a rodent of the timber stands. When great stretches of white oak covered much of the eastern United States, gray squirrels probably numbered in the millions. Basically, the gray thrives on mast foods like acorns, hickory nuts and beechnuts. Probably shagbark hickory nuts rate first on the menu with white oak acorns running a close second. Red oak acorns have a high content of tannin which is used in leather processing. Tannin is probably the reason gray squirrels avoid red oak acorns except when other sources of food are unavailable.

The gray's larger cousin, *Sciurus niger* (the gaudy fox squirrel) doesn't vary much in the diet category from the gray except corn ranks high with the big red. Also gray squirrels normally choose heavy stands of timber while the fox squirrel settles for small patches of woods or even two or three trees in the corner of a fencerow some-

times within sight of farm buildings. Perhaps it's the fox squirrel's unsatiable appetite for corn that keeps it close to the farmer.

Contrary to a popular myth, the eastern black squirrel is an ordinary gray squirrel and not a separate species. Through the melanistic process, the squirrel's hair darkens. The black mutations of the gray squirrel increase in frequency northward. The northern part of Pennsylvania, for example, has a ratio of about 40 percent black, but in Canada only 10 percent of the gray squirrel population is actually gray.

Scouting Pays

There are many ways to hunt the treetop artist, but the veteran squirrel hunter knows from experience that pre-season scouting is paramount to success. Finding squirrels may appear elementary, but it's not that easy. For instance, a patch of woods can be filled with confusing signs. Inexperienced hunters make the mistake of looking for heavy concentrations of acorns. That's fine if the acorns are the white oak variety.

It's almost a waste of time to hunt in timber that is dominated by red oak trees. Proof that the woods is void of squirrels can be seen in the hundreds of acorns that are strewn across the forest floor. The gray is an invet-

The author's partner, Bill Young, uses a Walther KKJ topped with a Unertl 6x—ideal for long-range shots.

(Right) All rifles used for squirrel hunting should turn in groups running 1-inch or better at 50 yards. Try different types and brands of rimfire ammo to see which performs best in your particular gun. Author prefers standard velocity match ammo.

when other types of small game are low in numbers, squirrel hunting gets another look. This is unfortunate since squirrel hunting has all the ingredients to be classed as a major hunting sport.

It isn't a sport for just kids and new hunters. It requires shooting skill, a comprehensive knowledge of the quarry and the intestinal fortitude to settle for defeat more times than for

Fox squirrels tend to live close to farmland and especially cornfields. You will note the 1-inch tubed scopes on the rimfires seen here. Why? They provide optimum clarity and light gathering qualities, something every squirrel hunter needs in his optics at dawn and dusk.

from early morn straight through the day to late evening. Some of my best shooting was after 9 in the morning and before the proverbial 3 in the afternoon.

Wind is supposed to be detrimental to a squirrel's movements across the crowns of high trees. The solid belief that the long tail is the squirrel's rudder and if blown about will keep him grounded is just a tale from the past. A big gray may tip the scales at 1½ pounds. It's only reasonable that a small, lightweight animal would have trouble navigating across thin limbs that are being tossed about by a vigorous wind. Still, a hungry squirrel has all the nerve needed to venture out on the thinnest limbs for a succulent bud

(Below) In the open woods, a rimfire rifle is tops. This photo is a good example of a hunter fully utilizing his surroundings to take a steady rest. With a good rest, accurate rifle and seasoned hunter, shots over 50 yards are not difficult.

erate hoarder, and when the caching fever is in full swing, the bushytail can bury a half-dozen acorns in 10 minutes. Put a dozen grays to work in a patch of white oak, and it will take a sharp eye to find an acorn above ground by the time the hunting season rolls around.

The pre-season scouter should search for sections of timber that have a high number of beechnut, hemlock, hickory or cherry trees. Wild cherries happen to be a favorite summertime dish. Any patch of woods containing a heavy concentration of one of these trees or a mixture of all will be worth taking a second look at.

Once the proper habitat is found, look closely for squirrel signs. A good set of binoculars is a must for scouting. Study holes high up in trees to see if gnawing marks around the edges and lower lip of the hole are visible. Squirrels gnaw around their den holes to keep nature from closing it in a healing process. A full-time den tree hole will be gnawed white. Escape holes will show little gnawing but will have a definite smoothness especially on the bottom edge. Look for escape holes in dead snags.

Scratch marks aren't a positive sign for gray squirrels. Most forest mammals climb trees and leave cuts and scratches in the process. The remains of chiseled nuts or acorn hulls are obvious signs. Pine squirrels normally gnaw holes in each side of a hard-shelled nut. Grays, on the other hand, gnaw two holes that practically straddle the centerline. The most assuring sign is overturned leaves where a cached nut has been dug up. The final determination comes by just sitting for a quiet hour or so to see if the signs in the woods point to squirrel.

There has always been a heated argument over the best time to hunt for grays. One faction claims the knowledgeable hunter will be on watch long before the sun breaks over the eastern horizon. "If you're not dug in ½-hour before the sky brightens, you're too late," an old-timer told me. The other faction, and this writer is a member, believe squirrels move throughout the day. I will admit that early morning and late evening are the best periods of the day for squirrel movement if weather conditions are right. The gaslight era hunter stopped before 9 in the morning and didn't start until 3 in the afternoon, but he missed a lot of good shooting.

Squirrels do feed early and in some cases when there is a bright moon, feeding will go on long after dark. Some veterans won't hunt the morning after a full moon believing implicitly that the gray isn't hungry enough to get out of bed. Feeding may take place at the beginning and end of day, but from years of hunting, I'm convinced that squirrels can be hunted

or nut no matter how strong the wind is. Under windy conditions, the hunter should watch the ground where the action will eventually take place.

Another old tale that has no real foundation is the emasculation myth. When I was a young hunter, I believed with a pure conscience that the nasty pine squirrel (chickaree) would castrate gray squirrels. It was also told that older, dominating male grays put the young males out of commission to cut down on romantic competition. There's no real truth in either of these fables.

The castration tale probably got started when a hunter killed a young male that appeared to be castrated. If the wood patch was infested by pine squirrels, the conclusion was obvious. When I was a boy, I saw a piney chas-

(Right) It always pays to look for signs. This hunter has just picked up an acorn cap out of the "digs" just in front of him. Squirrels can't be far away.

(Left) Some shooters like to walk, others like to sit. The choice is yours—both methods work.

ing a fat gray. (It was probably an irate chickaree mother putting up a brave front to save her family.) I joined in the chase hurtling over logs and brush piles hoping to see the red surgeon make a eunuch out of the gray. I lost sight of the squirrels and tore my new tennis shoes to boot.

It is now known that the testes of a male squirrel do not enter the scrotum until the young squirrel is sexually mature. The shrunken scrotum with little or no fur around it does appear to be cut. There is no solid evidence for the emasculation theory.

Which Firearm is Best?

The most touchy subject in the squirrel-hunting realm is over the type of firearm used. It boils down between the rifleman and the shotgunner. Each is very adamant about his particular choice. Shotgunners claim that rifle-toting hunters make the woods unsafe with screaming ricochets, and the rifleman is quick to point out that scattergun buffs don't make clean kills with their rice throwing devices. There is no middle ground; each side claims the other is a despicable sight in a squirrel woods.

While the shotgun/rifle argument has existed among squirrel hunters for years and is now gathering steam with the turkey hunting clan, there is no basis for this controversy. Each type of firearm has a distinct advantage under certain conditions. For instance, a rifle hunter in dense masses of vines and limbs is up against insurmountable odds. Here is where the shotgun is right at home. On the other hand, where the woods are open and the beech and hemlock tower 30 yards in the air, the rifleman has the edge.

There's no denying the scattergunner will kill three times as many squirrels as the rimfire advocate since he can take all types of shots within range. The rifle hunter will be lucky to get a shot at one out of three squirrels seen, and his success ratio might average two out of five. The shotgun hunter can blast through limbs and vines with a heavy charge of shot, but the rifleman has to wait until a clear shot is available. When squirrels are excited or on a food-foraging spree, the rifle toter will be hard pressed to get an open shot at a motionless target.

I'm not implying the shotgun hunter doesn't have a challenge on his hands, but with the expanding shot pattern, a veteran shotgunner will

(Left) These hunters are working as a team. The author on the left is using an Anschutz Model 54 topped with a Weaver T-6. The hunter on the right is using a Walther KKJ topped with a Unertl 6x, 1-inch target scope. Both rifles are chambered for 22 Long Rifle.

From top to bottom: Ruger 10/22 semi-auto Deluxe Sporter; Weatherby Mark XXII semiauto; Browning BL-22 lever action; Remington 541-S Custom Sporter. The author prefers bolt-action rimfires over autos or pumps because of their generally better accuracy. Whatever action type you choose, be sure to try a number of brands and types of ammo and use that which provides top accuracy.

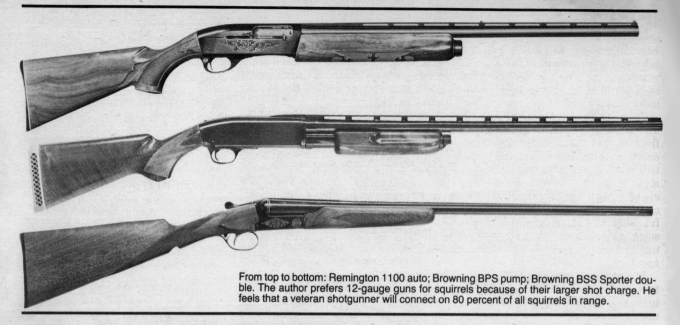

From top to bottom: Remington 1100 auto; Browning BPS pump; Browning BSS Sporter double. The author prefers 12-gauge guns for squirrels because of their larger shot charge. He feels that a veteran shotgunner will connect on 80 percent of all squirrels in range.

(Left) In dense forest, or during early-season hunts when the foliage is still present, a shotgun is super on bushytails.

connect on 80 percent of all squirrels in range.

In the gauge column, there's little doubt that the big 12 leads the pack. This may raise the hackles on the necks of the 3-inch 20-gauge crowd, but ballistics definitely show the larger shot charge of the 12-gauge keeps it ahead of the rest. It's true the 3-inch 20 can be stuffed with 1½-ounces of shot which seems to put it on par with the 12. In pellet numbers, they are equal, but the bigger 12 can generate a little more velocity. If only the weight of the shot charge is being con-

sidered, the 12-gauge can handle a full 1½ ounces of shot.

I've listened to both sides for a number of years, and it's all a waste of words. A squirrel under 30 yards is no match for either shell providing the proper shot size and the correct choke boring is used.

No one should argue against the full-choke for squirrel shooting. Gray and fox squirrels are small, tough animals. They can absorb a lot of punishment and still escape. The shotgunner who specializes in squirrel hunting should stick with the full choke bor-

ing because of the denser patterns that choke provides at longer ranges.

In the shot size column, more controversy exists. Some specialists insist that nothing smaller than No. 4 shot is adequate. From a ballistic viewpoint, No. 5s or 6s might be better. At 30 yards, a full-choke barrel produces a pattern roughly 30 inches in diameter. At 40 yards, it enlarges to nearly 4 feet. With only 169 pellets in a 1¼-ounce load of No. 4 shot, it's easy to see why the pattern would be spread very thin.

Unlike the rifle bullet, a shotgun pellet can't be guided to a predetermined spot. The shotgunner depends on pattern density; the denser the pattern, the more pellets in the target. A 1¼-ounce load of No. 6 shot contains about 280 pellets or 111 more than the 1¼-ounce load of 4s. With 111 more pellets in the same diameter pattern, there will be fewer gaps and fewer squirrels that get away.

The old belief that the 410 bore is the perfect squirrel outfit still exists. But with all the nostalgia the 410 bore has accumulated, ballistics show it is not a squirrel outfit per se. At 20 yards, the 410 is as deadly as the 12-gauge, but beyond that distance, the exceptionally thin pattern of the tiny shell works against the hunter. This is doubly true with the novice hunter who usually is stuck with the 410.

At best, the 3-inch 410 shell can be stuffed with ⅝-ounce of shot. With No. 5 shot, the count runs out around the 100 pellet mark. Going with the same load of No. 6 shot ups the total to 140, but velocity will fall. It's time to take the 410 bore out of the squirrel woods and replace it with a shell that is capable of handling an ounce or more of shot.

Squirrel hunting is a challenging and intriguing sport with any type of firearm, but the common 22 rimfire cartridge adds a new dimension. This tiny shell is really too small for varmint hunting other than extremely close range shots on chucks and crows. Compared to the more powerful centerfire cartridges, the 22 does seem insignificant—that is, until it's used in a squirrel woods where it speaks with great authority.

The shotgun hunter who is accustomed to a high ratio of success will be up the proverbial creek without a canoe or paddle when he switches to the rimfire. No longer is squirrel shooting just pointing and slapping the trigger at everything in range. The playing field wouldn't change one iota, but the rules will. The vines and limbs that succumbed to a load of No. 5 shot are now an impregnable fortress protecting the wary gray. There's no blasting through; patience becomes the name of the game. The hunter has to wait for the squirrel to move into a miniature porthole opening. Chances are, it won't happen. Frustration is an integral ingredient for the rimfire squirrel hunter.

The 22 rimfire has all the qualifications to be a super squirrel cartridge. Even with low velocity target ammo it has sufficient velocity and kinetic energy to drop a squirrel instantly at 60 yards. High quality target ammo in a fine rifle offers the ultimate in accuracy. For those who are long-range specialists, the 22 Winchester Magnum Rimfire is tops. It offers nearly double the velocity of target fodder, but due to its tendency to ricochet, care must be exercised in congested areas.

Rimfire rifles are very eccentric. No single rimfire rifle will consume all grades and brands of ammunition with the same degree of accuracy. In fact, I have found that it's a rare case for a rifle to meet my "five shots in 1-inch at 50 yards" requirement when any type of high speed ammo is used. This may seem relatively easy to accomplish, but range tests will prove only a few rifles will meet this criterion on a consistent basis even with target ammo.

Just because a rifle won't shoot into an inch or less at 50 yards doesn't mean you should discard it. A rifle that holds a consistent 1½-inch group

at 50 yards will be putting all its shots in ¾-inch at 25 yards which is close to normal shooting range for most hunters. No rifle should be relegated to the ranks of the unfit until there's ample proof it can't hold a fairly tight group at 50 yards.

Target ammo usually enhances the group potential of any rifle. It is manufactured to more exacting standards and uses a balanced bullet. Consequently, it is more consistent in every respect. It's also quieter. Top of the line target ammo bites deeper into the pocketbook, but its superb accuracy and low noise level pays off in the woods.

While there is roughly 200 feet per second difference in velocity between target fodder and high speed stuff (even more with some of the super rimfire ammo now available), target ammunition is more than adequate to make clean kills up to 60 yards. Beyond that distance, the common 22 shouldn't be used for squirrels.

Accuracy is a product derived from many ingredients: good ammo, a finely tuned rifle and good shooting. It never comes by pure chance. For the most part, bolt-action outfits have tighter locking systems and perform better in the accuracy column. But the other actions can't be overlooked.

I have shot super groups with the Marlin 39A and the Browning BL-22 while a friend swears by his Remington 572 Fieldmaster pump. The semi-auto, Mossberg Model 377 Plinkster, Weatherby Mark XXII and Ruger 10-22 series are excellent choices. The semi-auto won't duplicate the accuracy of the bolt, but, with the right ammo you'll do fine.

A super squirrel rifle is no better than its scope. I've worn out my statement that you can't shoot any better than you can see. While any scope is more efficient than open sights, not all scopes are for the squirrel woods. For many years, the rimfire rifle automatically carried an inexpensive 4x scope having a crosswire intersection so thick it practically covered a squirrel's head at 50 yards. Things are different now.

First, the 6x is a wiser choice. The extra magnification is beneficial to the hunter beyond 40 yards. Going to very high powers really defeats the purpose. The reduced field of view in a 10x or 15x makes it extremely difficult for the hunter to find his target and light transmission is reduced drastically.

A big game scope in a straight 6x or 7x variable will turn in a superb job. The only drawback is a focus problem.

Most big game scopes are focused by the maker to be parallax-free at 100 yards. This means that at ranges under 60 yards, the target may appear hazy or blurred. If a big game scope will be used only for squirrel it should be returned to the manufacturer to be made parallax free at 50 yards. It will make a distinct improvement.

The trigger is the only communication the shooter has with the shot he is about to fire; hence, the need for an adjustable trigger that can be adjusted for weight of pull and is free from forward play and overtravel. Unfortunately, this type of trigger is available only on a few expensive bolt-action rifles, but for the "purist," it's the only way to go.

Each hunter has a particular routine for hunting the wily gray squirrel. The shotgun buff may stalk his quarry hoping for the element of surprise. For him, a moving squirrel is fair game. The rifleman may "still" hunt by slipping quietly for a few yards stopping by a tree for partial concealment and a solid rest if a squirrel appears. The "sit and watch" method is by far the most common. Digging in and being quiet is a proven way to get squirrels.

The end result of a successful hunt is not just a game bag full of squirrels; it means some very tasty eating. Squirrel meat is delicious when properly cleaned and cooked. It makes a perfect side dish for a holiday meal.

Admittedly, squirrels are hard to skin, but here's a method I have used for many years. Cut off the feet and encircle the midsection with a slit just under the hide. Work the hide loose on both sides of the slit and with a firm grasp with both hands, pull the hide in opposite directions. Cut through the tail bone close to the rump, work the feet free from the hide and cut off the head. With a little practice, it takes only a few minutes.

If squirrels are the most underharvested game species as some biologists claim, it's a sad commentary for the hunting fraternity. Squirrel hunting is an exciting and challenging sport. Better yet, it's a perfect way to start the new hunter. There are lessons galore in matching wits with the scrambling high targets. The tyro discovers the importance of good habitat, learns the language of the woods and acquires a high degree of shooting skill. For many hunters, it leads to more exotic hunts, but for thousands of us, the flame that was ignited when we dropped our first squirrel still burns brightly as we accept the challenge of ol' longtail. ●

THE SUN was just chinning above the broken teeth of distant mountains when the buck came tiptoeing down a faint trail between tightly clustered pines. My hunting buddy Johnny Johnston grabbed his binoculars and focused on the animal, certain the buck had antlers but not at all sure how big. The sudden shock of the clear, 10x view nearly knocked him out of his tree stand, his heart doing double handsprings as the magnified picture penetrated his brain. The buck was a monstrous whitetail, a once-in-a-life-time trophy with six long, even points per side, eyeguards 8 to 10 inches in length, and massive main beams well over 2 feet wide.

As Johnny gazed in stunned astonishment, the big bruiser moved directly toward him, passed less than 30 yards away, and stopped to look the other direction in a car-sized opening between two trees. John had determined the exact distance to that opening with his bowhunting rangefinder, and he automatically drew his hunt-

made a smooth, rock-solid shot. He had held 25 yards, the distance from the tree stand to the deer was 25 yards, yet the arrow had hit fully 18 inches high.

"Did you try another shot from your tree stand at a pine cone or something else to see where you hit?" I asked. He shook his head no. As an experienced bowhunter, I was sure I knew what had happened. "If you'd shot another arrow, John, I'll bet it would have hit high, too," I continued. "Arrows shot downward from tree stands always hit high, exactly the same as rifle bullets when shot downhill. You have to practice aiming low to make downward shots hit where you want them to."

John managed to nail a smaller buck with his bow from the same tree stand near the end of the archery deer season—a buck he shot after practicing downward shooting a lot during midday hours. He held just below the deer's chest at 25 yards, and scored a perfect hit through both lungs.

of these excellent bow shots do not realize how important another shooting factor can be in hunting. This factor is the arching trajectory of an arrow.

The best bow-shot in the world cannot bowhunt worth beans unless he is thoroughly familiar with the trajectory of his gear. Trajectory control is very important in hunting with a rifle, but hitting game with a bullet is laughably easy when compared to the problems involved in lobbing an arrow into an animal's vital zone. A hunter with a rifle in the 270 Winchester or 30-06 Springfield class may have to worry about small holdovers at ranges between 300 and 400 yards and has to slightly alter sight placement for shots taken sharply up or down. However, a bowhunter who misestimates the distance to a deer by 2 yards will miss that animal clean on a 50-yard shot. Similarly, compensation for upward and downward shooting angles with a bow is enormous compared to that needed with a rifle. For example, on a long downhill shot

TRAJECTORY CONTROL—
Key to Bowhunting Success

by CHUCK ADAMS

Trajectory control is the single most important factor in consistently successful bowhunting.

Most Bowhunters Miss High Or Low

There is nothing particularly easy about accurately shooting a bow. A hunter must practice regularly on the target range to accustom his muscles to the strain and must make certain he develops proper shooting habits along the way. Unless he learns to draw, anchor, aim, release, and follow through consistently from shot to shot, he will never be a decent shot on targets or game. However, despite the difficulty of shooting a bow with pinpoint accuracy, many, many serious bowhunters learn to hit a Dixie cup at 40 or 50 yards after several months of practice. Unfortunately, a good share

ing bow, placed the 25-yard sight pin on the buck's fat gray flank, and let go with a smooth, even bowstring release. The orange aluminum arrow glinted dully as it sizzled toward the deer . . . and then the impossible happened. As if in a nightmare, the arrow whizzed over the buck's back and smacked a rotten stump beyond, missing the deer by fully 6 inches. The monster leaped in the air, jackknifed frantically, and charged away through the woods like a turpentined tomcat. Johnny hunted the same area for the rest of the season, but never saw the giant deer again.

Needless to say, my pal was heartsick over blowing such an easy setup at the biggest buck he had ever seen. He was a beginning bowhunter, but he had practiced diligently on the target range with his bow for 3 full months before season. His bow-and-arrow equipment was well tuned, and I'd seen him shoot 6-inch groups at 25 yards with machine-like consistency. He told me about the incident with the big whitetail buck immediately after it happened, and he was shaking his head in total bewilderment. He swore up and down that despite his shock over the size of the deer, he had

of 50 or 60 yards, a bowhunter might have to alter his aim by 5 or 6 *feet* to score a dead-center hit. The slow-moving, arching trajectory of an arrow can make shooting at game a bonafide nightmare unless a hunter knows the exact distance to his target and has plenty of uphill and downhill shooting practice under his belt.

As far as I'm concerned, trajectory control of an arrow is the single most important factor in consistently successful shooting at game—or more important than machine-like shooting on the target range. An average-to-good archer can keep most of his shots in a 6-inch group at 30 yards and a 12-inch group at 60 yards, yet not one in a hundred can consistently hit within 2 feet of the mark when shooting at unknown ranges out to 60 yards. Simple grouping ability is quite important in bowhunting, but preventing an arrow from hitting considerably high or low is far more difficult to achieve.

Arrow-Drop Statistics

Most non-bowhunters have no concept at all of just how much a hunting arrow drops in flight. An average 535-grain arrow shot from an average

(Left) Even at ultra-close range, a bowhunter must use the right distance pin or miss an animal clean.

(Below) This photo dramatically shows how critical aiming is with a bow. The four sight pins are set for 20, 30, 40, and 50 yards. A misestimation of only 2 or 3 yards will cause a clean miss or a poor hit.

compound hunting bow of 60 pounds flies about 190 feet per second—less than 1/15th the speed of an average deer-hunting bullet. If such a bow is zeroed at 15 yards, it will hit 12 inches low at 25 yards, 35 inches low at 35 yards, 69 inches low at 45 yards, and 116 inches low at 55 yards. The same bow zeroed for 25 yards will hit about 8 inches high at 10 yards and 46 inches low at 45 yards. Given the fact that the average whitetail deer has a vital chest zone only 10 or 11 inches in diameter, it is obvious that slight vertical aiming errors with a bow will generally result in crippling hits or complete shooting misses. A bow-hunter holding 25 yards dead center

Open-country animals like mule deer (opposite page) require accurate range estimation for killing hits with an arrow. A top-quality bowhunting rangefinder like the Ranging Model LR-80 (left) ensures such distance-gauging accuracy.

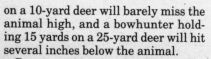

A little shooting at various target ranges shows how arching arrow trajectory is.

on a 10-yard deer will barely miss the animal high, and a bowhunter holding 15 yards on a 25-yard deer will hit several inches below the animal.

Range estimation becomes more and more critical with a bow as shooting distance increases. At 45 or 50 yards, a hunter who misestimates shooting range by 1½ yards will miss a deer clean, even if he's capable of placing all arrows in a 10-inch group at these ranges. Add to this the problem of altered trajectories on uphill and downhill shots, and controlling arrow trajectory is clearly the bowhunter's primary problem.

Minimizing High/Low Misses

There are several ways a bowhunter can minimize the chances of missing animals high or low. One common method is attempting to milk maximum arrow speed from a bow to at least slightly flatten trajectory. This can be achieved by shooting the lightest-weight projectile recommended by arrow manufacturers and/or using the fastest-shooting bow design available. The relatively new cam-operated compound bows available through some archery companies increase arrow velocity by some 10 to 15 percent over bows of more conventional design, which indeed flattens arrow trajectory and makes hits at unknown distances at least slightly more feasible. Unfortunately, bow accuracy of-

(Above and right) Shooting up or down dramatically changes point of arrow impact. An archer must practice such shooting to help him properly aim on game.

ten falls off when ultra-lightweight arrows or souped-up bows are used, and such setups are invariably more noisy to shoot than slower, more accurate combos. A noisy bow often spooks animals before the arrow arrives downrange, and flatter trajectory isn't worth a hoot if basic accuracy is not sufficient to hit game in the first place. Because of the built-in problems with flattening arrow trajectory, most knowledgeable bowhunters rely on other factors to help ensure consistent hits.

The smartest thing any hunting archer can do is purchase an accurate, good-quality bowhunting rangefinder. Such a rangefinder allows the hunter to take distance readings on handy landmarks where game might appear, and also lets a sneaky hunter take readings on undisturbed animals themselves. A top-notch archery rangefinding tool like the Ranging Model 50 or Ranging Model LR-80 takes much of the guesswork out of shooting at distant game, thus minimizing misses high or low.

Every bowhunter should practice diligently at estimating yardage by eye to help him out in situations where using a rangefinder simply isn't feasible. One excellent way to do this is strolling through the woods

and taking shot after shot at dirt banks, rotten stumps, grass clumps, and similar natural targets at unknown ranges. Two or more bowhunters can make a highly enjoyable game out of such activity, competing to see who hits closest to the mark on every target. A bowhunting rangefinder is by far the most accurate means of judging distance, but practicing estimation by eye adds another important skill to the bowhunter's shooting bag of tricks.

Practice Shooting Upward and Downward Angles

As my friend Johnny Johnston found out the hard way, shooting sharply downward completely alters a bow's normal level-ground trajectory. So does shooting at a significant upward angle. The only way a bowhunter can control arrow trajectory in such situations is practicing a lot prior to season at uphill and downhill targets to develop a feel for this sort of shooting.

Here are some general rules about

Successfully shooting at game with potential obstacles in the way requires a *thorough* knowledge of arrow trajectory.

taking uphill and downhill shots. Arrows always hit higher than normal on downward shots. How much higher depends on your bow, the weight of your arrow, and the angle of the shot. Arrows shot upward hit higher than normal for the first 20 to 30 yards, then begin to drop off as the tug of gravity begins to slow them down. On longer uphill shots of 50 or 60 yards, arrows usually hit *lower* than they will on dead-level shots. Only shooting practice will give you a handle on the uphill and downhill shooting peculiarities of your particular bow/arrow combo.

Going One Step Farther

A thoughtful, experienced bowhunter goes one step farther when learning to control the trajectory of his arrows. In addition to estimating range to the best of his ability and learning to compensate on uphill and downhill shots, he makes a point of knowing where his arrow will be during its entire flight from bow to target. For example, when shooting at a

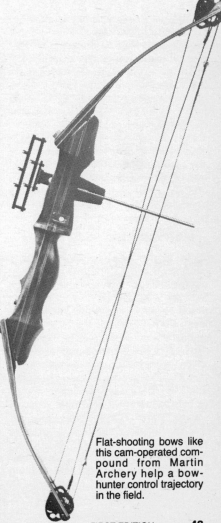

Flat-shooting bows like this cam-operated compound from Martin Archery help a bowhunter control trajectory in the field.

40-yard target, a savvy archer knows how high his arrow will be at 10, 20, and 30 yards. By learning the path of his arrow from start to finish, he can tell in advance whether his arrow is likely to clear brush and trees in front of the target. In addition, he can sometimes hit targets he cannot even see because of intervening obstacles.

Here are two examples of what complete trajectory control can do for a bowhunter. I once killed a dandy 6x6 bull elk in Montana at 45 yards. After using a rangefinder on the unsuspecting animal to determine the shooting distance, I held slightly low to compensate for the downhill slant of the shot. There were two tree limbs between me and the bull—one at 20 yards and another at 35. By placing my bowsights on the target, I could see that my arrow would go over the first limb and barely squeak under the second. My view of the bull was actually obscured by the limb 20 yards in front of me, but the arrow rose above my line of sight enough to cleanly miss all obstacles. The arrow hit the heart for a very quick kill.

Another time I shot a pronghorn antelope which I couldn't even see. The animal was standing behind a low hill with only its horns projecting above the horizon. The shot was dead level, and my rangefinder said the horns were exactly 60 yards away. Since the crest of the hill was only 40 yards in front of me, I knew the arrow would clear the rise and drop into the buck. I planted my 60-yard sight pin where I thought the buck's chest should be and let the arrow fly. It sailed over the hill out of sight and the horns disappeared immediately. A minute later I was gutting out my prize, a fine 14-inch trophy with long, even prongs. The arrow had hit the spine directly behind the shoulder, knocking the pronghorn flat on the spot.

Learning proper shooting form is extremely important in bowhunting. So is practicing diligently on the target range to condition shooting muscles and tighten target groups. However, control of an arrow's trajectory at random field-shooting ranges is far more critical in practical hunting situations. A sensible bowhunter uses a relatively flat-shooting setup, learns to estimate shooting range within a yard or two, and thoroughly familiarizes himself with the trajectory peculiarities of his particular bow/arrow combo. The end result is supreme fieldshooting confidence and far more game in the bag. ●

Open-country animals like pronghorns and mountain goats often require lengthy shots with a bow. As a result, exact range estimation is a must.

Hit Their Vitals . . . Get Your Vittles

THAT PIECE OF ADVICE is as good today as it was back when the early settlers and the mountain men depended upon big game as their main source of meat. Although our modern guns are far superior to the muzzle-loading rifles of yesteryear, most of us are not as good as the men who stood behind those old-time guns.

One hundred and fifty years ago most of the men were physically stronger and had more endurance because almost everyone lived in a rural or wilderness area where muscle-building hard work was a way of life. In most of those areas game was abundant and the hunting competition light because the human population was sparse. While modern sportsmen may "hobby-hunt" for several weeks a year, many of the old-timers

Proper bullet placement, or lack of it, can make the difference between success and failure in the field.

by LEONARD LEE RUE III

Whitetail buck, slightly quartering: (1) Brain; (2) Neck; (3) Shoulder; (4) Heart. Given the trophy nature of this animal, shots 1 and 2 would ruin a beautiful head of game. Shots 3 and 4 are, perhaps, best.

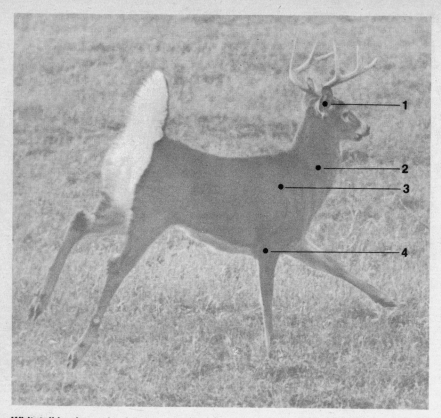

Whitetail buck, running full speed: (1) Brain; (2) Neck; (3) Shoulder; (4) Heart. Considering this buck is running full tilt, the torso is the easiest portion of the animal to hit; hence, a shoulder or heart shot would be recommended.

hunted continuously throughout the year and many hunted professionally almost every day of the year. Such men were far better woodsmen and marksmen.

Almost everyone at that time either hunted or raised farm animals to butcher for food. Up until the specialization of farming after WW II most farms were diversified enough so that most families raised their own meat. During the 1930s and early '40s, when I was raised on a farm in northwestern New Jersey, we always butchered three or four pigs and a steer each year for meat. The best way to learn the anatomy of an animal is to butcher it; and, the knowledge of anatomy is crucial to being able to make a clean kill. Most hunters today don't even butcher the game animals they have shot; they haul it off to the nearest meat locker. Hunters who do this deprive themselves of the pride in being able to do the job and, in addition, do not gain the needed knowledge of animal anatomy. The success of my latest book *After Your Deer Is Down* (Winchester Press, Tulsa, OK), shows that many hunters are trying to get back to the basics.

Everyone who hunts has a moral obligation to the game being hunted. If the hunter is not sure that he can

kill the game in the shortest time possible and in the most humane way, he should not shoot. No hunter should overextend either his abilities or the capabilities of his weapon. Throughout my many years of hunting — and game has been my main source of meat for most of my life — I have lived by that rule.

I have passed up hundreds of opportunities to shoot at game of all kinds because I wasn't sure I could kill it. This past spring I did not take a shot at a huge wild turkey tom because it stopped about 10 yards short of the spot I had picked out as within my known killing range. I do not want to wound game of any kind. I do not want to hurt any creature. I have known many hunters who will shoot at ranges outside their or their weapons killing capabilities in the hopes of wounding a head of game so they can get closer to it. Sportsmen like that are a discredit to all hunters. Wounded game may escape to die a lingering, painful death. Everyone, myself included, has wounded game, but I have never done it deliberately and I have always put the game out of its misery as soon as possible.

A few years ago I was up on the George River in Ungava, Canada, trying to photograph caribou. The

weather was bad, constant mist, snow squalls, bone-chilling dampness, but it wasn't bad enough. That fall it hadn't been cold enough nor had it snowed enough to force the caribou to leave the tundra and head south toward their traditional wintering grounds in the taiga.

I walked miles every day following their age-old trails through the stunted spruces and up on the eskers, the north-south gravel-sand ridges, that are the caribou's highways.

One morning I accepted the guide's invitation to accompany a hunting party that was going miles up the river in hopes of finding the forefront of the herd.

In migration, either north or south, the cows usually start before the bulls which follow along at a more leisurely pace. Miles above camp we encountered a lone caribou cow swimming the river. Since we needed fresh meat in camp, it was decided to take the cow. But because it is illegal to shoot a caribou in the water, the cow would have to be taken after it scrambled ashore but before it gained the protective cover of the dense riverbank alder and willow.

The hunting party consisted of four men in two canoes. The oldest man was 76 years of age and this would probably be his last hunt. I thoroughly enjoy seeing elderly hunters out enjoying themselves, and I hope to be in the woods till the day I die; however, that particular hunter, in my opinion, should have stopped hunting the year before. The elderly shooter was extremely wealthy and much more at home behind his executive desk than he ever would be out in the bush. He was dressed in a white shirt and tie and claimed those were the clothes he wore on all of his hunts throughout the world.

The caribou was tired from its swim but also very curious, as most caribou are. When it splashed ashore, it stood there broadside to watch the approaching canoes. The old gent raised his rifle and loosed a barrage of shots. He shot, and shot, and shot and shot again. The first shot hit the caribou in the paunch, the second went through the rib cage, the third into the animal's hindquarter, the fourth blew a hole in the tundra. The caribou didn't run, it didn't drop, it just sort of staggered and sagged, blood pouring from its rib cage, mouth and nostrils. I don't fault the shooting from a moving canoe, but I will condemn the man for what occurred next. With the bow of the canoe up on the beach, a well placed shot would have dispatched the caribou. To our exhortations that he finish off the caribou, he shocked us by replying that another shot wasn't needed, that the caribou wasn't going anyplace. After several minutes one of the guides could stand the tension no longer and neck-shot the animal, dropping it as if poleaxed.

Too many hunters depend upon the killing power of their cartridges and not enough upon shot placement. Far too many hunters are over-gunned, shooting rifles packing more wallop than is needed for the game being hunted. The rifle that packs a wallop on game also packs a wallop on the hunter. Consequently, when such a hunter pulls the trigger, he flinches in anticipation of the recoil and that flinching destroys accuracy. Most hunters don't shoot enough to become familiar with their gun no matter what caliber it is; the more powerful

the caliber the less likely they are to practice with it. The gun should be carefully sighted in on a benchrest and checked out again *after* the hunter has arrived at the area he intends to hunt. Despite the care in packing and handling, the sights (iron or glass) on any firearm may be knocked out of line in transit.

More hunters would kill more game cleanly if they would use the lightest possible caliber suitable for the game they are hunting. The hunter would be much more comfortable with such a gun, if he didn't take a beating each time he fired it. Increased confidence due to decreased recoil usually increases accuracy — it's an equation that seldom fails. Accuracy, of course, is really what shooting is all about. Knowing where to put the shot, and being able to put it there, results in meat on the table.

One last misconception should be cleared up. No bullet is really a "brush-buster." The heavier, more powerful cartridges and the projectiles they fire may achieve deeper penetration according to the shape of the bullet used and its construction. (On bears, for example, you need deeper penetration than you do on deer.) Admittedly, fast-moving lightweight bullets may disintegrate when they hit a twig, but even the heavy bullet may be deflected under the same set of circumstances. It remains that most game is killed in the open, even if that means only an opening in otherwise heavy cover.

Almost all domestic animals are mechanically and methodically slaughtered, under controlled conditions, with a blow to the brain. A sportsman's bullet impacting the brain of a game animal is equally lethal, but the brain case of any animal is a small target and hard to hit. For example, the brain case on a whitetail deer is about 2½ inches wide by 2½ inches long by 2 inches in height. The brain case in a moose is about 4 inches wide by 4 inches long by 3 inches high.

The Importance of Shot Placement

No trophy hunter is going to shoot a trophy animal in the brain — the shot will shatter the skull, negating any official measurement. However, it must be said that many *meat* hunters

Alaskan brown bear, side view: (1) Brain; (2) Neck; (3) Shoulder; (4) Heart. On dangerous game like bear, the author recommends a shoulder shot quickly followed by a heart shot. The first shot (shoulder) will stall or stop a potential charge — the second shot (if needed) finishing the job.

Silver-tipped grizzly, front view: (1) Brain; (2) Shoulder; (3) Heart. As with the Alaskan brown bear nearby (see same), a shoulder shot followed by a heart shot is recommended. (Also, note comments, in text, about frontal brain shots on bear.)

Pronghorn antelope buck, side view: (1) Brain; (2) Neck; (3) Shoulder; (4) Heart. Given the fact that pronghorns are the speed-demons of the North American continent, only shoulder or heart shots are recommended when this head of game is on the move. When standing as shown, the choice is yours; however, consider any trophy qualities before taking a brain or neck shot.

Pronghorn antelope buck, frontal view: (1) Brain; (2) Neck; (3) Heart. Considering the nice set of horns, a heart shot would probably be best.

bullet placement must be precise.

I have heard hunters say that brain-shooting an animal requires a shot that will place the bullet in "the animal's ear." Such hunters don't know their anatomy. A shot through the ear hole on any member of the deer family *may* cause the splintering bone to penetrate the brain; or if the shot is slightly to the rear of the ear hold, it may sever the skull from the atlas bone of the neck vertebrae. Either shot will instantly kill the animal, but neither shot is truly a *brain shot.*

The hunter who tries to shoot a bear in this same spot is going to be in big trouble because the ear opening of a bear is below both the brain case and the atlas bone connection. With both deer and bear, a shot on a line slightly higher and halfway between the ear and the eye will enter the brain and produce instantaneous death. Not many hunters can hit a target that

will go for a brain shot under ideal conditions; i.e., open cover, close range, a bullet that will penetrate, a sturdy rest, and a rifle that provides 1-inch or better groups at 100 yards. All of this, of course, must be coupled with an intimate knowledge of the anatomy of the game being hunted. Ordinarily, if a big game animal is facing the hunter, a shot placed slightly higher than an imaginary line between the eyes will enter the brain. However, a bear can be shot that way only if its nose is pointing down. Why? A bear has a sharply tapered, thick-boned skull, and if its head is horizontal to the ground, a shot placed above the eye may deflect off the skull plate. If the bear is charging, its head will be up and a shot through the center of the nose will enter the brain, while a shot in the center of the mouth will shatter cervical vertebrae. Either shot will drop a bear in its tracks, but

Trophy bull elk, side view: (1) Brain; (2) Neck; (3) Shoulder; (4) Heart. This is, truly, a trophy elk. A shoulder shot would instantly stop (or kill) this beautiful trophy animal, insuring it would be, if you will, "brought to bag." If necessary, a bullet in the heart would serve as the finishing shot.

small nor should they try unless they find themselves meeting all of the criteria mentioned above.

The cervical, or neck, vertebrae runs approximately up the center of the neck of each animal no matter whether it is viewed from the front, rear or side. The actual spinal column

Bull elk, running, side view: (1) Brain; (2) Neck; (3) Shoulder; (4) Heart. On the run, either a heart or shoulder shot is recommended.

Bull moose, side view: (1) Brain; (2) Neck; (3) Shoulder; (4) Heart. The choice is yours, but a shoulder shot will break 'em down fast, allowing for a finishing shot if necessary.

of a deer is about 1-inch in diameter but the vertebrae are about 3 inches across. The larger animals have proportionatly larger vertebrae. Smashing the vertebrae usually severs the spinal column providing an instantaneous killing shot.

A marksman hitting the atlas bone, the uppermost vertebra, where the spinal column joins the skull, will drop the animal in its tracks without spoiling any of the very tasty neck meat; however, it should be remembered that a shot in the neck of a head of trophy game may spoil the cape if the animal is to be mounted.

The shoulder blade, or scapula, is a good anchoring shot if the shot is a quick second shot to the heart will usually finish the job.

At this point it should be noted that an animal shot through the heart will die, but it may not die soon enough. Hunting history is rife with stories about animals that have charged the hunter or have run away after having their heart completely destroyed by a bullet — that's why I mentioned the 2-shot approach for bears.

I cannot stress often enough the importance of an *accurate first shot*, particularly on an unsuspecting animal that has been successfully stalked. A good candidate for a heart shot is an animal that is not alarmed, or has not exerted itself — it can often be

sharply to the rear. A shot placed here that misses the heart may break one or both front leg bones, or sever major veins and arteries or hit the lungs. This will cause massive hemorrhaging although the animal may run a considerable distance before dropping.

Lung shots are usually fatal although some game animals do survive them. In most cases the animals that do not drop instantly must be tracked. A good example is the bow hunter after deer. Often shooting from a treestand, the archer attempting a lung shot must get sufficient arrow penetration. If penetration is complete, a fast moving razor-sharp

Bighorn ram, frontal view, slightly quartering: (1) Brain; (2) Neck; (3) Shoulder; (4) Heart. This superb bighorn ram is a trophy of a lifetime. Remember, he can move fast. Go for shoulder shot first, heart shot second (if needed) and bypass potential trophy-ruining brain or neck shots.

Bull moose, charging, frontal view: (1) Brain; (2) Shoulder; (3) Heart. A moose in rut has a mind of its own. This one looks like it is about to pay the hunter a quick visit — intentions less than friendly. If you *must* drop a moose in water, under these circumstances, stop or slow him down instantly with a shoulder shot and take a second shot at the heart if need be.

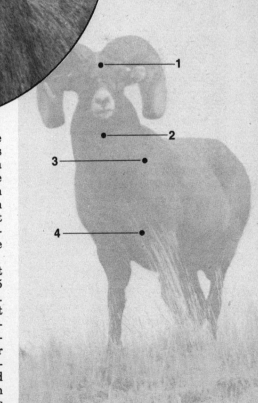

placed about two-thirds up from the bottom of that particular bone. This placement is critical because the scapula is a wide, flat, comparatively thin bone. In the deer family you can actually see the outline of the shoulder blade; however, that bone is well hidden, on bears, by that animal's long hair. The top third of the scapula covers the dorsal or thoracic vertebrae so that a shot properly placed here may shatter both the shoulder and the spine. This is the area of a bear's anatomy that's ideally suited for the "first shot." I say "first shot" because a bear is one game animal that, in my opinion, requires two, well-placed shots. Why? While a bullet in the scapula may or may not kill this animal instantly, it will prevent the bear from charging the hunter. If required,

dropped with a single shot to the heart. That same animal, if it has been frightened, or has run for even a short distance, will have adrenaline pumping through its entire body. An animal that is "hyped up" may run hundreds of yards with its heart shot out. And the meat of an excited animal will be much tougher in texture and poorer in taste quality.

A deer's heart, for example, is about 3 inches wide by 3 inches high by 5 inches long, not a really big target. On a bear, the heart lies just about at the bottom of the animal's rib cage directly behind the junction of the scapula and the humerus and on a deer the heart lies slightly above and behind the junction of the humerus and the radius leg bones. This junction on the front leg of the deer family points

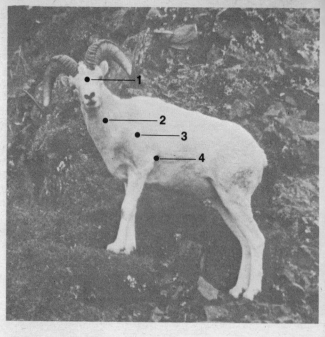

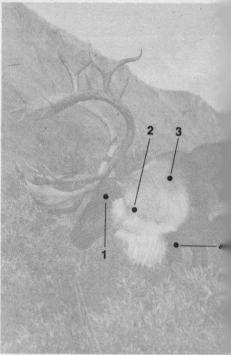

(Above) **Dall sheep ram,** side view: (1) Brain; (2) Neck; (3) Shoulder; (4) Heart. Consider the trophy aspect here. A shoulder shot followed by a heart shot would do the trick and save the trophy.

(Left) **Barren Ground caribou bull,** side view: (1) Brain; (2) Neck; (3) Shoulder; (4) Heart. Here're the problems: First, this is a record-book head of game. Second, the meat is *superb*. Considering both aspects, a well-placed bullet will break down the humerus (upper leg) on its way to the heart. The heart shot, in this instance, will require a bullet of sufficient caliber and construction to penetrate properly.

(Right) **Barren Ground caribou bull,** slightly quartering: (1) Brain; (2) Neck; (3) Shoulder; (4) Heart. Not a bad rack. A shoulder and/ or heart shot will do the trick.

arrow will come out the bottom of a deer's rib cage. If the arrow lacks velocity and/or sharpness, penetration will be incomplete and the animal will bleed internally leaving absolutely no blood trail by which it can be tracked. It is to insure such penetration that most states require a bow to have a minimum pull of 35 pounds. It's the hunter's job to insure broadhead sharpness.

The hardest shot on any game animal is when it is running directly away from the hunter. Unfortunately,

this is the shot that is most often presented. If the meat is the primary purpose of the hunt a majority of hunters will pass up a rear-end shot because of the possibility of hitting a ham and ruining a lot of meat. If a trophy animal is running away on the level, a shot placed in the base of the tail should hit the animal's spine. If the animal is running up a grade the shot will have to be held in the middle of the back. If the animal is running down hill a shot held below the anus should do the job.

An animal that stands facing the hunter offers a shot to the brain, the cervical vertebrae and possibly the spine; also the lungs and if lower the heart.

The accompanying photographs will show where the shot should be placed to hit the identified spots on the different animals at different angles. Know your anatomy, know your gun and know how to place your shot where you want it to go. You owe this to yourself and to the grand game animals you hunt.

●

Black Bear Tales . . .

. . . and other yarns tailor made for the bear hunter

by HAL SWIGGETT

"THERE HE IS!"

Stan Chee, our Mescalero Apache guide was 60 yards away, pointing and yelling. I was 10 feet away so I knew exactly where the bear was.

Bear hunting can be like that—black bearhunting that is. Often no close contact; most often no close contact. But it can happen when Murphy's Law prevails and according to long time friend Bill Jordan, "Murphy was an optimist."

Having hunted black bear in many of the western states and three Canadian provinces, and with all methods except dogs, I've found it can go from boredomsville to downright exciting. It can also make that transition in an instant. Or quicker. Such was the "There he is!" hunt.

I had hunted the Mescalero Apache Reservation in south-central New Mexico for mule deer, elk and black bear on several occasions. I had told numerous friends about my hunts, Anne Snow being one of them. She wanted a bear rug. Went so far as to ask me to bring her one. I countered with, "No way, but I will take you and let you get your own."

She accepted the challenge almost before it was out of my mouth. The hunt was arranged. At the last minute her husband, Bobby, decided to go along. Anne is a mighty good looking girl.

The author dropped this cinnamon colored heavy-coated black bear on the north fork of the Clearwater in Idaho.

The tone of the hunt was set that first morning—that it was going to be a different hunt I mean. The restaurant connected with our motel in Ruidoso didn't open until 6:30 AM. We wanted to be hunting long before that so a bit of a bribe encouraged the cook to be on hand 2 hours earlier. Bobby and I ordered a normal-type breakfast. Anne ordered a lettuce and tomato salad. See what I mean!

Stan Chee, our guide, is a friend of long standing. Born and raised on the reservation, he is also an outdoorsman first class. He almost can tell each animal by the hairs on its hide. Also knows where they will be and when—most of the time. That wasn't fair. All the time he knows *where* they will be. It is the *time* that sometimes varies—meaning every time a "fact" is stated about a wild animal the next one up will make a liar out of the "factee."

A water hole had been staked out. One used by elk, mule deer, whitetail and bear. It was at the base of a rather steep canyon. Thirty yards up the side there was a stump where an enormous ponderosa had been cut. Its base made an ideal stand. Anne, Bobby and Stan gathered around this stump. Pine boughs had been spread 2 days before to make it more comfortable. Also, a few branches had been added here and there to the light brush surrounding the stump to make the three bodies less visible. Actually, I was the arranger and the backup man too, as it turned out. I walked back down the

canyon about 500 yards and stretched out on my pickup seat.

Anne was carrying a Model 70 30-06 (pre '64 for those of you curious) and was shooting Federal 180-grain

ammunition. Bobby, for backup, had his then almost new Remington Model 600 350 Remington Magnum and 200-grain Remington ammo. I had my 6-inch Model 29 44 Magnum loaded with 240-grain Speer Jacketed Soft point bullets over 23.5 grains of H110. This load, by the way, has been very good to me over a lot of years. The M29 was in a Bianchi holster on a gun belt holding 20 rounds.

It wasn't yet daylight. Only 7,500-foot elevation mountain sounds were to be heard. Civilization, so far as we were concerned, was so far away as to be nonexistent. It got real quiet. Dawn was approaching. Then the sun came up. The day passed. Sort of fast at first with the expectation of a shot at any moment. Then it started dragging. By late afternoon it was hardly moving. But it *was* moving.

With the sun only inches above the mountain the mighty roar of Anne's 30-06 brought me to life. I was out of the pickup, gun belt in hand trying to buckle it on and run at the same time. No more than two or three steps and another shot. It sounded different. It also made me feel easier, but running was still in order.

All three of them were standing at the base of the canyon, between it and

The author's son, Dr. Gerald Swiggett, took his first black bear in Ontario, Canada, after years of trying to "Bonus-Out" while deer hunting.

Anne Snow took this black bear on the Mescalero Apache Reservation in New Mexico. She used a pre-war Winchester Model 70 in 30-06.

the water hole, looking as if they couldn't believe what had happened. Darkness was rapidly setting in.

As we headed across the clearing the story unfolded. The bear had come to water. Anne shot, at no more than 35 yards from her stand looking down at the bear. It went down, rolling, as usual, and got up just as fast—its feet in the right position, as usual. Bobby got off that second shot as it made fast tracks getting out of there. At that second shot it again went down rolling and was again up and off just as soon as its feet were under it.

Stan took Anne's 30-06. Bobby had his 350 Magnum. I had my 44. Anne said, "Where would I shoot it with this?" We looked—she had pulled her 38 Chiefs Special. As a single voice we said, "Stay behind us."

Bobby is a fine tracker. So is Stan, but it was fast getting dark, and we wanted that bear rather than let night take over and have it want us. Bobby tracked blood. Stan went to the low side, so I took the upper route in the general direction it had disappeared. Looking back every so often, Stan and I forged way ahead to try and find the bear. We stayed in the general direction Bobby was heading. The bear jumped ahead of us and Stan saw it, yelling to let us know. I took off down the mountain faster than I should have, but time was getting even more important. Two big ponderosa pine trees offered a gate to lower levels. There was low scrub brush in front and between them. I aimed to go between them.

Bobby said, from a full tilt downhill run, I stopped instantly, like I had hit a brick wall. He added that my 44 Model 29 was out and aimed so fast he didn't really see it happen—just instantly it was there. It could be that that bear suddenly raising up to full height with arms outstretched 10 feet in front of me had something to do with it.

When the 44 butt hit the palm of my left hand, (I know no other way to shoot except with the pair of hands God gave me) one of the 240-grain bullets took off for the bear's throat. I aimed just under the chin which was just below those beady black eyes that didn't look at all friendly.

This was happening, as you might have figured out, while Stan was yelling, "There he is!"

I missed. Not the entire neck, but the center where it counted. A hunk of meat and hide flew off the side. The bear slapped its neck, I think harder than the bullet hit, then sort of lunged forward. I don't know why I didn't die right there. The move turned out to be its way of getting those front legs back on the ground. A bear is several feet long. Now with its front feet on the ground, we were *mighty* neighborly. So neighborly, I knew it had halitosis. That, folks, is too neighborly for a wounded bear.

The bear had all the advantage, but it turned out it had decided that me and the 44 were meaner than it—at least it spun around and was off down the mountain galloping alongside a fallen log. One more 240-grain bullet from the 44 saw it on its way, but touched nary a hair. As the bear

These bear hunters were successful. They set up a small blind made of pine boughs directly above a water hole. A nice bear was shot immediately to the right of the shadow on the far side of the water.

One of the author's favorite bear rifles is a Remington 660 in 308 Winchester. Using that combination, Swiggett connected on this particular black bear.

crossed to the right, on reaching the end of the log, Bobby dumped it end over end with the 350 Mag.

In minutes it was dark.

The whole time I was in the face-off, Stan was some 60 yards back and to my right. Bobby and Anne were no more than 35 yards behind. There are three witnesses to this event, meaning my version could be biased, but all agreed it was that way. We field dressed the bear, placed it belly down over a stump, then stumbled our way back to the vehicles.

Next morning pictures were taken then the bear skinned. It turned out it was full of holes. Anne's first shot hadn't been all that bad, the bear just didn't want to give up. Neither had Bobby's shot as the bear made fast tracks away from the water hole. Stan had fired when he yelled on first seeing the wounded bear. We had paused to make sure we heard him. He had shot at the bear, however, and hit it again with the 30-06. Bobby's final bullet was there too. Then there was that hole in the neck. I simply missed my second shot.

Anyway—that bear had two 30-06 180-grain bullets through him, two 200-grain 350 Magnum bullets and the single 44 240-grain in the neck. It

looked as big as the side of a mountain when it stood up in front of me. Don't know what it would have looked like if it had been a big bear—it only weighed about 125 pounds when it was all over.

Other Black Bear Tales

Idaho, east of Pierce, which is east of Orofino, both being east of Lewiston on the North Fork of the Clearwater and maybe a gallon of gas distance in a medium-sized car from Montana, provided the big cinnamon colored black bear hide hanging on my office wall. It was estimated by those who seemed to know at 450 pounds.

The outfitter, Ray Tarbox, had given me 5 days to get a bear—then it was to be dogs. He wanted to use his hounds from the start but somehow that doesn't turn me on. After all, it's the hounds doing the hunting. Man has nothing to do with the success of the hunt other than to get there when the dogs bay or tree the critter. No patience extended. No sitting motionless for hours. No watching for that changing breeze that forces a change of position. No slow, careful, quiet, walk through the woods.

Ray had said, finally, "OK, we'll do it.

your way, 5 days then we pick up my dogs and get you a bear that morning." How's that for being sure of yourself—and your dogs?

The first day we drove logging roads as best we could looking for bear, bear tracks, signs that bear were really in the country. We saw it all. There were bear, bear tracks, and signs of bear.

Day number two we walked. Indications bear surrounded us were every place it seemed, though none were seen. Ray was out to kill bear too, along with guiding me, so shortly after noon we split, with a yonder ridge as the meeting spot an hour before sundown.

Ray was carrying a Model 70 Winchester rebarreled to 6.5 Gibbs. Rocky Gibbs was known for his sharper shoulder angle and shorter neck on the 30-06 case in an effort to gain more capacity, hence higher velocity. He had his fans too, I might add, one of which was Ray Tarbox who owned Gibbs rifles in several calibers. I had a Remington Model 660 308 Winchester topped with a V4.5 Weaver scope. Handloads consisted of Hi-Precision's 180-grain bullet over 43 grains of 4064, set off with a CCI magnum primer.

Mosquito/black fly proof headgear is a must for spring bear hunting in Canada. Same for snug cuffs and gloves. It was from this blind (the roots of an upturned tree) that the author's son killed his first black bear.

bear wan't visible until it crossed that intersection. As it did, I planted one of those 180-grain bullets on its shoulder. That is, I tried to. It was only because of the scope being on 1.5x that I could see it; sundown was near.

At the shot, it was gone. Until you've seen it, you will never believe how fast a big black bear can move. It went from a contented amble to the dash of a quarter horse instantly.

Ray was mighty quick with words: "How could you miss something that big that close?"

All I could think of was a small, 4 or 5-inch diameter tree I remembered in the edge of the scope. Ray headed for where the bear had been. I stopped to look at the tree. There was no mark indicating a heart shot on it. Not even a crippling shot mark on that tree.

Claw marks were deep where the bear had dug in to take off. Ray took off after those deep scratches in the trail. Moments later he called out, "Here it is, on his back and dead." It was too. I can't explain it, but most of the bears I've found dead were on their backs. Also, I'm sure it has happened, but I have never seen a black bear dropped in its tracks. They always have enough "git up and go" left to "git up and git" a little ways.

We field dressed it. It was for all practical purposes dark when we draped it, as best we could, over a log. Ray wanted the heart for breakfast. With my hands deep inside I insisted it didn't have one. Ray insisted it had to have one. Turned out Ray was right—only there wasn't anything left for breakfast. The trigger had been squeezed as that right leg went forward, so instead of breaking the shoulder and hopefully getting the heart, too, I had hit the heart dead center. It had literally exploded.

Our walk in the wilderness was pleasant but of no consequence. Heading for the Scout revealed, once again, God is in charge. As it darkened, which happens rather suddenly in mountains or thick forest, I had, totally without thought or plan, turned the scope magnification to its lowest power. Had it not been for that, there would be no bear hide on my office wall—at least not that bear.

To our left, maybe 50 yards away, an enormous bear stood up, looked around, sniffed the air momentarily and was back down. Had it left then, that would have been it. It must have heard us, smelled us, or at least thought it had because of that inquisitive gesture. Obviously satisfied all was well, it ambled on its way—the path of which intersected our trail 40 yards ahead. Cover was such that the

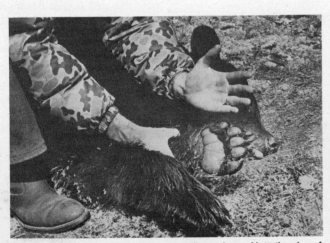

Believe it or not, this black bear is a small specimen. Note the size of the paw when compared to a man's hand.

Scouting ahead can be helpful. It's tracks like these that get a bear hunter's attention.

Baiting, where legal, is a bear-hunting reality. The can resting on the ground contains scraps of meat and bone. The rock and tree limb are designed to help keep a black bear occupied.

All because a scope had been turned down to 1.5x without even thinking about it. I'm convinced the bear would have been missed had the 4.5x setting been in place because of both dusk and closeness.

Another hunt in New Mexico—again on the Mescalero Apache Reservation. This time I was shooting a Navy Arms replica Remington Rolling Block (with the Vernier sight), chambered for the venerable 45-70 cartridge. Loads for that hunt were Winchester/Western (now it's Winchester only) factory loaded 405-grain bullets. The rifle shot well. A whitetail buck had already fallen to it. I wanted a black bear added to its victories before going on to something else.

Waiting at a spring, the Mescalero's like water hole watching and even prefer it to bait. (They could use bait on the Reservation even though it is illegal in New Mexico.) I had set my distance for a shot at 100 yards. Having hunted extensively with black powder, old cartridges, and handguns, I long ago learned to limit shots to proven distances for the gun/cartridge combo in use at the time.

Near sundown we saw the back of a bear in a gulley 150 yards or so across the clearing. It made two or three passes back and forth before coming out. It looked big and with a modern scope sighted rifle would have been an easy shot. Not, in my opinion, for the rifle in hand. Finally the bear did come out, walked to a huge ponderosa (they seem to come in only two sizes—huge and huger), stretched full length up the trunk and scratched. It appeared the bear was going to climb the tree. I even drew my legs under

me getting ready for a fast 135-yard dash because once it got a ways up that tree I figured it was my bear.

There was a momentary urge to shoot, even though the distance exceeded what I had set as maximum. It would have been a safe shot because the entire spine was exposed to a dropping bullet. Discipline is a feat I take pride in and, an art for that matter, that I would encourage all hunters to practice. It adds to, rather than detracts from, the sport. True enough, shots, good shots, will be passed up. Sometimes returning home without firing a shot will be the result. It's a great feeling though, knowing you had the choice. I really belive a man walks a little taller bacause of it.

The big bear walked off. Had I known how really big it was, a shot would have been fired. We found out how big that bear was the next morning when we came back after the one I killed a few minutes later. Scratches on the tree were finger-tip high to a 6-foot man stretching as far as he could. It *was* a big bear.

Near dark, (it seems to always be "near dark" when bear killing time rolls around) Stan and I got up and headed for the pickup. Standing near the spring and looking up on the side of the mountain (miles from where Anne killed her bear), there was a bear sitting on a log watching us. It appeared to be 80 yards away. The rifle came up—it was barely visible through the peep sight but the bead seemed steady on its chest—so the trigger was gently squeezed. The big 405-grain bullet hit squarely between its legs, dead center in the chest, and knocked it over backwards. The bear crawled a dozen steps up the moun-

tain before giving up, in spite of that center chest hit.

Canadian bear hunting is good, too. I've enjoyed the sport in Saskatchewan, Ontario and Quebec. One of the better hunts was in Ontario, near Sudbury, along the Georgian Bay. Ted Gorsline was the outfitter. A good bear hunter he is, I might add. Ted uses bait exclusively for spring bear hunting. He uses baits in a far different manner than I'd ever seen used anyplace—stateside or Canada. Normally an enormous amount of scrap meat and bones are piled up. Bears gorge themselves then lay up for 3 or 4 days.

Ted, however, uses teaser baits. Small amounts of scraps and bones from friendly butchers. Some are hung in onion sacks several feet above ground at a barely reachable height. Others are under cans held tight to the ground by heavy rocks or logs. Ted says if a man can barely lift it, even a young bear can toss it aside. He puts the weight on top to make the bear stay around for a while allowing time for a shot should there be a hunter in that particular blind. Up to a hundred baits are put out for his spring hunts.

My son, Dr. Gerald Swiggett, had bought a lot of bear licenses when we hunted throughout New Mexico, Colorado, Wyoming and Montana for mule deer and elk. He had never been allowed a shot though he did see a bear in Colorado. He had, also, never been on a bear-only hunt. I decided to take him to Ontario.

Spring bear hunting in Canada is the greatest, but then so are the black flies and mosquitos. Don't *ever* go into the Canadian woods in the spring without long sleeves with tight cuffs, a net head cover, and an ample supply of black fly/mosquito repellant. They will flat out eat you alive if not protected.

We carried lunches and planned to stay out all day every day. Lots of bears are not seen because there is a tendency among hunters to hunt only early and late. I've seen and photographed black bears all day long. Same goes for deer and elk. If you are hunting—*hunt*—you can rest when you get back home.

Gerald and I sat at baits for 3 days without seeing a bear, yet bears were hitting the baits every day. They were not hitting the baits we were watching during daylight hours, but there is no way to know that until a day has been spent waiting. The fourth day a really big bear came to my bait, rather headed for it, from the only spot I couldn't see to shoot.

I hadn't heard him. There wasn't a

sound. Suddenly a feeling that something was closer than it should be caused me to slowly turn my head. There was barely 12 feet between its eyeballs and my eyeballs as we stared at each other. I was in a blind made up of small logs and tree limbs with my back against a sizable tree. No way in the world to shoot to the right or back—and that was where it stood.

Something had to give, so I grabbed the Marlin 444 Remington and jumped up. The Aimpoint sight was flipped on with the same motion. Since we both started at the same time, it was 50 yards away and disappearing fast through the cover by the time I got up, swung the rifle over the obstacle course, and got on it. Only a glimpse of the south end of a north bound bear did I get. By then it was dark—as usual.

Next morning Ted had a blind selected for Gerald that was close by camp. The decision was to get him there before daylight, minus breakfast. Pickup time was set for around 10 o'clock.

Gerald shoots a 270 Winchester Model 670 and does his own loading. Nosler 160-grain bullets over 57 grains of 4831 is his load for bear or elk. His scope is a 6x Weaver. A bit more than needed for this type hunting where shots can be anywhere from 15 to 75 or so yards.

When we got there, Gerald had a bear. He had killed it at 6 AM, about 10 minutes after getting in the blind. He said the bear walked under the bait, then a few steps on toward the blind, and stopped with its front feet up on a rock to sniff the air, making sure it was safe.

It wasn't. Gerald's Nosler bullet hit about an inch off center of the throat and went full-length through the body. We found it in a ham. It ran about 30 yards before collapsing.

Canadian law allows party hunting. This means shooting can continue until all limits are filled. Conceivably by the same hunter. I suggested Gerald be taken to the blind where I had seen the big bear for the evening hunt. His first had been skinned, salted, and packed away in a cooler. Ted was busy so he described the location of the blind in question to a friend who agreed to provide transportation.

Dark-thirty we went after the bear.

As we drove up I commented this wasn't where I had seen the big bear. By then we could see Gerald standing beside the logging road. He was very excited as we got out of the pickup.

"I shot it—the big one you saw yesterday!" He didn't say "killed," and it

was dark. I asked, "Where was it the last time you saw it?" His response was quick, "Right where it is laying." What a relief.

This one had come to the bait, milled around, walked off, came back, seemed to sense something was wrong but wasn't sure enough to leave. Gerald, for some strange reason, knew it was a sow. He watched closely for any sign of a cub. There was none. The bear was around the bait several minutes, long enough for Gerald to be sure there was no cub with it. The sow was big—so Gerald put another of those 160-grain Nosler bullets in its direction. A perfect heart shot at 35 yards. It ran 20 yards and dropped. He already had it field dressed and drained.

Two bears on the same day after several years of wanting one and many licenses bought. Ontario is like that. His second weighed close to 250 pounds. A mature sow that appeared to have maybe just reached full growth and probably had never had a cub yet. Some say it takes 4 years for a sow to mature.

Bear hunting is great sport. However, most bear are killed by deer hunters who stumble on to one and get in a lucky shot. I prefer walking, bait or stands because that puts the hunter

on the same level as the bear and at a decided disadvantage. Yes, disadvantage, even over a bait. The hunter *must be motionless* and have the wind on the bear. It is not as easy as it sounds. Only those who haven't tried it belittle it.

Rifles for bear? Most anything good for mule deer is fine plus all the "woods" rifles, whatever that might mean. To this writer 243/6mm is not big enough. Start with the 270 and stop with the 30-06. Nothing bigger is needed, that's for sure. Any of the 7mm calibers, except magnums, are fine as is the 308 Winchester. Use one of the heavier bullets in your caliber for best results. Old-timers like the 30-30, and the 35 Remington and 45-70 are ideally suited for black bear hunting.

Scopes should either be low powered fixed, or low powered variable in 2x or 3x.

Where to go. All I know about is the West and part of Canada. New Mexico has a lot of bear. To try a hunt on the Mescalero Apache Reservation write to: Game Department, Mescalero Apache Reservation, Mescalero, New Mexico 88340. Southern Colorado, the Pagosa Springs area, has a lot of bear. Judd Cooney is a fine guide, totally dependable and trustworthy. He can

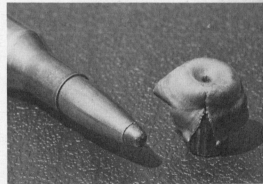

On the left is an unfired 160-grain Nosler 270 bullet. The slug on the right represents the same bullet after it entered a black bear's throat, completely traversed the body and came to rest in a ham.

The day the author had his eyeball-to-eyeball confrontation with an unwilling black bear, he was carrying his Marlin 444 topped with an Aimpoint optical sight.

be reached at Box 808, Pagosa Springs, Colorado 81147. Judd is a former Colorado state game warden.

Ted Gorsline is the best black bear outfitter I know in Canada. He can be contacted at 45A Henry Lane Terrace, Toronto, Ontario, Canada M5A 4D6.

Try a spring hunt. A black bear only hunt. You will be glad you did. ●

Using Today's DECOYS

Waterfowl habits and habitat are constantly changing. As a result, the decoys of today come in all sizes. Here's what to buy and how to use them.

by TOM ROSTER

TODAY'S DECOYS are not the same as yesterday's. In fact, today's waterfowl decoys are radically different from the waterfowl decoys of the past. As with all things new, they require some adjustments in thinking and in usage.

Yesterday's waterfowl decoys were usually constructed of wood, cork, or a wood fiber product and were about the same size as the species they were intended to imitate. There were many famous carvers who produced commercial lines of wood or cork decoys. The Carrylite Company was probably the most famous for producing a floating duck and goose decoy line made of molded paper fiber. Today, you can still buy a cork decoy from L.L. Bean, and if you know the right person, you may still be able to get a stool of decoys carved out of wood. Other than this if you're planning on buying a waterfowl decoy today, you can count on it being made of plastic.

Plastic is king in waterfowl decoys these days, and several types of plastic are used by the several different modern-day plastic decoy manufacturers. You'd have to be a chemist to keep the different types of plastic separate, but for the waterfowler, suffice it to say, today's plastic decoys can be categorized in groups.

Water Decoys

Most of today's decoys, like yesterday's, are floating duck or goose decoys. But today's plastic decoys come in a variety of construction designs and sizes that were not available in days gone by. Like the good old days, most of the plastic floaters in use today are of standard size. That is, the body size of the decoy is about the same size or a little smaller than that of the species of duck or goose it is

painted to represent. The development of the standard size decoy is logical enough. The makers were merely trying to imitate the chosen waterfowl species in every way possible from plumage colors, to head position, to body posture. Making the decoy the same size as the real McCoy seemed, I'm sure, the correct thing to do if you want total imitation.

On a commonsense level, standard-size decoys make lots of sense. From a practical and empirical standpoint, though, they often don't. The reason for this is that rapidly moving waterfowl, flying at various heights above the water, simply cannot perceive clearly the exact plumage patterns on a carefully painted decoy or real bird for that matter, nor can they gauge the actual size of the bird or decoy being observed as they circle or pass overhead.

Given this reality, a reality that is readily apparent if you do much flying in small aircraft, there is really no reason for a decoy to be the same size as the real thing. Nor for that matter is it necessary to have decoys with super detailed paint jobs. The perfect paint job and the perfect size is only of value when the observer is in very close proximity to the bird or decoy being viewed, and then only if the object of study holds relatively still.

Whether by reason or by trial and error, decoy makers seem to be discovering this because today there are three distinct sizes of floating duck and goose decoys for sale. The standard or life-size is still the most popular—largely due to tradition and price—but two other sizes are now gaining in popularity.

Those other two sizes are both larger-than-life-sized. The first size larger than standard is commonly referred to as magnum. Whereas a standard mallard decoy might be about 15 inches in length, a magnum-sized mallard decoy will measure 18-20 inches. The magnum plastic floaters,

therefore, are just slightly larger than the biggest adult of the species in question. The other size larger than life is the supermagnum. A super-magnum mallard floater will measure from 21 to 25 or 26 inches long, or about one-and-one-half to two times the size of a typical mallard.

Largely because of weight, wood decoys were seldom carved oversized. This is less true of cork decoys. The magnum and super-magnum sizes, it's fair to say, never really flourished until plastic became the major decoy production material. Because plastic decoys can be made hollow, the weight savings was so great decoy manufacturers began experimenting with sizes.

The principal idea behind today's magnum and super-magnum size floating duck and goose decoys is to increase the visibility of the spread. This is especially useful to waterfowlers hunting over large open water areas, or anywhere that ducks fly by at a good distance from the hunter's setup. As previously stated, ducks at a distance can't judge size accurately, and so it doesn't matter to them that the decoy spread they're eyeing from ¼-mile away is composed of individual decoys that are twice their size. While the size difference should become more obvious the closer they get to the spread, it doesn't seem to matter because both ducks and geese will pitch right in to rest and preen among decoys two to even five times bigger than they are.

The point is that from ¼-mile away a dozen or so standard-sized decoys may not be noticeable at all to passing ducks and geese. But magnums and super-magnums will show up just enough to get their attention. Just which size floater to use is a matter of both practicality, hunting environment, and cost.

If cost must be kept to a minimum, then the standard-sized decoys will be the least costly investment. But if suc-

cess is the goal, then I'll summarize size choices in one piece of advice: get the super-magnum. Whether you hunt a small pond or a large open body of water, my experience and the experience of most really good duck hunters I know is that today's ducks and geese seem to decoy the best to the biggest setup of the biggest sized floaters you can afford. This is especially true if you are hunting in competition with other decoy spreads. The more competition, the more the biggest decoy spreads made up of the biggest decoy bodies become imperative to success.

Why is this? My feeling, based on closely observing waterfowl for several years, is that today, once ducks and geese reach major wintering areas, they are tending to rest, move, and feed in ever larger concentrations. This is not because there are more ducks and geese; the fact is, ducks are generally declining in numbers, although Canada geese are generally increasing. Rather, I attribute it to declining suitable wintering areas both in total acreage and in the quality of the habitat left. What numbers of ducks and geese do survive, in other words, are being forced to winter on declining state, federal and private lands. They are being forced to artificially concentrate to survive. Hunters viewing these wintering concentrations are thus often deceived into thinking there are more and more waterfowl each winter. There are not; in fact, there are less. The numbers are just more confined.

So, in Grandad's day, widely dispersed groups of large numbers of waterfowl tended to move and feed in small groups and pairs. Today's more concentrated, diminished numbers of waterfowl tend to move and behave in larger and larger groups. They tend to do more things alike at the same time, simply because they have fewer choices of resting areas, and in some wintering areas, less feeding choices.

The relative size difference between the standard size goose shell (left) and the magnum (center) and super-magnum shell (right) is obvious. Today's super-magnum sized waterfowl decoys add a great deal of visibility when hunting over large, open water areas. To increase the visibility factor even more, use drakes predominantly and keep the distance between decoys large.

So, mass-flocking behavior is the common behavior of today's waterfowl.

To successfully hunt this situation, today's waterfowler must have the equipment and skill to pull large groups of ducks. The easily decoyed singles, pairs, and small bunches are much less common than they were even 10 years ago. More often than not, I now count on having to decoy bunches of 10 or more ducks, rather than less than 10. I plan for this reality on nearly every major wintering refuge, state, or private area in the continental U.S. other than the most pristine potholes in the prairie states of North and South Dakota.

Which brings me to the size of decoy spreads. Gone are the days for most waterfowlers in most areas where 12 decoys will consistently produce limit hunting. Today's bunches of 10 to 100 to 1000 ducks in a passing flock won't usually look at 12 decoys twice except in the most extreme of weather conditions. I've found that the waterfowler of the 1980s must learn to set large decoy spreads that imitate the large concentrations which characterize the behavior of today's waterfowl. That means plain and simply that today, on anything but the smallest potholes, a decoy spread must consist of at least 5 dozen decoys if you're after consistent success. If you want to be sure of decent shooting, I'd say no less than 80

decoys are required for most water spreads. Now certainly there are exceptions, but I'm saying that as a rule for day-in and day-out good hunting over water, today's waterfowler must be prepared to set large spreads of large-bodied decoys.

The final consideration in a floating

decoy today is plastic type and design. I'm not going to name the various plastics here except briefly. Rather, descriptions of the decoy types will be more meaningful. Today you can buy hollow plastic decoys. They come either with a rather flexible plastic shell or a hard, rigid plastic shell.

While pairs or small groups of waterfowl may be seen during migration, it is much more common, today, to encounter large flocks. Why? Shrinking habitat.

There are also hard plastic decoys filled with plastic foam. Hollow decoys are also available made from rubber or rubber-like vinyl. And finally, solid-bodied plastic decoys can be purchased made of molded, expandable foam plastic.

Of these choices the most delicate are the hard plastic, hollow decoys. If dropped or hit by a stray pellet or two, these decoys will crack or even shatter. Once cracked they will sink, and the cracks are nearly impossible to seal since it's quite difficult to find a glue that will bond well with many of the plastics being used in today's decoy construction. The hard shell exterior, foam-filled decoys are also a bit delicate, but if the shell springs a leak at least they won't sink. It's just that you will be forever draining water from them.

The solid foam plastic floaters are an unsinkable bet, but if not molded quite densely the tails tend to break off. This can be repaired with wood dowels for reinforcement and the right kind of glue. The hollow, vinyl inflatable decoys are probably the most rugged—you can literally throw them in a pile day after day without damage, but they are easily overinflated taking on a round bottom contour. This causes them to rock unnaturally in rough water. They are also very heavy in the magnum and super-magnum sizes. So the hollow vinyl decoys are best employed on sheltered waters and ponds.

The all-around most serviceable de-

These honkers were taken over a spread of two dozen super magnum (shell-type) decoys. Note the size difference. Amazingly, geese will flock to the super magnums long before they even wink at a spread of standard-size decoys.

This hunter enjoyed a limit shoot of both mallards and Canadian geese. He used a spread of magnum-sized Canadian goose and mallard floaters. Note the distance between decoys and the hole left to segregate goose and duck deeks.

Waterfowl, today, seem to be resting and flying in ever larger flocks once they reach their wintering areas. To have a chance at decoying such birds, today's hunter must set *large* spreads of decoys.

When using the new super-magnum (field-type) goose decoys, place them directly on the ground with lots of space between each decoy. Also try to use a ratio of about 80 percent feeder heads to 20 percent uprights to effect a contented feeding flock.

coys in my experience are the hollow plastic decoys made from a fairly flexible plastic. These decoys do not crack when dropped, hold a paint job well, are self-sealing when hit by stray pellets, and are relatively light.

The hollow plastic decoys made of blow-molded polyethylene are lighter, but polyethylene is more rigid and thus, brittle.

When transporting water decoys by boat, the weight of the decoy is of little matter. But if you are hiking your decoys in, then weight is everything. The best decoys for the hike'em-in hunter are the hollow, blow-molded, polyethylene decoys with hollow water keels in the standard size. The best decoys for the open water hunter are the solid foam bodied, or flexible shell, hollow decoys with built-in solid keel in super-magnum size.

When buying floating decoys another consideration is head position. A flock of ducks or geese with every head in the spread at the same height and in the same position is not as natural as one with a variety of head positions. Therefore, anytime you can get all you want in a given body size, keel design, and composition in a plastic decoy and still have a head style that allows you to turn the head, buy those decoys.

The last consideration is plumage color and ratio of hens to drakes in duck decoys. The least important consideration in a decoy is the faithfulness and detail of feather and plumage paint jobs. A solid brown decoy works just as well in pulling ducks as the most carefully painted ones on all except the most bright of still, calm, bluebird days. However, the brighter plumage patterns of the drakes in duck species show up from further away than the mottled and muted browns of the hens. For this reason your spread should feature a higher preponderance of drakes to hens. Duck decoys come packed usually six hens and six drakes per dozen. A better ratio would be 10 drakes and two hens. Trade all the hens you can for drakes or paint your hens to look like drakes.

Field Decoys

In days gone by it was rare to find any maker of wood or cork field decoys. What field decoys that did exist were full-bodied affairs that rested on stakes and were a bear to transport due to their bulk and weight.

Plastic has changed all that. Today's plastic field decoys are remarkably light, fairly durable, and nearly always of shell design rather than full-bodied. Like water decoys, field decoys are offered in three sizes — standard, magnum, and super-magnum. Unlike water decoys, most field decoy lines are available in goose rather than duck species.

As with water decoys there are probably more standard-sized decoys in use than the larger sizes. As with water decoys, the standard size shell decoys are about the same size as the goose they intend to imitate. Of the three available sizes the standard is the least expensive per dozen.

If the proper clothing is worn, there is no reason to "pit-in" when using today's shell-type decoys. You can lay down right in the decoys and rise to shoot. Note preponderance of feeding heads in this spread.

The available magnum goose shells are about twice the size of the actual goose being hunted and increase the visibility of the spread greatly without adding much weight. The super-magnum goose shells are truly something to behold, usually measuring about three to five times larger than the real McCoy. Unlike the magnum, the super-magnums are greatly increased in weight, making transportation the number one problem in using the super-magnums besides their usually steep price tags.

The biggest problem most hunters have with the super-magnum, though, is getting used to them. It's hard for a lot of hunters to accept the idea that a Canada goose would decoy to a plastic shell that looms up five times bigger than the biggest of honkers. But believe me, they do. In fact, I would say nothing is more deadly on Canadas than a spread of 3 dozen or more super-magnum Canada goose shells. And if you don't believe me, just try setting up a spread of 100 or so standard size Canada goose shells and 3 dozen of the super-magnums nearby. The Canadas, especially the larger races, will almost always work the larger shells in preference to the smaller ones, even though there's only a third the number.

So, if visibility is the goal (and it usually is in wide open field areas), and if money and transportation are not a problem, my advice for Canada goose and whitefront hunting is to set a spread of 3 dozen or more super-magnum Canada goose shells for optimum results. Five or 6 dozen are even more effective.

For snow geese, numbers, not body size seems to be most effective. For snows, 200 of today's standard-size shells will draw the white birds well. The magnum size helps, but isn't really needed for snows. The same goes for the super-magnum shells.

The greatest value of the magnum shells is in Canada or whitefront hunting where the hunters may have to pack their decoys long distances to set them up. Where mobility is a problem, the magnum size shells offer the best of both visibility and portability. When you have to pack your decoys, I'd select the magnum shells every time.

Besides snow goose hunting, I've found the best use of the standard size goose shells for ducks, not geese. I've taken all of mine and painted them like drake mallards. They make a great magnum-sized duck decoy for field-feeding mallards. When I hunt geese, I've gone exclusively to either

The author retrieves a pair of Canadian geese taken over a spread of six dozen magnum and Canada goose shells. It's results like these that make the new, larger-than-life decoys a real bargain.

the magnum or super-magnum shells depending upon transportation limitations.

One big advantage of the super-magnums is that they are so large and heavy you can set them directly on the ground without having to support them on stakes. Not only will they still show up well, their weight keeps them from blowing over in all but the worst of winds. Additionally, the super-magnum shells' large silhouette allow the hunter to hide among them by lying directly on the ground (assuming the proper colored camouflage clothes), without having to go to the hassle of digging a pit. This is a great

asset in the winter when the ground is frozen.

Today's decoys are larger and lighter than those of yesterday. The larger sizes when set in large numbers are particularly effective for eliciting good decoying response from ducks and geese which these days seem to be moving in larger groups.

Gone are the days when a dozen decoys will produce limit shoots. Good hunting today over decoys demands big spreads and a large dollar outlay. In this respect the lighter, plastic decoys of today allow the hunter to set a spread that offers maximum drawing power. ●

AT THE OUTSIDE limit of my shooting range, the buck made a sharp right-hand turn. He was now moving slowly and directly away from me. The entire length of the spine presented itself as a target. I earred back the hammer on the custom 54 long rifle, took a sight picture, held my breath, clicked the set trigger, and with a good lead and holdover, touched her off. The buck stopped. He backpeddled a couple steps. He could go no farther.

I was hunting with my little daughter, Nicole, not quite 4 years old. We were on foot at the time, and I had to pack her a distance and then let her walk a little while my arms rested. But we had our buck, just the two of us out there on the flatlands. I was pleased as I field dressed the 15-incher. Nicole helped by holding up a leg as I worked. The round ball had harvested another buck, and though I would collect three antelope that season, as I had three antelope tags, I would not grow bored with the speedy pronghorn.

Our camp was high above the plains, and Nicole and I made our way to the site, where we safeguared our buck from the forthcoming morning sun by situating it in the trees. We then began cooking our meal and laid back after a long and interesting day. "Sage hen for supper," I told Nicole, and she nodded in approval.

I've not grown tired of seeking the pronghorn antelope. Some say it's too easy a target to be a challenge. At times, the antelope indeed can pull

by SAM FADALA

fool tricks that will put it in the bag. I suppose I added the muzzleloader to my list of pronghorn-taking tools because this form of the sport increased the excitement. But I have had a devilish good time, too, watching a few "great bwanas" blow shots at the "easy pronghorn." I've had a chuckle or two as these sports told me getting an antelope was easier than buying a package of steaks at the supermarket, only to later run into herds grown wild from no more than a cursory contact with hunters.

But, we have to admit that the odds of putting a pronghorn in the freezer are truly very good. And that, surely, is not all bad. I don't think we have to face the ultimate challenge every time we go afield. If this were true, a great many of us would have given up on cottontails and squirrels a long time ago. No, there's nothing wrong

With over 100,000 antelope taken annually, Wyoming is truly the antelope harvest capital of North America.

On the fantastic Red Desert of Wyoming, these antelope stand out clearly and can be spotted from a very long distance. Even on such flat terrain, the antelope can be stalked by a hunter willing to belly-crawl over the ground. Watch out for the cacti!

ANTELOPE MECCA

Antelope are not always on the flattest part of their habitat, though they are certainly open-country animals. Here, a herd is negotiating a small hill. They are in a good place as far as a stalk is concerned.

with going out for a big game head that you pretty much know is going to be yours in a day or two of hunting.

I've hunted antelope in various areas, and I think a hunter can bag one in any state he chooses to hunt in. But we have to admit that Wyoming is the antelope capital of America. In recent times, the state has granted an annual tag number going beyond the 100,000 mark if one counts the additional antelope permits in that number. Wyoming has allowed a hunter as high as three permits, one "any antelope" tag, which he can use for a buck or doe, and two more tags which are legal for non-buck antelope only. Each and every tag for the state is issued on a drawing basis, however. This is good because it allows for a spread of hunters and a much more useful harvest.

One area may have a scant handful of permits issued, while another has a couple thousand. Game management of the antelope herds has been very successful because of the excellent policies followed by the fine Wyoming Game Department. But there is more to the game management unit and permit system than good management. There is also a much better chance for a quality hunt when the hunters are distributed throughout the habitat, not only by units, but also by time, for the entire state does not open in one fell swoop.

Private Land

The would-be Wyoming antelope hunter who lives in another state writes for his information early in the year. The very best advice I can give him is to be careful on the choice of area. But isn't antelope hunting good in all areas? Mostly. I am not worried about that. I'm concerned with *access*. About half of Wyoming is private property, and a lot of that private property lies squarely upon antelope terrain. A hunter does not have the right to pursue antelope on this land without permission from the land-owner, often *written* permission.

It is conceivable that a sportsman could arrive from out of state only to learn that most of his antelope hunting area is privately owned. Private property makes for excellent antelope hunting, to be sure, and some ranchers allow trespassing for a small fee. But the hunter should know *before* he reaches Wyoming just what he's going to find waiting for him by way of access. Since much of the private antelope hunting is widespread over the state, and since so much super anteloping is available on private grounds, it pays to check ahead. Naturally, if the hunter has signed on with an outfitter, then access is assured.

I often hunt on private ground, and before I put in for a permit, I check a land status map. If I find that I want to hunt a section that is private, I'll check with the rancher *before* I put in for that unit. The Wyoming Game & Fish Commission has branch offices around the state, and a hunter can call or write for names of ranchers.

Once in the area, the hunter is responsible for staying on the ranch he has acquired trespass upon. Therefore, it is up to the outdoorsman to get good directions from the rancher and to pay attention to those directions.

Antelope are curious animals. This buck has come in to see what was going on as the author waved a rag in the air. Trying to lure antelope in for a shot is not a practice that works all the time, but it can work some of the time.

Cindy Zollinger of Rexburg, Idaho, enjoys a trophy on the plains of Wyoming. She used a 7x57mm custom rifle to bag her buck. New hunters enjoy antelope because the game is usually in sight much of the time and success runs high.

hunters who have a lot of fun enjoying the field together is ideal. A group of hunters should set the ground rules before they ever leave home. Then there are no surprises later on when we learn that Charlie prefers getting up at 9 o'clock and Jim hates to drive.

Often, there must be some agreement as to who shoots first or who hunts with whom. If a fellow jumps out of the rig in the early morning light of the first day and bags a big buck, there should be no questions in the minds of his companions that it was his turn and his right to shoot first. These little pre-agreements can make for a much more agreeable camp.

Someone is always going to come off with the big boy of the party. I am, personally, much against competition in hunting. I think it spoils the hunt. Competition is great in tennis, on the football field, at work and in many acts of life, but on the hunt, it's mostly a waste of good time. A hunter has to be happy with his buck because it is *his* buck. On one hunt, two fellows from out-of-state bagged almost identical 13½-inch bucks. They were so ecstatic that their feet didn't touch the ground all the way back to the base camp.

In the camp, there were about a dozen outdoorsmen altogether. No one other than the two gentlemen had fired a shot that morning, for one reason or another. The antelopeless hunters took a good look at the hanging bucks and admired them. And at that time, the guide said something I thought was pretty clever. "Boys," he addressed the two beaming men who had tagged their bucks, "right now you have two great big bucks hanging there. But by this time tomorrow, they could both get pretty small." He was referring to the fact that one of the other boys would probably get a bigger head before the hunt came to a close.

Guns and Terrain

Antelope country is flatter than Switzerland, but it is not as flat as most folks think, at least not everywhere. The pronghorn hunter should bear this in mind as he proceeds to hunt his game. Antelope can be stalked. Those of us who have taken them with bow and arrow and muzzleloaders know this is true. I say this because I've noticed that a lot of antelope hunters think the only way they are going to bag a buck is to fire at one clear over into the next county. It is true that antelope will often present a challenging long shot. But it is also

But I like the private ranch, as it can often be another positive limiting factor. In short, the rancher will generally set a limit on the number of hunters as maximum for his spread, and he won't exceed that number for a given time period. This means less crowded conditions. Wyoming is a big state, and the hunter who visits this "Cowboy State" should enjoy the wide open spaces.

Permit in hand, the hunter is ready to collect Mr. Pronghorn in Wyoming. Planning carefully is going to, often, be the key to success. When I speak of success, I mean much more than bag-

ging a buck. In many units, over 90 percent of the hunters are going to do that. With a success rate of 90 percent plus, and that includes those tags belonging to "no show" hunters, a fellow ought to be taking an antelope back home with him.

But there is also success in the sense of enjoying every minute of the outing. It's then that the little things count for so much. The first of these, I think, is the getting together of compatible hunters. Sharing a trip is more than splitting the cost of the gas. It is also sharing the camping and the driving and the footwork. A party of

Antelope camps can be anything from elaborate to plain. The author, on an antelope/deer hunt in Wyoming, picks a small draw as a temporary home. Nothing fancy here, but the campsite was smack in the middle of both deer and antelope territory.

Dean Zollinger took his antelope buck with a 7mm Magnum. A great number of calibers are useful on the plains, but the so-called "high-velocity" numbers are generally the best in terms of long-range shooting, since they take some of the guesswork out of adjusting for trajectory.

true that a hunter can certainly get a lot closer than several hundred yards if he will remember that there are breaks in the land to conceal a stalk.

The hunter who does get close enough for a reasonably sure shot is going to enjoy that stalk and his chances of making a clean kill will be greater than they were from super long range. Of course, hunters generally overestimate the range out there on the flatlands. My son had bagged a nice buck one season and when the buck was hanging in camp a group of hunters stopped to admire it. "How far away did he get it?," they wanted to know, and we said it was a fairly long shot, about 200 yards. They laughed.

"Heck, I got mine at 700 yards," one of the guys said, and another piped up with a similar range.

"What are you shooting?" I asked. They were both using the 30-06 and factory 150-grain ammo. "How did you sight in?" I asked next. They had sighted in for 200 yards. "How high did you hold?" I then inquired. Turned out they had both held about a ½-foot over the backs of their bucks.

From where they said they hit their bucks, I figured they had been about 250 yards away from them, maybe 275. Had they truly fired from 700 yards, they would have had to hold several *feet* high. At 600 yards, sighted for 200 yards with factory ammo, the drop would have been over 80

inches, or over 6½ feet. These gentlemen were not liars whatsoever. They truly believed they had taken antelope at 700 yards. They had not. In fact, the antelope is a rather small target as big game goes, and when out on the plains, he presents a pretty modest target when he is 200 to 300 yards out there. I prefer stalking to long-range shooting.

Since taking up a long love affair with muzzleloaders, I have failed to harvest the bigger bucks I see each season. In fact, this past hunt I had what was surely a buck over 16 inches in horn length, and I stalked to within 200 yards of him. But with my muzzleloader, I felt 200 yards was too far. On the other hand, I did end up with a 15-inch buck, and I was thrilled to harvest this animal with a round ball. So it is up to the individual as to a choice of antelope artillery.

If I were absolutely pinned down to name the finest antelope cartridge in existence, I could not do it. There are so many great ones. As already mentioned, the antelope is not large and this means that even at longer ranges there is enough punch left in the smaller calibers to get the job done cleanly. The 243/6mm class is just right for most antelope hunting. Here we have cartridges of mild report and recoil, yet sufficient energy to drop an antelope on the plains. Light, handy rifles are available in these 24-caliber packages. For example, the new 6½-

pound Remington Model Seven will be available in both 243 Winchester and 6mm Remington chamberings.

The fellow who owns any of the 25s in the 257 Roberts class is also in business. The 250 Savage, 257 Roberts and all of the take-offs on these cartridges are excellent for antelope. The big brothers to these rounds, and now we are speaking of the 25-06, 257 Weatherby Magnum and that ilk, are no doubt among the finest of all long-range antelope getters. Loaded with any of the "big game bullets" now available, such as the Nosler, Hornady Interlock, Speer Grand Slam, and similar projectiles, these calibers will down a buck without undue destruction.

In the 270 to 30-06 class there are several rounds which make fine antelope cartridges. These are certainly more powerful than necessary for antelope hunting, but if a man owns any of the 27- to 30-caliber models, he's in business. I have heard the remark that these do not drop an antelope any better than the 243 and 6mm at up to 300 yards. Actually, there is some truth in this, but the reason has nothing to do with any of the cartridges named here. The fact is, defunct is defunct. When an antelope is hit correctly with one 6mm type bullet, he's done. Therefore, we often see no better performance from the larger calibers.

While it is, perhaps, less appealing to give the nod to many rounds for plains hunting, rather than selecting a few favorites, the truth stands clear—all of the high velocity calibers are good. If I were to pick one round for antelope hunting only, where long-range shooting happened to be paramount in the selection, where a shooter wanted to be able to practice and have a very effective caliber at longer ranges, then I suppose the big 257 Weatherby would get the nod. Owners of the 7mm Magnum class, firing the 139- or 140-grain bullet at, perhaps 3300 fps, would also have a bid for best rifle status.

At any rate, the shooter should pay much attention to his plains firearm, be it a 6mm, 270, 257 or 300 Magnum. The rifle should be sighted with great care. While all big game rifles should be so sighted, so the shooter knows exactly where his bullets are going, the long-range rifle is even more sensitive in this domain because the line of departure, the angle if you will, makes off-target sightings a disaster as range increases.

Look at it this way—if a rifle is slightly off the mark, and a deer hunter shoots at the chest area of a buck at 50 paces, he might be off a few inches. While this condition is not to be praised, being off a few inches at 50 yards probably won't account for a miss or a botched job of harvesting the game. But at 250 yards, the angle has turned into a real gremlin. No longer off by a few inches, as it was at 50 paces, the bullet can now be off many inches, and the result could be a miss, or much worse, a wound instead of a clean kill. In short, the antelope hunter should practice at a couple hundred yards, and it might behoove him to back off to 300 yards and set up an antelope-sized target to shoot at. I prefer a target a foot square. This will give the shooter a fairly good idea of the actual chest area vitals that he will be firing at.

Everyone knows how you actually get an antelope, and it does not seem to matter whether you are coursing the high country of Arizona, Nevada, Colorado or Wyoming. You drive around using a spotting scope and field glasses until you find a herd which contains a good buck, and then you stalk as close as possible, hopefully, and you get the buck. Let's be honest about it. It is often this way. But I submit that if this is all a man knows about antelope hunting, he's no antelope hunter.

The antelope range is shared by many other residents, including livestock. The needs and desires of a great number of people, from hunters to ranchers, must be met; therefore, management of the land is imperative for the best interest of antelope and livestock. This horse is sharing a big parcel of real estate with the pronghorn—location: National Grasslands in Wyoming.

Nicole Fadala, not quite 4 in this photo, has hunted antelope with her father, Sam, from her earliest days. Now, the two go together on several trips. Nicole is learning to stalk and to help care for the game once it is down. Author took this 15-inch buck with a .535-inch round ball from a Dennis Mulford custom rifle.

Furthermore, I'd find such routine pretty boring in no time. However, there is more to the Prince of the Plains than this. I again admit that antelope are easier to get than Arizona whitetails, but after a herd is stirred up a bit, this is not always the case. Also, when a person wants to hunt for a truly large buck, he may find that he's better off having more tricks up his sleeve than merely driving out, looking and shooting.

Species Traits

Knowing something about the pronghorn is what makes it enjoyable to hunt. It's truly a well-adapted animal. Its race goes back in time 20 million years and has made it on the plains because of many attributes. First, I suppose, is its speed. I have heard so many arguments about how fast an antelope can run that I'm no longer sure I know what speed to relate as factual. Some say it can hit 70mph. Others say that this is nonsense, and with a Wyoming tailwind it's lucky to do 35mph. I only know that I have been driving at 55mph, with witnesses in the car, and I have had antelope keep up alongside the car for short distances. I think an antelope can hit 55mph, therefore, though I don't say any antelope can do it. Surely, as in our own race, there would be at least some physical differences among the antelope individuals.

As for eyesight, there is again argument. Some say the antelope can actually magnify its view. I don't know if it can or not. I do know for certain that I have set up a tripod with a 20x Bushnell spotting scope on it, and I have searched for antelope herds on the flatlands. I have found herds so far off that they were truly invisible to the naked eye. And yet, the antelope seemed to be watching me. If I had a partner walk out away from me to my left, all heads moved in that direction. If I waved a hat in the air, all eyes followed the motion. They could see me. I'm sure of that.

Another wonderful trait of the antelope, though at times it makes some ranchers unhappy, is the breeding rate. For the first year of production a doe may drop but one kid. However, she will generally have two kids after that, a buck and a doe. Twins, then, are a rule, not an exception, and I have seen does with triplets, or what at least seemed to be three kids belonging to one dame.

These nervous feeders put down lots of food in a day and will often drink daily if they can find water.

Antelope are often seen bordering highways in Wyoming. They are generally awake for most of the day, feeding a good part of the time, though they will often bed down during the daylight hours, especially in windy weather. They will also, quite often, feed for an entire day on one range of ground.

The coal belt in Wyoming has attracted development, of course, but there are plans to safeguard the environment and replant mined areas. The author visited one such site and was impressed with the restoration project. Antelope, as with all game, need habitat as a foremost criteria for continuancy.

Hunters should note all of these things. Hunters should also be aware that the antelope will be feeding during the daylight hours. They, unlike most deer, seem to prefer the night for rest. Therefore, the serious 'lope hunter brings his lunch and hunts through the day.

They are not big animals, as we have suggested. The bucks will only dress at 90 pounds or so for the mature animal. Averages are always dangerous, for they include the very light and the very heavy. But I'd say that though one study showed average buck weight to be 127 pounds, doe weight only 105 pounds, the mature antelope buck can run 140 pounds, live weight.

Hunting Tips

There are a few tricks the wise antelope hunter can employ, and I'd like to mention three of them here. First, it is true that antelope can tend to lose some of their natural caution as the day wears on. I have had a devil of a time getting close to a skitterish buck, only to stay with him by keeping him in sight until late afternoon, at which time he seemed to calm down considerably. So I suggest that the late afternoon is a fine time to keep after a big buck. As with all rules of thumb, this won't work all the time, but it has paid off for me. As a black powder hunter, I found that one way to get that 75-yard shot was to stick to a buck until later in the day.

Second, it is good to know that antelope seldom jump a fence. I have seen them jump fences, so anyone who thinks that an antelope will *never* jump a fence, or cannot physically jump a fence, is dead wrong. In fact, my son Bill and I were escorting a friend of ours on a Wyoming antelope hunt. Debbie Kane had come from Colorado, where her husband is an excellent big game guide, to stay with my family for a couple days of antelope chasing. As Bill, Debbie and I drove along we saw, in one day, two cases of antelope jumping fences, and these were different antelope. They simply walked up to the fence and sailed over it like a rocket.

However, all in all, antelope seem to hate jumping fences. They will go through them when they must, but not often will they go over them. This is a good bit of knowledge to have, as we have seen a herd of antelope following a fenceline, and since they do not usually jump a fence, we have paced like crazy, gotten ahead of the herd, which was only walking slowly or we would not have had a chance,

and actually met the group as it worked along the fenceline. Antelope can tend to continue in a direction once they have established that direction. I have had 20-yard shots with bow and muzzleloader by spying an antelope on a trail and then positioning myself along that trail until the antelope actually walked up to me. So knowing about fences and the sometimes determined paths antelope take can be a bit of helpful knowledge for the hunter.

The third item is small, but can be useful. Antelope do make a sound. They emit a little yelp when they are disturbed. I have heard this yelp when I could see no antelope whatso-

ever. But because I heard the cry, I started looking and eventually found a herd or quite often a few separated animals. So, the "bark" of the antelope can be a signal which can lead a hunter to find a herd that may be hidden in a draw of beyond the crest of a hill.

We might also mention that an antelope can consume over a gallon of water on a very warm day, though they will take in much less than this on cooler days. However, a hunter who sees a windmill and a waterhole next to it should at least take a good look at that area. Often, antelope will frequent a place where good daily water is available.

Wyoming is unique in the fact that lands may be checkerboard, so to speak, in status. Here, on the vast Thunder Basin National Grassland, there is much open public domain. However, there is also intermixed private property. *The hunter must check land status before attempting to take game.*

The use of optics is paramount when it comes to finding antelope on the plains. Author uses a Bushnell spotting scope for locating antelope. He also carries binoculars.

The hunter knows that antelope can see wonderfully, and he knows they are fleet of foot. But what about hearing and the sense of smell? Frankly, although I live with antelope virtually in my backyard, I do not know the real facts on these traits. I have, however, had antelope walk right up to me when the wind was at my back. Deer, I think, would have bolted. My friend Kenn Oberrecht and I were in a sandy wash, having just stalked and then passed up a buck, when all of a sudden here came a herd of 40 antelope right in the bottom of the same wash we were sitting in. The wind was at our backs. But every one of those animals walked right past us. I can assure anyone that had we moved, the antelope would have bolted like quail in the short grass, but smell us they did not seem to.

Hearing? I have made stalks in which I was not perfectly quiet. And the buck seemed to pay no attention to small noises that I made. But then I have to admit that I have seen an antelope raise its head as I cocked the hammer on my frontloader, this from 75 paces distance. I suspect the antelope can hear fine. He simply pays more attention to the messages received by the eye than those taken in by the ear, or the nose for that matter.

How about luring a buck right to you? I have done it. But I have only lured bucks up a few times out of dozens of tries. Let me just say it can be

accomplished. By lying flat on the ground, I waved a hat in the air one time, and a buck we just could not close in on walked in 200 yards closer and the fellow I was with downed him. I have tied a handkerchief to a twig, and had antelope walk closer to it, though they did not come right up and sniff it.

On one occasion, while hunting near Buffalo, Wyoming, I got a chance at a bow and arrow shot at an antelope by pouring some of "Tink's #69 Doe Lure" on a rag and fixing the rag to a bush. The animals, in this case, did walk right up to the rag, which I am sure they saw long before they smelled it. But when they got a hundred yards from it, since the wind was coming from the rag to them, I'm fairly sure they smelled the lure, for they walked right into the rag.

All in all, there are several ways to bag a buck. I like to set up a good camp and enjoy the chase. I have elected for a muzzleloader as my hunting tool, though I have a strong urge to tote a 257 Weatherby one of these seasons so I can bag one of those big boys that always seem to hang back about 50 yards farther away than I care to shoot with an old-fashioned thunderstick. One of the more enjoyable antelope hunts is a fine camp, but a hunt which is primarily on foot. I like to slip a daypack over the top struts of my packframe and just wander out all day long in

what I know to be "hot" antelope country. That is fun, because one will generally see more than antelope that way.

While some snobs feel that they are too good to consider antelope a top trophy, I don't give a damn. I'm still going to chase the plains for them. It hardly matters which plains they are. Wyoming is a big first choice because there are so many permits, but other states have fine antelope herds, too. New Mexico is noted for big bucks, so is Arizona. And a buck taken by a good friend of my son Bill will rank way up in the top couple heads in the world. That buck was harvested in Montana, a fine antelope state.

Although the winter kill can destroy many antelope and in some places studies show that half the fawn crop is devoured annually by coyotes, the race continues to thrive. The antelope will be here as long as man wants him to be. When the habitat is turned into a parking lot, of course, then the antelope will fail. Until that time, hunters will be able to go on the plains and harvest this renewable resource. While not the most cunning of North American game, finding and harvesting a big antelope buck can provide the hunter with a very worthwhile and long-lasting experience. And Wyoming has quite a number of opportunities for the hunter to enjoy. ●

Centerfire bullets for big game are all the same, right? Wrong! Here's a look at what works best.

Big Game Bullets —

What works best for reloaders. by RICK JAMISON

These two bullets are 180-grain Hornadys recovered from an elk. Although the bullet at bottom lost its core, both bullets penetrated just as deeply and inflicted an equal amount of damage.

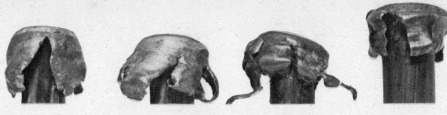

These bullets were all recovered from game—they represent four different brands. From left: Nosler, Sierra, Hornady, and Speer. All illustrate excellent expansion characteristics at different ranges.

(Left) The hunter after large game has entirely different bullet performance requirements than the shooter going after varmints. In this case it's penetration *vs* rapid, explosive expansion.

THOSE WHO RELOAD metallic centerfire ammunition, do so for a lot of different reasons. For many, reloading provides ammunition that is more accurate than anything available from the commercial manufacturers. For others it's a matter of economy. Lastly, and more importantly, there's the hunter/handloader who is anxious to turn out a variety of accurate, powerful ammunition, that will solidly anchor big game or turn a varmint inside out.

It's the hunter/handloader who, unfortunately, often overlooks the most important component of his reloads — *the bullet*. Selecting the right projectile for the right job is, perhaps, the most important element of any hunting handload. Selecting the proper (or improper) projectile for the kind of hunting you intend to do will play a vital role in your cartridge's over-all efficiency in the field. Accuracy, retained velocity, bullet penetration and expansion are not controlled by case size and powder charge alone.

Every year there are dedicated hunters who go afield and hunt with home-brewed ammunition loaded with bullets they have complete faith in. When the moment of truth arrives, those hunters expect their projectiles to fly fast and flat, crash through bush without being deflected, penetrate to the animal's vitals from any angle, not destroy meat, drop any size animal instantly and not waste energy by coming out the other side.

Unfortunately, it doesn't always work that way. However, let's forget about the hunter and talk strictly about the bullet, and what this tiny hunk of alloyed lead encased in an alloyed sheath of copper, nickel and zinc must do.

The first thing that any hunting bullet must do is quickly travel from the gun muzzle to the animal. In these days of large-capacity cases and belted magnums it's no secret that a fast moving bullet carries more energy to the target and has a flatter trajectory. This flatness of trajectory is important because range estimation for a hunter is not so critical when trying to make a hit at extended ranges.

Bullet velocity, however, is not determined by barrel length and case capacity alone. Once a bullet leaves the gun's muzzle the velocity that it will carry to the target is totally dependent upon the projectile itself. The more streamlined a bullet is, the greater its ability to overcome air resistance and to retain velocity (and energy) downrange at the target. The term *ballistic coefficient* is the numerical result of a mathematic equation that reflects a bullet's ability to overcome air resistance. Ballistic coefficient figures can be readily found in the various loading manuals. In short, the higher the ballistic coefficient, the better the bullet's ability to overcome air resistance and retain velocity. Another term which relates to a bullet's ability to retain velocity is *sectional density* which is the ratio of a bullet's weight to its diameter. If two bullets of a given diameter start out at the same velocity, the longer, heavier bullet will generally retain its velocity to a greater distance as long as shape of both projectiles are the same.

In practical terms, a boat-tail bullet generally retains its long-range velocity slightly better than a flat-base bullet while a "spitzer," or pointed bullet, retains more velocity than a round nose bullet.

As already mentioned, a heavier bullet retains its velocity to a greater distance if diameters, shapes and initial velocities are the same. However, this statement is the clincher for, as handloaders know, heavier bullets usually can not be fired safely at the same muzzle velocities that lighter bullets can. Hence, bullet weight *vs* velocity is a tradeoff. There is a point at which using a heavier bullet gains the shooter nothing because he sacrifices so much initial velocity that the trajectory curve is more arched. (The bullet drops more.) Slower bullets also drift more in the presence of a cross wind. It's generally thought that heavier bullets drift less in high winds though many people overlook the fact that wind drift is also a function of the bullet's time in flight. The

(Above) The boat-tail spitzer bullet (right) has a very slight advantage over a flat-base spitzer for extreme long range shooting as it retains more velocity and energy at greater distances.

(Right) A spitzer bullet, left, is generally much better suited for long-range shooting than the round nose bullet, right. The spitzer bullet retains its velocity and energy to a much greater distance downrange than the round nose design.

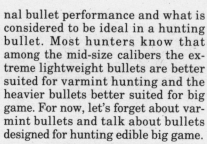

nal bullet performance and what is considered to be ideal in a hunting bullet. Most hunters know that among the mid-size calibers the extreme lightweight bullets are better suited for varmint hunting and the heavier bullets better suited for big game. For now, let's forget about varmint bullets and talk about bullets designed for hunting edible big game.

The Game Bullet

One of the foremost criterion for any big game bullet is *penetration*. It must penetrate enough to reach the animal's vitals. A second generally accepted criterion is that the bullet should destroy ample tissue along its path. The third criterion is that the bullet should impart adequate shock to disable the animal quickly. Fourth, it's preferred that the bullet destroy a minimal amount of meat.

There are all sorts of ways that various bullets meet these criteria, and there are almost unlimited variables that can alter a given bullet's performance. The manufacturers control bullet performance by manipulating core hardness, jacket thickness and toughness, and over-all design of the jacket and core.

Variables that may be imparted to the bullet by the shooter and his individual rifle include, among others, rotational velocity resulting from the

barrel's rate of twist, the distance that the animal is from the shooter, the angle or position of the animal, the amount of vegetation or brush that the bullet must penetrate before meeting the animal, where the bullet impacts the animal, and others.

While the bullet manufacturer has the capability to alter the performance of his product, he really has his work cut out for him in trying to make a bullet that will perform well in the face of all the variables the hunter and his rifle may impart.

One of the most common complaints that hunters have regarding a big game bullet is that the core and jacket separate on impact. A few

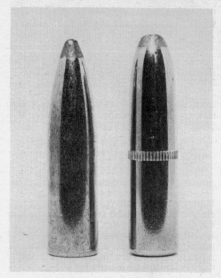

The hunter who seeks his game in the wide-open spaces should make certain that his selected hunting bullet will expand well at extreme ranges.

more time that that wind has to act on a bullet, the more the bullet will drift off course. This is yet another reason for selecting a fast, streamlined bullet.

When it comes to hunting bullets, it's the terminal performance of a projectile (the moment a bullet impacts the game) that most hunters are concerned with. There's a lot of discussion and disagreement about termi-

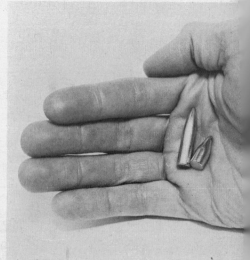

This photo illustrates extremes in available 30-caliber bullet weights. At left is the Speer 200-grain Spitzer alongside the 110-grain Speer Spire Point. The 200-grain bullet is designed for controlled expansion and penetration on large game while the 110-grain Spire Point is designed for rapid, explosive expansion on smaller varmint-size game.

years ago, I shot a five-point elk with a 30-06 rifle loaded with ammo using 180-grain Hornady spire point bullets. The elk was about 75 yards away and was trotting almost broadside to my position but at a slight angle away from me. I fired twice. Both bullets hit the elk about 4 inches apart and both penetrated through the ribs and chest cavity, stopping under the hide on the opposite side of the animal. Both bullets destroyed almost an identical amount of tissue and penetrated the same, yet when I recovered those two bullets, one's core and jacket were intact while the other was recovered in two separate pieces about 1-inch apart. Either bullet would have killed the elk quickly. However, had some hunters found only the single bullet with the separate core and jacket,

(Right) There is a large range of bullet types from which to choose in any given caliber. The serious sportsman would be wise to select a proper hunting bullet for the terrain he hunts in, and his own hunting habits *before* going into the field after game.

This photo illustrates the carcass of a mule deer shot with a 300 Winchester Magnum rifle and a 180-gr. Nosler Partition bullet. Many shooters would consider the 300 Winchester Magnum to be entirely too large for deer hunting, saying that the round destroys too much meat. However, if a bullet is selected properly, very little meat destruction results, as shown here. (All blood-shot meat has already been cut away.)

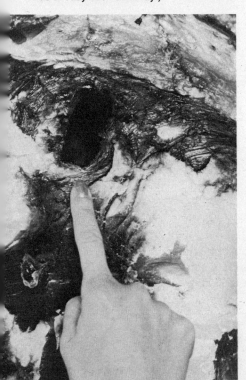

they would have considered that bullet to be a failure. As long as a bullet *penetrates well* and does the job I can't see what difference it makes if the core and jacket are recovered separately.

Another area where considerable disagreement occurs regarding ideal performance is in the *amount* of penetration a particular bullet may or may not provide. Many hunters feel that ideal performance is achieved if a bullet penetrates almost through an animal (particularly on a broadside lung shot), lodging just under the skin on the far side. For some reason, this is thought to be better performance

than if the bullet completely exits the animal. The reason generally given by those hunters is that they don't want to use a projectile that expends the bulk of its energy on a hillside after it exits the far side of the animal.

Unlike these hunters, I prefer to have a bullet that penetrates completely through the animal and is still traveling at a good clip when it exits. It has been my experience that the exit hole is a major contributor to a good blood trail, and believe me, this *is* important. Even when an animal is hit vitally, it may still travel some distance before going down. In dense cover, a good blood trail can make the tracking and eventual location of the animal a quicker and easier chore. Also, when a bullet stops within the animal's body (and this point is generally overlooked), the tissue-destruction channel becomes increasingly smaller as the bullet's velocity decreases. If a bullet stays inside the animal, the last few inches of penetra-

tion generally do relatively little tissue damage. On the other hand, if a bullet completely exits the game, the amount of tissue damage is greater because the wound channel travels fully through the vitals of the animal's body.

Some hunters feel it is paramount to put game down instantly. This is generally accomplished with a large bullet diameter that expands with a very large frontal surface and is fired at good velocity. Such bullets frequently destroy more tissue than other types of bullets although they don't always penetrate quite as much.

I, too, have hunted in areas of the eastern United States where I felt that it was important to put a deer down quickly, possibly at the sacrifice of some meat. Under those circumstances it is better than risking the loss of the entire deer to another hunter because it ran 50 or 100 yards.

Some years ago I used a 243 Winchester loaded with 100-grain Hornady bullets while hunting in the south central region of Pennsylvania. I was accustomed to hunting mule deer in the West where there was no worry about another hunter claiming a dying animal, even if it traveled several hundred yards before going down.

Just after daylight, I was making my way up the mountainside when I heard something crashing through the brush. I stopped and instantly turned toward the noise just as a big-racked whitetail came running down the mountain at me. Instinctively raising my rifle, I suddenly realized that the buck was going to pass less than 20 yards in front of me.

When I fired the big buck went down, floundered a bit and regained his footing whereupon I shot him again—he stumbled down the mountainside out of sight. Sensing I would have an easy time finding the buck, I looked down at the ground trying to locate my empty cases. Hardly had my eyes met the forest floor when I heard a volley of gunfire about 75 yards below.

(Above) Even the same bullet will perform differently, sometimes drastically so, when fired in different cartridges. Though these cartridges (both loaded with 150-grain bullets) are capable of taking large game, the small-capacity 308 Winchester, left, does so with much less velocity than the large-capacity 300 Winchester Magnum, right. As would be expected, the 300 Winchester Magnum is more likely to promote rapid bullet expansion than is the small 308 Winchester. Bullets should be selected for the velocity of the cartridges they'll be fired in.

(Left) Hunting game in dense-cover areas requires bullet performance different than that which would be considered normal on game found in the open plains.

(Below) These are all 180-grain 30-caliber bullets and, as the sectioned view illustrates, each is constructed differently. A serious hunter would be wise to select the one *best* suited to his needs *before* going afield.

I quickly picked up the two cases and started tracking the big buck; he had left distinct hoofprints in the soft leaf litter on the forest floor. I didn't see any blood along its trail but that didn't surprise me for I doubted that the 243 slugs exited such a big buck, particularly at such close range.

The buck had gone perhaps 100 yards and met the gunfire of three hunters from Ohio who had ventilated the buck's body liberally. At that point, there was no telling whose bullet hole was whose, and one of the hunters had already tagged the buck.

Not wanting to spoil a hunt with an argument and since I preferred not to cut my hunt short anyway, I started after another buck. Three days later, I bagged another whitetail buck which wasn't nearly as large as the first.

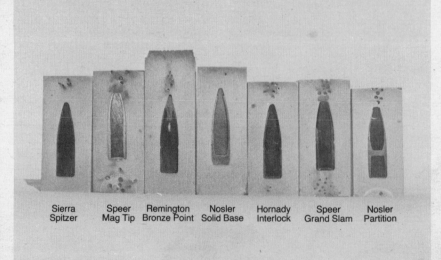

| Sierra Spitzer | Speer Mag Tip | Remington Bronze Point | Nosler Solid Base | Hornady Interlock | Speer Grand Slam | Nosler Partition |

Had I been shooting a larger caliber rifle loaded with ammunition using a bullet designed to destroy more tissue (and penetrate completely), I have no doubt that I would have claimed the big buck. From that point on I decided that I would use a larger caliber when pursuing large game in such heavily hunted areas.

Some bullets expand to the point where they present a relatively small frontal diameter in relation to other bullets. Bullets of this type, when compared to those that mushroom rapidly, nearly always penetrate more assuming the velocity of both is the same. One bullet that expands with a relatively small frontal diameter is the Nosler partition. The jacket of this bullet generally peels back to the partition and the sides of the frontal section fold back close to the bullet's shank forming a small frontal surface. Consequently, the bullet usually penetrates deeply creating a relatively small wound channel along its path, and then exits the animal on the off side.

The expansion of more conventional bullets can vary, however, depending upon impact velocity. For example, when using the 250-grain Speer Hot-Cor in a 358 Winchester on both elk and bear at close range, the bullet performance was excellent. There was minimal jacket peel-back or expansion due to the reduced velocities and the heavy bullets normally used in that small-capacity cartridge. Certainly, the 358 Winchester might give less than ideal performance if the range were several hundred yards. However, I know what sort of performance to expect from the bullet/cartridge combination and use that round only when I'm hunting in dense, short-range cover.

The place where a sportsman hunts may well dictate the ranges at which he will expect to see game. If he prefers to hunt thick cedar swamps or hardwood thickets, the ranges are likely to be short. On the other hand, if he hunts canyon or mountain country or sits along the edges of clear-cut areas in dense forest, the ranges are apt to be long.

Some hunters claim to take only lung shots on broadside-standing animals while others prefer to jump game out of a bedding area and shoot the animal as it departs. In the latter instance considerably more penetration with less tissue destruction is desirable.

Perhaps the sportsman's own hunting/shooting style is the biggest factor in selecting a bullet that will provide the best performance. For this reason, it seems to me that a hunter must determine for himself which bullets best suit his needs. In this day and age it's impossible to expect to shoot enough big game to get any sort of meaningful evaluation of a hunting bullet's performance. Certainly, no sportsman should go into the field to "test" a bullet while hunting. If the bullet being tested is a poor one, he may have a disappointing experience. Besides, a single bullet won't tell all.

Conduct Your Own Bullet Performance Test

A hunter can, however, easily determine the performance of a given bullet in relation to other bullets by simply shooting them into an expansion medium. Shooting bullets into an expansion medium is not just for the ballistics expert. Actually, it's no more difficult or time-consuming than patterning a shotgun.

There's a variety of media that can be used to check bullets for expansion. Some that have been used successfully include: water, clay, Duxseal, and ordnance gelatin. One that I use all the time and that works quite well is water-soaked newspapers. You can either save your old newspapers or obtain some at the local newspaper office in the form of "spoils." These are the papers that are ruined when setting up the press and getting the proper inking. They're generally discarded and are given away for the asking.

If you're using newspapers it's best to bundle them into 8- or 10-inch stacks, leaving them folded just as they appear at the newsstand. The bundles are then immersed in water overnight, allowing them to swell up.

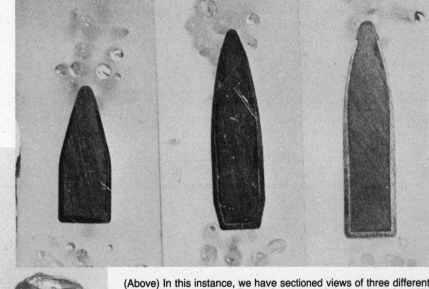

(Above) In this instance, we have sectioned views of three different 30-caliber Speer bullets. From left are the 110-grain spire point, 165-grain boat-tail, and 200-grain spitzer. Note the thinness of the jacket on the 110-grain bullet as compared to the other two projectiles. Bullets like this 110-grain Speer are designed to expand rapidly—they're not for big game.

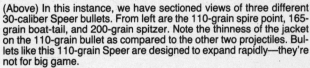

(Left) This photo illustrates the 180-grain Speer Mag Tip bullet (left) and its expansion characteristics when fired from both a 308 Winchester rifle (center) and a 300 Winchester Magnum (right) at a distance of 50 yards. Note how expansion characteristics differ drastically depending upon the velocity at which the bullet is fired.

(Above) Bundled, water-soaked newspapers offer an excellent expansion medium for checking bullet performance.

(Right) Here's a 180-grain Speer round nose after being fired from a 300 Winchester Magnum into a wet newspaper expansion medium at very close range. Note how the bullet expanded very rapidly and that the core separated from the jacket. Such a combination might be more ideally suited to a lower velocity, 30-caliber cartridge, such as a 308 Winchester, for the same close-range shooting.

Hornady's Interlock line of hunting bullets is another example of bullet construction designed solely for the hunter. When sectioned, you can see an internal, protruding ring of jacket that securely grabs the base of the lead core. That "ring" serves to retain the core within the jacket as it passes through game tissues.

Of course, the subject of hunting bullets wouldn't be complete without the mention of the famous, time-tested Nosler Partition lineup of hunting bullets. Like the Hornady and Speer offerings, Noslers come in a wide

If you haven't already guessed, those bundles get very heavy so be sure to tie them securely and avoid making them too large. Also, don't wedge the bundles down into a smaller container before they're soaked — they will expand considerably and can become jammed tight if you aren't careful.

The newspapers should be used as soon as they're removed from the water. I generally use a 4-foot thick section when shooting expanding, centerfire rifle bullets. In my experience, most bullets will be stopped within the first 2 feet of the medium. The newspapers have an advantage in that the strings around the bundles can be cut and pages flipped until the bullet is recovered. Then, you can make notes regarding depth of penetration, size of destruction cavity, recovered bullet weight, frontal diameter, percentage of weight retention, etc. Or, if you prefer, you can simply eyeball them in order to keep things simple. A hunter can learn a lot by this process. The answers the test medium provides will tell you which bullet is likely to give the best performance without having to test it on live game.

I want to emphasize the fact that an expansion medium gives only a rela-

tive bullet performance comparison. It, by no means, should be considered as being directly comparable with animal tissue. No artificial expansion medium can do that. The best we can expect to get from these tests is a *relative* performance comparison with an artificial medium. Once a shooter begins conducting bullet expansion performance tests, he'll suddenly discover that all bullets perform differently.

Another way to determine the approximate potential performance of a bullet is to simply cut a bullet in half. By "sectioning" a bullet one can determine the internal structure. For example, even in conventional bullets one can see the variations in jacket thickness between different brands, and the amount of jacket thickness tapering an individual bullet may possess.

Speer's line of Grand Slam bullets was designed to specifically meet the needs of hunters. Each Grand Slam bullet possesses certain characteristics that can be readily seen once a bullet is sectioned. Each Grand Slam projectile has a lead core that is much harder at the base than it is at the nose; and, after sectioning and polishing, the differences in lead-core hardness are apparent to the naked eye.

range of calibers suitable for big game use. Each Nosler Partition bullet is composed of two separate cores — the frontal nose core and the base core, both being separated by a beefy, internal, gilding metal partition. The Nosler is designed to expand only to the partition, and no farther, so that the base core remains intact allowing the bullet to penetrate deeply.

As you can see, there's a lot involved in deciding what it takes to make a big game bullet. It depends upon the hunting country — the terrain, vegetation, and expected range. It even depends upon the sportsman's own style of hunting — whether he takes only broadside lung shots or whether he'll shoot a departing animal. It depends on bullet placement. There's no over-estimating the importance of shot placement. The species and size of the game is another variable when it comes to selecting a bullet. The particular cartridge that the projectile will be fired from, as well as the projectile's velocity are other variables that must be dealt with. By conducting your own tests in a uniform expansion medium you can determine for yourself which bullet you think will perform best for your particular hunting task. ●

The Mag Seven's Enough

by CLAY HARVEY

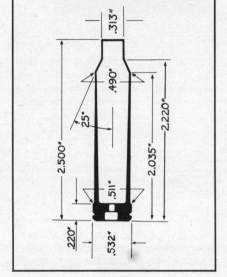

"...If I were restricted to one caliber for all game on this continent, it would be the 7mm Remington Magnum. *There would be no second choice.*"

THE BIG bull had its hackles up. It knew something was amiss, just couldn't point an antler at what it was. My hunting croney, Dave Jacobson, was as skittish as the bull. The rut was on; the elk had been lying up in the timber, which made them hard to locate and even harder to see clearly. This old boy, a fat five-pointer, was partially screened by alders; only its neck, part of its rack, and a little shoulder peeked through the shrubbery. Dave insisted upon a clear shot, a clean kill; the chance offered was too risky. So he was waiting the bull out. The tension was palpable. All the bull had to do was turn and head off in another direction, and the chance would be blown. He snorted and took a step, completely exposing a shoulder. Dave put a round through the rib cage and decked it. His rifle was a 7mm Remington Magnum.

All day I had been trying for a coyote. I'd shot at one roughly 400 yards out, just missing it. My elevation was okay — I was using a very flat-shooting load — but my offhand shot landed a little left of where I'd intended. The yodel-dog took off at an angle, and before I could work my bolt, Rick Jamison dropped him. (Rick was smarter than I; he shot from prone.) Later in the day I missed another, which was running flat-out at 300 yards or so, by consistently shooting behind him. Again, my elevation was fine; the bullets were impacting in line with the coyote's tail.

Finally, Rick called one in close enough. As I raised my rifle, it spotted me and scooted off down a ravine, traveling directly away at about 70 yards. I shot it up the spout; the bullet traversed its body and exited the skull. Dead coyote. My rifle was a 7mm Remington Magnum.

The foregoing yarns illustrate the practical limits for the 7mm Magnum, with elk (and moose) at the upper end, coyotes and javelina at the bottom, bracketing deer, sheep, and such in between. I'm sure there are those who might advocate true varmint shooting (prairie dogs for example) with a Big Seven, and others who may sanction the pursuit of the big bears. Not me. In the case of varminting, the caliber slaps back a mite hard for me to enjoy shooting it, especially repeatedly, in shirtsleeves, and from the prone position common to varmint hunting. As for grizzlies and the like, I'd feel more comfortable with something that throws a slug about the size of my foot. For everything in between, I'd feel nary a handicap if all I had to hunt with was a Seven Mag.

Warren Page, the late shooting editor for *Field & Stream,* was a Big Seven fan. His favorite big game rifle was a 7mm Mashburn Magnum built on a Mauser action. He dubbed the gun Old Betsy and wrote of it often. Page used Old Betsy to account for nearly 150 animals, ranging in size from an 80-pound African gerenuk to a 1600-pound moose. Page killed grizzly with his Belted Seven, and wrote that he'd not hesitate to take on a brown bear with it. His score on elk included two

During the author's pack-in elk hunt in Idaho, his partner Dave Jacobson dropped a nice bull elk with one round through the rib cage—it was an instant kill. The rifle? A Remington 700 in 7mm Remington Mag.

As a premier hunting rifle, any 7mm Remington Magnum should be equipped with both scope and iron sights. The author is fond of a good set of well regulated, Express-type sights as seen here on this Interarms Whitworth. Experienced hunters agree that an auxiliary set of iron sights can, in an emergency, save the hunt of a lifetime.

one-shot kills in excess of 400 yards. He took more than 50 trophy animals in Africa and India alone.

Page liked 160-grain Spitzers and 175 Nosler semi-Spitzers, doting on the high retained energy and flat trajectory of the former, the incredibly deep penetration of the latter. With the semi-pointed Nosler Partition, he shot a monster British Columbia elk that made the Boone & Crockett listing. The bullet had to bore through some heavy brush to get to the shoul-

The 7mm Remington Magnum, since it is available in so many rifles from so many factories, has a wide variety of throat lengths. The illustrated cartridges, bullets upside down, provide graphic evidence of such disparities. The cartridge at far right is a 7mm Weatherby Magnum. (Mark V rifles are free-bored.)

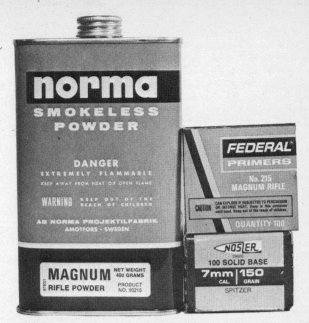

Norma MRP (Magnum Rifle Powder), Federal Magnum No. 215 primers and Nosler 150-grain 7mm Solid Base bullets make for some of the finest loads possible in the 7mm Remington Magnum. The author's favorite load in his own Interarms Cavalier consists of 66 grains of Norma MRP coupled with the other components listed above.

der, but the Nosler just plowed on, nicking one branch and cutting clean another the size of a man's thumb. The slug hit the elk right where it was supposed to and dumped him. No follow-up shot was needed. On such occasions are intimate relationships based, replete with confidence and trust.

In the year of its birth, 1962, the late Jack O'Conner, then shooting editor for *Outdoor Life,* took a 7mm Remington Magnum to Mozambique and Angola. There he slew all manner of livestock, from smallish gazelles up to elk-sized kudu and zebra. Most of his game was taken with one shot; many of them fell in their tracks. He allowed as how the 150-grain Remington factory load seemed to drop more critters where they stood than the stouter and slower 175-grain.

However, when it came to penetration, the 175-grain load was the berries. O'Conner smacked a hefty sable through the lungs; the bullet sailed on through and wounded a hapless bull grazing on the far side!

O'Conner was of the opinion that the Big Seven was adequate for brown and polar bear, a conviction seconded by Bob Chatfield-Taylor, a hunting partner of Jack's. In 1963 Bob used a 7mm Remington Mag to drop a big brownie with one shot while O'Conner watched.

Bob Hagel, noted big game hunter

and scribe, has written that he'd much rather dig an angry bruin out of an alder thicket with a 7mm Magnum loaded with 175-grain Nosler bullets than with a 358 Winchester stuffed with 250-grain loads. (Given his druthers, Hagel said he'd prefer a 340 Weatherby to either. Wise man.)

Bob, too, has noted the remarkable penetrative abilities of the 175-grain Nosler Partition bullet. In his excellent tome, *Game Loads and Practical Ballistics for the American Hunter,* he wrote the following:

The hard fact is, and I've tried it on enough big ones to know, that the 175-gr. Nosler 7mm bullet from one of the big 7s will penetrate as deep as any expanding bullet we have in any caliber from any cartridge, the 458 included.

Many other experienced hunters, like Elmer Keith and Rick Jamison, have gone on record as opposing the 7mm Magnums on large dangerous game. Rick likes the 300 Winchester Mag as a minimum, prefers something even heavier as an ideal. Keith

In Alaskan tidewater country like this, a 7mm Remington Magnum isn't enough gun for a brown bear, which contradicts the thinking of some according to the author. A better choice for brown bear would be the Colt-Sauer 458 Winchester Magnum shown here.

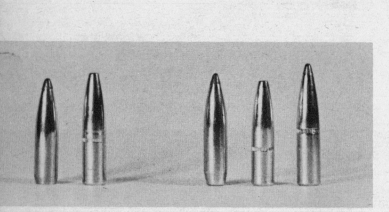

From left to right: 150-gr. Nosler SB; 175-gr. Speer Grand Slam; 160-gr. Sierra SPBT; 160-gr. Speer Grand Slam and the 175-gr. Hornady SP. All of these bullets have proved to be good performers in various handloads.

On the right is an unfired Nosler 175-grain semi-pointed Partition bullet. To the left is an example of the same bullet after it was recovered from a bull elk.

would likely feel naked without a rifle having a bore large enough to house a cantaloupe. They each have a point.

Although I'm positive no one would advocate the Big Seven as *necessary* for pronghorns, deer, sheep, goats, caribou, and black bear, I'm equally certain few would quibble with the fact that the cartridge will get the job done in a businesslike fashion. If long-range shooting is likely, few cartridges exceed the Mag Seven's downrange ballistics. At 400 yards, Federal's Premium boat-tail factory

load retains 1930 foot-pounds of energy. There are only two factory loads, in non-proprietary calibers, produced in this country that will surpass that: the Federal Premium 300 Winchester Magnum loading, at 2230 foot-pounds; the 225-grain pointed 338 Winchester Magnum loading, at 2005. The Big Seven beats all the rest. Thus, we underscore the 7mm Magnum's area of usefulness, from coyotes through moose.

One distinct advantage the 7mm Mags have over many other car-

tridges is rifle availability. From many factories in numerous nations comes a constant flow of 7mm Magnum-chambered rifles, in bolt, semi-automatic, and single-shot actions. Roy Weatherby offers a proprietary Big Seven, the 7mm Weatherby Magnum, in his Mark V series of bolt guns. Schultz & Larsen chambered their version of a belted Seven, dubbing it the 7x61 S&L. The Remington version, far and away the most popular, has been chambered by Husqvarna, Remington, Savage, Winches-

COMPARISON OF ALL-AROUND CARTRIDGES

Cartridge	Bullet	Velocity (fps)					Energy (fpe)					Bullet Path (inches)		
		MV	100	200	300	400	ME	100	200	300	400	100	300	400
264 Win. Mag.	140 PSP	3030	2782	2548	2326	2114	2854	2406	2018	1682	1389	+1.8	−7.2	−20.8
270 Win.	130 PSP	3110	2849	2604	2371	2150	2791	2343	1957	1622	1334	+1.7	−6.8	−19.9
284 Win.	150 PSP	2860	2595	2344	2108	1886	2724	2243	1830	1480	1185	+2.1	−8.5	−24.8
7mm Rem. Mag.	150 PSP	3110	2830	2568	2320	2085	3221	2667	2196	1792	1448	+1.7	−7.0	−20.5
7mm Rem. Mag.	150 SPBT	3110	2920	2750	2580	2410	3220	2850	2510	2210	1930	+1.6	−6.9	−19.7
7mm Rem. Mag.	175 PSP	2860	2645	2440	2244	2057	3178	2718	2313	1956	1644	+2.0	−7.9	−22.7
30-06 Springfield	180 PSP	2700	2469	2250	2042	1846	2913	2436	2023	1666	1362	+2.4	−9.3	−27.0
30-06 Springfield	200 SPBT	2550	2400	2260	2120	1990	2890	2560	2270	2000	1760	+2.3	−9.0	−25.8
300 Win. Mag.	200 SPBT	2830	2680	2530	2380	2240	3560	3180	2830	2520	2230	+1.7	−7.1	−20.3
338 Win. Mag.	225 PSP	2780	2572	2374	2184	2003	3862	3306	2816	2384	2005	+2.7	−9.4	−25.0

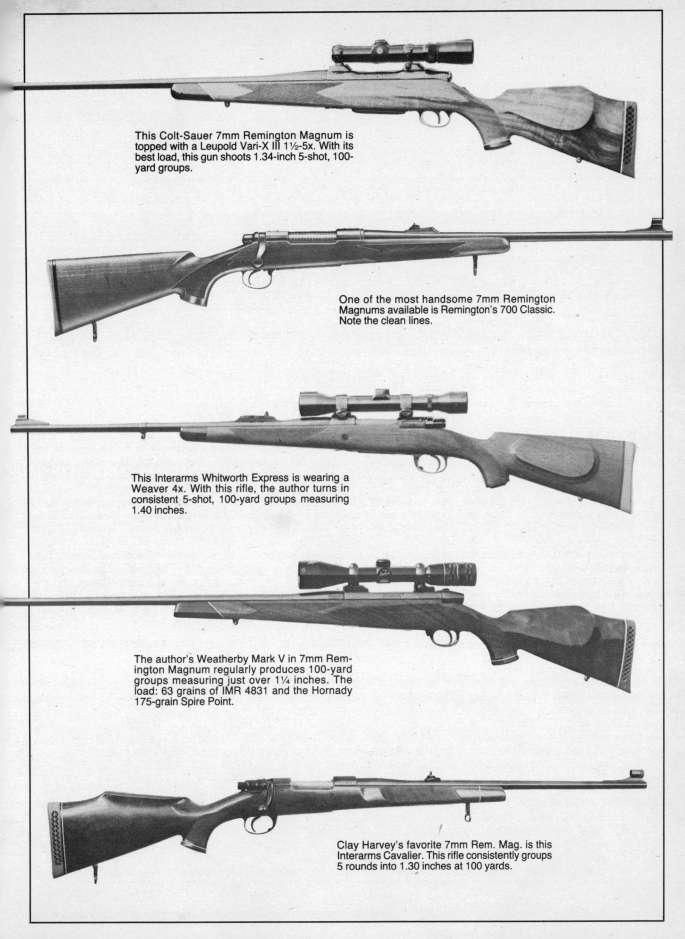

This Colt-Sauer 7mm Remington Magnum is topped with a Leupold Vari-X III 1½-5x. With its best load, this gun shoots 1.34-inch 5-shot, 100-yard groups.

One of the most handsome 7mm Remington Magnums available is Remington's 700 Classic. Note the clean lines.

This Interarms Whitworth Express is wearing a Weaver 4x. With this rifle, the author turns in consistent 5-shot, 100-yard groups measuring 1.40 inches.

The author's Weatherby Mark V in 7mm Remington Magnum regularly produces 100-yard groups measuring just over 1¼ inches. The load: 63 grains of IMR 4831 and the Hornady 175-grain Spire Point.

Clay Harvey's favorite 7mm Rem. Mag. is this Interarms Cavalier. This rifle consistently groups 5 rounds into 1.30 inches at 100 yards.

ter, Ruger, Thompson-Center, Weatherby, Steyr-Mannlicher, Tradewinds, Mauser, Interarms, Sako, Smith & Wesson, Parker-Hale, Krico, Colt-Sauer, Champlin, Heym, DuBiel, BSA, and some more I don't know about or have never heard of. The 7mm Magnum is nothing if not *available.*

I've owned a bevy of them. To date, I've worked with a pair of Colt-Sauers, a Remington M700 Classic, a Whitworth Express, a pair of Interarms' Cavaliers, a Golden Eagle, a Ruger Number One, and one of Weatherby's Mark V's. My favorite of the lot was a Cavalier (built on a Mauser action by Interarms). It wasn't the most accurate; nearly every Big Seven I ever tested would average a tad over 1¼ inches for several five-shot groups with a favored load or two, and the Cavalier was no exception.

Nor was it the most handsome. The Remington Classic and the Whitworth Express pleased my visual palate more readily than the somewhat bizarre lines of the Cavalier. It wasn't the most carefully crafted; the Colt-Sauers got the nod there. Reliability was less than perfect; case ejection was a bit iffy on occasion. The action was rough; not terribly so, just not up to the velvet slickness of the Colts or the Golden Eagle.

Alas, it wasn't perfect. But I liked it. Why? For one thing, like many Big Sevens it would put string after string of shots in the same place on the target, whether in humid lowland North Carolina or the arid elevations of Arizona. For another, it never seemed to kick much. Obviously, the oddly-shaped stock had virtues that escaped the eye. Aside from those minor details, and the fact that I shot it a whole lot, I'm not sure just why that rifle sneaked its way into my heart.

I've never hunted big game with a Seven Mag. I live in the East; a magnum just isn't needed there. I did intend to tote the Interarms Whitworth Express after an Idaho elk, but UPS didn't cooperate. I went on the hunt, but the rifle sat in a warehouse in Montana. Too bad; I had a humdinger of an elk load cobbled up for that trip.

Which brings up the issue of good loads for Remington's Seven Mag. My favorite in the Cavalier was 66.0 grains of Norma MRP under the 150-grain Nosler Solid Base bullet. That's the load I used coyote hunting. It clocked a little over 3100 fps and shot flat as hell. Nowadays, if I were after a load specifically for coyote-sized animals, I'd start with Speer's new 130-

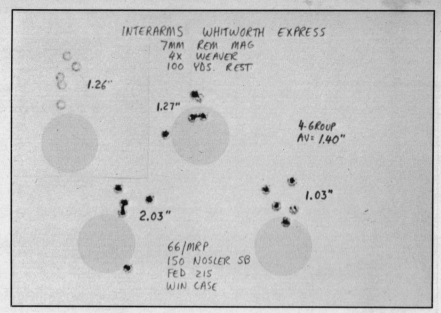

These groups are representative of typical 7mm Remington Magnum accuracy. In this instance the groups were fired with the author's Interarms Whitworth Express. The best 5-shot, 100-yard group is in the lower right portion of the photo and measures 1.03 inches.

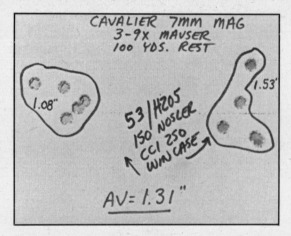

The 5-shot, 100-yard groups shown here are also typical of 7mm Remington Magnum accuracy. They were fired from the author's Interarms Cavalier.

7mm REMINGTON HUNTING LOADS

Load	MV fps	ME fpe	Remarks
150-gr. Nosler Solid Base/66.0-MRP	3104	3201	Fine load for medium game
150-gr. Nosler Solid Base/53.0-H205	2855	2715	Very accurate in Cavalier
160-gr. Speer Grand Slam/65.0-MRP	2980	3164	Good velocity
160-gr. Sierra SPBT/64.0-WIN 785	2889	2965	Accurate
175-gr. Speer Grand Slam/62.0-MRP	2860	3178	Good elk or moose load
175-gr. Hornady Spire Point/62.0-MRP	2853	3164	Accurate
175-gr. Nosler Partition/78.0-H870	3008*	3515	Very fast and accurate
150-gr. Winchester Power Point Factory	3089	3172	Fine load for medium game
175-gr. Hornady Frontier SP Factory	2682	2797	Most accurate factory load
175-gr. Remington PSP Factory	2792	3029	Good big-game load
175-gr. Federal PSP Factory	2824	3100	Good velocity

Approach all handloads from 10 percent below these charge weights and work up carefully, in one-tenth grain increments, watching for excessive-pressure signs! Do *not* exceed these charge weights.

Loads chronographed in 24-inch barrels
*Ruger Number One 26-inch barrel

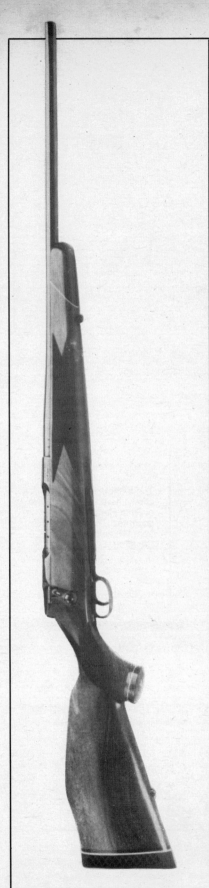

The Colt-Sauer bolt-action is available in 7mm Remington Magnum. It's noted for its strong, smooth action and clean lines.

From left to right: Winchester 785, Norma MRP and Hodgdon H205—all fine propellants for handloading the 7mm Rem. Mag.

grain boat-tail Soft Point. A wise powder selection should kick that little slug out of a 24-inch barrel in excess of 3300 fps. That's fast.

For deer, sheep, or antelope, I'd opt for the above-mentioned 150-grain Nosler recipe. With bigger game on the menu, I'd load up 78.0 grains of Hodgdon H-870 behind a 175-grain Nosler Partition for about 3000 fps.

If I had to stick to factory ammo in the 7mm Remington Magnum, I'd carry 150-grain Winchester Soft Points for everything up to caribou in size. I've tried it for accuracy and velocity in a half-dozen rifles; it always does pretty well. For the really big stuff, I'd buy a box of Hornady Frontier 175-grain Spire Points. It's not the fastest factory load on the market, but does it

shoot! One other load, which I haven't tried, shows promise; the 160-grain Nosler Partition load that Federal makes up for their Premium line. From where I sit that load looks good on paper.

In closing, let's be clear on the issue. If I planned never to hunt game larger than elk and knew that *most* of my hunting would entail the pursuit of deer-sized animals, my list of cartridge candidates would be lengthy. The Seven Mag would not be on it. But, if I were restricted to one gun and caliber, for use on all game on this continent, my list would be very short. It would contain only one cartridge, the 7mm Remington Magnum. There would be no second choice. ●

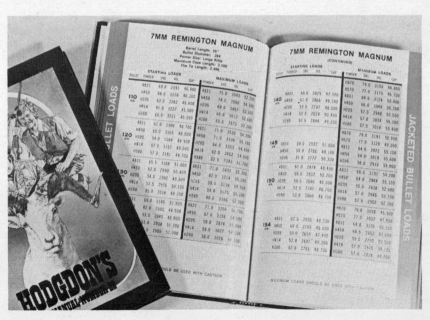

Whatever 7mm Rem. Mag. loads you choose, be sure you consult a reliable loading manual and start at the bottom load (for the powder and bullet weight you select) and work up carefully a tenth of a grain at a time, never exceeding maximum recommended powder charges.

John Amber
on
Custom Guns In The Field

John Amber's love for custom guns is, indeed, well established. But, the question remains, are they suitable for the field?

As SOME of you may recall, I've written about custom guns more than once over the many years; about made-to-order firearms in general and, to be sure, about those made for me—or acquired by me. Looking back, and rereading some of the things I said in print, I'd have argued that my coverage of the subject had been quite complete.

But no! I was, I must admit, brought up short not long ago by a question from an eastern reader. What, he wanted to know, did I do with my bespoke rifles and shotguns?

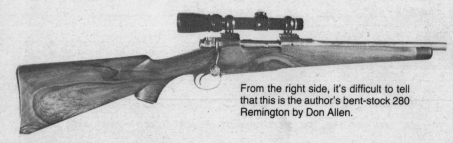

From the right side, it's difficult to tell that this is the author's bent-stock 280 Remington by Don Allen.

Did I hang 'em on the wall, there to be ogled and exclaimed over by random visitors, or did I ever take them on hunts near or far, exposing them to the rigors of the elements and the ever-present chances of possible damages?

Legitimate questions, I now realize, and I'm embarrassed to put down here—as I said to my inquirer—that the actual use of custom guns in the field just never occurred to me. If I'd ever given this matter a thought at all—and I don't think I did—I would have assumed, I'm quite sure, that

gun owners everywhere had bought those sporting arms to hunt with, custom made or not.

I can and do tell you that such an attitude was mine from the very beginning, but it was an unconscious position, one I didn't rationalize at the time—nearly 40 years ago—nor one I'd be writing about now were it not for my inquisitive reader.

I just said that, in effect, it never struck me to do anything with a gun—any gun—but to use it, and I offer some evidence now, good evidence, I believe, that I have done just that.

The time was 1946. I was back on the job at Marshall Field's Gun Shop. During my time in the Navy, I'd dreamed about making a big game hunt, and here was the chance. Three of my customers, good friends as well, were planning a lengthy pack trip into British Columbia. Did I want to join them? I nearly lost my job and my bride, but I went! That was a 60-day trip for 11 of us, about 45 of those days on horseback. There were 34 animals in the string. A truly great and fully satisfactory hunt, full of adventure and close calls, but I won't go further on that hunt here.

I'd bought early in 1937 one of the new Model 70 Winchesters, the caliber 30-06, and I'd mounted a Lyman Alaskan 2½x scope in the Echo side mount. That rifle would be my main arm, if only because of the scope. However, at an auction some months before I'd bought two Griffin & Howe rifles—one a 7x57 Springfield with remarkably trim, slim lines, the other a Sauer Mauser in 30-06, fully engraved by Kornbrath.* The bolt handle was unaltered, and I wanted to leave it that way, in its original form. But that G&H was with me on the B.C. trip, and I used it to kill the grizzly I took, which I knew would be a short range shot—as it was. This handsome G&H was a spare rifle essentially, of course, but I carried it on numerous occasions during that hunt. The only damage was a bit of blue wear on the barrel and a few minor scratches in the wood. This was one of the several guns sold for me at Christies in 1982, and it was in the same

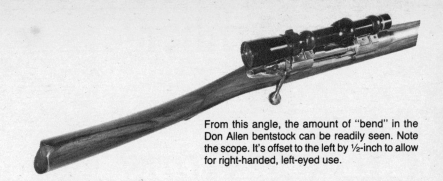

From this angle, the amount of "bend" in the Don Allen bentstock can be readily seen. Note the scope. It's offset to the left by ½-inch to allow for right-handed, left-eyed use.

---

*Both of the G&H rifles, plus several others, are described and pictured in Lucian Cary's story, "Griffin & Howe," published in GUN DIGEST 28/1974 and in G.D. Treasury, 5th ed.

condition I've just described.

Now, to jump ahead a bunch of years, I'll describe briefly the rifle that Don Allen of Northfield, Minnesota, put together for me, with the able help of Herman Waldron, and T.J. Kaye, master metalsmith and top engraver respectively, plus good work by Mark Lee of the Allen shop.*

Now, this bent-stock 280 Remington, a long favored caliber, was made on a pre-1964 M70 action. The variety of jobs performed on it, in metal and wood, make it one of the most fully customized rifles I own—and one of the most expensive!

---

*For full details of this rifle and various others made for John Amber see Gun Digest Review of Custom Guns, ed. by Ken Warner, pp. 16-25.

But I meant it for hunting use, and I've shot it extensively in practice and in working up handloads. To that end I took the rifle to Europe in 1979, intending to use it on a hunt in Austria for roe or red deer. It was not to be! The customs agents in England and Germany seized the rifle temporarily (I had no proper papers, which was my fault), returning the piece to me on my leaving those countries. Alerted by this *contretemp á deux,* I phoned the Austrian consulate and got the bad news—I could not enter Austria with it either. I should have shipped it to Steyr, Daimler, Puch, my hosts to be. I gave up, sending the rifle home by air, unblooded.

Through the many years from the mid-1940s to 1980, say, I've laid by a

This Don Allen custom rifle is one of John Amber's favorites. Chambered for the 280 Remington, it was specifically made to accommodate right-hand, left-eye usage. The rifle was built around a pre-'64 Model 70 action. Note the offset Leupold scope.

On one sunny Tennessee day, John Amber and Jim Carmichel of *Outdoor Life* did some bench testing of the author's Hagn single shot in 7x57. The last 5 rounds fired that day (all reloads using 175-gr. bullets) went under an inch at 100 yards, using *iron sights*. That, my friends, is superb hunting accuracy.

fair number of custom rifles and shotguns, most of which I used or fully intended to use. However, during the past decade, circumstances and my physical condition changed, and a lot of my good intentions went by the board.

As an example, the 375 Weatherby I'd had Roy make, one of a pair done in restrained styling, I used for a lot of African shooting on two safaris, but there has been no good chance to use the tip-up 270 single shot that Renato Gamba made for me.

Rifles that I've used on Western hunts for elk, deer and antelope are: the 264 Magnum M70 made by Dale Goens in full stock form, engraved by Jack Prudhomme and silver mounted; the 6mm John Warren-engraved Sako rifle, also full stocked; the BRNO 270 stocked for me by Maurice Ottmar, who at one time did most of the stocking for Champlin Firearms Co.

I used in Alaska, on two hunts there, the 7mm Remington Magnum that Al Biesen did for me years ago, and the 338 Magnum on a Champlin action that the Oklahoma company made for me. This same 338 was used

with good results in Africa also, killing several Cape buffalo without fuss or feathers.

Well, I'm getting on now, and shooting from my left shoulder (which I must resort to with most of my long guns) is still awkward and clumsy. For those reasons, among others, I may not find it feasible to get into the hunting field with certain of my rifles. Included in that lot would be a 458 side-by-side DB rifle made by John Fanzoi of Ferlach in sidelock form; a 375 H&H DB side-by-side, also a sidelock, by Victor Sarasqueta of Spain; the very special Browning 30-06 over-under with the gold-inlaid and fully engraved action by Louis Vrancken; the Bergstutzen over-under DB rifle, calibers 375 H&H and 22 Hornet, made by Dr. L. Kortz of Brusselles/Ferlach and, my latest, a side-by-side DB rifle received in January of this year (1983). Made by Visini of Brescia, it is offered by them at an attractively-low price. A quite plain rifle, without ejectors and the checkering merely fair, but stocked to my dimensions and certain trim added—a trapped grip cap, a Pachmayr butt pad and my initials gold inlaid.

So far I've given scant attention to my custom shotguns. Among these are two side-by-side 12 bores by Abbiatico & Salvinelli—one the handsome and unusual Castore 270, an outside-hammer gun with automatic hammer cocking and selective ejection; the other A&S's best sidelock double with *bulino* engraving by Fracassi.

Then there is a Griebel-engraved Model 21 in 20-gauge, the receiver showing several birds and dogs in raised gold; a Merkel 12-gauge over-under in 203 grade but with special game scene engraving; a Francotte sidelock 12 that shows Joseph Fugger's first engraving for Abercrombie & Fitch; one of AYA's best doubles, the Model One sidelock, made for me with an extra pair of barrels; my much-used Stiegele of Munich 16x7x57R over-under, which has brought me several head of game, including a great wild boar at Bill Ruger's Blue Mountain Forest facility.

I must at least mention here my latest single shot rifle, the action made by Martin Hagn of West Germany. I consider the Ruger No. 1 action the

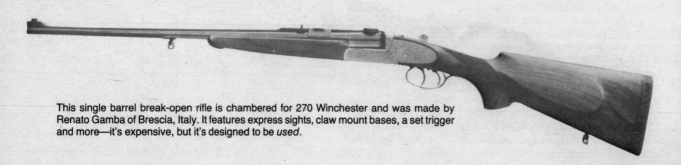

This single barrel break-open rifle is chambered for 270 Winchester and was made by Renato Gamba of Brescia, Italy. It features express sights, claw mount bases, a set trigger and more—it's expensive, but it's designed to be *used*.

very best of its type ever evolved, which is to say in the spirit of the late 19th century, and in the manner—but highly improved and strengthened—of John Farquharson and Alex Henry. On the other hand, the System Hagn represents the ultimate in modern design. Protected by several patents, this compact dropping block action is made without a single screw; all parts are held and positioned by pins of adequate strength. When the buttstock and fore-end are attached, no pin is visible! All movement is contained within the receiver; nothing attaches to the barrel. At any point in the opening and closing position of the underlever, the breechblock remains tight and unshakeable; there is no detectable movement of the block in *any* direction.

At the same time, the Hagn is one of the most handsome of single shot actions, graceful and well-proportioned. The lever is of elegant and simple design, but could easily be altered or reformed as desired by a custom gunsmith.

My system Hagn rifle is the essence of slim, svelte line and gracefulness. At 7¼ pounds it is as agile and responsive as a finely balanced shotgun. Made in 7x57 standard rimless form, it shoots well with open sights. Jim Carmichel shot it extensively one sunny afternoon in Tennessee.

With almost no exceptions, I've at least shot all of the rifles and shotguns mentioned; some were shot extensively, these needing more shooting to find a good handload or, now and then, because it was a nice day and I felt like shooting. I don't think it is any great secret that I dearly love to shoot a rifle.

As I've tried to show, I carried into the hunting field whichever rifle or shotgun was called for by the game in view or the country. Often enough the particular gun selected was deliberately one of the custom efforts, and for what, to me, are perfectly valid reasons. First, such made-for-me rifles usually shot tighter groups by virtue of their special barrels and via my tuned and mated handloads. Thus, naturally, I had more confidence in them than I'd have put in a standard rifle of the same caliber. Second, in light of the fact that one doesn't actively hunt 60 minutes of every hour, it is satisfying and pleasant to contemplate—as Cap Crossman pointed out some 50 years ago—a handsomely engraved, well-stocked and perfect-fitting example of the gunmaker's art. Sybaritic? Perhaps, but don't put it down until you've experienced it. ●

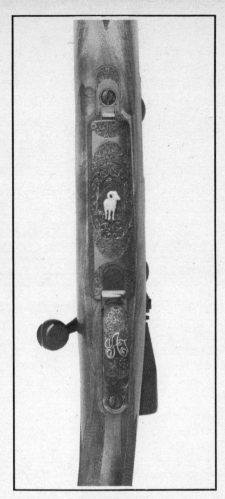

Once completed, the Don Allen bentstock rifle was engraved by Tommy Kaye. The trigger guard bears the author's initials in gold while the raised gold figure on the floorplate is that of a European moufflon. Rifles like this aren't just for the looking. Considering the lavish care taken in inletting, the quality of the barrel, and a host of other functional plusses, the rifle shown will print under an inch all day long. It's not just for "looking" — it's for shooting.

Amber's first post-WW II custom rifle was this Mauser 98 bolt action Griffin & Howe 30-06. The engraving is by Kornbrath. This superb example of the gunmaker's art accompanied the author on his hunt in British Columbia in 1946.

This example of the single shot Heeren rifle (in 11.15x60R Mauser) was made in Strassburg/Baden, Germany, about 1900. This small, strong, beautifully made action is ideally suited for the hunter who likes his rifles on the light side.

Aoudad Hunting American Style

by DICK EADES

Slowly but surely this exotic game animal is turning into an All-American trophy!

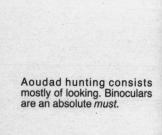

Aoudad hunting consists mostly of looking. Binoculars are an absolute *must*.

"HUNTING imported animals is unsportsmanlike!" "Animals not native to this country are half domesticated and easily taken by anyone with a rifle!" "Hunting on a game ranch is like shooting the neighbor's milk cow!" These and many similar statements are often heard when someone mentions hunting one of the numerous species of non-American game animals now found in this country.

However, disparaging comments like these are made only by those who haven't tried hunting imported game. First of all, it must be said that imported game is anything but domesticated. Ranchers who raise exotic game animals take great pains to see that these animals remain wild. Unless their paying customers/hunters find hunting exotics a challenge, the ranchers would soon be out of business.

Foreign game animals furnish some of the most exciting and challenging hunting on this continent today. They aren't pen-raised animals turned loose for a hunt, but are animals descended from imported stock. Many exotic game animals have existed here for several generations and have adapted so well to our climate and topography that they furnish better hunting here than do their counterparts in their native lands.

An excellent example of a well-established exotic is the African aoudad

or Barbary sheep. Native to the Atlas Mountains of North Africa, the aoudad, pronounced "ow-dad," ("aw-dad" if you're from Texas) is an outsized sheep with an amazing talent for becoming invisible when hunted.

To be precise, the aoudad is the only representative of the genus *Ammotragus lervia* although there are several subspecies. Biologically, it is very closely related to the true sheep and, for simplicity, most people call it a sheep. Large rams will weigh somewhat more than 300 pounds and may display magnificent curved horns measuring more than 30 inches from base to tip. Oddly enough, American specimens are slightly larger than those still taken in their native land.

The first aoudad in this country, outside of zoo specimens, were released in New Mexico and Arizona in the early 1900s. In the 1930s Texas joined New Mexico and Arizona as a haven for free ranging aoudad. Then in the 1950s, Texas *officially* released breeding stock, and numerous private herds were developed in the ensuing years. Although no one has taken an exact census of animals on both public and private lands, the state now has several thousand available for hunting. The largest single herd, thought to contain as many as 2,000 animals, roams the rugged Palo Duro Canyon in the Texas panhandle. This particular herd has been classed as *game* by the state with legally established hunting seasons and regulations. Animals on private lands are not subject to game laws and may be hunted at any time of the year with agreement of the land owner.

Like many sheep, the aoudad is most at home in rough terrain. They are surefooted and hardy, living well on rocky hillsides, near-desert flatlands and cactus-scarred canyons. Although not particularly nomadic by nature, they are not deterred by ordinary cattle fences and can jump clear of a so-called "deer fence" when pressed.

My first experience with aoudad came when I stumbled into a small herd while quail hunting some years ago. Several ewes and a huge ram calmly watched me approach within 100 yards before slowly turning and walking down a canyon as I stood in full view. So this was the behavior of a "wild" sheep!

More than a year later, I was offered a chance to hunt aoudad in the rugged Glass Mountains of west Texas. Remembering my first encounter with aoudad, I felt sure the outfitter was being overly cautious when he told me to plan on spending "at least 5 days" to try for a trophy.

We spent those 5 days (and one extra) tramping over some of the roughest terrain imaginable. Those mountains are composed of rocks, varying in size from a pea to a grand piano; every rock has a few sharp edges and most of them roll when you touch them. I returned home with more sore muscles that I hadn't known existed and an assortment of cuts, nicks and bruises that would do credit to any living victim of a big-city mugging. To top it off, during the entire trek, I had seen only two aoudad. The nearest one was perched on a cliff about 600 yards away, laughing as I took a knee-wrenching tumble while trying to get a better look at it.

Hobbling back to our base camp, I saw an aoudad taken by another member of our party. If I had any notions of abandoning the hunt, they quickly evaporated as I stared at those heavy, curving horns that taped more than 31 inches on each side. The spectacular horns, coupled with a sandy, tawny mane flowing from the deep chest, and long-haired "chaps" on the forelegs, convinced me that the aoudad must be one of nature's most striking trophies.

That particular hunt ended when I ran out of time and was forced to temporarily abandon the aoudad. The score was aoudad 1, Me 0.

The outfitter/guide/hunting partner on the Glass Mountain fiasco was Dr. Joseph Burkett who originated the Burkett system of scoring game trophies. In addition to his work as a tropaeologist, Joe is a darn fine guide for both native and exotic game animals. He operates his business from Rte. 2, Box 195A, Fredicksburg, Texas 78624. My lack of success was in no way Joe's fault but simply a matter of bad luck. He had been responsible for the taking of the monster that had fired my imagination. It's just a question of managing to be in the right place at the right time. (Sound familiar?)

My next opportunity for a try at aoudad came when Joe Burkett offered to put me on to a good ram from a herd near his home where hunting conditions were more charitable than those in the mountains. Gently rolling hills with a few deep draws and creek beds offered good habitat for the aoudad and there would be no high altitude climbing or rock sliding when it came time to get within reasonable shooting range.

After weeks of false starts during which we were unable to coordinate our available time, Joe and I exchanged enough telephone calls to make Ma Bell grin with delight. Finally, we settled on a date and time to meet at a small cafe in Fredicksburg. I gathered my hunting gear and drove into town late in the evening, sure that we would sight the grandfather of all aoudad the following morning.

The only thing we saw the following day was a ferocious rainstorm. Buckets of rain poured down on the roof of the motel, and I felt sure I would need a life preserver to make the few yards to the cafe where we were to meet. Undaunted, Joe insisted that we drive on out to the ranch, " . . . in case the rain hasn't hit there, yet."

The rain had not only visited the ranch, it had left behind a sea of mud. Not ordinary mud but a stubborn mixture of sand and loam that clung like glue to truck tires, boots and anything else it touched. We made a short but soggy tour of the pasture where Joe had last seen aoudad, but the ram we wanted had better sense than we did. It had apparently holed up someplace dry to wait for a break in the weather. After staring glumly at the drab weather and listening to the hourly weather forecast for an entire day, I gave up and headed north. Score: aoudad 2, Me 0.

I had almost made up my mind that the aoudad simply wasn't my game when a telephone call from Hubert Zink, Executive Vice President of Heckler & Koch, offered one more chance at a Texas aoudad. Hubert informed me that H&K was about to market a new 30-06 autoloader and wondered if I might be interested in accompanying him on a hunting trip to test the new rifle.

I'm usually ready to go hunting, but when Hubert told me that we would be after aoudad, guided by Joe Burkett, I was particularly anxious to get moving. Again, we would hunt in the Texas hill country, this time near Kerrville. Hubert arranged to have a then-new HK940 rifle shipped to me in advance so I would have time for test firing and sighting in.

The HK940, a delayed recoil, roller-locked action, autoloader, is an addition to the company's line of similar autoloaders which includes the M770 in 308 Winchester and the M630 in 223 Remington. The HK940 is an en-

larged version of the earlier, proven models. The roller-locked system offers recoil attenuation similar to that of a well designed, gas-operated system, however, the mechanism is considerably simpler.

In addition to the unique locking system, HK940 rifles are offered with polygonal-twist barrels rather than conventional rifling. Without getting involved in the technical aspects of polygon bores, they are formed without lands and grooves; the barrel walls themselves impart a spin to the bullet. Aside from the obvious elimination of gas cutting, the polygonal bore reduces internal friction and allows the bullet to achieve 5 to 6 percent greater-than-normal velocity.

The H&K rifle came fitted with a 4x Schmidt und Bender scope with a quick detachable mount. Range tests proved that best accuracy was obtainable with 180-grain bullets. For most purposes, I prefer a lighter bullet but the aoudad is a fairly large and hardy animal. Remington Bronze Point bullets were selected for their fast-opening characteristics.

Since the terrain we planned to hunt might offer shots at any range from point blank to 300 yards or more, the rifle was sighted in to strike 2 inches above point of aim at 100 yards. Such a sight setting would enable me to use an "on-target" hold to 250 yards.

We met in San Antonio and discussed the forthcoming hunt with Joe Burkett and his assistants. Joe had thoroughly investigated the ranch where we planned to hunt and had seen several aoudad a few days before.

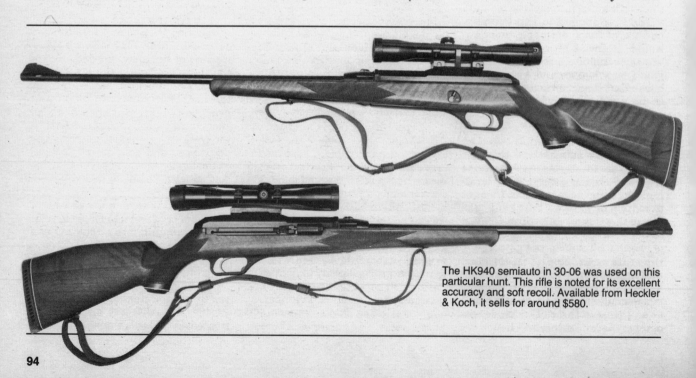

The HK940 semiauto in 30-06 was used on this particular hunt. This rifle is noted for its excellent accuracy and soft recoil. Available from Heckler & Koch, it sells for around $580.

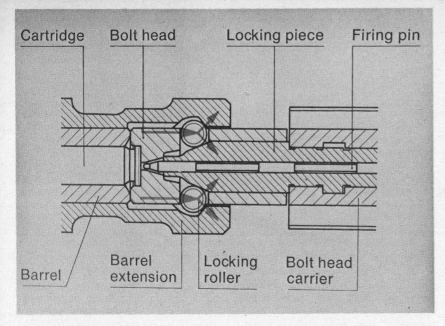

Cartridge   Bolt head   Locking piece   Firing pin

Barrel   Barrel extension   Locking roller   Bolt head carrier

Diagram of the locking system of HK940 rifle shows relationship of bolt, rollers and locking piece. It's this roller-locked system that helps account for smooth operation and soft recoil.

Like many H&K products, the HK940 features polygonal "rifling" which can be seen here (right) in comparison with conventional rifling (left). As can be seen the polygonal bore is much smoother. As a result the friction of the bullet is reduced as it travels the length of the barrel, somewhat increasing muzzle velocity.

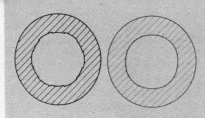

He felt sure we could locate a decent ram but warned that all our travel on the ranch would be on foot. Recent rains had left the ground too soft for vehicles except on established roads.

Our party was made up of four hunters and myself, Joe Burkett and his crew. Two of the hunters hoped to take mouflon and two were after whitetail deer. I alone was after an aoudad. The ranch covered a bit more than 5,000 acres so we should have no trouble in staying far enough apart for a safe hunt. We would strike out early each morning from Joe's ranch, some 25 miles from where we would hunt, and return each night.

Within a few hours of our arrival at the hunting ranch, one of the mouflon hunters had connected, and the other had seen several desirable rams but wanted to shop a bit before shooting. The deer hunters had another problem! There were so many good quality bucks that it was difficult to make a choice. It was the only time in years of hunting that I have heard hunters growling about passing up a buck because he was, "only an eight-pointer."

The only thing I derived from the first day's hunt was plenty of exercise from walking. We knew the aoudad herd was on the ranch but the big question was which part they had claimed as their own? They were somewhere in roughly 8 square miles of hills, brush, creeks and pastures.

During one of our infrequent rest stops, Burkett mentioned that the average hill country aoudad is somewhat smaller than those we had hunted in the mountains. This news was disappointing since I had hoped for

one that would break the magic 10-inch mark. According to Joe, this was highly unlikely since the older rams in this area usually support horns in the 24- to 26-inch category. No matter, we had yet to see one of any kind, large or small.

The morning of our third day, we decided to walk to a section of the ranch not previously covered. Joe knew of a steep, rocky, creek bed that seemed suitable for aoudad. We topped a small rise and stood looking

The Schmidt und Bender 4x scope used by the author is shown complete with an H&K detachable mount. Unlike some detachable mounts, this one works. We were able to remove and re-install the scope at will with no detectable change in zero. The optical clarity of the scope is superb. It's imported by Heckler & Koch.

A three-shot magazine comes as standard with the semiauto HK940. An optional 10-shot magazine is available. Note that the same magazine is used for 30-06, 9.3x62mm and 7x62mm.

down the long slope toward the dry creek bed. Dropping to his knees, Joe and I scanned the brush lining the creek with our binoculars.

After a few minutes searching, he turned to me and said, "There's your ram." I turned to see which direction he was looking. To my surprise, he was pointing almost exactly to the spot I had been glassing. Raising the binoculars again, I peered at the brushy shadows and tried to make an aoudad out of the dappled, leafy shade. No luck.

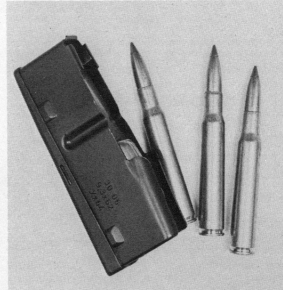

After what seemed several minutes, I glimpsed a faint movement in one of the darker shadows. Bringing the 7x glasses to bear on the spot, I connected with an indistinct outline of a reddish-brown animal. The horns were hidden in low-hanging branches and part of the body was obscured by brush. I wasn't sure if the animal I saw was the one Joe spotted or if it was a different one; there was no telling if it was large or small. Suddenly, I saw another standing a few feet away. The binoculars quickly revealed seven or eight animals, standing very close together. The reddish-brown hair was excellent camouflage, and there was no way to tell one from another. (Aoudad ewes have horns shaped much like those of a ram but generally smaller.) The last thing I wanted to do was work this hard for a trophy then muff it by shooting an undersized animal. We were within 200 yards of the herd but unable to get a

Looking down the slope into a dry creek bed, I was unable to spot the aoudad herd until one chanced to move slightly. Even after pinpointing their location, keeping an eye on the big ram was difficult.

Dick Eades (left) and Joe Burkett pose with the aoudad which was taken after miles of walking and hours of glassing likely spots. The ram was finally located in a dry creek bed.

clear view due to intervening brush. From their actions, we decided they were unaware of our presence.

Joe suggested that we try to change our position to one which would permit better observation and maybe a clearer shot. We moved slowly down slope and into a small stand of oak trees which put us 25 or 30 yards closer to the herd. I managed to fit myself behind a tree with a low fork that pro-

vided some concealment and a good rest for the rifle. Abandoning the binoculars, I studied the animals through the rifle scope.

One set of horns looked considerably larger than the others. After a lengthy, whispered conversation, we confirmed that we were looking at the same animal and that it was a respectable ram. The next problem was waiting for a clear shot.

I sat with rifle cradled in the tree fork and followed the slow movements of the herd for a time that seemed better measured by a calendar than by a watch. Each time I would get a good look at the ram, a ewe would amble up directly on the off side of it and stop. I couldn't risk shooting the ram and having the bullet pass through and kill a ewe, so the waiting game continued.

After a small eternity of milling around, the herd animals changed positions, and the ram stood clear of all the others. Unfortunately during the movement, the ram had repositioned itself so that its head and shoulders were completely obscured by a small clump of scrub trees. I hesitated, wanting to plant my shot directly in the shoulder. "It's the best shot you're going to get," Joe whispered. "Take it as close to the tree as possible."

I planted the wide cross hairs of the Schmidt und Bender — the vertical hair edging the tree trunk and the horizontal planted in the middle of the large, tawny body. As the shot rang out, all hell broke loose in the brush along the creek. Aoudad spewed from the cover in all directions. The ram wheeled and took off up the slope, quartering toward us in a pounding run.

Pulling the rifle free of the tree

Hanging the aoudad, while waiting for a truck, was no small job. We were unable to get the hind quarters completely clear of the ground even though the branch the aoudad was suspended from was about 6 feet high.

We trotted to the animal and found that its run had been made on reflexes alone. The Remington bullet had destroyed the heart and exited on the off side, leaving a neat, quarter-sized hole.

As we stood looking at the aoudad, Joe turned to me and asked, "What did you do, bring this one here yourself?" I missed the point of the question until he drew a tape measure from his pocket and ran it along the curve of one of the horns. It measured 30½ inches, crown to tip! Apparently this brute didn't get the word that hill country rams don't get that big!

After dressing the ram, we tried to drag it to the top of the slope where a road passed near enough to permit loading it into the truck. This task proved to be more than we could handle so we left to recruit help from our other hunters. The best efforts of four of us were required to hang the ram from a tree beside the road to await the truck. Even with help, we were thoroughly winded before the ropes were tied off to support the animal's weight.

Later that evening, after we had remeasured the horns to confirm their size, I counted score again. This time it was aoudad 2, Me 1. There were a few times when I was ready to concede the game, but I'm glad now that I didn't. The oversized aoudad will be one of my favorite trophies. There's no question that I earned it, every inch of horn and hair!

Line-up of the game taken during our hunt shows the relative size of the aoudad to other animals. In anyone's language, it's *big*!

fork, I stood and tried to get the cross hairs on the ram again. Before I could again apply pressure to the trigger, it disappeared from the scope field. About 30 yards from its starting point, the big ram had slammed into the ground, running full tilt. The massive horns plowed a long gash in the dirt where it went down.

Black Powder

THE SMOKE obscured my vision. I knew the round ball had found its target because the big animal was reared back like a rodeo horse, on two legs, high in the air, hunks of damp soil flying up like debris from a bomb strike. My brother, photographer Nick Fadala, was behind me. We had a plan. But the plan had changed in quick order. I was to raise my hand, and when my hand dropped to my side, that would be a cue for Nick to start the motor on his 35mm camera. But it didn't happen that way.

The bull bison decided that it wanted to share the piece of earth I was occupying. It was not charging. It simply wanted to use the ditch I was in for its own trail and my body happened to be in the wrong place. When I looked up, instead of seeing the bull going the other way, it was moving in my direction. At 20 paces, I decided that all signals should be forgotten. I raised the rifle, a custom 54-caliber longrifle made by Dennis Mulford, and I held for the brain. I had been told that if I

decided to make a head shot, the projectile had to strike either right or left of the center of the skull. "I have witnesses to the fact that a fellow bounced two 30-06 bullets off that 'boss' in the center of a bull's head," I was told.

I held left of center, and the 225-grain pure lead ball entered and passed through the right hemisphere of the brain. The ball was lost forever on the plains as it exited out the back of the head. With only half a brain to power its hulk, the bull was still able to rise. I had reloaded, and a second ball was fired behind the shoulder. This ball was recovered. It made its way totally through the big chest area of the bull, knocking a piece of rib bone through the hide on the offside. That ball we did recover. It was resting where the bit of rib had been. It had, in effect, taken the place of that section of rib which had flown through the hide.

"Anybody who thinks you just pop all bison through the safety of a corral should get out here on the plains," my

brother told me. He went on to say that he was certainly happy that the bull went down to a clean harvest on the plains rather than falling to the grim reaper of the slaughterhouse. "Too noble a beast for that fate," Nick said as he examined the fine head. "Boy, are we going to have some meat," he added. He finished his commentary on the proper way to harvest a bull bison, and I listened. And then I said my piece.

"Nick, they'll just think we banged him through a fence anyway," I said. My brother looked at me.

"The hell they will," he smiled. As he spoke, he patted the side of his motor-drive camera.

"You didn't catch that, did you?" I asked.

"I think so," he replied. "I think so. When I saw your rifle muzzle coming up, I took aim through the viewfinder and touched off my own shots."

When the film made its rounds to the processing plant and back to me, it was evident that Nick had only

Can Kill!

by SAM FADALA

Photos by Nick Fadala

missed the first split second of my shot. The rest of the story was clearly printed on celluloid. I had spent 20 years trying to locate a situation where I could take a bison out in the open, without any "help" from anyone, and pretty much on my own terms. And there was only one way I truly wanted to harvest that animal—I wanted to do it with a black powder rifle.

I hunt with modern arms, too, and I have no intention of ever closing the closet door on my firearms of modern style. But there are times when I prefer pushing the hands of time backwards. I want to add a bit of challenge to the chase. The tool of the hunt has to then be historical and aesthetic. That is how I rank the muzzleloader— challenging, historical and aesthetic.

I began hunting with a muzzleloader about 15 years ago. There was only one big question in my mind— would the frontstuffer be enough gun for big game? As far as I was concerned, if black powder arms were not truly lethal, then I'd confine my muzzle-loading to the shooting range.

On the face of it, the question seems ridiculous. One might suggest that since game all over the world has been decked with smokepoles long before the smokeless powder arm was a twinkle in the inventor's eye, that would prove that black powder was truly lethal. Actually, this is not logical. The old-timer hunted with black powder all right, and all manner of game has been dropped with "thundersticks," but that proves nothing. After all, what else did the hunters of yesteryear have to hunt with? Nothing else in the firearms line. That's for sure.

So I began a serious testing program which included actual in-the-field experience, coupled with shooting into all sorts of test materials, and added to these I also began to compile data from reliable sources, mainly other black powder hunters, as well as good publications on the topic. Fifteen years later, having hunted with black powder in several states and dropping a number of game animals, I can say that the muzzleloader is a viable hunting tool, even for today's conditions. How does it compare with a modern firearm? I would say that in every respect a modern firearm has the potential of being more potent. Caliber for caliber, the modern arm is simply stronger in the ballistics department.

There is not a caliber or load for "standard" frontstuffers being used today which cannot be bettered by some modern caliber. But watch out! We have to be careful here. This is not to say that we cannot have or do not have some powerful and very practical black powder power in the hands of modern "downwind" shooters. We do have. We always did.

Smokepole Punch

Before going into the loads and practices that can make black powder shooting a truly reliable way to bag big game, I'd like to point out a few facts about smokepole punch. First, the old-time arms for big game hunting, and I include elephants here, rendered their thunder from the use of truly large projectiles. This is an important aspect of gaining "power" from a frontloader. Of course, things can get out of hand here. A black powder cartridge gun of yesteryear is a perfect example. This was the two bore as manufactured by William Moore of London. While a cartridge gun, it was indeed a black powder firearm. Two-bore means, in effect, that it would only take two missiles to equal a full pound of lead! In truth, a conical bullet was used. This bullet did indeed weigh in at 3,500 grains, and it was backed by 800 grains of Fg black powder. The muzzle velocity was declared as 1500 fps, and the muzzle energy was and still is 17,490 foot-pounds.

Compare that with my 7mm Magnum, which I feel is a powerful weapon, and you have the 7mm pushing a 175-grain bullet at about 3000 fps for an energy of almost 3,500 foot-pounds. My 458 drives a 500-grain bullet at 2100 fps for a muzzle energy of under 5000 foot-pounds.

But we are not going to hunt with a two bore, so what kind of energy can we look at in our standard black powder arms? A very popular muzzleloader caliber for today is the 50-caliber. Firing a .490-inch round ball at 2000 fps at the muzzle, the muzzle energy here would be about 1573 foot-pounds, since the .490-inch ball in pure lead weighs 177 grains. That is not an awful lot of energy. Nor is it a popgun load. My 54-caliber handles a 230-grain .535-inch ball at 1975 fps for a muzzle energy of 1993 foot-pounds.

The ball loses velocity very rapidly. At 100 yards from the muzzle, the 50-caliber .490-inch ball mentioned above might be doing only 1120 fps with an energy rating of 493 foot-pounds. This brings us to our first rule of black powder hunting, which is to *get close*. Since energy is rapidly lost in the round ball, then the secret to success in terms of lethality is to get close. This is fine. After all, we elected to add the muzzleloader to our battery so that we would experience the extra challenge and thrills that come with that challenge. I do not lament the fact that I have to get closer with a thunderstick. I welcome the fact.

Well, since the ball loses velocity so rapidly, why not turn to the conical? There is no doubt that a conical will better the ball in terms of retained energy. There are, however, a few fac-

This buck was taken at about 20 yards distance with a .530-inch round ball of 224 grains weight fired at a starting velocity of about 2000 fps. The author's son spotted the buck in the brush, feeding, and a stalk was made for a close shot. Getting close is imperative if the full lethality of a muzzleloader is to be reached.

tors to observe. In the first place, normal conical shooting is going to result in muzzle velocities below those of the round ball. In fact, while well-constructed firearms with good barrel steel, such as offered by several companies today, can produce a muzzle velocity of about 1800-2000 fps for a ball, that velocity drops, usually, to 1300-1500 fps for a conical, such as the Minie or the Maxi.

Therefore, we find that trajectories are quite similar between the two missile forms. While the ball begins its journey faster than the "bullet," the elongated projectile retains its velocity better and out to 125 yards both print very similar parabolic curves. Furthermore, while some may fume over the statement, having hunted several states each season with black powder, we have managed to compile a great number of autopsies with ball and conical harvests, and wound channels look much the same for the two. I have found no better killing effect with the conical *at black powder ranges!* Of course, if the shooter were to insist upon firing from longer ranges, then he would have to take the conical for its superior external

ballistics.

In plain language, the conical does not generate enough velocity to make it explosive on big game, and it is still below the effect of the modern bullet at high velocity. In other words, the black powder shooter who uses a conical should still get close and place his shot. He should still consider his rifle much more primitive than a modern tool, and he should enjoy the fact by accepting the challenge.

In the final analysis, at close range, black powder lethality does not favor ball over conical or conical over ball. There is one exception—if smaller calibers are used, then a conical may be selected so that greater mass can be gained. As for penetration, I have shot through bull bison, bull elk, bears, mule deer, antelope and other game with the lead pill, and with witnesses to verify this fact. The ball will penetrate when the range is held to under 100 yards. In choosing ball or bullet for a black powder rifle, accuracy should be considered as the foremost criterion for the selection of one over the other.

Caliber is the key to black powder power. We have already admitted that we cannot, nor do we wish to, obtain modern velocity from a smokepole. Therefore, our lethality stems from a projectile of good mass. Also, the large caliber simply provides a better wound channel than the small caliber when we do not have the terrific shock wave associated with high intensity cartridges. As we all know, a fist-sized exit hole on the offside of that whitetail deer taken with a 243 did not emanate from the bullet itself. After all, there is no way to get a tiny 243 bullet to expand to a diameter of 4 inches, but I have seen a 4-inch exit hole on a buck. The shock wave made that hole.

With the round ball, we can actually figure the increase in muzzle energy by using a simple formula. We will not produce an exact figure, but an extremely close one by doing the following: divide the smaller diameter ball to the third power into the larger diameter ball to the third power. If we have a 50-caliber ball going against a 54-caliber ball, we treat the matchup like this:

$$\frac{.530^3}{.490^3} = \frac{.148877}{.117649} = 1.2654336$$

So, we say in theory that the .530-inch ball belonging to the 54-caliber arm will be 1.2654336 times "stronger" in kinetic energy than the .490-inch ball belonging to the 50-caliber arm. If we give both of these round balls a starting velocity of 2000 fps, the .490-inch ball at 177 grains will be worth 1573 foot-pounds of muzzle energy. The .530-inch ball at 224 grains will be worth 1990 foot-pounds at tne muzzle. Is the .530-inch ball exactly 1.265 times "stronger" than the .490-inch ball at the same muzzle velocity? Well, if we take 1.2654336 times 1572, the muzzle energy of the .490, we end up with 1989.2616, rounded off to 1989 foot-pounds. We are within 1-foot-pound of the actual muzzle energy of the .490-inch ball. It works out.

So we lean toward increased ball size for our lethality in the muzzle-loading ball-shooter. Similar caliber increases for the conical-shooters are also very important. As an example, if we have a 370-grain Maxi in 50-caliber at 1500 fps we arrive at a muzzle energy of 1849 foot-pounds. But a 625-grain Maxi for the 58-caliber at 1500 fps gains a muzzle energy of 3123 foot-pounds.

Lethality and remaining velocity also go hand in hand. Unfortunately, one of the more serious fabrications coming from the world of black powder suggests that since round balls

At longer ranges, the round ball will not flatten very much in its production of a wound channel. Up close, it will. But on thin-skinned game, even though the ball flattens, it penetrates well enough at close range. This buck was shot at 10 yards, yet the ball penetrated across the breadth of the animal, coming to a stop in the opposite shoulder blade.

lose velocity so rapidly, then there is no point in trying to gain a good muzzle velocity in the first place. This is false. It is quite true that as the muzzle velocity increases above the speed of sound (especially the speed of sound in terms of the "slipstream" behind the ball) more *percentage* of velocity is lost. We can look at this example: Our rifle is a Browning Mountain model in 50-caliber, and we are allowed to use as much as 120 grains FFFg by that company in that rifle.

However, we find that 120 FFg instead of FFFg gives us plenty of velocity. In fact, we obtain an average velocity of 1974 fps with that charge in the 50-caliber Browning. With 70 FFg, we have reached a muzzle velocity of 1602 fps. The school of thought which says that starting velocity is of little consequence had best take a good look at the figures here. The .490-inch ball at 1602 fps has a muzzle energy of 1009 foot-pounds. The .490-inch at 1974 has a muzzle energy of 1532 foot pounds. At 100 yards, here is what happens: **1602** starting velocity has dropped to **961** fps; **1974** starting velocity has dropped to **1113** fps. The loss in percentage for the

1602 fps load has been 40 percent. The loss in percentage for the **1974** fps load has been 44 percent. So, the lower starting velocity does show a better *percentage* of retained velocity, but the raw figures still remain strongly intact. The fact is that the 1974 starting velocity is still worth 487 foot-pounds at 100 yards and the 1602 starting velocity is worth 363 foot-pounds. That may not seem like much, but if we look at a percentage again, we find that the higher velocity ball is 25 percent higher in energy.

Therefore, black powder lethality certainly goes in favor of the higher velocity ball. Incidentally, on hard objects, such as telephone books and department store catalogs, which are both very destructive of projectiles, the higher velocity ball tends to have no more penetration ability than the lower velocity ball. On game, as well as on gelatin block tests and clay block tests, the higher velocity balls have surpassed the penetartion of the lower velocity balls.

A strong feature of the all-lead ball or conical is the fact that lead is high in the molecular cohesion department. In short, it sticks together rath-

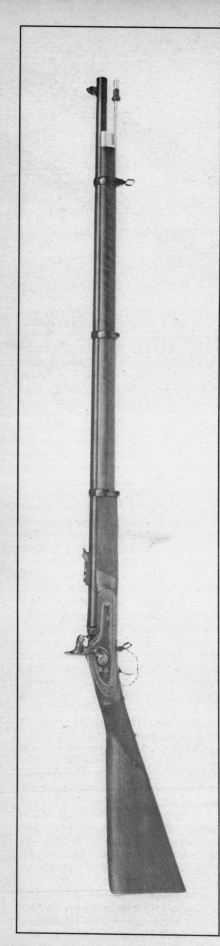

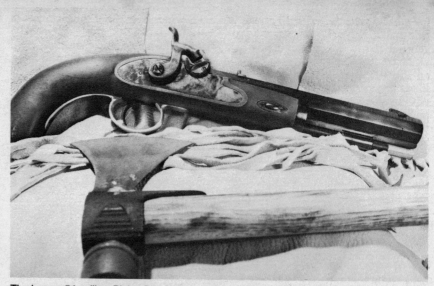

The Lyman 54-caliber Plains Pistol is especially useful for those who own a rifle of the same bore size. This pistol will manage as much as 40 grains of FFFg for a muzzle velocity of 952 fps.

er than fragmenting. This fact means a better chance for penetration. A fragmented projectile has ceased to penetrate as well as it was penetrating before it broke up. I have collected many lead projectiles from game and in all cases so far, the recovered weight of either ball or conical has been exceedingly high. The very last mule deer buck I harvested was stalked to 5 yards distance and shot at 10 yards as the buck broke away. The .535-inch ball was fired at a previously chronographed muzzle velocity of 1975 fps, so at only 10 paces, the pill was still scooting along at pretty high velocity for a black powder missile. That ball weighed 230.0 grains before it was fired. I know because I pre-weigh all of my projectiles before taking them into the field for a hunt. The recovered weight, after penetrating from under the spine all the way into the shoulder bone on the opposite side of the buck was 228.0 grains. The ball only lost about 1 percent of its original weight.

Handguns and Shotguns

We have not spent a moment on handguns or shotguns in our lethality discussion, but most of the figures already stated apply. The most powerful black powder handgun I have tested is the big Navy Arms 58-caliber Harper's Ferry 1855 model. I chronographed the 525-grain Minie at 802 fps with a muzzle energy of 750 foot-pounds. We certainly must adhere to the current practice of using Newton's idea of energy. Therefore, low velocity missiles take a real beating as the formula squares the velocity. However, there is not a perfect 1.00 positive correlation between actual "killing power" and energy ratings. I submit that a 58-caliber bullet of 525 grains at a muzzle velocity of 802 fps is what any shooter would call a very strong force indeed.

The black powder shotgun delivers ballistics that are not terribly far from modern ballistics, though the modern shell-shucker does win the contest. In fact, some truly well made shotguns will take loads which gain up to 1400 fps with 1⅛ ounces of shot, and I've chronographed as high as 1300 fps for 1¼ ounces of shot in a 12-gauge muzzleloader. Of course these loads were okayed by the gunmaker. I never load beyond the recommended charge of the manufacturer.

We also have not touched upon the smaller calibers for small game hunting. In fact, at close range, the smaller muzzleloader calibers have more than enough punch for small game. I have taken a quantity of cottontails, squirrels and up to wild turkeys with the 36-caliber firing a .350-inch 65-grain round ball. With only 30 grains of FFFg in my Hatfield flintlock, this little ball scoots out at just shy of 1800

One of the military style rifles available for the black powder deer hunter is the Parker Hale Whitworth Military Target rifle imported by Navy Arms. This rifle amazed shooters in the 19th century, and was praised in the famous book *The Gun* by W. W. Greener for its fine accuracy. This rifle, designed to fire conicals, has the proper twist to manage the longer, bullet-type missile. The twist is 1:20, or one turn in only 20 inches with a bore size of .451-inch. Barrel length is 36 inches.

fps muzzle velocity. With 40 grains of FFFg GOEX black powder, the ball gets out at 2023 fps. The only problem with the 36-caliber, and even the 32-caliber, is that with even modest loads, small game should be taken with head shots to preserve the edible meat. There is plenty of lethality in that squirrel rifle caliber for close-range small game hunting and wild turkey taking.

I think we have established that the bigger calibers are best for big game, whether we are using the round ball or the conical. On the face of it, and to oversimplify the matter, the larger projectile of pure lead, with its fine ability to hang together as a unit,

ever, when Baker and the boys met a herd of elephants, they apparently tried to down the whole pack.

This meant having some real force of power at hand. Sir Samuel often used his 4-ounce rifle. No, the rifle did not weigh 4 ounces, the projectile did. Let's see, that is 1,750 grains of lead, or a bit larger than your average 180-grain 30-caliber bullet of today. But

Black powder power and bore size go hand in hand. The caliber must be suited to the game. Here we have two fine hunting rifles. Above is a 54-caliber custom rifle made by Dennis Mulford of Iowa. The rifle fires a .535-inch ball at about 1975 fps muzzle velocity. Below is the beautiful Muskrat model from Ozark Mountain Arms. This 40-caliber rifle fires a .400″ (bore-sized) ball of 96 grains at 2000 fps. The latter can be a deadly rifle for deer-sized game in the hands of a good shot and a patient hunter who will wait and work for that close shot.

makes a long wound channel, and the larger the ball or conical, the larger the wound channel. Of course, the old-timers knew this. I like to refer to Sir Samuel Baker as one world hunter of the 19th century who relied upon shear force of caliber with good powder charges to down his game.

Baker was an Englishman who had a chance to live in Ceylon. To the world of history he is better known as a traveler of the Nile. To the world of shooting, he's known for his ponderous big bore rifles. Baker was, of course, a product of his times, just as we are products of our times. We would consider the amount of game he dropped a bit too much, but it seems that most of it went to good use. How-

more interesting to me is the fact that Baker often went away from this elongated missile to the round ball for his elephant shooting. He said, on page 136 of *The Rifle and the Hound in Ceylon,* the Arno Press edition, that: "With these elephants the 4-ounce rifle is an invaluable weapon; even if the animal is not struck in the mortal spot, the force of the blow upon the head is so great that it will generally bring him upon his knees, or at least stop him. It has failed me once or twice in this, but not often; and upon those occasions I had loaded with the conical ball (elongated projectile). This, although it will penetrate much farther through a thick substance than a round ball, is not so effective in elephant-shooting as the latter." So, Baker preferred the sphere of lead, the round ball, even for elephants, and he, with witnesses looking on, shot through water buffalo with round balls from a very long distance.

Anyway, this is neither here nor there, and I would not want to present the idea that a ball is deadlier than a conical. It is not. However, in speaking of lethality, the good load, not an overload for these are useless, but a good safe load which will deliver reasonable black powder velocity, combined with a projectile of good size spells punch for frontloaders. That, in the proverbial nutshell, is the story.

In preparing such a load, we must turn to the gunmaker for his "maximum" rating. A maximum rating does not mean that the gun is about to blow up. What it does mean is this—the load is up to snuff for big game when the caliber is right. That is all it means, and we do not exceed it, ever, for many reasons. We do not exceed that load because of obvious safety factors, because we do not wish to strain the rifle. And we do not exceed the load because the law of diminishing returns steps in and takes over.

In short, we can sometimes add more powder and all we get for it is a minimal increase in velocity, but a lot more noise, blast, recoil and smoke. That is a waste, because pressure can rise *out of proportion* with velocity increases. Black powder may burn in such a manner that as much as 57 percent of the load is not turned into a gaseous state. The 57 percent means that we have deposits of fouling in the bore, and it also means that we have to propel some of the solids from the bore. The sum total of such solids and the projectile combined is known as the "ejecta." We want to load our black powder in a safe manner and a sensible manner. Overloads do not pay off in added power.

At this point, there well could be someone in the crowd who has his hand up. He wants to say something, and I have a good idea what it is. "I

Ball size grows in mass way out of proportion as caliber increases. We can figure the exact theoretical perfect weight of a pure lead round ball by a simple formula: ball diameter to the third power divided by .5236 divided by 2873.5. Here we have a series of round ball. On the far left is a .350-inch ball followed by a .395-inch, .440-inch, .490-inch, .530-inch and .570-inch. The little .350-inch ball goes 65 grains, but the .570-inch ball weighs 278 grains on the average. Even though it is not nearly double the size of the .350-inch, the .570-inch far outweighs the smaller ball.

One of the most important factors for the ball-shooter to remember is the dimension of the sphere to be used on game. Compared here a 36- and 58-caliber balls. The 36, in .350-inch size weighs 65 grains. The 58, in .570-inch size, weighs 280 grains. Although the 58 is *not* double the caliber size of the 36, the 58-caliber ball outweighs the 36 by 215 grains. This extra mass makes all the difference in striking power.

This selection of 50-caliber projectiles shows a Maxi ball on the far left which, in this specific case, weighed 367 grains. In the middle is a .490-inch Speer swaged round ball (weight 177 grains), while on the far right is a 50-caliber Minie which goes 350 grains. Although the ball is the smallest of the three projectiles, the author has done well with this type of missile on mule deer. In spite of the bad press the round ball often receives from its detractors, it is a very effective tool within the confines of its range. The elongated projectile holds its velocity much better, of course, but is still difficult to hit with at longer distances (and becomes very hard to connect with much beyond normal round-ball range).

have a little 40-caliber rifle at home," he begins, "and I've taken 12 white-tail bucks with it with only 13 shots. Bet you don't know too many guys with a 30-06 who have done much better." The worse part of the guy's argument is that he's right—in a way.

But we are talking lethality. We are not talking hunter prowess. Given that little 40-caliber with a .395-inch ball of about 93 grains weight, in the hands of a good shot and with an accurate rifle, why, there's no doubt that the deer is going to drop. I do not consider myself good enough to hunt the big western mule deer on a day-in and day-out basis with a 40-caliber myself, but I have a very fine Muskrat (Ozark Mt. Arms) in that caliber, and I have taken antelope with it.

The rifle in question is highly accurate, light to pack, steady to hold, easy to shoot straight, and when a little 40-caliber pill goes through the head or neck of a game animal, that game animal is generally headed for the freezer, provided the brain or neck bones have been hit. So I do have sympathy for the good shot who owns an accurate rifle of "smaller" caliber. But all in all, what we have said about a larger projectile at a reasonable velocity still bears up under the scrutiny of both field experience and the laws of physics.

We can move away from the subject of black powder lethality by saying that frontloaders are indeed viable tools for the harvesting of big game. But they are not on par with modern arms. Nor would we want them to be. If they offered no greater challenge,

and if they did not have such historical attraction to go with that challenge, I doubt that we would have such a substantial body of black powder shooters today. It is the slow-loading, hands-on, do-it-yourself, get-close approach which attracts us.

One windy day my older son, also a black powder shooter, and I were out trying to put a mule deer in the pot. The day was nothing short of miserable. A self-respecting coyote would have been in his burrow, but we were trying to wrap up our home state hunt

so we could pack our smokepoles over to Idaho for another black powder hunt coming up. So we were out there fighting the elements. Finally, it just got to be too much. "Let's bag it and head for the hearth," I suggested, and Bill was not too put out with my idea. "But," I added, "we can hunt our way back slowly just in case."

On the way out, I put the 9x35s on a desert cliff and in a virtual depression in that cliff was the head of a mule deer buck surveying the thousands of acres which lay below it. Bill and I stalked the side of the cliff, and I peeped over the ridge only 5 yards from the buck. I went back and measured this so I could be certain of what I am saying. It saw me the moment I saw it, and it launched out of that depression like a brown rock from a Roman catapult. I had set the trigger, and the 54 was ready to go. At 10 yards, also measured, the buck was hit by a round ball and dropped immediately.

"After all of these years," I said to myself, "you still get a thrill from the great sport of harvesting meat for yourself now and then instead of having someone else do it for you." And I had to admit that the single-shot frontloader certainly added a lot of charm and memory to that harvest. Had I missed, that buck would have been having lunch with his *amigos* in the next county. There would be no way to stuff another patched ball and charge downbore in time for a second shot.

The black powder firearm remained in the hands of hunters all through our country's history and surprisingly, perhaps, these old-time shooting irons never completely faded away. Even when modern repeaters and cartridge guns were available, at least *some* shooters stayed with the muzzleloader. One of my heroes used a muzzleloader, though in the late 19th century, before his death, he could have turned to a cartridge gun if he had wanted to. But he stayed with the frontloading smokepole.

This was Nessmuk, George W. Sears. Sears was a hunter and an avid outdoorsman, and he wrote *Woodcraft,* a fine book on the outdoors.

Nessmuk, toted his shooting bag and his "possibles" on his hunts. He was a backpacker, living with the game on at least some of his hunts. He says, "My rifle was a neat, hair-triggered Billinghurst, carrying 60 round balls to the pound, a muzzleloader, of course, and a nail-driver. I made just three shots in 10 days (of a long backpack trek), and each shot stood for a plump young deer in the 'short blue' " (p. 82 of the Dover reprint).

His rifle was in the area of about 43-caliber, and I have no doubt he could shoot it. He made up for lack of "big power" with an abundance of accuracy. I like to think that for most of us today, where time is often a limiting factor, we are better off to carry enough punch to make up for a shot that is not exactly through the brain. Of course, placement of the projectile is still the most important factor.

I have been on both ends of the continuum. I have taken venison at a few hundred yards with a scintillating speedster of the 257 Weatherby class, and I have stalked in and bagged a buck at a few yards with the ancient lead pill. Both are valuable experiences, and both ways can produce clean one-shot kills—humane harvests that no one can argue with. Within its range limitations, the lethality of the old muzzleloader is without question a fact. All that is asked by the old-time black powder firearm is reasonable caliber size for general big game hunting under "usual" conditions and a comparatively close-range shot. There is something aside from the value of extra power in that close-range muzzleloader harvest, too, and that is the greater chance for ball placement. After all, therein lies the real thrill of the hunt, finding the game and then taking it cleanly with one well-placed shot. The venerable frontloader is capable of doing just that. Black powder lethality—it is for real. ●

The type of impetus which is possible from a huge Minie ball, such as shown here on the left, is definitely not necessary for the harvesting of mule deer, although the hunter is welcome to use this force if he wishes to do so, and if the rifle in question happens to shoot such slugs accurately. The Minie shown is 58-caliber and weighs 625 grains. It is called the Shiloh Stakebuster. For comparison, a Hornady 308-caliber bullet is shown on the right. The author has been using only the round ball in 50- and 54-caliber for the past few years and, with proper loads from high-grade rifles, has had first-rate success in harvesting mule deer and other game.

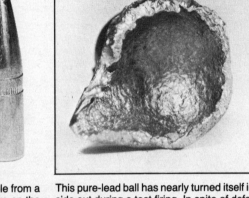

This pure-lead ball has nearly turned itself inside out during a test firing. In spite of deformation, the author has seen a .530-inch ball totally penetrate the chest cavity of a bull bison. Though the ball was flat as a frizbee, it maintained all but .1 (one-tenth) of one grain weight of its original mass.

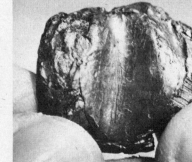

This .530-inch ball was extracted from a bison after having penetrated the entire breadth of the chest cavity and knocking a piece of rib *through* the hide on the offside.

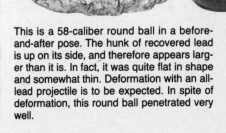

This is a 58-caliber round ball in a before-and-after pose. The hunk of recovered lead is up on its side, and therefore appears larger than it is. In fact, it was quite flat in shape and somewhat thin. Deformation with an all-lead projectile is to be expected. In spite of deformation, this round ball penetrated very well.

USING A lung-powered varmint call to con a clever coyote into believing that you've laid out a free smorgasbord for it takes the skill of a trumpet virtuoso, the larceny of a used car salesman, and the self-conviction of a Supreme Court justice!

You are in fact matching wits with an animal that has evolved through a million generations into one of the swiftest, deadliest hunters in the world — suspicious by nature, and equipped with senses of sight and smell a dozen times more acute than your own. Count on the coyote to use all of its faculties to verify if your winsome wail on the call truly signals *hasenpfeffer* on the hoof or just a hammy hoax!

As one of the biggest predators prowling the range in the contiguous States and Mexico, the coyote comes to a call confident that it can steal a meal from whatever animal has the rabbit in its fangs. This arrogance accounts for those infrequent occasions when a greedy coyote bores in on the call like an overdue freight train. However, it's usually the untutored pups that make a beeline for your stand. Old, seasoned dogs will swing wide to pick up your scent.

When coyotes approach in packs, one member usually circles downwind. I once called up a trio of prairie wolves on the desert flats of New Mexico while nestled into the shade of a stunted mesquite atop a rise. Camoclad from cuffs to cap, I watched them approach like a military infiltration team, with first one, then the other, darting forward from prickly pear patch to ocotillo cluster, to sagebrush clump, never clear of cover for more than an instant. Suddenly one "ki-dog" dropped into a shallow dry wash, as the other two continued to work their way toward me. Just as I riveted one under the cross hairs of my rifle scope and squeezed the slack from the trigger, I heard a frantic barking from behind — *downwind!* Both coyotes in front instantly swapped ends, throwing up clouds of sand in their haste to depart.

At least half of the battle in successful calling lies in choosing the proper stand — *well clear of dry washes that coyotes can use to get downwind unobserved*. If you can back up to a cliff with the wind in your face, so much the better. But such ideal locations are few and far between. Seek out high points, such as just below the crest of a ridge, with a commanding view of a valley and opposing hillside, preferably with the sun at your back, hunkered in the shade of a tree or bush. A rocky outcropping is good if you can find a safe perch. Coyotes seldom look up until nearing their destination. Even the crotch of a tree can often place you above the normal range of its penetrating pale yellow eyes. Allow some knee-high brush in front of your position to encourage a frontal approach. Otherwise coyotes may hang around the fringes of cover, reluctant to cross open ground, or worse, circle downwind.

Man gives off stronger odors than he imagines, even after a Dial shower. It pays to avoid perfumed deodorants, hair spray and after-shave. Smoking on a stand guarantees zero results! Even smoking in the car beforehand permeates hair and clothing with a stench that oozes out for hours after.

Dating back to the mountain men of frontier America, trappers have brewed a variety of malodorous concoctions from well-aged coyote urine, glands, and diced intestines, simmered for days in foul-smelling caldrons to eye-watering purees, bottled, then sprinkled on trap sets. Happily, today's commercial scents are less objectionable to humans, and perhaps

Conning The

Home-made portable camouflage blinds can be set up in any location to afford cover for the caller. Blinds like these allow more freedom of movement and concealment than simply backing up into brush.

even more attractive to wild canines.

Buck Stop Lure Co., Inc., of Stanton, Michigan, markets a wide array of trapping lures that work just as well for coyote calling. They include Coyote Lure, Fox Lure and Bobcat Lure, compounded of glands, secretions and musks, preserved and fixed. Also offered are UR-N-All scents containing concentrated urine of coyote, fox or bobcat. Packaged in small plastic bottles with caps that dispense a drop at a time, the scents can be applied to boots, cuffs and hat brims, and high on surrounding brush to disarm the coyote's most formidable defense, its long thin inquisitive nose. Buck Stop also markets plastic pin-on scent pads with tufts of wool to accept the smelly drops. Doff these before entering the house, and you'll improve your welcome from the better half!

Before sitting on your stand, use a stick to dislodge snakes, centipedes, etc., that might be there ahead of you. That stick can also be used to remove rocks that might later impress your posterior painfully. Avoid a cramped position that will later force you to shift your body, likely just at the moment a suspicious critter is viewing you from cover with a justifiably jaundiced eye.

If you should back your behind into a cholla cactus as I did once down in Mexico, you'll value a pair of tweezers higher than gold. Don't cozy up to a verdant poison ivy, poison oak or poison sumac!

Aside from its obvious benefit to your epidermis, insect repellant is essential to successful varmint calling. No coyote will go near a caller waving his hands like semaphores, warding off mosquitos, chiggers and blackflies. Ticks can become unwelcome hitchhikers, threatening tularemia. Cutter's Insect Repellant Cream or Stick offers long-lasting protection without giveaway odors.

It's not macho or even smart to be miserable from cold when varmint hunting in the winter. Frozen fingers can't find, much less feel, the trigger. Hand warmers that burn volatile fuel give off odors foreign to the wild. A new, *no-smell*, approach to cold hands comes from Hot Mini of America, Inc., of San Francisco, California, in the form of a pocket-sized plastic "Heat Treat" pad that chemically creates 130-degree heat for a continuous 24 hours when exposed to air. Action can be interrupted by returning it to its sealed plastic bag.

Other hazards haunt hunters of

predators. Occasionally, a coyote or fox will barrel in and bite first, and identify its prey later. Predatory owls and hawks are often first to answer a varmint call and have been known to lift a hat or even a scalp. I once had an almost hair-raising encounter with an eagle that had the wing span of a Piper Cub! It swooped down at me like a Kamikazi. At the last instant, I stood up and waved it off. With a piercing scream of alarm, the huge bird lifted up and over my head, leaving a wake in the air like that of a supersonic transport.

If you have a stand that really inspires confidence, you can go to the trouble of setting up a portable blind that you constructed of chicken wire covered with camouflage cloth, or use one of the Mini-Blinds from Sports Haven, Inc., Seattle, Washington. In forested areas, an aircraft aluminum Climbing Tree Stand from Baker Mfg. Co., Valdosta, Georgia, affords sufficient elevation to see a wide area and places you above the normal range of coyote's vision.

Where to Find 'em

You'll get nothing but practice calling an area where the coyote population is nil. You can locate productive

Clever Coyote

by **JOHN LACHUK**

While matching wits with a coyote isn't easy, it *can* be done — that's what makes the coyote a varmint-hunting challenge that's second to none!

Several times California varmint calling champion, Don Egger, and the author survey one night's kill in Owens Valley area of Southern California. Desert coyotes are generally smaller than their mountain-grown cousins.

Low deserts are another favorite haunt of the coyote. Here, author (right) admires partner's kill.

Hunting partner Bill Sims looks on as author examines downed coyote. Note that Sims is wearing insulated, camouflaged coveralls—they're excellent for cold climes.

territory by idling along rural dirt roads, watching for tracks and droppings. A coyote's dog-like tracks show four toes and claw marks, about 2 inches wide by 2½ inches long, usually with dirt thrown up behind. Seemingly always in a hurry, coyotes run or dog-trot rather than walk. Even fresh tracks don't necessarily indicate a coyote within hearing of your call. It could be miles distant. If you locate coyote feces, spread the feces with the toe of your boot. If they contain short hair, the coyotes are eating principally rodents. Long hair indicates rabbits are the main fare. The presence of coarse seeds probably means that cactus apples are a staple.

Where there is food, there you'll find coyotes. Shallow marshy areas with ducks in residence are good for calling. Coyotes love to invite ducks to breakfast. Farmers and ranchers can direct you to the most recent serenade grounds of *Canis latrans* (baying dog). Locals usually welcome polite, serious-minded varmint hunters with sense enough to direct their fire well away from buildings and stock. When approaching a rural residence to ask permission to hunt, *leave your guns in the car.* Don't give the appearance of an invading army!

Coyotes in easy to reach areas are probably well educated to the ways of varmint callers. A four-wheel-drive rig can get you off the beaten track into the less accessible regions of forest or desert. When opening the doors of your rig, hold inward hard on the arm rest, to prevent the loud "click" of the latch releasing. Avoid "clinking" sounds while loading your rifle. Squelch talking and laughing on your way to the stand. Walk into the wind — far enough to leave the popping sounds of cooling metal and the smell of gasoline far behind. Take the shortest possible route to your stand, without crossing over the area from which you expect critters to approach. Don't allow binoculars and calls to "clink" together!

Calling alone is less productive and less fun than working with a companion. Two men can watch twice as much ground for incoming critters. After hunting together for awhile, good friends can almost sense what the other is thinking, making for a sort of silent communication necessary to calling success. Adding a third hunter seems to multiply confusion by six times, and should, in my opinion, be avoided for the most part.

It's not uncommon to spot coyotes from the road while traveling to or from your stand. Resist the natural impulse to leap out and blaze away at the retreating rear. That only wises up the breed for generations into the future. Instead, drive until a rise or gully hides your rig. Leave it and establish a calling site as near as possible to where you saw the coyote, without revealing your presence by sight or sound. Then call as usual. Odds are you'll bag a critter or two.

When a storm is in the offing, critters are loath to answer a call. They have done their hunting early and are already snug in their dens. Somehow they can predict bad weather better than a satellite. They will stay holed up during a storm, but immediately after, they are hunting hot and hungry! In a high wind, coyotes answer a call grudgingly if at all. Wind hampers their senses of smell and hearing, making critters reluctant to trust either. The sound of the call carries well downwind, but so does man-musk. So your most likely response will come from upwind, but only a short distance. For best results, make short stands — from 5 to 10 minutes — close together, always moving into the wind.

After calling, the average wait for a coyote is 15 to 20 minutes. While foxes answer a call with little or no caution, the average coyote wants more time to size-up the situation.

Night Hunting

Predators are principally nocturnal in nature. If the law allows, you can enjoy a whole different world — a wierdly exciting one — by hunting at night. You can park your rig along

Author approaches coyote downed by .240 PSP. Note that the type of country favored by coyotes includes plenty of brush.

Author (left) surveyed woolgrowers in Wyoming on coyote predation. All were adamant in their condemnation of the predator.

Four-wheel drive outfits like the author's Jeep Gladiator allow you to reach out-of-the-way areas where coyotes aren't so well educated to callers.

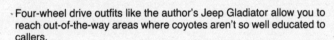

Importance of camouflage clothing is clearly demonstrated here. The author (center) is sitting between the two Burnham Brothers who are in camo clothes. Note how the author stands out.

The author's two favorite coyote rifles are the 240 Weatherby Magnum Mark V, with Bushnell 4x-12x (left), and a custom 240 Page Super Pooper, with Bushnell Lite-Site 3x-9x.

one of the dirt roads that customarily follows a mountain ridge, and hunt an entire canyon, driving a quarter to a half mile between stops. On the flatlands, seek out any available high spots. However, I can't recommend a railroad right of way.

One night in New Mexico, I parked on a rise where my partner and I began calling. Instead of the customary pair of bright dots in the distance that signify critter eyes, we were greeted by a Cyclops that matched our varmint call wail for wail. That smoke-belching "varmit" grew to immense proportions as it bore down upon us. As the one huge light grew more intense, it reflected off of two glistening ribbons that made a straight line from it to us. *We were parked on the railroad tracks!* In a sudden flash of insight we both jumped into the Jeep, and I started the engine cranking pronto! But in my haste, I managed to flood it, and the starter ground on in vain, as that menacing beam seemed

Also helpful for night shooting is Bushnell Lite-Site, with switch atop ocular bell that turns on a red dot at the center of the crosshairs.

Author's Ruger Mini-14 Ranch Rifle sports a Bushnell scope and Burnham Brothers Mercury Switch Shooting Light, that goes on and off with a twist of the rifle.

ready to engulf us. My partner opened his door prepared to bail out, when the engine finally coughed to life and pulled us off the tracks just as the freight train roared passed our back bumper!

Hunting from your vehicle offers the distinct advantage of using high candlepower lights plugged into the cigarette lighter, capable of picking up eyes several hundred yards distant, and revealing the entire animal a football field away. It's critical, however, to properly identify your target before shooting. Occasionally, a curious deer may come loping lazily in to the sound. In rural areas, roaming ranch dogs and house cats often respond. Infrequently you could summon up a cow or bull. If you shoot just at "eyes," you could alienate the whole community. Entire counties have been closed to shooting for less!

Among the finest hand-held lights available is the "Nite Tracker I" from Lighting Systems, Inc., Erie, PA, a 200,000 candlepower spotlight wrapped in a black high-impact polyethelene case complete with pistol grip, 15-foot power cord and trigger switch that can be locked on if desired. The Nite Tracker III reaches 300,000 candlepower with a 150-watt sealed beam quartz halogen bulb. Lighting Systems offers a leak-proof rechargeable portable battery pack that affords 90 minutes of constant use with the 160,000 candlepower Nite Tracker IV. This battery pack

From left to right, some of the lights used by the author for night hunting predators: Dark Blazer Super II hand lantern, Burnham Brothers' Scope Lite, Optronics Blue Eye 3000, and Mag-Lite four "D" cell flashlight. Also shown are two filters, amber and red, to make lights less noticeable to predators.

Johnny Stewart markets the new Searcher I Lexan "bump" helmet complete with integral light, powered by portable rechargeable battery pack.

Some of the items carried by the author when varmint hunting include Safariland holster, nickeled Colt Commander and Bushnell Compact 7x binoculars, compass. Also shown is a selection of calls, a good belt knife, a bottle of insect repellent and a camouflage cap.

serves to sever the umbilical cord relationship.

Optronics, Inc., Fort Gibson, OK, offers their "Varmint Lite," that features 200,000 candlepower spotlight, push button switch, and 10-foot coil cord, all in a vented pistol-gripped plastic housing. Unique is their "Blue Eye" spotlight with the bulb partially shielded by a blue coating that eliminates glare wavelengths of light — it's available in either 200,000 or 300,000 candlepower. The cord, however, is too limiting, requiring a 10-foot straight extension for optimum mobility around the vehicle.

The premier flashlight by far is the "MagCharger" from Mag Instrument, Inc., Ontario, CA, housed in a black anodized machined aluminum tube and rotating bell, that focuses from flood to spot with a quarter-turn. A precision reflector concentrates the light from a pin-type halogen lamp,

Mouth-blown calls (from left to right): Green Head Rabbit Call; three calls from Lohman (long range Jack Rabbit, medium range Cotton Tail, and close range Coaxer); Sure Shot Predator Call; Scotch Combo Call; Scotch Long Range Rabbit Call; Weems Wildcall and Weems Allcall.

delivering a brilliant white 30,000 candlepower. The five half-cell "D" sized battery pack is recharged by a combination holder-base that can be screwed to the kickpanel or door of your rig, with a cord plugged into the cigarette lighter. The MagCharger can be rejuvenated while traveling between stands, or plugged into the wall socket back home.

Certainly, there's nothing quite as handy as a conventional flashlight, and if that's what you want to use, you would be wise to consider the Krypton Star lamp bulb. The bulb is simply a replacement that boosts candlepower by as much as 400 percent. They are available from Carley Lamps, Inc., Torrance, CA. They replace the conventional PR bulb in flashlights compatible with standard batteries, as well as alkaline cells and rechargeable units.

The accepted "MO" on a night hunt is to have one man handle the calling and light, while the other devotes himself to the rifle. Scrambling to get the light and the rifle aimed at the coyote at one and the same time often results in a tangle of lamp cord and gun, or a scuffling of feet accompanied by hoarse whispered oaths and a suddenly vanishing critter. Highly helpful is the Burnham Brothers' Shooting Light that couples to your rifle scope with an upside-down Weaver-style detachable mount, and directs a pencil beam right down the bullet's path. A pair of Duracell 9-volt batteries direct current through a mercury switch that cuts the light when you rotate the rifle to the right. Aim at the critter, and the light is magically on. The famed varmint-hunting Burnham Brothers of Marble Falls, Texas, also offer a 50,000 candlepower scope light without the mercury switch, that plugs into a 12-volt rechargeable gel cell battery pack with shoulder strap.

Critters become understandably shy when burned with the main beam of a bright light. In years past we just held the light high and played the fringes along the horizon to pick up eyes. When the gunner was ready, we lowered the light for positive identification before firing. Lately, the cus-

tom is to cover the light with a red or amber filter, which apparently doesn't alarm game.

Calling

Calling methods vary little between night and day. I usually begin with a series of muted wails from a mid-range cottontail call to bring in any critters that happen to be nearby. Starting out with a loud blast from a long-range jackrabbit call is likely to scare off any critters in the near vicinity. If nothing pops up in a few minutes, I blow the long range call, long and hard, to get the attention of critters far and wide! If the terrain is open, allowing me to spot incoming coyotes from afar, I continue with the jackrabbit call until something is sighted, then switch to a cottontail or squeaker call intermittently, with long pauses, to draw them into rifle range. In close cover, I use the long-range call once or twice, then drop back to a squeaker.

Most varmint calls consist of a wooden or plastic tube about an inch in diameter, 4 to 6 inches long, con-

A lineup, from left to right, of close range squeaker calls: P.S. Olt CP-21, Burnham Brothers squeaker, Lohman squeaker and common rubber bulb squeaker offered by most varmint call makers.

Here's another series of popular predator calls. From left to right: Burnham Brothers Long Range Fox Call and Deluxe Predator Call; new Circe plastic Long Range Predator Call; two Faulk's walnut predator calls; P.S. Olt walnut #33 Predator Call; and Olt plastic T-20 Fox-Coyote call; two plastic Johnny Stewart calls (both "pitch-variable" by biting down), the SPC-3 and PC-1.

taining a plastic or metal reed that can be made to emit a variety of banshee-like wails, imitating the cries of a rabbit in the clutches of some relentless predator. Long-range calls produce the gravelly squall of a jackrabbit. Mid-range calls have less volume, and the higher pitch of a cottontail. Squeakers, of limited volume, mimic mice and rats, especially toothsome to bobcats and foxes, but also attractive to coyotes.

Father of modern varmint calling was the late Morton Burnham. His two sons, Winston and Murray, began producing varmint calls for sale in the early '50s, thinking that a few hundred would probably saturate the market. Over a generation later, Burnham Brothers' calls are still going strong including their two-piece plastic Long-Range Fox Call and walnut Deluxe Predator Call. Burnhams' rubber band squeaker call is a classic that has been widely copied. Other early call manufacturers include Circe Calls, Phoenix, Arizona; P.S. Olt, Pekin, Illinois; Weems Wild Calls, Fort Worth, Texas; and Lohman Mfg. Co., Inc., Neosho, Missouri. The following bird-call companies also offer fine varmint models: Faulk's Game Call Co., Inc., Lake Charles, Louisiana; Green Head Duck Call Co., Lacon, Illinois; and Sure-Shot Game Calls, Groves, Texas.

Johnny Stewart Game Calls, Inc., Waco, Texas, offers two black plastic varmint calls, long-range and short-range, both uniquely variable in tone by tensioning with the teeth when calling. However, Johnny's real claim to fame is his pioneer efforts in devel-

oping electronic game calls. His latest, and best, is the Deluxe Cassette Tape Game Caller, which plays 30-minute cassettes of an infinite variety of varmint calling sounds, from rabbits to birds. Totally self-contained, the unit is readily portable via a handy shoulder strap. A long-range high fidelity speaker comes with 25 feet of cord, allowing the sound source to be placed well away from the caller's position. Johnny also markets an extremely useful Lexan plastic "bump" helmet with attached high-intensity light with flip-up red lense, powered by a rechargeable portable

battery pack. The Burnham Brothers and Bill Anderson, Abilene, Texas, also make portable cassette players.

Scotch Game Call Company, Inc., Elba, New York, makes a unique "Shaker Call," with rubber bellows, tipped by a conventional wood tube containing a metal reed with a long range pitch. Scotch also makes several walnut and plastic mouth calls, including a bite-adjustable squeaker.

All of the call makers also offer records or tapes with sample calling and instructions. Given patience and determination, anyone can learn to blow a varmint call. You have to learn to

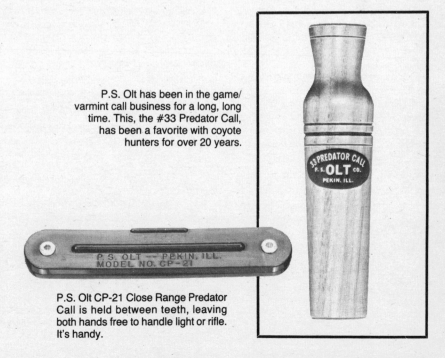

P.S. Olt has been in the game/varmint call business for a long, long time. This, the #33 Predator Call, has been a favorite with coyote hunters for over 20 years.

P.S. Olt CP-21 Close Range Predator Call is held between teeth, leaving both hands free to handle light or rifle. It's handy.

power the air with your diaphragm, rather than just puffing with your cheeks! It's not a matter of simply blowing hard. It's the volume of air rather than its velocity that delivers those raspy mellow tones that coyotes find irresistable.

Camouflage clothing is essential to successful daylight calling. Camo jackets and pants, or one-piece coveralls are recommended and available from the Burnham Brothers, Bob Allen and Lohman Manufacturing. Headnets and gloves made from netting are also in order if you're serious about the sport. Kane Products, Inc., Cleveland, Ohio, make zip-on camo covers for rifles, called "Gun Chaps," offering both protection and concealment. Parallex Corp., Bensenville, Illinois, sells camo sticky tape that can be used to disguise and protect your shiny rifle and scope. But the neatest trick yet is camo holsters from Uncle Mike's of Beaverton, Oregon. With closed-cell foam sandwiched between layers of tough Cordura nylon, these are the lightest, most rugged holsters I've yet seen. It protects the gun and keeps it handy — yet it costs less than a third of what most leather holsters do. Also from Uncle Mike's is a padded rifle sling of the same abrasion-resistant nylon.

Coyotes have been increasingly depicted in Bambi-like terms by the popular press, when in fact it is a ubiquitous, sometimes dangerous pest. Despite steady encroachment on wilderness areas by urban sprawl, the coyote has inexorably extended its range from the Plains States, in all directions. Significant coyote populations now touch both coasts and penetrate both borders. Recent reports show that they have infiltrated the Adirondack Mountains of New York and spilled over into the eastern border areas of that state. In California, coyotes inhabit the Hollywood Hills in numbers, drink from swimming pools and dine on poodles. Recently, one even attacked a young girl in her own backyard.

Coyotes are death to antelopes, especially fawns. They prey upon beavers, otters, wild turkeys and ground nesting birds, not to mention sheep and other domestic livestock. Even before the turn of the century, woolgrowers estimated annual losses to coyotes at over $15 million, a piddling sum by today's standards. One year the author surveyed sheep ranchers in Wyoming on the subject of coyote depredations. All were agreed that the prairie wolf was their greatest enemy.

Despite their relatively small stature, usually from 25 to 35 pounds, coyotes are difficult animals to stop. The lightest practical caliber is the 222 Remington, and I regard that as marginal. Better results are had with a 22-250, 224 Weatherby, or 220 Swift. When the wind begins to bend the path of 22 bullets, a 6mm bore such as the 243 Winchester, 6mm Remington, or 240 Westherby asserts its advantage. The author has his favorites — a 240 Page Super Pooper and his 240 Weatherby — the former equipped with a Bushnell Lite-Site.

Once you sample the thrills of varmint calling, especially coyotes, I predict that you'll become a confirmed addict of this exciting sport — and learning to match wits with a consumate hunter is half of the fun! ●

Bill Anderson's electronic caller is reasonable in cost, effective, and backed by wide array of available cassettes.

Sometimes coyotes get so close that hunter and animal alike are startled. As often as not, it results in the critter escaping unscathed.

Here's graphic proof that steel shot can kill; however, the author suggests confining your shots to 35 yards or less when using this less-than-best waterfowl load—in this case 1¼ ounces of No. 1 steel shot.

GRANTED, a full game bag should not be the criterion for an enjoyable day afield. But if I have to be placed into one of the groups represented by these comments I'd opt, as would almost any hunter, to be among the successful group. Far too often the quality of the hunt is reduced due to limited game or available land to hunt. Yet one type of hunting that will frequently do away with such problems is often overlooked by today's shotgunners. That type of hunting is of course waterfowling. Generous bag limits combined with plenty of available hunting water make ducks and geese very attractive quarry. Any water from a tiny trickling creek to a mighty tidal river, from a

Hunting Waterfowl

by EDWARD A. MATUNAS

"Walked 6 or 7 miles and never saw a thing." "Couldn't find more than 2 acres of unposted land." "Three of us hunted for 6½ hours, and we bagged only two birds."

"What a day! Birds poured in like it was a required flying test." "Had plenty of shots and filled my limit before 11 AM" "Took a real trophy sized goose and everyone limited out."

small farm pond to a great lake or saltwater sound can be a fine and productive hunting area. How often has anyone been ousted by a *No Trespassing* sign in the middle of a large river or saltwater bay?

From a weather standpoint, waterfowling can be an arduous sport. But one can learn to dress properly and remain comfortable in some horrendous weather. Waterfowling eliminates the need to walk a great many, often fruitless, miles in search of your in-

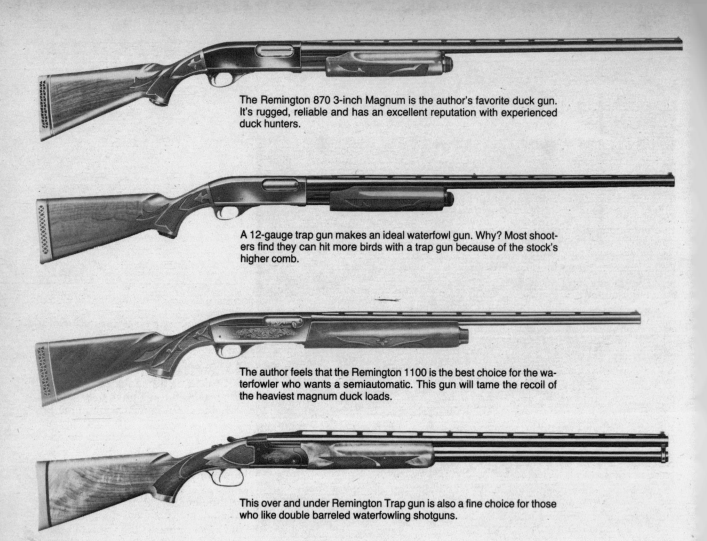

The Remington 870 3-inch Magnum is the author's favorite duck gun. It's rugged, reliable and has an excellent reputation with experienced duck hunters.

A 12-gauge trap gun makes an ideal waterfowl gun. Why? Most shooters find they can hit more birds with a trap gun because of the stock's higher comb.

The author feels that the Remington 1100 is the best choice for the waterfowler who wants a semiautomatic. This gun will tame the recoil of the heaviest magnum duck loads.

This over and under Remington Trap gun is also a fine choice for those who like double barreled waterfowling shotguns.

tended quarry. The duck and goose hunter frequently conducts his shooting from a stationary blind, a small boat or canoe that is easily paddled, or perhaps from a leisurely-paced hunt alongside a small stream. Such hunting is not strenuous and can be enjoyed by almost anyone.

Locating Waterfowl

Good duck and goose hunting usually begins with the location of bodies of water situated near your home. Perhaps the best way to find all the available water is to obtain a topographic map or two of the area in which you live or would like to hunt. Also, if you live along the coast or near a navigable river, a chart of the local waterways will reveal many a fine duck hunting area. Both topographic maps and charts are highly detailed and everything from tiny creeks and swamps to the larger expanses of water will be shown. Topographic map catalogs can be obtained free of charge from the following sources:

For areas east of the Mississippi River:

U.S. Geological Survey
Map Distribution Center
1200 Eads St.
Arlington, VA 22202

For areas west of the Mississippi River:

U.S. Geological Survey
Map Distribution Center
Federal Center, Building 41
Denver, CO 80225

For charts of coastal areas and inland waterways:

U.S. National Ocean Survey
Distribution Division
Riverdale, MD 20804

Study the maps or charts of your area, carefully noting all streams, ponds, marshes, swamps, lakes and rivers. Then well before season get out and inspect each body of water firsthand. In some cases smaller bodies of water may be totally contained on private land. Asking before season for access to this water will give you time to determine if it is water you want to hunt. Also, you will find most land owners surprised to have a re-

quest to hunt their water. This reaction usually brings a positive response to your request. If you take the time to look the water over before season, you will begin to get a feel for the most productive areas.

It is important to realize that water which is home to a great many waterfowl on one day may be devoid of birds on another day. The reverse is equally true. There is no substitute for learning which water is being frequented by birds on what kinds of days. This can only be accomplished by firsthand investigation. Keep a log of your visits to local water. Entries in your log can, at a later date, give you vital insight as to where to hunt. Notes should include date, time of day, temperature, wind direction, wind velocity, sky condition (sunny, overcast, rain, snow, etc.) and other facts that are noticeable and unique to the area. The height and direction of tide flow are, of course, important on any water affected by tides. Before too much time has passed, you will be able to note if birds are arriving in the area or departing during the period of your observations. With effort you will be

The Winchester Model 23 with Winchoke is ideal for those who like waterfowling with a side-by-side.

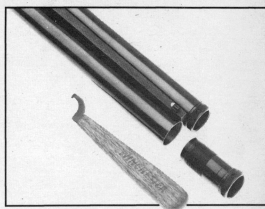

A close up view of the Winchokes on the Winchester 23. Interchangeable chokes allow this waterfowling shotgun to be used for other applications.

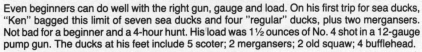

Even beginners can do well with the right gun, gauge and load. On his first trip for sea ducks, "Ken" bagged this limit of seven sea ducks and four "regular" ducks, plus two mergansers. Not bad for a beginner and a 4-hour hunt. His load was 1½ ounces of No. 4 shot in a 12-gauge pump gun. The ducks at his feet include 5 scoter; 2 mergansers; 2 old squaw; 4 bufflehead.

Not your best choice of clothing for duck hunting. This hunter's street shoes and slacks don't get it; but, worst of all is the hunter's coat and the way it stands out against the brush. Dull-colored or camo clothing designed for rough use is best.

able to learn where the birds feed although it may be a substantial distance from the water.

Waterfowl are migratory and will not always be present in your areas at all times of the year. Spring migrations are a good time to be afield investigating the birds' favorite areas. Come fall hunting season the returning birds will favor the same places used in the spring. During other periods of the year, local waterfowl populations will give good indications of what areas will be frequented when the migrating birds are flying through. Persistent observation will also give you the opportunity to see how content birds sit upon the water. You will begin to notice how birds tend to bunch up when they are nervous and about to depart. From such observation will come, if you are sharp, your first lessons on how to set out a decoy rig. Keep your eyes open and notice the groupings of birds. Equally important is to notice those groups which do not seem to attract other birds.

Don't do all of your studying from dry land. Use a canoe or boat to get out on the water. Try to discover out-of-the-way spots that others are not likely to hunt. Most waterfowlers seldom go more than 15 to 30 minutes across the water from the boat launching area. Traveling 45 minutes to 1 hour across the water may well put you on almost virgin hunting water.

Ducks and geese are very hard to kill. A bird fairly centered in a pattern of sufficiently large shot may be mortally wounded but still manage to fly a mile or more before falling from the sky. Such birds are wasted unless you can see some value in helping the local crows and gulls to an easy supply of food.

When hunting over open water, always watch any ducks you have shot at until they have flown out of sight. On many occasions you will be able to observe birds falling to the water after they have flown a considerable distance. When hunting regions where the surrounding cover quickly conceals the birds from sight, you may never be aware of such fallen birds. So when you have a choice, hunt the open water.

The proper selection of gauge and shot has earned the author's son, Eric, a limit of teal, as well as one black and one mallard duck. His 12-gauge, 1⅝-ounce loads of No. 4 shot prompted this smile.

Foul weather is duck hunting time. This fine brace of mallard fell to the author's son Eric, during a 45-minute out-behind-the-house hunt.

PRIMARY WATERFOWL HUNTING LOADS

Gauge	Shell Lgth. ins.	Shot Wgt. ozs.	Dram Equiv.	Type	Actual Vel. fps	Comments
12	3	1⅞	4	Magnum	1210	A heavy load useful when BB or #2 shot is required.
12	3	1⅝	4	Magnum	1280	Fine waterfowl load.
12	2¾	1½	3¾	Magnum	1260	Fine waterfowl load.

SECONDARY WATERFOWL HUNTING LOADS

12	3	1⅜	3¾	Magnum	1295	Absolute minimum load for geese.
12	2¾	1¼	3¾	Hi-Velocity	1330	Fine load for teal.
16	2¾	1¼	3¼	Magnum	1260	Good teal load.
20	3	1¼	3	Magnum	1185	Absolute minimum load for ducks.

SPECIAL WATERFOWL HUNTING LOADS

| 10 | 3½ | 2¼ | Max. | Magnum | 1210 | Should be used only |
| 10 | 3½ | 2 | Max. | Magnum | 1210 | by shooters who have plenty of experience. |

Shot Sizes, Gauges and Loads for Waterfowl

It has been fashionable with some outdoor writers to suggest small size shot, 6s and even 7½s, are sufficient for waterfowl. Such writing, in my opinion, is evidence of a lack of experience or a deficiency in the writer's ability to observe what happens when birds are struck by small pellets.

I started my own duck hunting using small pellets and quickly discovered that a No. 7½ pellet even when

SUGGESTED SHOT SIZES FOR WATERFOWL

Weight Ozs.	Geese	Brant	Large Ducks	Small Ducks
2¼	BB, 2	2, 4	2, 4	4, 5
2	BB, 2	2, 4	2, 4	4, 5
1⅞	BB, 2	2, 4	2, 4	4, 5
1⅝	BB, 2	2, 4	2, 4	4, 5
1½	BB, 2	2, 4	4	4, 5
1⅜	2, 4	4	4	5
1¼	4	4	4	5

started at a full 1330 fps would not penetrate the skull of a medium size duck if the range was much over 20 yards, and the small pellets seldom, if ever, broke wing bones. Autopsies performed on several hundred ducks also proved that even No. 6 pellets frequently failed to penetrate deep enough into a bird to reach the vital organs.

Besides inflicting mortal wounds, the goal of any waterfowl hunter should be to bring down birds where they are shot. To do this you will need to use a load that will break wing bones. The one universally effective pellet size for ducks has proven to be No. 4. I base this on 30 years of experience, a great deal of hunting and the taking of large numbers of ducks. How much experience? Well, in my home state, duck hunting for sea ducks (scoter, eider, and old squaw) begins usually around the 25th of September and runs until mid-January. "Regular" ducks and geese come into season about mid-October and stay legal until mid-January. From the middle of January to its end we enjoy a generous scaup duck season. During the more than 4 months available for waterfowl shooting each year, I average some 45 days of hunting. Our easily filled bag limit on sea ducks is seven birds per day. You can quickly see that the number of sea ducks I and my companions have taken has been considerable. Modesty prevents me from putting a figure on the total sea ducks, "regular" ducks and geese that we have put into my boat, but it has been more than sufficient to be certain about the best loads to use. My experience rather than my ability with the pen says that the small pellet sizes, i.e. 7½ or 6, are near useless cripplers of game despite any limited amount of ducks brought to bag with such tiny spheres.

Equally evident is the fact that the next larger shot size, No. 5, is useful only for small ducks or at short distances on large birds. I have met a great many shooters who will disagree with my position on shot size. I have also met a great number who agree with me. Invariably those who disagree simply have shot far too few ducks on which to base an opinion. I don't think that 10 years of ducking with an average annual bag of 50 or 60 birds qualifies someone as an expert. You will of course draw your own conclusions. But if you start with my suggested loads and shot sizes, I can assure you that the despair of watching crippled ducks escape will not often fall upon you.

Dug into a small hillside, this blind blends very well into the surrounding marsh as attested to by the Canada goose being displayed by the author.

While standup blinds in open fields are a no-no, this one, set back far enough from the water and built to blend with surrounding growth, does indeed become a camouflaged place of concealment.

Natural blinds are the best. The author's oldest son, Edward, has just popped up from concealment to drop a pair of incoming goldeneye. Even from this shooting position he is still well-concealed.

Your boat can become a floating blind if it is properly disguised. The use of burlap to completely cover the boat as well as positioning the boat alongside a natural background (such as this rocky shoreline) has enabled the author to shoot hundreds of ducks in a single season. In front of the boat is a spread of diving-duck decoys and to the left is seen the edge of an equally large spread of puddle-duck decoys. Time after time the author has proven that divers and puddle ducks can be hunted simultaneously given a location that both types frequent.

The effective camouflage of a boat blind (arrow) can be clearly seen in this side view. To incoming ducks these hunters and their boat become simply some more of the rocky shoreline.

As with the need to keep away from small size shot, there is an equal need to refrain from use of the small gauge guns. Such guns are best suited to the gentle efforts of bagging woodcock, quail and grouse in the uplands. But for the hardy waterfowl one is not adequately armed with anything less than a 12-gauge gun.

The best 12-gauge loads have proven to be the 1½-ounce, 2¾-inch Magnum and the 1⅝-ounce 3-inch Magnum loads. These shells, when combined with No. 4 shot, will prove to be the match for any duck fairly centered in the pattern at ranges up to 50 or 55 yards. They will also be adequate for geese when No. 2 or BB size shot is used. When one is hunting primarily for geese, the 1⅞-ounce 12-gauge, 3-inch loading has some definite advantages when combined with the larger shot sizes, BB's and No. 2's. The heavy 10-gauge is a specialty item and lighter 12-gauge or smaller loads put a needless handicap on your efficiency.

A good shot who confines his shooting to 40 yards or less will be able to get along very well with a 1⅜-ounce load of No. 4 shot. A 1¼-ounce load is a marginal performer past 30 yards, hence the standard 12-gauge high velocity load is at best a secondary choice. The same applies to the slower moving 16-gauge 2¾-inch Magnum 1¼-ounce load and the even slower 3-inch 20-gauge 1¼-ounce load.

Don't make the mistake of using less shell than is required to always get the job cleanly done. Even when shooting over decoys, the ranges can run from 35 yards or more. Then there will be days, not at all infrequent, when the best you get will be shots at ducks skimming the outer edges of a stool of decoys, some 40 or more yards away. Use enough shell and prevent flying cripples that would otherwise eventually die and be wasted. The accompanying tables show my primary and secondary recommendations for load selections. The secondary selections are for use only by gunners who are extremely sensitive to recoil or who, as beginning duck hunters, do not own a 12-gauge gun. In any event, all secondary load users should limit the maximum shooting range to 35 yards.

I have listed the 10-gauge loads in a "special" category. These loads simply produce too much recoil to be effectively used by anyone other than an extremely experienced hunter. The 10-gauge is only for those who can shoot heavyweight guns well and not mind the huge helpings of recoil. For these shooters such big guns can be effective for longrange pass-shooting especially when the targets are big Canadian geese.

If you hunt in an area where steel shot must be employed, you have my sympathy. At the least use 1¼-ounce steel loads, avoiding the lighter 1⅛-ounce loads. A 3-incher becomes almost a necessity with steel shot in order to use the heaviest payloads which are considerably lighter than the heaviest lead loads. And keep your shooting confined to 40 or, better yet, 35 yards.

Shotguns and Chokes

When selecting a waterfowl gun, give serious consideration to buying a dependable one. The wet and freezing conditions encountered while duck hunting will often cause firearm failures in many a well thought of upland gun. The Remington 870 pump is my shotgun of choice for waterfowl. It is available in both right- and left-hand configurations. It can be easily stripped to its basic parts with only the aid of a simple punch.

The Ithaca 37 is also a dependable shotgun, but you must remove its buttstock in order to completely disassemble the action. If you hunt saltwater and therefore must strip your gun after each trip, you will quickly become disenchanted with this procedure.

Many shooters will perform their best on waterfowl when using a higher than normal comb buttstock. For

If flights of ducks consistently refuse to decoy, you can bet your decoy spread is not set out properly or of sufficient quantity or quality. Your own spread may be guilty of all three problems.

Shown here is the author's favorite never-fail, calm day, diving duck decoy spread. You should set your decoys to match the natural formations of content, resting or feeding ducks.

this reason trap grade 12-gauge shotguns make excellent waterfowl guns. Or you can purchase a trap buttstock and install it on your existing shotgun. For most shooters this will pay off in additional birds harvested.

If you prefer a semi-automatic shotgun due to its lower level of perceived recoil, the Remington 1100 is a rugged choice, and it is easily stripped to its basic parts. I cannot overstress the importance of easy stripping and cleaning of a duck gun. They will get wet inside and out on most trips. If you want the gun to last, you will need to be able to accomplish this task easily. If it is not easy to do, you will find yourself neglecting the chore or wishing you had purchased a different gun.

A good double gun can be used. If it is tightly built, you will not have to strip the action unless the gun is accidently submerged. The Winchester 23 (with Winchoke) is an excellent double gun candidate for waterfowling. I have used a 23 with Winchoke quite successfully. I prefer to use the modified and the improved-modified tubes for most waterfowl shooting.

Chokes for a single barrel duck gun should be modified, improved-modified or full depending upon the skill of the shooter. The less experienced hunter will do best with a modified barrel, limiting his shots to a maxi-

mum of 40 yards. The skilled scattergunner can use a full-choke barrel with 55 yards being the maximum range. You can forget the advice of the inexperienced duck hunters who claim the improved-cylinder choke to be a cure-all for hitting hard flying ducks. Over decoys at short ranges,

ducks are relatively easy targets and here a tight choke is no real handicap. However, at the ranges where most waterfowl are killed (30 plus yards) an improved-cylinder choke would prove a very definite handicap and would result in a large number of cripples.

Mounted birds like this bufflehead are the best possible source of input on how a decoy should be carved and painted. The author maintains a large number of such birds, mounted by his oldest son.

Here's what a good decoy should look like. Compare this drake bufflehead with the real thing shown nearby. Note the slight exaggerations of the head crest and white head feathers as well as the muted details of the remainder of the decoy. Decoys like this work when others are being ignored by the ducks.

Waterfowl Shooting Methods

Some duck and goose shooting can be done without the aid of a blind. Such jump-shooting can be a lot of fun. You may move quietly along a stream or stalk a small farm pond. When the prey is aware of you and jumps, you shoot, assuming you are within range. It's a lot of fun and enables you to enjoy a quick hunt in a great number of different places. Or you may choose to paddle a winding creek or river and jump your ducks in this manner. Such shooting can be extremely enjoyable, and covering a lot of distance on the water will almost insure that you see sufficient birds.

Some waterfowlers will spend the first 2 hours and last 2 hours of daylight in their favorite blind. In between they jump shoot. Such a routine can be a very rewarding method of hunting.

For the most part, however, duck hunters as a whole hunt from blinds. By definition a blind is any hiding place that allows you to see approaching birds but does not permit the birds to see you. To accomplish this feat a blind must blend into the surrounding landscape. Taking advantage of natural camouflage is the best approach. Learning to build a well-concealed blind and using natural cover effectively is not difficult.

What seems to be extremely arduous for many hunters is the need to keep out of sight and motionless. I can't begin to count the times I have watched would-be waterfowlers in a distant blind who just couldn't keep out of sight and immobile. Such hunters feel that they just must be standing to survey the sky for miles around. Frequent short walks to get warm are also part of these non-successful hunters' routines. If you want to bag ducks stay well down inside your blind. Do not let your head or gun protrude. When you do move, do so carefully and slowly. For the most part only your eyes need to be moving. And keep conversation to a minimum! Sound travels easily and for great distance under the conditions usually present over water. I have "overheard" would-be duck hunters from ½-mile away when on the water.

Some decoys need more detail than others. Wood ducks, for instance, are very ornate birds. Wood duck decoys, therefore, must be somewhat more intricate than some other decoys. The two shown are superb examples of what a wood duck decoy should be.

These Canada honkers are way past any practical range, yet they drew gunfire from several sky-busters. Knowing when *not* to shoot is important. Why drive birds higher up when they may drop into the next gunner's range?

If these "snow geese" look like legitimate targets, hold your fire and return to the waterfowl identification books; these birds are swans not snow geese.

To be a successful duck hunter you must:
- Use the right gauge and load
- Use a reliable gun
- Be well concealed
- Keep quiet
- Be at least a fair shot

Please notice that this list of requirements ranks shooting ability in the least important position. Do your bit, and the ducks will come in close enough for even a fair shot to take his toll.

Waterfowl Decoys

Nothing will add more to your effectiveness as a waterfowler than a proper spread of good decoys. I would like to make a few points on decoy quality based on personal observations and 30 years of waterfowl hunting. Nothing will replace decoy quality. You are better off with 2 dozen magnum size cork bodied decoys than you would be with 4 dozen of lesser quality or smaller decoys. The painting of decoys should reflect the natural identification marks of the bird it represents. You need not paint every feather but each feature that stands out on a duck in the field should be accented or even slightly exaggerated.

For example, the backs of scaup are grey and black, each color appearing in a rippled pattern. At a distance this feathering appears grey. Therefore your decoys should have grey backs or, if you want to take the trouble, grey backs with rippled black lines. Some of the scaup decoys available today have white backs. Why? Because the manufacturer finds that less than savvy duck hunters like to buy decoys with lots of white on them. But such decoys are far less effective than those properly painted.

Often you can make very effective decoys if you have a supply of cork for bodies and pine for heads and tails. Take a look at the accompanying photo of a mounted bufflehead and the bufflehead decoy carved by my son, Edward. Note how the crest of the natural bird is slightly exaggerated on the head of the decoy. Also observe how the predominant white feathers on the head are also slightly overstated. Likewise notice the extent to which other details are left somewhat muted. Believe me, decoys like this will result in birds going out of their way to the decoy. The pictured decoy has actually been "pecked" by several female buffleheads that were allowed to land in a spread.

Some decoys need to be less elaborate, others more detailed. A good black duck decoy can be painted a solid flat black with only its face being lighter in color. Wood duck decoys are

Good decoys look real or real ducks look like decoys. Either way, can you spot the real from the artificial?

the other extreme. They need to be quite detailed to look "real." Use decoys that are lifelike at 15 yards distance, and you are on the road to success. Use larger than life decoys and you will need fewer of them to pull birds from greater distances. Always match the natural lay of real ducks when setting out your decoys and never place them closer than 4 feet apart. I prefer to keep my decoys at least 8 to 10 feet apart when hunting big water. Proper decoy setting means the careful placement of each block not the helter-skelter tossing of decoys over the side of your boat. Such tactics seldom produce spectacular results.

Bird identification is an important and enjoyable part of duck hunting. With federal restrictions on specific ducks, you need to be able to tell one duck from another in its natural habitat. Learning to do so is not at all difficult. You simply must be willing to read good books that are complete with color photos. Also read any available state supplied literature on the topic. A half-dozen good books from the local library can help you to quickly become an expert.

I suggest the following two books as being particularly good for learning waterfowl identification: *Ducks, Geese and Swans of North America*, by Francis Kortright, published by Stackpole; and *Water, Prey and Game Birds of North America*, by Alexander Wetmore, published by the National Geographic Society.

You need to learn what not to shoot as well as legitimate target identification in order to prevent the "I-thought-it-might-have-been-a" syndrome. Trips to the local zoo or museum of natural history will help you along your way to becoming a pro.

When learning to identify ducks in the field, try also to develop a feel for what ducks and geese look like when they are within legitimate range. Even some so-called pros waste a lot of ammo and needlessly cripple birds

It's refuges like this that help insure the future of waterfowl hunting. These geese are enjoying a bit of rest, courtesy of "Remington Farms" in Maryland.

Honest, this photo was taken with a 100mm lens from the author's blind—not a zoo. Properly placed, a blind can be surprisingly productive even without decoys.

because they don't know the difference between a bird 50 yards away and one 65 or more yards away. A considerate hunter never fires at waterfowl past 55 yards. Hunters who talk about 90-yard shots fit into a category charitably described as "game cripplers." Ballistically, no shotgun is capable of clean, sure kills past the 55 yard mark regardless of the prowess of the hunter.

When waterfowl hunting, try new techniques frequently. Also follow hunches. When I started waterfowling, one of the truisms I was taught was never to mix puddle duck decoys and diving duck decoys in one spread. It's good advice. However, where I do most of my duck shooting, divers and puddle ducks are divided almost equally. So I tried a spread of divers with another spread of puddle ducks starting some 15 yards or so to one side. I have been hunting both types of ducks simultaneously and very successfully ever since. They said it couldn't be done!

The waterfowler does need a substantial amount of equipment: a means of water transportation, life preservers, 2½ to 3 dozen diving decoys, 17 or 18 puddle duck decoys, warm clothing, hip boots, a good shotgun and plenty of heavy loads, etc. Or he can need only a handful of 12-gauge shells and a good 12-gauge gun and an hour or so to spend walking along a local creek. Regardless of the amount of gear owned or the selected method of hunting, waterfowling may well prove to be the best road to enjoyable shooting with plenty of game. If you haven't already tried it you're missing out on some very fast-paced shooting. Good luck! ●

Duck calls can be useful if you know how to use them. If you're not really good with them you will do better by leaving such equipment at home.

A good pair of binoculars such as these Leupolds are essential if you are going to learn much about waterfowl.

The Hunter's Edge

by JIM WOODS

Selecting the right knife for the right job is one of the most important things a successful hunter can do.

HUNTING has become more and more specialized in the last few years. This is due to a couple of factors. First, game has become more scarce as have game lands, both a result of creeping urbanization. Also, sporting arms manufacturers have produced specialized hunting guns and specialized cartridges, too. Their ability to sell hunters on the need for specialized arms and ammo—small game gear, varmint rigs, medium game guns, and big bore equipment for big game—has been as much of the problem of hunting specialization as it has been the solution.

Hunting cutlery has seen every bit as much this same broadening of the manufactured and actual needs for specialized equipment. A hunter who has several different rifles to suit all his hunting needs may well have several knives with which to accomplish all his hunting-related cutting chores.

Just how many knives do you need to take with you on a hunting trip? If your answer is not two or more, you could be "under knifed." Suppose you've got your deer down. First you're going to gut the animal, and you want to accomplish this, of course, without puncturing the paunch and fouling the meat.

So don't use a scimitar-curved blade that looks like it was designed to do hand-to-hand battle. However, turn that blade edge up and take a look at the design. Notice that the point is

pointing down, and if you could draw a line through the lower edge of the handle out through the knife's point, you'd see that the point is in line with, or even extending lower than the plane of the handle. It's called a "trailing-point," and you can see that if you start pushing that high curve through your deer's stomach muscle layer, that point will be raking the paunch, and you're going to have a mess on your hands.

If the back of the knife blade is straight from the handle to the point, it's referred to as a "straight-point." Such a blade has generally less utility than the trailing-point design.

The best blade shapes for puncturing or piercing, intentionally, are the

Mark Roper makes these three skinner models. The dropped point (top) would be a good caper, the swept point (middle) is a proper skinner, and the larger dropped point (bottom) is an ideal utility knife.

clip-point and saber-point designs. These are the ones where the back of the blade takes off straight from the handle, then darts out of line and forms a point with the cutting edge somewhere around halfway down the width of the blade. If the detour is a straight-line or an angle from the back, it is a clip-point; if it's a sweeping, dropping curve, it is a saber-point. Bowie knives generally are characterized by a saber-point, or clip-point—so much so that hunting knives with such shapes are often referred to as "Bowies."

Perhaps the best suited design for most hunter's chores is the "dropped-point." The dropped-point is lower than the back of the blade, viewed cutting edge down, but the point gets there in an outside curve, much like you might picture the trajectory curve

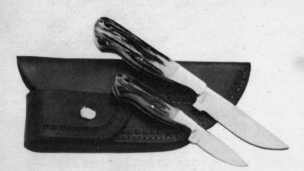

Here is a fine knife set for the serious hunter, put together in a unique sheath. The large knife will do a fine all around job on big game, the smaller knife is for caping and small game use. Crafted out of 440C steel and serialized, it's made by Jerry Poletis.

Schrade's new-for-1983 "Third Generation" pocketknives include several that will serve the hunter well.

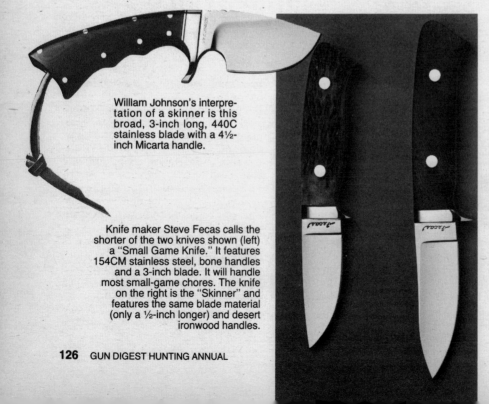

William Johnson's interpretation of a skinner is this broad, 3-inch long, 440C stainless blade with a 4½-inch Micarta handle.

Knife maker Steve Fecas calls the shorter of the two knives shown (left) a "Small Game Knife." It features 154CM stainless steel, bone handles and a 3-inch blade. It will handle most small-game chores. The knife on the right is the "Skinner" and features the same blade material (only a ½-inch longer) and desert ironwood handles.

of your rifle's bullet. The curve is opposite to that curve that forms the familiar Bowie saber-point.

Among knifemakers, the dropped-point can fall anywhere from almost a straight-point, to a point at the center of the blade's width. Likewise, the cutting edge curving to meet the point can be a very shallow curve, resulting in an extremely pointed blade, or can have a full skinning curve belly, resulting in a more blunt point. A dropped-point blade is probably the very best all-around hunting knife shape, but the variations are many, so you can still pick a blade that suits your personal likes.

A dropped-point blade does its best work when opening a deer for gutting. In this job and position, however, for which it was designed, it's not a "dropped," but a "raised" point. As the cutting curve of the blade slices through the skin, the point is raised away from the paunch, aiding in avoiding a miscue.

One approach to a dropped-point skinner has the dropped point actually higher than the back of the blade as it leaves the handle. Such a blade starts a sweep like a trailing-point, then reverses into a dropped-point. The curve is designed to provide a long cutting edge as you peel the hide. To get the full use of the design, you start your cut with the portion of the edge nearest the handle, then sweep your hand down and in an arc; use the blade's edge all the way to the point on each stroke. The skinning curve will not do you much good if you take short, chopping strokes in separating the skin from the meat. Such a blade shape is the tool of an experienced skinner.

Another blade for the experienced skinner is a caper. In general, caping blades are short, narrow, and thin to permit turning some tight curves around head structures. The best commercial approach to an ideal caping shape is the pocketknife spaying blade. You can usually make sure you're getting such a blade if you order a "stockman's" pocketknife.

A knife for caping is almost always a second, or third knife taken along for handling game. Caping use calls for a special knife; you can't do an effective caping job with a 4-inch long, ⅛-inch thick, 1¼-inch wide general purpose knife. The blade is too rigid and too bulky.

If you are going to be a one-knife hunter, a compromise design is going to have to be your lot. But rather than

compromise, consider taking along two or three knives. You don't have to carry them all on your belt; leave the butcher knife and caper back at camp. Or take the small caper along in a dual sheath with the all-purpose knife, or even in your pocket.

Chances are you've got more than one long gun for hunting, or if you're a one rifle man, you've picked a caliber in which you can use various bullet weights and styles for different game. It makes just as much sense to pick a couple, or more, knives to do the balance of your hunting chores. You just can't do all the cutting jobs with a single knife or single blade shape.

There are any number of supplemental and combination cutting tools that hunters can put on the job when the basic sheath knife runs afoul of chores it's not suited for. A belt knife makes a poor axe, even though some are big and husky enough to bring down trees. A knife pressed into shovel work is inefficient, but you can dig a garbage pit with one if you've got the time. But, just as these chopping and excavating jobs are best performed with implements designed for those tasks, so are certain game field dressing jobs better handled by specialized tools.

Folders

A folding hunting knife can do most all of the chores that the straight blade knife can do. However, it should not be subjected to those non-knife duties that a belt knife is so often misapplied to—substitute shovel and axe

work. The hinges may not stand the side loading forces that result from digging or hacking. For that matter, unless you choose your folding knife from among the largest and huskiest available, you may find that the common chore of splitting a deer's pelvis is beyond your knife's capability.

Folding knives come in blade lengths from around 2 to over 5 inches. A good mid-range approach might be a 3- to 4-inch blade to combine the advantages of compact size with a blade big enough to accomplish most field and camp chores. Folder blade configurations include many of the shapes found in straight blades—dropped-point, trailing-point and clipped-point. Generally, if your choice is a folding knife, you won't give up any utility just because you can't find your choice of blade style.

Nearly all the folding knives available from all manufacturers have blades of stainless steel. This is good simply because the knives can't be thoroughly cleaned very easily in the field. The use of stainless prevents collected blood and salts from corroding the blade, or at least delays the damaging process long enough that a later cleaning will usually head off the problem. For those knives that are not of stainless, a soaking in fresh water as soon as possible after use is advisable to neutralize the blood and salt. After that, a liberal dose of one of the aerosol moisture displacement lubricants is a good idea.

Whatever the blade size, shape, or steel, a very handy feature to look for in a folding knife is a blade lock. The most common approach is the "lockback" design. The lock mechanism consists of a bar usually extending the full length of the handle, fitted with a pivot point, and held in the locked position by a spring steel rod or leaf fastened at one end at the butt or pommel of the knife. By pressing the bar against the spring, via a notch in the back edge of the handle, the bar pivots and separates from the blade tang. Once the tang is free of the locking bar, the blade can be closed by hand. A good lock will be well fitted at the junction of the locking bar and the blade tang.

Lock systems are important for holding open the folding blades—but first the blade must be capable of opening and closing. The key to any folder is the hinge mechanism.

The cheapest hinge to manufacture is merely a length of hardened wire of the diameter to fit holes in the blade tang and the bolsters. In a properly priced knife, and if you are aware of

Harold Corby calls this 4½-inch clip point knife his "Field dressing Model." It's well named.

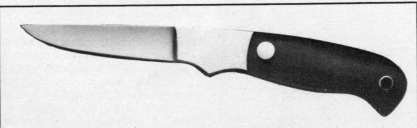

This slender 2¾-inch blade of 154CM stainless, with Micarta handle, is called the "Mini-Fisher" by maker Don Hethcoat. Designed for fishermen, it would also make an ideal caper.

Western Cutlery combines a deep pouch and a unique snap-strap to produce a good compromise sheath that rides high on the belt.

These Uncle Henry skinning blades come with deep-pouch sheaths. This type of sheath secures the knife against loss much better than the traditional snap-strap sheaths do.

For this convenience, you get a bit weaker knife than a straight blade just because the hinge cannot be as strong as a solid bar of steel. The folder can't be cleaned as easily as a straight blade, but this is largely made up for by the use of stainless steel and brass that is corrosion resistant, at least in the better quality knives. As with straight blades, you can get as much quality as you wish to pay for, but the quality is more difficult to determine in a folder. Straight blade construction details are laid out in the open; folders hide theirs behind pins, rivets, liners and bolsters.

Pocketknives

Not quite as husky, but every bit as useful to the hunter, are pocketknives. Some hunters get by with just a pocketknife for all cutting chores, but pocketknives were the first personal cutlery to provide specialized tools.

The patterns and combinations of pocketknife blades are identified by names very descriptive of the knives' use. Practically everyone recognizes the term, "Boy Scout knife." It has a large, general purpose spear-point blade, a combination screwdriver/bottle opener, a punch, and a can opener. Sometimes called the "camper" or "utility" knife, it supposedly holds all the tools necessary to get along in our prepackaged, canned or bottled, world of convenience.

A more exotic "camper" knife is the equally recognizable Swiss Army knife. It goes the Boy Scout version several functions better, up to and including a corkscrew for the wine bottle.

The term "jackknife" is used to describe any of the large, two-bladed knives. Jackknives must have two, and only two blades; and to be a true jack, both blades should be hinged at the same end. However, any large, hand-filling pocketknife may be acceptably called a "jackknife." Usually the handle shape of modern jacks is of the "hunter" design. That pattern is flat-backed, but the point-housing end of the body curves into a horn shape, while the open side of the body, in which the blades nest, is sculptured into a double-dip profile. However, the traditional Barlow, a modified "sleeve-board" pattern, is a longtime standard jackknife design.

Some patterns of pocketknives, the names of which relate to animals, are especially good choices for hunters. Two common ones are the "trapper" and the "stockman." The blade combinations described by these models'

the quality you are purchasing, it's not necessarily a poor system. Wear on the hinge wire and the mating holes in the blade will eventually cause the knife to be unsafe or unusable. When that happens you discard it and buy another.

The refinement of the system is the machined hinge pin that is precision made and fits a precision hole in the blade. Properly done, it's the best of knife-hinge arrangements. However, metal wears on metal, and the hardest metal wins. Hinge pins should be of the same metal as the blade and should be tempered to the same de-

gree of hardness as the tang of the blade. Thus equal, wear is minimized or eliminated entirely. Large diameter hinge pins are preferable to thin ones since the large ones give more bearing surface.

Folding knives are compromises. One of the primary advantages is their compactness. They do ride the belt, if a pouch is used, with less trouble than a straight-blade knife. A short sheath won't snag the passing bushes nor will it gouge you in the ribs when you sit in a vehicle. Without a pouch, they can be toted around in the pocket.

names will be the same, regardless of manufacturer or size of the knife. The trapper is a double-ended knife; that is, one blade hinged at each end—a saber-clip shape and a round-ended spaying blade. The stockman, also double ended, has the same two blades as the trapper, but adds a sheepsfoot blade.

The all-around pocketknife is the stockman design. The saber-clip is time-proven for general purpose use, and the sheepsfoot is an efficient cutting wedge. The blunt-end spaying blade is the best commercial answer to a caping design.

Pocketknives are, as they have been for years and years, practically indispensable tools for everyone. Sometimes they are the tools you depend on to keep all the other tools working. Any hunter can find use for one in the field, or in the pickup truck, or in camp. No pocket should be without one.

This attractive Thuya burl handled, 3⅜-inch blade, by Billy Mace Imel, is a good design for skinning.

Skinners

A skinning knife is a necessity for most hunters. That is, it's necessary unless your brand of hunting calls for a guide to do all the work. If you do skin your game, your knife is probably a skinner first and an all-purpose camp knife second, and that's a good way to go if one knife is all you carry. A skinner will usually serve well for field dressing, camp chores, and even butchering. However, a specialty knife for any of those chores may not be the best skinner.

There are a few things to look for in picking out a skinning knife. First, assuming you may want to keep the hide, you can do without cuts through the skin. So stay away from severely pointed blades; it doesn't take much of a miscue to puncture the hide.

One of the most used skinning designs ever is the very pronounced curve "buffalo skinner." The blade on such a design sweeps to 2 inches or more higher than the handle, but the back edge of the blade meets the cutting edge in such a way that the point is reasonably blunt. For pure skinning, it's still one of the very best designs. The long blade and extreme curve provide a long cutting edge. If it's used properly, in a long, sweeping stroke, it separates a sizable strip of hide in a hurry.

A hunter with the wrong blade shape, or a small penknife, will skin with short, jabbing strokes. Not only is he doing a lot of unproductive work, but he runs the risk of puncturing the hide, and he'll have a difficult fleshing chore left over too. A long, sweep-

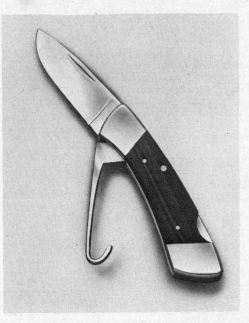

A blade just can't always do all jobs, so, the entrail hook on this Edge Mark Turkey Hunter becomes a useful, but very specialized hunter's tool.

ing stroke with the right knife, on the other hand, separates the hide and carcass cleanly and quickly.

Your skinning knife, if it's the only knife that you intend to take afield, must be capable of doing its primary job—skinning—well. Pick a full-bellied, broad-bladed, ligweight one, for best results. If it's designed for something else, you can bet your hide that you will wish that you had bought one labeled "skinner."

Blade Steel

No matter what the knife's func-

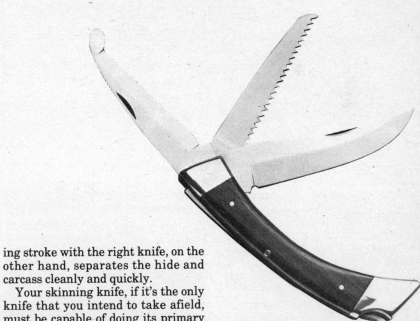

Browning's combo knife has a long-clip skinning blade, a saw and a round tipped gutting blade that won't penetrate the paunch.

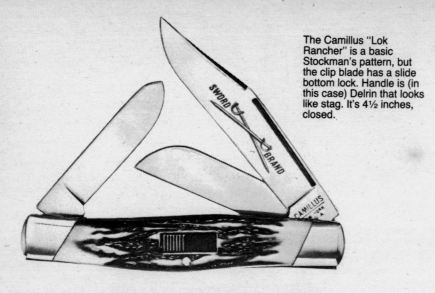

The Camillus "Lok Rancher" is a basic Stockman's pattern, but the clip blade has a slide bottom lock. Handle is (in this case) Delrin that looks like stag. It's 4½ inches, closed.

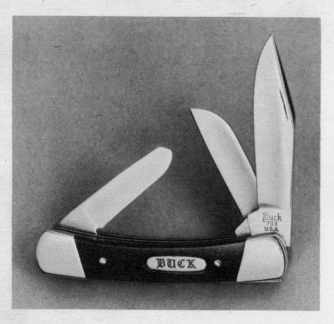

The Buck "Colt" is a classic Stockman's pocketknife pattern, complete with clip, spey and sheepsfoot blades. This one is 3¼ inches closed.

There is more selection in handle material than in blade material. And, you don't have to have an education in anything serious to select that material. All the commonly used knife handle materials have some pros and cons, but probably the biggest factors to be considered are whether it's attractive to the eye and "friendly" to the touch. A handle is to the blade as a stock is to the barreled rifle action. It fits the tool to the user's anatomy and gives it function.

Knife handles and handle coverings have been made of a wide variety of materials for a number of years. Wood has been a longtime favorite, probably due to availability and ease of working, but just any wood won't do, at least for very long. The wood for knife handles must be dimensionally stable under conditions of changing temperature, humidity and use. It should be hard and dense to preclude absorption of moisture and oils that will cause it to rot away.

There are a few American-grown woods that work well as knife handles. The two used most frequently are maple and walnut; two that just happen to be used most commonly as rifle stocks. Rifle stocks, of course, must be stable and dense, so it reasons that stock material could be used for knife handles. Cherry wood should be okay, as are some other fruit and nut-tree woods.

The African and South American hardwoods, generally classified as "exotics," are available in quantity and meet the demands of stability, density and hardness, plus they have the added desirable feature of "character." Many of them (for instance, cocobolo, rosewood, pau-ferro, goncalo alves, and ebony) are used more often as knife-handle material than our home-grown walnut.

More and more, woods for knife handles are being impregnated with phenolic resins. Micarta is the name used most often; however, Micarta is a Westinghouse trade name, and all such resin-treated woods are not Micarta. However, for most knife users, "Micarta" is a recognizable identity of the type of material. Others are Pakkawood or Fibron. All describe wood that is improved through lamination and/or impregnation.

One advantage of wood so treated is that the grain and figure of the wood are preserved, from a cosmetic standpoint, to stay good-looking forever, never to be soiled by dirt, blood, or oil. Also, more and different woods can be used for knife handles—softer woods

tion, the user must take a little bit of interest in the steel from which the blade is made. Most knife users are not metallurgists, so its not vital to get deeply into steel formulas. Basically there are just two choices—carbon steel or stainless steel. The latter is a bit of a misnomer, because it seems to indicate that stainless steel does not contain carbon. Such is, of course, not the case.

Carbon added to iron creates steel. There are other components, but the percentage of carbon in the iron is a primary determination of the steel's characteristics. Tool steel will contain controlled amounts of carbon—about one percent—plus manganese, phosphorus, sulfur, silicon, chromium, molybdenum, nickel, vanadium, or tungsten in varying amounts.

When the chromium content is increased, the steel's resistance to corrosion, or rust, also increases. When the chromium percentage is relatively high, on the order of 15 percent or greater, the resultant material is stainless steel. More properly, it is "corrosion resistant" steel, because even stainless can eventually rust.

Conventional carbon steel, even though properly maintained through drying and oiling, can still deteriorate through oxidation, and the results can't be seen with the naked eye. Put a carbon steel knife away for a time, the length of time varing according to several atmospheric factors, and the edge will dull due to microscopic oxidation. Good stainless is not so affected; however, a stainless knife should still be dried and lightly oiled.

with good figure that normally wouldn't work, and laminates of straight-grain wood laid in eye-appealing patterns. More practically, the structure of the wood is made impenetrable to destructive moisture, blood, and salts. When it's sealed to tang, guard and rivets with epoxy, the handle is as durable as the steel to which it is attached.

Micarta, unlike the other materials, is not just a wood product. Knife handles of linen-based Micarta are available in a myriad of colors—green, tan, and burgundy among the more popular. Perhaps the most attractive Micarta is the paper-base material that results in "ivory" Micarta. It has the appearance and color of ivory, but has none of the faults of real ivory. It won't shrink, crack, or chip.

Micarta and its copiers are not the only man-made knife-handle materials. Several thermosetting and chemical-catalyst plastics are very useful and find wide application for knife handles. Don't be turned off by plastic-handled knives.

Although its popularity has declined in recent years, the stacked leather-washer handle has a lot going for it. It is comfortable to hold with just a barely noticeable springiness to it. Unfortunately, it tends to get slippery with use, and it's susceptible to moisture absorbtion and subsequent rot. However, leather rot takes a lot of years so that's not a consideration of real importance. Leather-washer knife handles are passing from the knife scene primarily because they require too much hand work in a world gone automated.

There are some knives that have no handle covering; some that have no handle. All-steel knives with a skeletonized handle frame milled from the same bar of stock as the blade are supposedly popular with backpackers and others who are concerned with weight savings. However, all-steel knives are both cold and slippery—two attributes to do without when working with animal blood and entrails.

Sheaths

One knife accessory that isn't given as much attention as it should by purchasers and users is the sheath. A sheath is as important as the handle and blade, assuming of course that the knife in question is not a folder or pocketknife. Part of the following does apply to pouches for folders, though.

A sheath for a belt knife serves

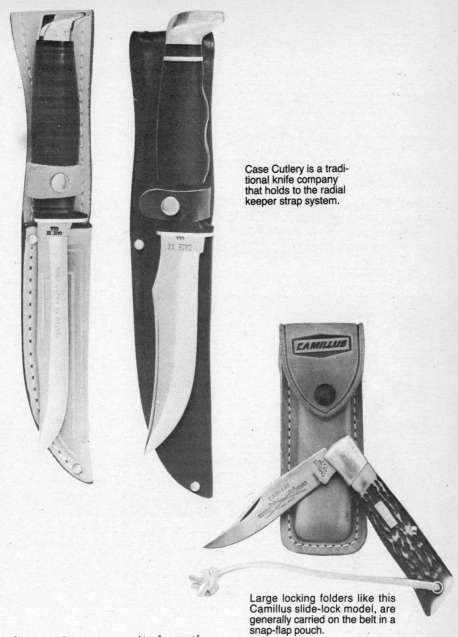

Case Cutlery is a traditional knife company that holds to the radial keeper strap system.

Large locking folders like this Camillus slide-lock model, are generally carried on the belt in a snap-flap pouch.

three main purposes: it places the knife in a handy position for access; it protects the knife from loss or damage; and it protects the wearer from his own knife. A good many sheaths position the pommel of the knife just above the belt. However, it's really just a bit too high a position for easy extraction and insertion. Two or 3 inches lower is a much easier access position, but a knife so positioned is not as secure as a higher-riding one.

You should be able to sit without your hip-mounted sheath digging into the seat, ground, or saddle. If the sheath tip strikes the seating surface, it's either hanging too low or it's just too long. A 4 to 5-inch blade knife generally will not inhibit the wearer from sitting if the knife's pommel is positioned at or around the beltline.

Laterally, the best position is just aft of the pants' belt loop that usually is located at the hip, or within 2 to 3 inches behind that belt loop. Any farther back and it becomes an access problem; farther forward and it gouges the wearer's leg when he sits.

An exception would be in the case of the cross-draw sheath. Such a sheath must be positioned in front. However, such a front mount is more a combat carry, or an affectation of one, rather than a practical carry for the hunter. If the hunter has no physical handicaps that dictate special access to the knife, the hip-carry is the most useful.

Protecting the knife presents more options than where to carry it; and protection of the knife is not totally separated from protection of the wearer. That is, a sheath that protects the knife from loss or damage will usually protect the wearer from injury as well.

Sheaths made of wood, metal or horn are for the knife collector exclusively. The very best hunting belt-knife sheath material is heavyweight, stiff leather. If the sheath isn't stiffened either by its own weight, or by sewn-in stiffeners, it doesn't present a straight track for insertion of the blade. A knife that goes in crooked can snag and penetrate soft and flimsy leather.

Knives are held in the sheaths by two basic methods—keeper straps and compression. Keeper straps come in several designs and positions. They may encircle the knife handle radially, or may cross diagonally over the guard. Either way, they usually fasten with snaps. If the radial keeper strap is employed, it should be low on the handle, right at or barely above the sheath mouth. A high strap can permit the knife to be pushed upward, out of the sheath, exposing the blade's edge where it becomes a danger to the wearer and the sheath. The diagonal, cross-the-guard, keeper holds the knife securely enough when the wearer is in the upright position, but when squeezing through brush or scooting over rocks, this design is easily snagged and lifted open. The knife can be pushed out and lost, or become a personal danger.

Either kind of keeper, radial or diagonal, once it takes a "set" into a fastened position, tends to block entry to the sheath and is subject to being cut as the knife is inserted into the sheath. Thus, putting the knife away is a two-hand operation. One hand holds the keeper out of the way while the other directs the knife.

A deep pouch sheath protects the knife and user better than a snap-strap keeper. Also, it's more convenient with its one-hand operation for inserting and removing the knife. A pouch, shaped to conform to the knife it holds, keeps the knife in place by compression. The whole sheath fits snugly all around, and if properly constucted, will hold the knife while the sheath is upside down, and even when shaken vigorously.

Deep sheaths permit just a finger's width of knife handle to protrude, and it takes a firm finger grasp to extract the knife. Because it is so secure, it protects handle, blade, and the wearer.

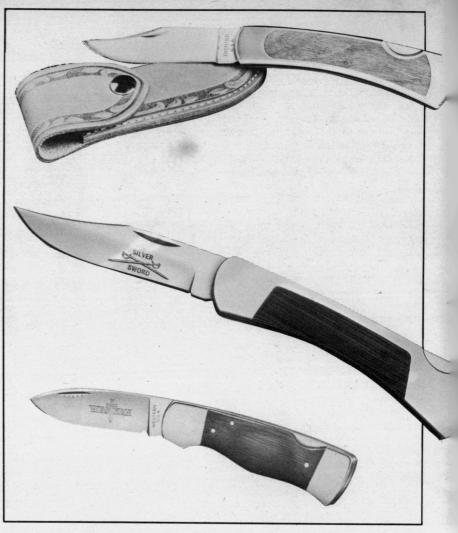

Lock-back folders are the most popular knives sold. Every maker has them in a variety of styles and decoration. (Top) Imperial Frontier "Diamondbrite;" (Middle) Camillus Silver Sword "Sheriff;" and (Bottom) Western Lock Blade. Most come with a carrying pouch.

Part of the security of any knife sheath is in the belt loop. A folded hanger loop is none too secure, as the knife will slip around on the belt. Two vertical slots, if not fitted tightly to the belt, permit the sheath to twist around. Either of these problems result in the knife not being where you expect it to be, and as a result it is vulnerable to damage or, worse, may damage the wearer.

The best loops are the single, wide one stitched to the back of the sheath, or the pair of snug-fitting slots backed up by a leather panel. The latter may be achieved by sewing a slotted panel to the sheath back and installing an additional panel inside the sheath to back up the slots.

If you give consideration to these several things—blade shape, blade size, blade steel, fixed or folder, any number of handle materials—plus sheath style—you can see that you are indeed dealing in specialized hunting gear when you pick a hunting knife. The good news is that a knife that's a joy to use in the field is also a joy to shop for.

There are several hundred custom knifemakers and 3 or 4 dozen knife factories and importers who stand ready to supply a knife for any purpose. There is no reason for hunters today to settle for anything but the very best tools for the job, whether it's firearms, ammunition, or hunting knives. Treat your cutlery system as you do your firearm system—first define the job you want to do, then acquire the equipment necessary to get the job done *properly*. ●

To be a trophy your elk
must have a rack that runs
over 50 inches, right?
Wrong, because . . .

Every Elk Is a Trophy Elk

by CHUCK ADAMS

I RECENTLY READ a magazine article bemoaning the fact that huge bull elk are few and far between on public hunting land. The writer's conclusion was that public elk herds produce "junk animals" not worth going after, and that serious nimrods should pay big bucks to hunt on private western ranches where elk are less disturbed and more apt to reach trophy proportions before being culled. I have hunted several such ranches in the past and fully enjoyed the quality trophy-hunting experience they provided. However, I strenuously object to the notion that elk with headgear less than 40 inches wide and 50 inches high are not worthy of a serious hunter's attentions. As far as I'm concerned, every elk is a trophy elk, be it spike bull, cow, or monstrous 6x6 wallhanger.

I recall one 10-day elk hunt I enjoyed high in Colorado's San Juan primitive area. Eight of us packed in several miles on horseback, set up a cozy camp, and opened the elk season by canvassing every inch of ground for several miles around. There were elk in the area for sure, evidenced by numerous fresh tracks in the heavy timber, droppings wherever lush grass grew, and old rubs where bulls had polished their racks in preparation for rutting season. However, nobody saw a legal antlered bull during that day or the next, and by the third morning of season we were all wishing cows were legal game. There were other riflemen in the area to complicate the situation, and over breakfast we all decided to take stands in the heavy timber in hopes of ambushing one of these sneaky, hunter-shy animals. By using this strategy, two of our party nailed spike bulls by the end of the hunt—a 25 percent success rate on a par with Colorado's statewide elk-harvest statistic. I've never hunted elk more difficult than those in the San Juans, and I've never seen hunters happier than we were with those two young spikes. A giant "rump-scratcher" would have been nice indeed, but we weren't all sad with the trophies we ended up dropping on the ground.

All Elk Are Alert and Wary

The elk is an incredibly beautiful and cagey creature, a former plains-dweller with the adaptability to head for the hills when white men swept across the continent's open ground. Less flexible animals like bison and pronghorn antelope bit the dust en masse before this human onslaught, but elk simply shifted ground and continued to multiply and prosper. In the heavy timber country it now prefers, the modern elk is a solid test of any hunter's skills, using a first-rate nose, razor-keen eyeballs, and ultra-ultra-sensitive ears plus a nimble brain to detect and avoid its human enemies. The hunter who drops any elk can pat himself on the back and can also look forward to meal after meal of tender, grass-fed meat. A bald-headed cow or a runty "raghorn" bull with antlers the size of a deer's might never grace a status-hunter's hall, but such an animal will provide any challenge-oriented hunter with ample outdoor sport.

Top elk-producing states like Colorado, Wyoming, and Montana are heavily hunted these days, placing extreme pressure on elk herds and lowering the percentage of bulls reaching the trophy age of 4 to 8 years old. Those bulls which do gain maturity have done so because their habit patterns help them avoid the waiting guns of hunters. As a result, all elk on public land are tough to hunt, and the mature bulls in public herds seem to dig holes and pull the sod in after them when the opening-day guns go off. At least one outdoor writer might have concluded that taking public-ground elk is no trophy-hunting prop-

Montana that required more diligent hunting and better shooting than near Boone and Crockett bulls laid low on seldom-hunted tracts behind closed gates. Anybody who claims that those near-record bruisers are better trophies than cow elk reaching maturity through the school of hard knocks will get an argument from me.

High-country elk habitat is beautiful—a bonus on any hunt.

osition, but in my mind there is no trophy like an elk taken in fair chase on heavily hunted property. Years of hunting pressure have made these elk warier for the simple reason that the dummies were shot off long, long ago. The smarter, sneakier animals survived and reproduced their kind, populating the forest with a strain of bon-afide super-elk. Anyone who has hunted elk for days on end without seeing more than fresh tracks and fresh droppings knows exactly what I mean.

Nice trophy bulls shot on private, controlled-access land are impressive on the wall, but in reality such elk are far less difficult on the average than their harder-hunted brothers. I've seen cow elk taken in Wyoming and

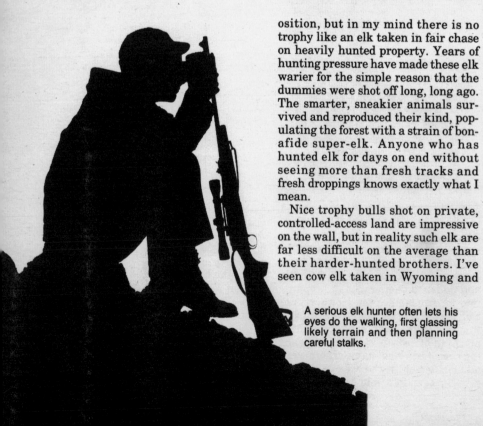

A serious elk hunter often lets his eyes do the walking, first glassing likely terrain and then planning careful stalks.

What Is A Trophy?

The dictionary defines the word *trophy* as, " . . . a prize difficult to achieve or attain." This definition certainly applies to any hard-hunted elk. If you don't believe it, ask my good friend Bob Smith. Bob has the bug to take a Pacific-Coast Roosevelt elk with his hunting bow and has been trying unsuccessfully for the past three seasons. Meanwhile, Bob has taken nice buck deer with his bow each and every year plus a wide variety of other wary game. Bob is not being a nitpicker about elk, either—any fat cow will suit him fine. The trouble is, he prefers hunting public ground where every elk is as slick as Houdini in the ultra-dense cover typical of coastal Roosevelt-elk habitat. Knowing my pal the way I do, I'm sure Bob will eventually shoot an elk with his bow, and when he does, it won't matter how big the animal happens to be. According to the dictionary definition, Bob's elk will be a trophy, even if the only appendages on its head happen to be big, fuzzy ears.

No elk is especially easy to hunt. It is to be expected that lightly hunted elk are somewhat easier to shoot than heavily hunted elk, but even elk on completely protected tracts of ground display an innate wariness typical of the species. The fully protected Tule elk in my native California are an excellent example. The second largest herd of these animals resides less than 75 miles from my home, giving me the opportunity to stalk and photograph them regularly. Although the oldest elk in this herd have never heard a hunter's gun, they still hang in heavy cover throughout midday hours, never stray far into the open at peak feeding periods, and depart posthaste when approached by curious spectators or camera buffs. The biggest Tule bulls are seldom seen except during the September rutting season, holing up away from men and younger, less wary elk throughout the balance of the year. Elk are skittish by nature, even when undisturbed by regular hunting harassment.

A recent study by the Oregon Fish and Game Department disclosed that the heavily hunted elk in this state almost never stray farther than 20 yards from dense lodgepole cover. This finding does not at all surprise me, for elk become incredibly spooky in areas frequented by two-legged predators. The elk I've hunted on relatively lightly hunted private ground

This is a nice public land trophy that was challenging to bag.

Be it a giant animal or a small-racked young one, the hunter has to work hard for elk—before and after the shooting.

have sometimes strayed several hundred yards into completely open meadows, but even these elk have fled for cover at the slightest hint of danger. By comparison, elk I've encountered in traditional public elk hotspots like northern Wyoming's Big Horn Mountains have almost never been more than two or three quick strides from cover, acting more like whitetail deer than the plains animals their ancestors used to be. Elk are spooky by nature, and they quickly learn to use cover to full survival advantage.

I remember one elk hunt I made with my dad in the central Big Horns several years ago. With four other hunting companions, we carefully still-hunted through a densely timbered thicket along the flank of a large, grass-covered ridge. This thicket was roughly 400 yards wide and ½-mile long, and the country all around was wide open grass intermixed with old logging clearcuts. We actually smelled elk in the thicket at several points during the hunt, and one of us jumped a heavy animal that crashed away unseen. The numerous trails in the jungle were pounded to a pulp with the oblong, cow-like tracks of elk, yet when the six of us emerged from the far end of the timber stand we hadn't seen an animal. Three hours later we were sitting on a point across the canyon from that thicket, glassing for elk as the sun sank in the west. Fourteen elk cautiously emerged from the trees just before dark, including a fat branch-antlered bull and two spindly-horned spikes. The animals had sneaked back between us during the drive—either that, or they had simply tucked in tight like wary rooster pheasants. We ended the 7-day hunt without taking a single shot at an elk, despite spotting distant animals nearly every day.

(Left) An accurate, scope-sighted rifle like this 30-06 Sako is just the ticket for wary public-ground elk. If you miss a shot, you may not get another.

(Below left) Elk meat is first-rate table fare, especially from younger animals like this spike.

(Below right) Telltale tracks are often all a hunter finds in good elk habitat, even though cagey animals abound.

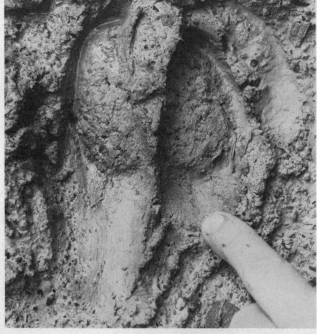

Some Tips on Shooting Elk

When it comes to shooting difficulty, any elk can frustrate a hunter to tears regardless of how big that elk happens to be. In fairly open timberline country where early-fall elk are often found, the most common hunting technique is glassing meadows at dawn and dusk, stalking elk in likely locations, and trying to make an accurate, killing shot. As a general rule, such shooting is extremely challenging—partly because distance is deceptive in the high country and partly because shots are often long.

When still-hunting or stand-hunting the dense timber where hard-hunted elk invariably disappear, a rifleman usually gets mere snapshots at animals moving rapidly through tightly clustered trees. Elk sometimes crash away loudly when taken by surprise, but more often slip quickly away with the stealth of a hunter-wise coyote. As a result, a rifleman seldom has ample warning to take a deliberate, well-planned shot in heavy cover.

The serious elk hunter equips himself with a medium-weight, fairly maneuverable mountain rifle which will function equally well in long-range and close-range shooting situations. An elk is a big, tough animal requiring plenty of stopping power, making the 270 Winchester about as light as any serious elk hunter should go. The most common rifle seen in the western elk woods is probably the good ol' 30-06 Springfield, but the 7mm Remington Magnum and the various 300 magnums are also popular with those in the know. A 4x fixed-power scope is ideal for a variety of elk-hunting situations, but many elk hunters prefer variable scopes to cover both dense-cover, midday jumpshooting and long-range sniping at dawn and dusk. Even a well-equipped gunner with a

(Left) A haunch of well-cooled elk meat provides many fine meals for the camp.

deadly shooting eye will find any elk to be a genuine shooting trophy, regardless of sex or level of antler development.

The most difficult elk shooting I've ever encountered has been in central Montana's Little Belt Range, which harbors a sizable herd of Rocky Mountain elk. When open-morning guns go off in the semi-open high country, the elk scatter like quail and charge downhill into ultra-dense thickets of spruce layered chest-high with deadfall logs. The best bet for dropping an elk in the Little Belts is taking a stand along the edge of heavy timber to ambush elk fleeing from hunters driving the ridgetops. The trouble is, these elk are usually galloping full tilt when they pop into view, their momentum increased by their downhill direction. A 500-pound cow or 800-pound bull may be a big animal, but such an animal seems to shrink to jackrabbit proportions as a hunter tries to swing the crosswires far enough ahead for a solid chest-cavity hit. There's an incredible amount of space around a hard-running elk, and most of this space seems to be behind the animal. At least that's where most of the bullets seem to go!

Elk as Table Fare

Regardless of size or antler development, any elk is a top-notch trophy on the dinner table. In the table-fare trophy-judging category, the younger,

From top to bottom: Ruger 77, Remington 700 BDL, Winchester Model 70 and the Weatherby Vanguard. All are available in calibers considered popular with experienced elk hunters, i.e., 270 Win., 7mm Rem. Mag., 30-06 and the family of 300 Magnums.

smaller elk take the highest prizes. Elk are primarily grazers, waxing fat on sweet grass which grows throughout western mountains. As the old saying goes, you are what you eat—and elk compares favorably with domestic beef in texture and flavor because both kinds of meat are primarily produced with grass. There is absolutely nothing superior to the meat from a young cow or spike elk on the barbeque grill or in the oven, and even a bull with massive antlers and several years behind him makes gourmet eating when properly prepared. When an outdoor writer refers to public-land elk as "junk animals," it immediately becomes obvious that the fellow has never settled his teeth into young, tender elk steak. Such "junk" is fit for any king!

Aside from hunting challenge, shooting difficulty, and gourmet delight on the table, the elk is a trophy animal in one more important way. On a scale of one to 10, the elk's typical high-country habitat rates a solid 12 in terms of breathtaking scenic beauty. No matter whether you drop an elk or bomb-out trying, you can take home the trophy memory of gorgeous landscapes composed of lush mountain meadows, pristine stands of pine, and merrily bubbling streams. Whether the elk win or lose, every hunter can savor the brushstrokes of a flaming autumn sunset over lofty purple peaks, the heady smell of bacon frying above a small pine-knot fire in a wilderness hunting camp, and the invigorating feel of legging it up a steep, needle-littered hillside through crisp, rarified mountain air. These intangible delights make all elk trophy animals, even if these trophies end the season laughing at hunters in some lodgepole thicket dense enough to strangle a half-grown chipmunk.

Anyone who judges the success or failure of an elk hunt solely on the size of trophy antlers taken is severely cheating himself. A giant rack of horns is certainly one legitimate elk-hunting trophy, but there are other rewards every bit as gratifying. Hunting challenge, shooting difficulty, first-class meat, and breathtaking scenery are all important elk-hunting benefits—benefits to be enjoyed even if the elk you shoot turns out to be a slick-scalped cow or spindly-horned spike bull. For this reason I'll say it once again. Every elk is a trophy elk—bar none! ●

An enjoyable time around the mountain campfire is a pleasant part of the elk-hunting experience. It's memories of scenes like this that make every elk a trophy elk.

SPAIN'S BIG GAME

Red stag, ibex, boar and more— they all add up to hunting experiences that are second to none.

by FRANK PETRINI

IF I HADN'T known better, I'd have thought I was hunting the Texas hill country. That beautiful patch of rolling hills, studded with stunted oak and scraggly cedar breaks is where I make my home, so it's not easy to fool me on such things. It's also the home of the largest whitetail deer herd in the U.S. and some of the best turkey hunting I've ever experienced, so I've had plenty of opportunity to spend days, months and, in fact, years roaming over it, gaining intimate knowledge of it. So, you might say, I had no excuse for getting confused.

Where I was standing, dusk was just rolling in and the September air, cool just like in Texas at that time of year, fanned my face. Just a few minutes earlier the red fireball hung seemingly still in the crimson sky, and the late afternoon air was calm and silent save for the buzzing, from time to time, of a few horseflies. Now, with evening coming, the air was filled, instead, with a cacophony of sounds—bawling and coughing, from

a dozen different thick areas of oak cover on the surrounding hillsides.

While it seemed like Texas, I knew that I was thousands of miles away from that place I call home as I stood on that hillside, one of many in the Montes de Toledo. To be more specific, I was in Spain and, as I was just finding out, in some of the best deer country in the world. Only it wasn't whitetail country. Here, we pursued the red stag instead.

The western red deer, or the species *Cervus elaphus* or, in that specific part of the world, the *Cervus elaphus Hispanicus,* to the uninitiated, are part of the deer family just like whitetails, muleys, moose and elk. But they're more like North American elk than any of the others, and if it weren't for the difference in coloring, a red stag is also a spitin' image of an elk except for being a few pounds lighter.

The red stag, as the name implies, is reddish in color, perhaps more of a reddish gray. But the coloration is more even overall than that of an elk where the light tan body and rump are contrasted sharply with the dark chocolate mane and snout. And while the average bull elk will run between 400 and 600 pounds, a mature red stag will go 300 or 400 pounds.

I've hunted stag before, back in the 1960s in Germany. These were the Eastern variety but more than distant cousins. I was looking for a real trophy then and was unsuccessful. I didn't know about Spain then. And maybe things weren't as good back then. But I can tell you about now.

The number of red deer throughout Spain is estimated at 350,000 animals. Except for 500 in the ancient hunting ground of El Pardo, just north of Madrid, the majority of

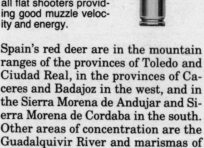

The 30-06 (shown), 7mm Remington Magnum and the 270 Winchester are three good choices for stag, ibex or other big game in Spain. Why? They are all flat shooters providing good muzzle velocity and energy.

Spain's red deer are in the mountain ranges of the provinces of Toledo and Ciudad Real, in the provinces of Caceres and Badajoz in the west, and in the Sierra Morena de Andujar and Sierra Morena de Cordaba in the south. Other areas of concentration are the Guadalquivir River and marismas of the Huelva province.

The very best trophies seem to come mostly from the Montes de Toledo and Sierra Morena where a good typical trophy will have antlers at least 34 inches in length with 12 or more points or tines. In the field such a stag has the bearing and majesty of the elk. In the opinion of this hunter, it and the elk are in a class by themselves as game animals.

There are a number of game preserves run by the Spanish government, but these are principally for hunting the exclusive Spanish ibex and high-ranging chamois, in particular abundance in the Pyrenees and Cantabrian Mountains. The ibex is the true monarch of the mountains on the Old Continent and is the number one trophy in Europe. It's hunted, again in high places, such as the Montes de Gredos.

Licenses to hunt in the Government Game Reserves are obtained through the Spanish State Tourist Department in Madrid. But the number of permits is strictly limited.

Probably the best bet for visiting hunters who don't know their way around Spain is to book a hunt through the sporting agency of Caza y Naturaleza, S.A. (CAZATUR). CAZATUR books hunts for the Western or Spanish red deer, wild boar, European mouflon, fallow deer, the Continental or European roebuck and the Spanish ibex *(Capra hispanica).*

CAZATUR conducts hunts in five different areas in Spain but their main hunting facility, "Sierra del Castano", is probably the best bet for hunters pursuing the red stag, wild boar, mouflon and fallow deer. It contains some 37,000 acres and lies 125 miles south of Madrid in the province of Ciudad Real, in the district comprised of the municipalities of Luciana and Piedrabuena.

CAZATUR representatives typically meet their clients at the Madrid International Airport and help with firearms clearances and then provide car transportation to the hunting lodge some 2½ hours away.

The facilities at "El Castano" include electrical lights, television and more than 100 kilometers of jeep roads to allow getting within reasonable hiking distance of the most remote hunting areas.

The main lodge offers the trophy hunters one of the most impressive big game trophy collections in the world, with heads lining the walls and full-mount trophies at floor level, making a unique museum for the outdoorsman.

While the country around "El Cas-

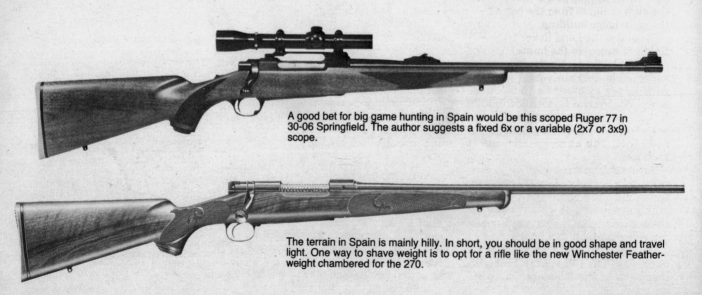

A good bet for big game hunting in Spain would be this scoped Ruger 77 in 30-06 Springfield. The author suggests a fixed 6x or a variable (2x7 or 3x9) scope.

The terrain in Spain is mainly hilly. In short, you should be in good shape and travel light. One way to shave weight is to opt for a rifle like the new Winchester Featherweight chambered for the 270.

The author hunted southern Spain at the "El Castano" lodge which is nestled in 37,000 acres of rolling hills. Note the similarity of the terrain to the southwest portion of the U.S.

tano" is much like the rolling hills of central Texas, the climate also helps to fool disoriented Texans. The vegetation is much like that of other areas along the Mediterranean, predominantly evergreen and cork oak trees, pines and eucalyptus trees. The shrubbery consists of dwarf oaks, young oaks, turkey oaks, mastic trees, rockrose, heather, Spanish broom, sage, strawberry, rosemary, and thyme. Herbs abound in the form of clover, brome grass, wild oats and other short grasses. All in all, in appearance, it's much like the rolling Texas Hill country.

Land Rovers are used to carry the hunters to the prime hunting areas, although in many cases the prime hunting areas, such as for fallow deer, are right around the main lodge. Indeed, during the rut, Red stags "bugle" off in the darkness just outside the glow of lights from the porticos of the main lodge building.

In spite of the Land Rover transportation, it behooves the hunter to be in reasonable shape for the hiking involved. The terrain varies greatly, with slopes as great as 15 to 40 degrees. The maximum altitude is 3020 feet at the highest point throughout the area with the lowest elevation at 2100 feet. The average altitude is 2460 feet.

Successful hunting requires covering a lot of country so while the altitudes may not be strikingly high, climbing up and down a number of them every morning and afternoon can cause considerable fatigue.

Of course good hiking boots are a necessity. The soil is clay-like with many stones and boulders. There are large volcanic formations in addition to granite outcroppings and rockbedded terrain of various geological elements. Such formations can be rough on boots and can literally destroy those of poor quality. The tough, Vibram sole is recommended.

The game herds in Spain are controlled strictly and managed through the use of modern game management techniques. CAZATUR employs game managers to oversee the herds and provide the correct habitat for maximum support of the various game herds but also to insure the largest number of trophy quality animals for hunting.

CAZATUR books about 100 hunters from all over the world every year and, combined, they take 150 to 200 red stags plus 60 to 70 Spanish ibex. Approximately 85 percent of these animals are in the medal class. All trophies are measured by the SCI (Safari Club International) system and scored for Bronze, Silver, and Gold medals. The trophies are also measured using the method used by the Government Conservation of Nature Department (ICONA) which is called the "old formula." Any trophy fees charged are based on the ICONA rating, which in many ways and situations is much stricter than the SCI system.

Choosing the Right Rifle

Choosing the proper rifle takes a bit of care and thought. Quite a bit of the shooting is over long distances with 300 and 400 yards relatively common, although it's not that unusual to get a stag at 200 yards when they're acting foolhardy during the rut. Even closer shots are not that unusual during that time. My Gold Medal stag was dropped at 100 yards but other hunters at El Castano while I was there experienced considerably longer distances, with 250 yards about the average.

For the hunter pursuing more than one game animal (as many do when traveling such a great distance to hunt) choice in rifle and caliber should be based on the more difficult species. For example, hunting Spanish ibex or chamois, requires long-range shooting much like, or even more than, the red stags. Flat shooting cartridges like those you might choose for mountain goat and sheep in the U.S. are your best choices. The 7mms, including the popular 7mm Remington Magnum, along with the 270 Winchester and 30-06 Springfield are probably the most popular calibers among hunters from the U.S.

The red stags are big animals and, while they resemble the American elk, they're not as tough as a bull elk. I have always felt that the American elk seem to require more "killing" than their size would indicate. Not so with the red stags. In choosing a cartridge for use on them you'd be wise to think in terms of a good mule deer cartridge. For this reason it's hard to beat the good old 270 WCF with a good quality 130-grain Soft Point bullet (my choice for my most recent Spanish hunt). This is certainly a top choice for all-around use. Other equally good choices include the 308,

Hunters from all over the world are coming to southern Spain for trophies. This Belgian hunter took his gold medal fallow deer in the Toledo mountains.

As they enter the rut, red stags will rub their antlers on shrubs and saplings. Broken, worn saplings like these are solid indication that red stag are "working" the area.

During the rut the hunter will frequently find areas of apparent fighting among the mature red stags.

7mm-08, 7x57mm, 7mm Remington Express, plus a number of popular wildcats like the 7mm JRJ (developed by hunter and writer Jon Sundra).

You can pack one of the magnums if you like, but except for the 7mm Remington Magnum, you'd probably be overgunned. Certainly there are few uses for the additional power of the 300 Winchester Magnum and even less for the 338 and 8mm Magnums.

A top quality telescopic sight is a must. A decade or more back I recommended a fixed-power scope for most hunting uses, primarily because the zooms, or variables, just weren't up to the heavy uses put on most hunting rifle scopes. The point of impact changed relative to the point of aim in most of those variables as the power was changed.

Then, in the 1970s, the scope manufacturers licked most of these problems. The variables began to find uses in all areas of hunting. And I recommended them wholeheartedly.

I still do. For red stag, fallow deer, or ibex a 2-7x or 3-9x variable, by one of the top manufacturers, would be hard to beat. However, on my Spanish hunt I went back to a fixed power. In this case it was a 6x Zeiss, one of the new glassware items by that famous company to be introduced in this country last year. It performed beautifully. Not once did I regret not having the variable feature, and it was awfully nice not having to fool with the variable knob. The 6x seemed the perfect power for this type of long-range shooting. Even at more than

300 yards—the distance over which I shot my wild boar—it was more than enough.

When I was on the fixed-power kick years ago, I usually recommended a 4x tube for all big game hunting, with the belief that a 6x sight was harder to hold off-hand. But after shooting fallow deer, red deer and wild boar with the 6x Zeiss on my 270 Winchester I find no drawbacks in the use of that power. The benefits of increased magnification are welcome on long-range shots. Besides, no one shoots offhand at 300 yards, at least no one in his right mind. And at these longer distances the hunter usually has the time to drop to a sitting or prone position where the 6x is most welcome. Zeiss also markets a 4x and a 3x to 9x variable which I have yet to try. I can, however, vouch for the 6x as an all-around long-range big game rig. It's just about optimum.

Hunting Methods

Most hunting at El Castano and other reserves operated by CAZATUR is done by stalking. A personal guide usually drives the hunter to the hunting area in the early morning, before first light, and again in mid-afternoon, and then you and the guide stalk, glass and hike through the prime hunting areas.

To a lesser extent "stand" hunting is employed. This, as in most of Europe, is usually done from tree stands. I spent one evening in a densely camouflaged tree stand near a small creek and saw a large number of red stag as they approached the water in early

evening but none were bigger than Bronze and I was holding out for at least a Silver medal stag. In spite of my lack of success at it, I suspect this type of hunting will present the closest shots since the stands are located in prime hunting areas where the animals are known to frequent and are seen quite regularly by the game managers.

Between these two hunting methods, stalking and standing, the U.S. hunters, as you might guess, prefer the former. Why this is true I can't say except that Americans are probably too impatient for long sitting vigils; at least walking is some kind of action. Europeans generally prefer the stand (or sitting) technique, of the two methods.

The most popular hunting technique in Spain is the *monteria*, or commonly called "drive" hunting here in the States. I've participated in quite a few of these types of hunts in Germany, and there are many similarities with the method as employed in Spain.

Hounds are used to drive the game to the posted or standing hunters. As many as 20 or 30 animals are frequently used and their movements are controlled by a horn blown by a drive master. Neighbors often participate as hunters and as drivers (or beaters) along with the dogs.

As practiced in Spain, and indeed all over Europe, drive hunts resemble military operations with large numbers of hunters, beaters, and dogs. The hunters are strategically placed in various hunt positions. In the

Spanish *monteria*, the hunt positions are usually assigned by drawing a number out of a hat so there's fairness in assigning the best stands. After that, the hunters are directed to their stands and the operation seems to fall into complete chaos and confusion, although it's clear by the end that someone was, in fact, in control.

The *monteria* is the most productive way of harvesting game. Indeed, in Spain, as many as 35,000 Red stags are taken each year with this hunting method. And it is the prime method for harvesting wild boar and stags. The record take for such an operation is 360 trophy stags killed in a day's *monteria* at Las Alarcones in 1973. The previous record was 238 trophies taken in a day in 1969 at San Calisto. Obviously this method finds little use with the mountain game, but for red stag and boar, it's the main technique of the native Spaniards.

The season for red stag extends from early September to mid-February. The rut normally commences about the tenth of September and continues for about a month and, of course, is the best time to hunt these large animals. It's also the most exciting time with the "bugling" which, in the case of stags, is more reminiscent of cows bawling and coughing than the characteristic "bugling" attributed to the American elk. In the early dusk this activity can be eerie and exciting, and adds to the pleasure of the hunt.

When hunting any open, hilly terrain, be it in Spain or the southwest U.S., a spotting scope can come in handy. This particular spotting scope is Weaver's new offering; however, don't overlook spotting scopes from Bushnell, Zeiss and Swift—they're all top quality performers!

As with any foreign hunting these days the Spanish hunts are expensive. However, the trophy potential is high, much higher than comparably priced hunts elsewhere. CAZATUR has a number of package hunts plus hunts packaged with tours of the surrounding country (the prime hunting areas are close to all the areas rich in history). For example, an 8-day "Huntour" which includes hunting and taking a stag, mouflon, fallow deer and wild boar along with tours through the ancient city of Toledo and the national monument at Almagro and other places including the old winery at Valdepenas has a price tag of $3,480. Ten- and 15-day "Huntours" are also available. In addition, mountain hunts for ibex, mouflon, chamois, and roe deer are also available through the late spring and summer for up to 15-day hunts at varying prices. Most any arrangement and package can be put together.

Prices quoted usually include all expenses excluding airfare to and from Madrid. This includes room, board, one guide per hunter, transportation and trophy preparation, salting, etc.

For the most up to date information, contact CAZATUR, Velazques, 22,4 dcha, Madrid-1, Spain, or Apartado de Correos (P.O. Box) 50.577, Madrid, Spain. For the hunter longing for real trophy hunting, long gone in some places in this world, Spanish hunting could be the answer to your prayers. ●

In wide open country you can save miles of fruitless stalking by spending a lot of time glassing probable areas before moving. This technique worked well for the author in the hilly country of southern Spain.

While stalking and still hunting is commonly employed, the *monteria* (drive hunt) is still very popular in Spain. The *monteria* is a prime technique for harvesting wild boar.

WYOMING . . .

"Given a country of diversified topography, whose physical conditions are favourable to the support of a large stock of big game and it is a comparatively easy matter for the future to rectify the effects of overhunting in the past. Thus in Wyoming, one of the finest natural game countries in the world, there is now to be had excellent hunting for elk, deer, bear, sheep and cougar, while in 1912 when an open season for moose is to be allowed, there will be opportunities to secure some grand old bulls from the large number at present harbouring in the forests. The outlook therefore is most encouraging and English sportsmen who are meditating a hunt in the western wilds might do worse than turn their attentions to the famous hunting grounds of Wyoming, where, if all indications do not deceive, everything favours the hunter's returning with something more satisfactory and tangible than a lightened purse and pleasant memories."

SUCH WAS THE OPINION of an English gentleman, Lincoln Wilbar, Esq., of Bournemouth, England, after returning from a hunting trip to Wyoming in 1909.

Probably several western states could have merited such reviews around the turn of the century, but comparatively few states could honestly qualify for such statements in this day and age. However, the state of Wyoming is a pleasant exception. The quality of hunting that Wyoming now affords sportsmen has come about through a carefully planned wildlife management program. Very little has been left to chance.

As early as 1869, there were concerns over the wildlife situation in Wyoming. At that time the First Territorial Legislature passed, "An Act

a wildlife management success story

by AL LANGSTON

(Opposite page) Wyoming has more bighorn sheep (currently 5,000 animals) than any other state as a result of an aggressive restocking program. (Below) Wyoming didn't have any wild turkeys until 1935, when the state traded a few sage grouse to New Mexico for 33 birds. There has been such tremendous growth that over 3,000 turkey licenses are available each year. (Right) Harvests on Wyoming's sage grouse (males may weigh up to 6 lbs.) are around 80,000 per year! Since sage grouse and antelope seasons often overlap, many antelope hunters carry their shotgun along for a little added sport.

For the Protection of Game and Fish in The Territory of Wyoming." Although this piece of legislation was largely ineffective, concern had been shown and the first step taken.

In 1875, a hunting season from August 15 to January 15 was set on big game. Game animals were to be killed only for food and then only when necessary for human subsistence. However, once again, no provisions were made to enforce the law. During the next two decades, various measures were enacted for the conservation of Wyoming wildlife until 1899 when the legislature created the office of State Game Warden. It was then that tighter measures were taken to protect Wyoming's game animals. Several seasons were closed and limits on big game were set at two deer, two elk, three antelope and one mountain sheep. Residents were required to buy a gun license for $1 to hunt in counties other than their residence.

In spite of the seeming liberality of these laws by today's standards, a start had been made toward establishing a sound conservation program.

An Antelope Success Story

The game laws remained relatively unchanged until 1909 when the legislature closed the season on antelope. At that time some estimates had the Wyoming pronghorn population as low as 5,000 animals. In his writings on the antelope situation, Lincoln Wilbar penned the following, "Antelope are comparatively scarce and entirely protected until 1915. The general impression seems to be that they are practically a doomed animal . . ."

Anyone who has ever hunted antelope in Wyoming knows that the pronghorn is far from doomed and is thriving in the 1980s. Currently, antelope are on the increase in several western states and in Wyoming now number more than 300,000 animals. The dramatic increase in hunting opportunity for antelope is easy to see when harvest figures for the 1930s are compared with present day reports. In 1934, for example a total of 1,500 antelope were bagged. Compare this with somewhere in the neighborhood of 80,000 taken in 1982. Such a dramatic increase did not happen by mere chance. When the season was reopened in 1915, it was done with restrictions to insure the herds could continue to increase. The antelope responded well to this protection and in 1923, the herd had built up to an estimated 14,000 animals. By 1926 the pronghorns had topped the 20,000 mark, and by 1936 the number had increased to 35,000 head.

By 1950, Wyoming's total big game count exceeded 200,000 animals for the first time since the turn of the century. Of these 200,000 animals, 76,000 were antelope.

Wyoming has more antelope than any other state—the population numbers nearly 300,000 animals. Around the turn of the century many thought the antelope would soon be extinct. It is now commonplace for a Wyoming antelope hunter to see anywhere from 200 to 1,000 animals in a single day of hunting.

Here's the author with a nice pronghorn taken in Wyoming's Red Desert country. The antelope sported 14½-inch horns. Langston says average pronghorns of 12-14 inches are fairly easy to come by, but getting 15 inchers can be tough. Rifle is Ruger M-77 in 270 Winchester.

Nowadays antelope are managed on an area-by-area basis with 109 such game management areas spread across the state. Every spring a combined aerial and ground census of these animals is taken by biologists and game wardens. These big game surveys are not taken until the spring for a very important reason. Wyoming is frequently subjected to harsh winters. Depending on the severity of these winters, the antelope population may be reduced by as much as 75 percent in some areas. So game counts are not taken and final seasons and quotas are not set until after the effects of the winter are known. The Game and Fish Commission then sets the seasons around the first of May. Sportsmen, who do not understand this, frequently complain about the practice, saying they would like to know the exact seasons and quotas during the winter months in order to put in for vacation time in advance.

Admittedly the spring season setting is inconvenient for some nonresident hunters, but it's one of the reasons why the hunting is so good. Every effort is made to accommodate both hunters and wildlife, but if a decision is to be made pitting the convenience of hunters against the well-being of the game herds, the decision will invariably favor the animals.

This might seem like a rather hard-nosed approach to some hunters, especially in light of the fact that it's the hunter who picks up the tab for wildlife management. But few complaints are heard from sportsmen once they've actually experienced a Wyoming antelope hunt. First-timers will usually ask, "Which areas offer the best antelope hunting?" This is somewhat like asking which of the Great Lakes has the most water. They all have plenty to float your boat.

Success ratios vary from a low of around 70 percent in a few areas to a

high of close to 96 percent in others. When all 109 areas are averaged, the statewide success if an amazing 92 percent! In most areas of Wyoming, it is possible to see over 200 antelope per day, and in some the hunter may see more than 1,000! An individual may hunt anywhere from 20 minutes to 2 days depending on how big a pronghorn he decides to hold out for. In spite of the great numbers of antelope, hunters should be aware, as with any big game animal, that antelope of record book proportions rarely come easy. It is not too difficult to bag a better than average buck in the 12- to 14-inch range but getting a 15-incher can be tough. Nevertheless, the animals are there, and it appears that the Wyoming Game and Fish Department is doing its best to keep the hunting a quality experience.

Deer

A similar success story could be told for deer. People often talk of the good ol' days when referring to deer hunting, however talk of this type usually comes from those who have never had the chance to participate in those grand old days they hear so much about. I've talked to old-timers who lived in Wyoming, in the '20s who said they considered themselves very lucky to even see several deer in a season, let alone bag one. One 70-year-old native I talked to told me that in those days seeing a deer was such a big event, when it happened,

The Wyoming Fish and Game Department regularly conducts trapping operations for antelope, with Arizona, Kansas, Nebraska and Texas receiving animals for transplant in recent years. The labor for these operations is made up of game wardens, biologists, and wildlife students from the University of Wyoming.

(Right) Sometimes antelope are trapped for the purpose of conducting studies on migration patterns and land use. Many of the studies are precipitated by proposed energy developments on critical wildlife habitat. Those studies help determine how much impact a development will have and help the Fish and Game people to lessen the impact if necessary.

(Left) Wyoming places great emphasis on maintaining a quality hunting experience for sportsmen. It should be said that a better than average hunter success ratio is one of their prime goals.

Elk hunters in Wyoming welcome the fact that the hunter success ratio is among the highest to be found anywhere. One out of three Wyoming hunters get their elk for a harvest of around 17-20,000 animals in an average year. (Wyoming Fish and Game Dept. photo)

you went to school and told all the kids about it. But in the 1980s seeing a deer is such an ordinary occurrence it hardly merits conversation among classmates, much less hunters.

Basically, the deer in Wyoming are managed in order to provide a quality hunting experience — something that is becoming increasingly hard to find in other states. Several important management techniques have been largely responsible for the hunting being as good as it is. One technique is to spread out hunting pressure by dividing up the nonresident pressure into various areas of the state. To accomplish this "spreading out" of hunting pressure, the state has been divided into eight general regions for nonresidents, each of which has a specific license quota which varies from year to year to compensate for fluctuating deer populations. This prevents a disproportionate number of the 33,000 nonresident deer hunters who come to Wyoming each fall from all going to some area that has a glowing reputation and causing too much hunter impact. It should be mentioned that nonresidents can apply for whichever regions they wish and that all licenses are issued by computer drawing. In addition there are some deer areas within these regions managed by what Wyoming refers to as the "limited-quota" method. To obtain these limited-quota licenses, hunters must apply for the specific limited-quota area rather than the region. A set number of resident and nonresident licenses are available for each

limited-quota area and of course all these licenses are issued by drawing. Once a hunter has a limited quota license for an area, that is the only area he can hunt. This applies to both resident and nonresident hunters. Now, I realize all this might sound a trifle complicated, but it really isn't. It's all explained quite clearly in each of the big game application booklets.

When the limited quota system was first instituted, there were many complaints. But as hunters got more and more used to the system and realized its benefits, the criticisms subsided. The limited quota system was not necessary 30 years ago when the hunting pressure was much less, but the system has largely been responsible for maintaining good hunting success in areas that receive heavy hunting pressure or in areas where the terrain and open spaces make for an easier harvest. The limited-quota system, then, is just one more example of the Wyoming Game and Fish Department keeping pace with the changing times. Whatever else might be said, the proof is in the deer success ratio. Currently around 64 percent of Wyoming deer hunters get their deer, which represents the highest success for deer hunters in the West. Like antelope, the extent of the deer management success can be shown by comparisons with the old days. In 1935, 819 deer were bagged in Wyoming. Compare that with the most recent harvest of over 66,000, and it's easy to see the amazing progress that has been made. Of course there are

many more hunters now than there were in the '30s but there are also a lot more deer.

Although thought of primarily as a mule deer state, Wyoming also has an expanding population of whitetails. Most Wyoming whitetails are found in the Black Hills in the northeast corner of the state, but there are a lot of whitetails around the communities of Wheatland, Cheyenne, and Buffalo to name a few. In all, Wyoming's population of deer is around 50,000 whitetails and 400,000 mule deer.

Elk

Elk hunting and management in Wyoming has a long and colorful history. Around the turn of the century, elk were facing a serious problem from tusk hunters. A tusk hunter would kill an elk and take only the two canines (which are similar to ivory) from the animal. The tusk

The good old days are *now* as far as Wyoming deer hunters are concerned. The herds have improved to where the harvest has risen from 819 in 1935 to over 66,000 today. Last year 64 percent of Wyoming deer hunters brought home some venison.

hunters were especially active in the Jackson Hole area until one Charles Gobel, leader of a particularly notorious band was caught and jailed. Gobel, however, was released after spending the winter in jail and resumed his unlawful activities with the coming of spring. This prompted the legislature in 1907 to pass a law making the killing of big game animals for heads, antlers and tusks a felony punishable by a prison term of up to 5 years.

One of the greatest problems the elk faced was loss of their winter range due to increased development of the land. The growth of Jackson Hole put the large elk herds of the region in a serious situation, and during the severe winter of 1909-1910, thousands of elk died from starvation. That winter, an estimated 20,000 to 30,000 elk came into Jackson Hole. The ranchers did what they could for the animals and furnished hay and labor to feed them. That year the Wyoming Legislature appropriated $5,000 to buy hay for the elk, and in 1913, Congress appropriated $20,000 to carry the elk through the coming winter. That same year the National Elk Refuge was established, giving the elk a place to winter.

Although elk are now being fed each winter in Wyoming, it is not believed by most biologists to be a panacea to pull the animals through the winter. Many biologists favor habitat preservation and improvements over feeding. Feeding is tremendously expensive and can facilitate the spread of disease when animals become crowded together. This has caused the people at the Wyoming Game and Fish Department to take a hard look at setting up additional feedgrounds. On the positive side, there is no evidence to suggest that the feeding has created a herd of semi-domesticated elk. Elk hunting still requires a lot of know-how, effort and, of course, a little luck if a hunter is to be successful.

Some elk areas have been designated limited quota for the same reasons already explained for deer. There is a nonresident quota of 12 percent of the average of the 3 previous year's license sales. This usually works out to around 6,000 nonresident licenses and the nonresident has around a 50

percent chance of drawing one of these licenses. Once a license is drawn the hunter has an excellent chance at success. While Wyoming hunters usually harvest several thousand fewer elk than neighboring Colorado, the success ratio is much higher with about 33 percent of Wyoming hunters harvesting 17,000-20,000 elk each year. The Wyoming success ratio is by far the highest among leading elk states.

Elk have always been fairly numerous in Wyoming, and since only a limited portion of the state offers good elk habitat, the population increases haven't been as dramatic as with deer and antelope. But even with that, the current harvest is a lot higher than the old days with about three times as many elk bagged now as in the '30s.

Moose and Sheep

Wyoming is by far the leading state in the lower 48 for moose hunters. It's not easy to get a moose license, (the odds are about 12-1 statewide), but if a hunter is successful in the draw, he'll likely get a moose. The success ratio is about 86 percent with some 1,400 animals bagged annually. Compare this with a total of 86 moose bagged in 1930 and decide for yourself if it really was better in the old days.

Similar success could be cited for the bighorn sheep program. Once again, the sheep numbers are among the highest in the West, and further growth has been slowed by limited habitat although new sheep areas have been created by transplants to

areas that have been historically occupied by sheep. There are around 5,000 bighorns in the state and about 360 licenses are available each year. As with all game animals, maintaining thriving bighorn sheep herds is much more involved than simply setting seasons and issuing licenses. A great deal of research has taken place on the bighorn's behalf during the past several decades. It appears that much of this research has centered around ways to effectively trap and transplant sheep while keeping the stress level to a minimum in an effort to reduce capture mortality. To their credit, the Game and Fish Department maintains a full-time research laboratory and staff with headquarters at the University of Wyoming and a wildlife research facility near the town of Wheatland. That 3,081-acre facility is called the Sybille Research Unit and the projects undertaken there are geared towards game management. Studies on wildlife diseases, nutrition, reproduction potential and many others have also been conducted. That laboratory has made great inroads towards reducing the lungworm problem which has decimated so many bighorn sheep in the past.

Much of the success of reestablishing big game populations in Wyoming has resulted from trapping and transplant programs. Through the years, Wyoming has provided bighorn sheep, moose, antelope and elk to a number of states wanting to supplement their own herds. And several

The Shiras moose is Wyoming's largest game animal and one of the toughest for which to draw a permit. But once a license is obtained, the hunter will have an 86 percent chance of success. Nearly 1400 moose are harvested each year in Wyoming—the most of any of the lower 48 states. The Fish and Game Dept. is careful to see that good herds are maintained to provide quality hunting for sportsmen.

WYOMING BIG GAME HARVEST—1981

Species	Number of Hunters	Harvest	Hunter Success Ratio
Antelope	73,708	67,801	92%
Deer	103,345	66,090	64%
Elk	56,815	18,713	32.9%
Moose	1,588	1,369	86.2%
Bighorn Sheep	337	174	51.6%
Rocky Mt. Goat	8	7	87.5%

areas of Wyoming now have populations of bighorn sheep, antelope and elk due to an aggressive restocking program from herds having surplus animals. The world famous Whiskey Mountain bighorn sheep herd near Dubois provides about 60 sheep for relocation each year.

In recent years, Wyoming has provided sheep for Utah, Nevada, Idaho and California; moose for Colorado; and antelope for Texas, Kansas, Nebraska, Utah and Arizona. Elk from Yellowstone National Park and Jackson Hole have also been transplanted in many areas of Wyoming and all over the United States.

But it is not always Wyoming that provides the animals; the state has also been the recipient. Back in 1935 Wyoming received 15 Merriam's turkeys from New Mexico in exchange for some sage grouse. Those 15 birds were introduced in the Laramie Peak area just west of Wheatland. Finding suitable habitat, the birds increased rapidly, and in 1942, the population was estimated at 600 birds. By 1950, the Laramie Peak flock had increased to the extent that trapping and transplant operations were initiated from the original flock. To date, the most successful turkey release was made in the Black Hills in 1951 and 1952 with a transplant of 33 birds. These turkeys multiplied so rapidly that in 1955 a season was held and 400 permits issued. Nowadays over 3,000 licenses are available for the spring and fall hunts with the bulk of those licenses being issued for the Black Hills area. In 1981, the harvest was 1,678 birds for a success ratio of 51 percent. Not a bad trade for a few sage grouse!

One of the big reasons for the success of Wyoming hunters is that the wildlife of the state is managed by biologists and game wardens rather than politicians. In other words, the Department has not had to go to politicians each year to request funding for wildlife. The sole means of financing the Department comes from license fees and Pittman-Robertson and Dingell-Johnson funds. Not a penny has come from the state legislature since 1937. Obviously, this funding autonomy from state lawmakers allows the wildlife managers of the department to make the decisions that are truly best for wildlife rather than having to justify each and every management decision to non-wildlife professionals. That the system has worked is proven by the high demand for Wyoming licenses and the lofty hunter success ratios which are among the highest of all Rocky Mountain states.

The bottom line is the people of Wyoming along with the Game and Fish Department are justifiably proud of the state's rich wildlife resource. It will be an uphill battle to keep and maintain the quality hunting of this exciting and wildlife rich state . . . but I sure wouldn't bet against it. ●

CHUKAR—
The Bird That Won The West

by PAULA DEL GUIDICE

They're tough, fast and provide one of the finest wingshooting experiences you'll ever have.

ONCE WHILE fishing in Utah, a local angler, hearing that I was from Nevada, asked me, "Isn't there anything in Nevada but sagebrush? I mean, aren't there any *trees* or anything?" I giggled to myself because, after all, sagebrush *is* Nevada's state flower. But those of us who are devoted chukar hunters know that where there's sagebrush, there're chukars, especially if there're plenty of rocky hills, water, and tasty chukar morsels such as cheatgrass in the mixture.

In the late 1800s, chukars were introduced to most of the United States as well as a dozen or so Canadian provinces to supplement those game birds that were on the wane due to increasing amounts of land going to farming and development. In all but the far western states, these populations failed to take hold due to the extreme winters that prevail in these agricultural areas. Farmlands didn't provide enough adequate cover or roosting and nesting areas.

Chukars are able to withstand cold temperatures, but deep snows hide available feed. I remember one particularly cold winter in my hometown of Elko, Nevada. The snows had accumulated to such levels on the outskirts of town that the nearby chukars couldn't find any available food.

An opportunity for a clear shot on chukars is a unique situation. This hunter has taken advantage of his chance.

Into town they swarmed, looking for tidbits to fill their tummies. It was quite a sight! The chukars were more confused than the local residents were delighted. Unfortunately, many of the displaced birds met an untimely demise when house cats found out how much fun they were to play with.

These Euroasian creatures finally found their "heaven on earth" among the sagecovered rocky inclines in the semi-arid West. The birds prefer the rough terrain of canyon country. They like the inhospitable territory that requires hunters to muster all their courage and endurance to tackle. Chukar populations are now established in Arizona, California, Hawaii, Idaho, Montana, Nevada, Oregon, Utah, Washington, and Wyoming as

well as in Mexico and British Columbia.

Habits and Habitat

You'll have a good chance of finding chukar near rocky outcroppings and eroded canyons. Canyons are especially suitable for chukar if there is a small creek or river at the bottom. Most coveys are found within a mile or so of water during dry seasons. However, when insect populations are dense, the birds can go longer without any apparent water source. The chukar feed in the stubble or topside draws, but roost on the precipitous walls or steep ledges of canyons. The wary birds prefer the exotic cheatgrass to nibble on, but will feed on the stubble of grainfields if it is available. So don't neglect the edges of fields, especially if there are rocky hills or water nearby.

Once you've scouted the most likely chukar habitat, you'll have no difficulty distinguishing chukar from their desert neighbors. Although it's difficult to discern the male from the female of the species, males are usually larger than their female counterparts and have leg spurs. The birds are blue-gray in color on the upper portion of the body, wings, and breast area. The outer tail feathers are brown-colored and the lower part of the face and throat are white-colored. The legs and beak are vermillion-colored. Both eyes are encircled by vermillion rings. Above the beak, a black band stretches across the face and eyes, then curves down along the neck

and over the upper breast. The belly is tan, and the flanks are a paler tan color highlighted by distinctive vertical black and brown bars. Chukars are slightly smaller than ruffed grouse, averaging about 15 inches in length and weighing in at about 1-pound or so.

Chukars are found in the same areas as pheasants, quail and Hungarian partridge, particularly if you hunt near agricultural areas. It is not uncommon to go home with a mixed bag of these birds doubling the delight of a successful chukar hunt.

Now that you've located the perfect spot for chukars and know what to look for, you'll have to find where the coveys are hiding. The easiest way is to look and listen. You'll know you're in chukar country when you hear their tattletale call: Chuk, chuk, chuk, chuk, chuk-ar! The birds tend to jabber to each other becoming silent when disturbed. You can purchase chukar calls at nearly any wellstocked sporting goods store. Try blowing it when the birds have clammed up, and they'll usually answer. They won't come towards a call, but their answer will tell you where to look for them.

An old-fashioned method that remarkably resembles the chatterings of a chukar are two silver dollars clicking together. Use the edge of one silver dollar held in one hand against the flat side of another dollar held in the palm of your other hand. The only problem with this technique, used by my father during his chukar hunting

This wary hunter takes a classic shot on a downhill-flying chukar. (The bird is located just above and to the left of the shooter's shoulder.)

days, is it's best to use pre-Eisenhower dollars—the ones with silver in them. The newer ones just don't have the same sound. Some hunters learn to develop a reasonable facsimile of a chukar call using only their vocal cords.

Carry a pair of binoculars with you. Usually chukars will be visible in their feeding areas. It is not uncommon for a single bird to perch on a prominent rock as a sentry for the rest of the covey that averages approximately 20 in number, but can range from just a few to nearly 40 birds.

Check heavily used dusting areas near water sources such as creeks, rivers, springs, watering tanks, and other water supplies for feathers, tracks, and droppings. Because the birds' feeding activity peaks during the mid-morning hours, searching for fresh chukar sign can be done during a noonday lunch break or before your hunt begins.

How to Get 'em

You'll need to change your hunting tactics in order to bring chukars home in your bag. Chukars have very odd habits that will perplex even the most experienced wingshooter. These confounded game birds insist on heading downhill when airborne and they have the uncanny ability to run like the dickens uphill.

Shots are made on most normal upland birds when they're on the rise. Wingshooters weaned on doves or quail are likely to shoot over the tops of chukars before settling down and

discovering the system that works best on these curious birds. One of the best ways to increase your bag is to wait out your shot just a bit before squeezing the trigger. A lead just underneath a bird will also increase your success.

One tendency an inexperienced chukar hunter may have upon discovering a sitting covey is to chase them until they flush. This approach is foolhardy, at best, and should only be attempted by the strong of lung, mighty of heart, and loose of marbles! Those little critters can scamper up hillsides with amazing quickness. A full-grown hunter fully clad in hunting garb with binoculars bouncing can look pretty silly while chasing these mini-roadrunners up a steep incline. Those birds won't even pause to get in a good laugh before they disappear leaving such a hunter panting and sweating in their dust.

One of the best ways to outsmart the red-legged partridge is to position part of your hunting party near the bottom of a slope and the rest of the hunters at the top of the slope. Chukars scared by the hunters near the bottom will run uphill while those flushed by hunters near the top will fly downhill. Make certain you know your shotgun ranges and spread your hunters out adequately.

One season, while feeling particularly full of myself after outwitting a bag limit of chukar, I smiled quite smuggly while my mind slowly unwound the hands of time back to nearly 20 years ago and my first chukar

hunt. I couldn't help but chuckle in retrospect. It was very early, the sun hadn't even come up yet, when I heard noises coming from our kitchen below my room. Sleepily, I crept down the stairs to join my Dad, my older brothers, Tom and Dick, and Dad's friend Wally Blohm. They were quickly preparing for an early-morning trek after chukars.

When I discovered I wasn't to be included, I cried my eyes out. Well, that had always turned the trick before and it did again. I ran upstairs to don my clothes, including my best anklets and school shoes, hardly your standard hunting garb.

We headed off toward Palisades, near Carlin and about 30 miles from Elko, Nevada. My brothers were hardly enthused about their little sister tagging along. After walking about a mile from the car, I'd managed to step in a huge mud puddle, grow two blisters on my heels, develop an extreme case of hay fever, and make a general nuisance of myself forcing my doctor father to take me back to the car, foregoing his own hunting, to treat me.

After an early lunch and an allergy pill, I immediately locked the keys to the car in the trunk. So much for my first hunt . . . However, my life-long love affair with the outdoors was born, even out of my misery. The rest of the crew managed to bring out a bunch of birds, so the day wasn't completely lost.

This more recent hunting trip had been much more fruitful, however. I was working my way down a hillside when I discovered a large, rather flat area. A covey of chukars flushed unexpectedly nearly blasting me off my feet and unnerving my cool completely. I was lucky to drop two birds with my first two shots. The rest of the covey had seemingly vanished while I replaced the spent shells in my gun. Yet, as is common with these birds, several stayed behind until they panicked and got up in a hurry. I dropped two of the next three birds. The action wasn't as furious the rest of the day, but I managed to bring out eight birds.

When chukars fly downhill, they tend to curve around the hill laterally until landing at approximately the same elevation from whence they came. Occasionally one or two will alight on rocks and outcroppings. These will be worth a closer look.

Although many chukar hunters prefer to work without dogs, a close-working dog can save you plenty of steps when used to retrieve dead birds

Chukar are distinctive birds. Their unique coloration and odd habits make them a challenge for the shotgunner.

Chukar love this type of brushy terrain—plenty of cover and lots of food.

and cripples. In the rough terrain these birds dwell in, the extra steps saved might just keep you in boot leather for an extra season. Most any close-working dog trained well on signals will work on chukars, although it might be wise to choose one that is accustomed to rough footing and hot weather. A dog trained to circle below you as you hunt will help pin chukar in, forcing them to flush. This might help if there are fewer numbers in your hunting party.

Those who prefer not to use dogs insist that, due to the extraordinary flight and running tendencies of the birds, dogs only serve to push them ahead without coercing them into flight. I prefer to work behind a good dog. Any help I can get reducing walking time over rocky territory is more time I'll have trying to outwit these sly critters.

Chukar Guns

The gauge and gun you choose and the type of action you use is left entirely to your own personal convictions. The gun you choose must be lightweight for convenience sake. Most hunters prefer shot sizes in 6 or 7½, favoring 6's if their gun's choked tightly.

A modified choke will work well for all-around chukar hunting purposes. This will allow you to score most often on the varied types of shots you'll encounter. Many hunters prefer double guns, though, choked improved and modified.

Many Europeans use slings on their shotguns when toting them afield. Americans have been hesitant to use slings because they feel that swivels on the shotgun are aesthetically unpleasing. For that reason, I like to compromise with one of the new slip-on shotgun slings that won't mar my gun in any way. A slinged shotgun will, I assure you, make your hunting much easier. It'll leave your hands free when negotiating steep hills and rocky chukar terrain and might save your favorite shotgun from bumps and bruises if you lose your footing.

Where to Hunt

Although chukar hunting is good in almost all of the semiarid portions of the West, there are areas in nearly every state where chukar populations are concentrated. Washington, Idaho, and Nevada are usually the top three western states for chukar harvests.

Washington and Idaho

In Washington, the eastern part of the state provides the type of habitat chukars crave. Some of the best areas for hunting are right near the Idaho state line. The southeastern area near Clarkston and right across the Snake River from Lewiston, Idaho, provides excellent wingshooting possibilities. Hunting in that part of Washington will most likely place you near grainfields with the Snake River Canyon nearby.

Most seasons are set during the summer after brood counts are made. Your best bet when planning chukar hunting trips is to check with state agencies for their latest season information. In Washington, contact: Washington Department of Game, 600 North Capital Way, Olympia, Washington 98504, (206) 753-5700.

Idaho provides excellent chukar hunting in many parts of the state. Idaho typically has one of the longest seasons for chukar providing hunters with ample opportunities for honing shooting skills. Chukar populations are well-established along the Oregon border, especially in the Hell's Canyon area along the northeastern corner of Oregon.

The red-legged birds are also well-suited to the habitat in the Snake and Salmon River Canyon areas. Because many of these areas are inaccessible, some crafty hunters have taken to floating these rivers in search of the cunning game birds.

Hunting is also good in the Snake River Plain along the southern part of the state near Twin Falls. Your chances of bringing out pheasants with your chukars are also good in this agricultural part of Idaho.

Check with the Idaho Fish and Game Department at 600 South Walnut, Box 25, Boise, Idaho 83707, (208) 344-3700, for detailed information on Idaho chukar populations, including season dates.

Nevada

In Nevada, good chukar hunting prevails in the northern portions of Washoe, Humboldt, Pershing, Lander, and Elko Counties along the borders of Oregon and Idaho. During the past season, I asked many hunters where the best spots were near Reno and met with the same replies, "Don't bother." Thinking that the birds must have experienced a bad hatch, I asked Mike Hess, staff biologist for the Nevada Department of Wildlife, whether or not my assumptions were correct. Hess laughed and replied, "It wasn't a bad year for chukars, just a bad year

Not only do chukars provide challenging hunting opportunities, but serve as excellent table fare as well.

for hunters!" Apparently the early season precipitation caused the birds to scatter. The birds were out there, they were just difficult to find.

Most of the best hunting in Nevada is on public land administered by the Bureau of Land Management. The ranges south of Denio, north of Winnemucca, provide excellent chukar range. Other prime areas are the mountains in the Independence Range north of Elko and the Granite Range in northern Washoe County. For season dates and population information check with the Nevada Department of Wildlife, P.O. Box 10678, Reno, Nevada 89520, (702) 784-6214.

Oregon

Oregon's best chukar populations are in the excellent habitat provided by the Snake, John Day, and Deschutes River Canyons. The Snake River runs along the Idaho-Oregon border in the northeastern section of the state. The Deschutes runs in the northcentral part of Oregon close to the Washington border southeast of the Dalles as does the John Day River. Another good area is near the Malheur River east of Burns, Oregon.

California

California's birds are located in the White Mountain Range of the Inyo National Forest northeast of Bishop. There are also chukars found as low as in the desert area of Death Valley. Write to the California Department of Fish and Game for season dates and population information. Their address is 1416 Ninth Street, Sacramento, California 95814, (916) 445-3531.

Utah

Utah has pretty good chukar populations north of Logan towards the Idaho border. Hunting is also good northwest of the Great Salt Lake in the northern corner of Utah. Contact the Utah Division of Wildlife Resources, 1596 W.N. Temple, Salt Lake City, Utah 84116, (801) 533-9333.

Arizona, Colorado, Montana, and Wyoming host only fair numbers of chukars and harvests in the past several years have typically been low.

Most sportsmen, as well as game biologists, believe that chukar populations can't be overhunted and, in fact, in many states are underhunted. Chukars are no pushovers in their new habitat. After the last hunter collapses in weary frustration, chukars will remain the victor—king of the West. ●

Chukar hunting from the ridgetops, near good cover (and close to water), will ultimately bring success in areas with good chukar populations. The use of dogs in rocky terrain such as this will save a hunter from plenty of frustration.

THE RIPPING boom of my partner's 20-gauge semi-auto cut a swath through the frosty morning air. A quick second shot followed by excited yelps from my beagle, Cory, told me a rabbit was on the loose. I lost little time in scrambling onto a large rock that allowed a clear view of a forgotten tram road that wound through the heavy stand of pine trees.

While the chase headed away from us, Milt yelled that the rabbit had exploded out of a fallen tree top, jumped a small creek and was hiding behind a solid mass of underbrush. Milt retaliated by taking two quick shots that did nothing but reduce the weed population.

I knew from past hunts in this area that the rabbit would make a wide circle and come back on the tram road or cut below to the bottom and take advantage of the brush along the creek. Hurriedly, I yelled my thoughts to Milt, warning him to concentrate on the creek area. It was now a wait and watch game.

As Cory's voice grew louder, I caught a glimpse of the wary cottontail along the old road, but it wasn't headed in the right direction! My advice had been wrong; the rabbit was coming in from behind Milt, and I couldn't yell a warning since any loud noise could send the bunny on a tangent around him. Whether it was fate or some sixth sense that caused my partner to turn isn't important; he stopped the loping cottontail with a load of 7½ shot.

I had learned many years before that once the chase is headed toward the hunter, it's imperative to remain silent and motionless. Most of the time, the rabbit is well ahead of the dog and even minor noises or movements are instantly detected by the approaching rabbit. Its sharp vision and acute senses keep it alive, and the hunter will never see that cottontail unless he obeys this cardinal rule: *Watch hard and freeze tight!*

The common cottontail is a genuine American native spread across the entire North American continent and is found above sea level but below the

by DON LEWIS
(Photos by Helen Lewis)

Shotguns &

timberline. It doesn't exist in other parts of the world. Every citizen of this continent is familar to some extent with the long-eared rascal that has big feet and eyes that are situated on the sides of its head, permitting it to have almost 170-degree vision. It's not 2 feet long, seldom weighs 4 pounds but does carry a large powder puff of white fur on its rump that earned it the nickname "cottontail."

It's hard to conceive that the cottontail is America's number one game animal.

The briar patch dweller doesn't derive much peace in its short life; it's fair game for both man and predator. If luck is on its side, it may see its fourth birthday, but 2 years would be about average. Man and predators seek it for food, but disease, parasites and bad weather take an enormous toll. True, the cottontail is prolific and literally cranks out offspring. The female can have four litters a summer and often breeds on the same day it gives birth. This should swamp the land with thousands of rabbits, but the high death rate among nesting rabbits holds the population pretty much in tow.

The cottontail might be on practically everyone's menu, and it seems it

The cottontail rabbit is the American hunter's No. 1 target year after year. It's a favorite of shotgunners.

Farm land under cultivation makes ideal rabbit habitat. Here, a corn field surrounded by pasture land and dense thickets makes for ideal rabbit cover.

is defenseless. If that were true, rabbits would be on the endangered species list. The speedster of the thicket has a few things going for it. Its unique eye arrangement allows it to see backward and forward. Its large ears twist and turn to pick up the slightest sounds, and a muffled cough or a slight shuffle of the feet is enough warning to change its course. Two powerful hind feet are its best means of defense. When pushed hard, these oversize feet can propel it 5 yards per jump, and some hunters claim a run-

Cottontails

The one thing that cottontails can do better than any other variety of small game is *hide*. When a cottontail breaks out of late season cover like this, it usually manages to surprise the dickens out of the man doing the hunting.

The end of a successful hunt! Note the abundant young trees and grass. Cover like this is a natural for rabbits.

ning rabbit spends more time in the air than on the ground. Old hotfoot is no pushover.

As prolific as it is, the cottontail can't live without good habitat. Many hunters confuse cover with habitat. Habitat provides both food and cover. When farmlands are abandoned or not used for agricultural purposes, the land grows sour and lacks important organic matter the rabbit needs. On land such as this, there is no shortage of cover, but food such as grain, alfalfa, clover and other legumes is missing. Without these, the rabbit cannot exist. In this respect, there is a direct correlation between the cottontail and man.

The rabbit's insatiable appetite puts it on unfriendly terms with botanists, farmers and nursery owners. Its victims spend large sums trying to thwart its efforts in dismantling flower beds, gardens and fruit orchards. A variety of snake-like garden hoses, whirling windmills and special powders are used with little success, but a small mesh fence several feet high is a workable solution. With all the accolades that have been heaped on old thumper on TV and in print, the rabbit is a destructive pest to those who work the ground for a livelihood.

The brown speedster leaves many telltale signs for the hunter. Where rabbits are in good supply, well-worn paths crisscross through weed patches and crab apple thickets. Chewed apples, stripped bark from young trees and droppings are positive signs. On bitter cold days, rabbits tend to hole or take refuge in swale bottoms, under brush piles or any cover where

they are out of the wind. A rabbit's fur is very thick, but it's not windproof.

The hunter without a dog has to be on the alert. His quarry has an assortment of quick escape methods plus the element of surprise. All the action is packed into the first 3 or 4 seconds. When a scared rabbit hits two 10-foot jumps per second, it's nothing more than reflex shooting for the hunter. There's no time to lose: it's swing and shoot.

The hunter with a beagle can relax. The beagle isn't the greatest router, but its super-sensitive nose can unravel with ease the cottontail's twisting, turning escape route. In fact, some hunters won't shoot when the rabbit is routed; part of their satisfaction comes from listening to the hounds.

It's a mistaken belief that the dog "circles" the rabbit by forcing it to return to the area it was routed from. This is not true. A rabbit circles instinctively, and the diameter of the circle depends a good bit on available food supplies. Where food is plentiful, the rabbit may live its entire life on less than 5 acres. Unless pushed very hard, a rabbit will not leave the area it knows foot-by-foot. In this case, the chase may last less than 10 minutes. In areas where food is scarce and predation is high, the rabbit is more wary and will make a ½-mile circle. Unless the rabbit holes, it's a sure bet to return.

A rabbit runs in short spurts ahead of the dog. Farm rabbits may allow the dog to get within a yard or so before taking off. Rabbits that match wits with predators can be 200 yards ahead of the wailing beagle. Rabbit hunting has a sophisticated side; the hunter must have comprehensive knowledge of his quarry to be ultimately successful.

Picking the Best Rabbit Gun

Since I cut my shooting teeth on rabbit hunting about the same time that President Roosevelt made his famous, " . . .nothing to fear but fear itself" speech, I have used the 5 decades since then to analyze the rabbit-gun problem. It's true a special gun is not needed and that practically any type of shotgun will suffice, but it goes deeper than that. Waterfowlers and pheasant hunters take great pains in selecting the proper outfit, and, in my book, the rabbit hunter should be just as selective. His shooting is just as demanding.

One of the first considerations when selecting your outfit should be stock length. Stock length on a shotgun is vitally important. The measurement from the face of the trigger to the end of the center of the buttplate determines a good bit how quickly the hunter can shoulder the shotgun. The old method of nestling the buttplate in the crook of the elbow to see if the index finger can curl around the trigger has been a standard for determining the "fit" of the hunting shotgun. While there is merit in this system, it's not infallible.

If the "fit" of the shotgun is measured just in stock length, the rabbit hunter's scattergun should come to the shoulder in one fluid motion when the hunter is wearing hunting gear. The latter is extremely important. New guns are normally purchased in early fall when the weather is warm and the buyer is wearing light clothing. At that moment, the stock can be a full inch too long. This error will not surface until the temperature is down and the hunter is wearing heavy clothing.

Unfortunately, most shotguns on the market today carry stock lengths running out to 14¼ inches. For every hunter this length of stock will fit, there are two it won't. The long-stock theory is supposed to be based on statistics showing that today's male is taller and built on a larger frame than hunters from the gaslight era. Statistics can show whatever comes out of the computers, but the fact remains there are tens of thousands of us who are not built like professional football players. To offer just one stock length makes about as much sense as a shoe manufacturer cranking out only size 12 boots.

There are too many variables to settle for just one stock length. Neck and arm lengths along with cheek thickness enter into this complex problem.

(Above) Beagles and bunnies are a natural. Many seasoned rabbit hunters won't even tote a gun into the field unless the beagle's nearby. Given the rabbits taken here, it's easy to see why the beagle is a favorite.

This father/son team is using 20-gauge shotguns. The father is shooting an Ithaca Model 37 pump, while the son is using an H&R Model 490 Topper singleshot.

The fit of the shotgun is as personal as a toothbrush. It's a combination of many factors. In simple terms, the rabbit shooter will be better off with a stock length that doesn't interfere with quick shouldering of the shotgun in any type of weather, and it should have sufficient drop to allow the shooter's eye to sight parallel with the top of the barrel. When the cheek falls on the comb, the eye should see along the top of the barrel not into the middle of it.

Older hunters should take a second look at their shotguns. As we grow older and our muscles stiffen and reflexes slow down, the shotgun seems to grow longer. That extra inch of stock can spell disaster. As important as this aspect of the rabbit gun is, many hunters refuse to recognize stock length as their Achilles heel. Not me. At 62 and at a height of just 5 feet, 9 inches, I cut my hunting shotgun stocks to 13⅜ inches from the face of the trigger to the end of the buttplate or recoil pad. The stock that will not come to the shoulder in one sweeping motion and fit immediately into the shoulder pocket will work against the rabbit hunter.

Drop is another term that needs little explanation. It's a vertical measurement in inches from an imaginary line coming back from the top of the barrel to the top of the heel or the end of the stock at the butt pad. Placing a straight edge on the barrel and allowing it to extend back over the stock will permit a measurement from the straight edge down to the heel. Comb drop is measured from the straight edge down to the front of the comb.

Shotguns manufactured from before the turn of the century until the mid-1930s carried, what I consider, excessive drop. Some rabbit hunters will disagree with me because drop is essential to the rabbit hunter. The modern shotgun doesn't have a lot of drop, and the Monte Carlo design runs somewhat downhill to the shooter's face. This allows the comb to slide

gauges runs from 1,100 feet per second up to 1,400. Larger gauges have larger shot charges.

Rabbit hunting can't be classed as long-range shooting, and this rules out tight chokes, and with heavy brush and vegetation making up most of the rabbit's habitat, long barrels are a nuisance. The hunter who takes advantage of the benefits offered by the 26-inch barrel, bored Improved Cylinder in single barrel outfits and Improved Cylinder and Modified in two-barrel guns will ultimately be more successful. A compact shotgun delivering a quick-opening pattern is essential to the rabbit hunter.

During four seasons, I stepped off 62 rabbit kills made by myself or hunting partners. My statistics show that 34 rabbits, or 55 percent, were taken under 25 yards. Another 18 cottontails, or 29 percent, were stopped between 26 and 35 yards. The remaining 10 kills were made over 35 yards.

I'm sure my rough measurements were far from being accurate to the very yard, but they did prove beyond a

I pattern a shotgun by first firing a number of shots from a benchrest using double sandbags. I aim the shotgun much like a rifle being careful to use the same sight picture for each shot. Repetition is the name of the game here. It takes only a few shots to show where the pattern is forming in relation to where the gun is being aimed. The next step is to find out if the shotgun hits where the shooter thinks it's being pointed.

This is more or less reflex-type shooting. The gun is brought quickly to the shoulder in a sweeping motion with the butt pad fitting in the shoulder pocket. The shooter slaps the trigger the instant the muzzle hits the target. The idea is just to point and shoot. It's surprising how many shotguns won't impact on the target even though they splattered it thoroughly from the benchrest. The error is not with the gun; it's the shooter's fault. In most cases, the shooter does not keep his face on the comb of the stock.

A lot can be done for a shotgun today in regard to pattern density and

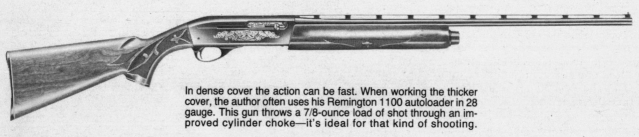

In dense cover the action can be fast. When working the thicker cover, the author often uses his Remington 1100 autoloader in 28 gauge. This gun throws a 7/8-ounce load of shot through an improved cylinder choke—it's ideal for that kind of shooting.

under the cheek instead of biting into it when recoil is heavy. Guns with little drop normally shoot high and are a boon to the pheasant hunter who is shooting at a rising target. The rabbit hunter is shooting downhill so to speak, and his shot charge should impact right where the eye sees the muzzle pointing.

Our forefathers were taught by their forefathers who believed implicitly in sheer power and tight patterns. Back then, very little was known about internal or external ballistics. High brass shells, long barrels and tight chokes were in vogue. The desire for "power" was such that big gauges like the 8 and 10 were used with ear-splitting amounts of powder and massive charges of heavy shot.

Today, after two world wars and the attendant ballistic research, we know that many of the old beliefs have no basis. For instance, a long barrel doesn't shoot any farther than a short one. Barrel length beyond 25 inches offers no appreciable increase in velocity. Neither does one gauge shoot harder than the others. Velocity in all

shadow of a doubt that in my area 84 percent of my successful shooting took place under 35 yards. Only 10 kills or 16 percent were made at the shotgun's normal patterning range of approximately 40 yards. The rabbit hunter should be interested in what type of pattern his scattergun offers at 25 yards instead of 40.

Not many hunters take time to pattern the shotgun. It is just taken for granted that the smoothbore shoots where it's pointed. That unwise belief has cost many a hunter years of frustration. A few years ago, when I ran a commercial shooting range, I ran across a perfect example of what I just mentioned. The customer brought a well-made double 12 bore. He complained that he missed everything that ran or flew. Ten shots from a solid rest on my shotgun patterning range proved why; neither barrel was on target. One barrel shot high and to the right, the other put its shot charge a full 2 feet above the aiming point. If he'd patterned the shotgun when he purchased it, he wouldn't have had 5 years of frustration and failure.

impact point. Briley Manufacturing in Houston, Texas, Nu-Line Guns in Harvester, Missouri, and Prodash Choke in Pompano Beach, Florida, can fit most any shotgun with interchangeable chokes. Nu-Line Guns can move the pattern nearly a foot towards center. Sometimes hunters will blame poor shooting for their misses when the fault actually lies with the gun. This is why it's of the utmost importance to pattern the rabbit gun at close range.

The brush-type scattergun should be a "fast" gun, and hopefully, this will dispel another fable from the past. Whether it sounds logical or not, a "fast" gun is not necessarily a super lightweight outfit; neither does it have to be short or compact. The fast gun is a balanced outfit that feels a bit muzzle heavy but carries its action weight centered between the hands and has a stock length compatible with the hunter. Weight is of little significance. A truly balanced shotgun can be handled faster, pointed quicker and will produce more kills than one weighing considerably less.

This hunter is waiting for his dog after bagging a cottontail. Note the shotgun. It's a Winchester Model 1400 autoloader complete with screw-in choke.

There is still some controversy over the proper gauge for the rabbit patch, but basically, all gauges of the same barrel length and choke boring will form patterns the same size in diameter. Perhaps the 410 bore can be ruled out here since its pattern is slightly smaller. A 28-inch barrel bored Modified will have a 3-foot pattern at 30 yards from the larger gauges. At 40 yards a Full choke offers a 4-foot pattern with a Modified adding ½-foot more. Dropping down to rabbit-shooting distances, the Full-choke has a 2-foot pattern at 25 yards, Modified ups it a few inches and Improved Cylinder runs out beyond 3 feet.

Since a shotgun is not aimed like a rifle, but is pointed, a wider pattern will make up for small pointing errors. Since a large pattern at close range is important for the cottontail hunter, it's also a necessity to have the pattern saturated with shot pellets. The more a pattern spreads out, the thinner it becomes. When large shot is used, pellet count is way down and a wide pattern will have many open gaps. Since every pellet that strikes the quarry contributes to the

kill, small shot is a must for briar patch dwellers. Large shot has a higher ballistic coefficient making it fly farther, and it does offer more kinetic energy. These factors are of prime importance to the waterfowler and pheasant hunter, but are of no real consequence on a 25-yard rabbit shot.

Old-time hunters stuck with 4s and 5s, but back then rabbits were all over the place, and the hunter picked only the choice open shots. A 1¼-ounce load of number 4 shot contains 169 pellets. Going up to 5s pushes the count to 213. However, number 6s offer 281 and with 7½s the count jumps to 437. The 1¼-ounce load of 7½ has 224 more pellets than the same weight of number 5 shot has. For very thick brush or briar-type shooting, I have used with good success a 1⅛-ounce load of number 8s that contains 462 pellets, and that's a lot of pellets coming out of a 20-gauge.

The type of action is up to the individual. It can be as much psychological as physical. I'm an advocate for the two-barrel shotgun. In a sense, two barrels of different chokings represent two different shotguns. I stick

with short barrels and open chokes like Improved Cylinder and Modified. One of my rabbit outfits carries interchangeable chokes bored nearly wide open and super tight.

Rabbit hunting is not for a select few, nor is it a safari-type hunt in some distant land; it usually takes place in a weed patch or swamp bottom. The common inexpensive single shot gives the same results as the custom over/under. The complexity of rabbit hunting is its simplicity; it has no peer when it comes to the excitement of untangling a maze of rabbit tracks in a new snow. The insignificant cottontail doesn't rate being mounted or having its hide displayed in the hunter's den, yet, without the briar patch speedster, the hunting fraternity wouldn't generate many new converts.

Cottontails mean something to almost everyone. They are pests to the landowner, the staff of life to the predator, and the hunter's most provoking target. The rabbit is the most important game animal in the lower 48 states. May he hold that position for decades to come.

HUNT SOUTH AFRICA!

by TED GORSLINE

"Our biggest problem is getting U.S. hunters to come here—once they give it a try there's a better-than-even chance they'll be back again."

"THE SOUTH African white rhino is a remarkable conservation story. Once almost extinct, it is now again plentiful enough to hunt though it definitely is not the symbol of what South African hunting is all about. White rhino hunting is expensive—the most expensive shooting in the country. However, when you start talking antelope, South Africa is one of the best big game bargains in the world today. At least 2,000 Americans figured that out and went there last year. You can go on safari and shoot six or more antelope, air fare included, for the price of shooting a single white rhino.

The variety of animals in South Africa is enormous. In all there are 36 species of big game including all the big five. However, you must shoot white rhino instead of black rhino since the latter are protected.

Most South African antelope hunts today cost less, on a price per head of game basis, than many of the guided hunts in western North America. For example it can cost $6,000 and up for a 50 percent chance to shoot a dall sheep or a big horn ram, or $9,000 or more for a 50 percent chance to shoot a grizzly bear—air fare not included. On top of it, you have to buy the expensive licenses whether you get a bear or not.

In South Africa you face the manipulation of two fees, the daily fee for the services of a hunter, vehicle, tracker, skinner, cook and your accommodations; and the trophy fees which are paid to the landowner or government if a hunting concession is involved. The longer the hunt, the lower the trophy fees; the shorter the hunt, the higher the fee. For example on a 6-day hunt you might have to pay $2,500 for a Cape buffalo whereas on a 30-day hunt, on which you have shot lots of other game, you can probably get one for $1,000. But it's possible to hunt for 10 days for $3,000, pay rinky-dink license fees of about $10 for animals like the magnificent kudu, after which you only pay a trophy fee (for kudu about $450) if you kill (or wound) an animal.

Some game animals like the heavily tusked wart hog are very cheap, $60 being an average trophy fee for each pig shot. Even the handsome blesbok which is found *only* in South Africa is normally available for a trophy fee of less than $200. It varies from ranch to ranch.

The taxidermy fees are generally much cheaper in South Africa than they are in North America. For example a greater kudu head, about the size of an elk head, can be mounted for $200 (U.S. dollars) and the taxidermist can arrange to send the trophy to North America by ship which is not that expensive.

Choosing the Right Rifle

The hunting is now so well organized and the standard of the outfitters so high that all you really have to do on safari is shoot and shoot well. You are sure to see game. So it's important that you choose the right rifle, scope and ammo combination, and that you practice enough to shoot well.

The rifle you will shoot most is your antelope rifle, and all things considered the magnums like the 7mm Remington using 175-grain bullets, the various 300 Magnums (Norma, Winchester, H&H, and Weatherby) using 180-grain bullets, the 338 with 250-grain bullets, and the 8mm Remington Magnum with 220-grain bullets are the best basic antelope calibers. European calibers like the flat shooting 8x68 using bullets like the 187-grain RWS H-mantle bullet at 3,180 fps are excellent too. The standard brand U.S. bolt-action rifles like the Remington 700, Winchester 70 and the Ruger 77, or any rifle based on a 98 Mauser-type action are all good. Flat-shooting rifles of this genre are fine for any antelope from the little bushbuck right up to the 1,500-pound Livingston's eland.

In general it's a good idea to use heavily-constructed bullets like Noslers because some of the antelope, like the wildebeeste and sable, are

Huntable, yes, but few shooters take advantage of the availability of giraffe in South Africa. Trophy fee: about $800.

The nyala, a brush-dwelling antelope, is plentiful in South Africa. Trophy fee: about $600. (Photo courtesy SATOUR)

Gorsline took this 26-inch nyala using a 375 H&H and 300-grain Silvertips.

Professional hunter Ron Sparrow was with the author when he downed this nice warthog. The author used a 375 H&H. Trophy fee: $60.

The fact is that most South African hunting is seldom far from a safari vehicle. You often spot animals from the safari car and then get out to stalk them. And I've never felt the weight of a rifle during a stalk. So you can shoot a long-barreled, heavy rifle to help tame the recoil or you can even hollow out the butt of your rifle and put lead shot inside to help deaden the kick.

Telescopic sights are important for hunting the larger antelope. Not all shots are long; in fact most shots at kudu and brush dwelling nyala, for example, are at close range—so you don't want too powerful a scope. You should either use a fixed 4 power scope or a variable in 3x to 9x. They are both good and the variable will help you to compare trophy heads. It's a good idea to use Dual X or tapered cross hairs.

Your large antelope rifle will double as your leopard rifle, and you will want to be able to see the cross hairs clearly in dim light because most leopards are shot over bait in the evening. For this same reason the scope should have good light gathering qualities.

Dangerous Game

If you want to spring for the money there is dangerous game hunting for the big five. Cape buffalo can be had at trophy fees of $1,000 to $2,500 and lion for up to $3,000. White rhino run between $5,500 and $7,500. Leopard trophy fees run about $1,500 U.S. dollars right now and elephant are going for about $3,000 and up. These prices fluctuate according to the balance between the South African rand and the U.S. dollar. As I write, the prices would probably work out to about 10 percent less than quoted above but those prices are fairly typical.

tough. It helps to be able to drive the bullet into a vital area regardless of the angle the antelope is standing at. And the angle you see may be the only angle you will ever get. More importantly, the heavily constructed bullets won't devastate the smaller antelope like the bushbuck. You are not hunting varmints.

Most of the antelope, with the possible exception of the handsome water buck, are good to eat. But if you plan to shoot many of the smaller antelope too, like the reedbuck, then it's a good idea to include a light, flat-shooting 243, 6mm Remington, 25-06 or 257 Weatherby Magnum in your battery. Again, as a general rule of thumb, use the heaviest bullet weights available for the particular caliber. If there is a bottom line in a rifle for South African antelope hunting it is that it be flat-shooting because you never know when you are going to get a shot at an exceptional animal 300 or 400 yards away. When this happens you want to be ready.

The only reason for going to one of the standard calibers like the 30-06, 270, 280 Remington (7mm Remington) or 308 is because you already have one that you can shoot well (and this is an excellent reason for sticking to it) or because you are bothered by recoil. It's better to be accurate than overgunned, but if you can handle the

recoil, you should choose a rifle that will let you squeeze out the last few yards of range.

It's true that you can handle 95 percent of the shooting with a 30-06, but if the critter in that last 5 percent is a 56-inch kudu and he escapes, you'll regret it. The largest kudu and nyala I saw in Africa, and both are normally brush dwelling antelope, were between 350 and 400 yards away. I didn't shoot because I wasn't sure of my gun and my ability to use it. When this happens there's seldom a chance for a reply. In my case there wasn't, at least not for really big animals.

The kudu have really bounced back in South Africa. The good numbers are a result of conservation efforts coupled with the reality that plentiful game means a source of income for South Africa's landowners. Trophy fee: about $450.

Some of the largest elephant to be found in Africa reside in, and seldom stray far from, Kruger National Park. While the park is strictly off-limits to hunting, surrounding private lands can be productive. Trophy fee: about $2300 and up.

South Africa has the best white rhino hunting in the world, but the hunting for lion, leopard, elephant, and buffalo is not as good as it is further north in places like Zimbabwe and Botswana. There just aren't the large numbers of animals to choose from because most of South Africa's lion (2,500), buffalo(25,000), and elephant (7,000) are in Kruger National Park and the hunting for these species is generally along the border of the park. It's a problem of choice. The only lion you get a crack at, the one that wanders out of the park, may not even have a mane. Herds of buffalo with as many as 700 animals are sometimes out of the park and, in the near future, it seems that Cape buffalo will become even more widespread.

Ranchers have been reluctant to reintroduce buffalo onto their property because they can carry the same diseases as cattle. However, a disease free strain of buffalo exists in Addo Elephant Park, and it would appear that these animals will soon be used to reintroduce the Cape buffalo onto large stretches of private land. South African Cape buffalo seem to have thick and heavily bossed horns although horn spread is not exceptional, 43 inches being a very good bull. But the bulls are real handsome and chunky old helmet heads. There are some huge elephants in Kruger National Park, perhaps the very largest in all of Africa. The largest bulls, and there are a few like this, carry an estimated 150 pounds of ivory on each side, but these really big chaps never seem to leave the park.

White rhino are most common in Zululand, and leopard are found in a great many areas in the western part of the country. It seems that wherever there are scrub covered mountain ranges in the Transvaal, there are leopards. White rhino are found on a great many private ranches, and they are not aggressive compared to black rhino. They can actually be tamed. However, wounded white rhino *do* charge. Hunter Rob Deane showed me the skull of a big bull white rhino that his father Norman dropped in full charge at just 9 yards.

Your heavy rifle for dangerous game should either be a 458 Winchester using 500-grain soft points for lion or solids for rhino, buffalo, and elephant or a 375 H&H Magnum using 300-grain soft-nosed bullets (or Silvertips) for lion and 300-grain RWS solids for buffalo, elephant and rhino.

South African hunters have mixed feelings about which is the most effective caliber. Rob Deane from Zululand Safaris, the oldest safari company in South Africa, has shot hundreds of buffalo and elephant and can't see much difference in the killing of the two. They both work. Ronnie Sparrow, who has dumped charging buffalo at a few feet, likes the 458 Winchester. Both calibers have their advantages. The 458 is, undoubtedly, the better rifle in a thicket and has an edge as a stopper; the 375 H&H is adequate in all situations and, because it has a trajectory almost identical to the 30-06, it can double as an antelope rifle.

I used a 375 H&H with 300-grain Silvertip bullets on nyala and warthog, and it dropped these little critters so fast that it was shocking.

Other Species

As mentioned, some species of South African game like the blesbok and the bontebok are found nowhere else in Africa. And shooting a Rowland Ward sized antelope of these two species, or of about six others including the red hartebeeste, is not that difficult. But it's not easy to shoot Rowland Ward sized kudu, because they are a very popular antelope, and many really big kudu have been shot in the past.

An interesting aspect of South African big game hunting is that there is no bag limit on some species. You can keep shooting as long as you are willing to pay the trophy fee. For example, you can shoot five wart hog for just $300 and some European hunters, who are addicted to wild pig hunting, actually go to South Africa just to shoot warthogs.

The seasons are months long too, year round in some cases, but the best hunting is in the cooler months from June to the end of September. In addition when you hunt in South Africa you are hunting one of the few countries in all of Africa where most game populations are managed on a scientific basis and where most animals are actually increasing. Any animal that is legal to shoot is not rare, threatened, or endangered. You are just hunting the natural surplus. Even black rhino are increasing in South

This white rhino bull charged the author and his professional hunter Ron Sparrow—the gentleman taking dead aim. At the last moment the rhino turned, not a shot fired. Pulling the trigger would have been expensive. Tophy fee: $7500.

The black rhino is fully protected in South Africa. Fortunately, the decline in the black rhino population has been stopped. In fact, South Africa is the only country on that continent where the black rhino is increasing in numbers. (Photo courtesy SATOUR)

Africa, and it's doubtful that the same can be said for any other country on the continent. However they are not plentiful enough to hunt.

The Future

Just like America, South Africa had a grim history of game decimation around the turn of the century. But a few farsighted individuals like Paul Kruger, who is the equivalent of America's Teddy Roosevelt, began setting aside large game reserves. This certainly helped to turn the conservation problem around.

The real reason for the boom in

A member of the antelope family, the little Klipspringer weighs in at about 35 pounds. Trophy fee: about $100. (Photo courtesy SATOUR)

South Africa offers the hunter an opportunity to bag sable. The weight runs from about 400 to 500 pounds. Trophy fee: $1000. (Photo courtesy SATOUR)

throughout South Africa as biltong (a kind of dried meat or jerky). Finally, the same animal that will be sold as venison can first be sold as trophy. When you pay the trophy fee for an animal that you have shot on a ranch, you only get the hide and horns. But then who is going to fly a 1,500-pound eland carcass home anyway? In effect, the rancher can sell the same animal twice, the head and horns go to you and most of the meat to someone else.

The result is that nowadays it is often more profitable for a rancher to have wild game on his land than cattle; and one rancher told me that he is going out of the cattle business to let his land revert back to its original state. If anything, antelope populations can be maintained at higher levels now than they could in the pristine past. Much of the South African ranch country is semi-desert, and in an attempt to make things better for the cattle, most ranchers drilled wells on their property years ago. These artificial water holes made for cattle now help to pull the herds of game through the periods of drought that tend to devastate antelope populations in places like South West Africa. The result is that antelope which disappeared many years ago in parts of South Africa, because of indiscriminate shooting (many ranchers thought the antelope competed with cattle), are now increasing at a remarkably fast rate. There are even auctions, just like U.S. cattle auctions, where the object of the sale is antelope for restocking. Some antelope, like the bontebok, which was once considered to be an endangered species in South Africa is once again plentiful enough to hunt.

So it's odd but true that one of the greatest boosts to antelope conservation in South Africa today is the American trophy hunting market. Like it or not, game populations are exploding in South Africa while the situation in much of the rest of Africa varies from uncertain to grim, both from a game conservation point of view and from a political stability point of view. South Africa is certainly worth a try. Professional hunter Francois Loubser, who guided me to a good kudu says it best. "Our biggest problem is getting U.S. hunters to come here in the first place. That's the hard part. Once they give it a try there's a better-than-even chance they'll be back again."

For details about South Africa hunting contact Dennis Engesser, Sharps Travel, 91 Yonge Street, Toronto, Ontario, M5C 2R3, Canada. ●

South African antelope populations today is economic. Wild animals that were formerly their "own owners" now legally belong to the owner of the land they live on and he can sell them in several ways. If an animal is truly rare, it cannot be hunted, but it can be sold to other ranchers to use as the basis of new breeding herds. More common antelope are sold as meat on the European market, especially in Germany, Belgium and France where antelope are marketed as "venison." Antelope are also sold widely

Move Fast

Mule deer, unlike whitetails, migrate from one area to another—but they don't all at once. This trophy straggler didn't move fast enough.

EACH YEAR the outdoor and hunting magazines are filled with deer lore. Like most would-be hunters at the ripe age of 14 or 15, I eagerly pored over these magazines cover-to-cover and began to mold my hunting tactics. From all I read, I doubt there is a single big game animal that has had more words written about it than the American deer, be it mule deer or whitetail. As a result, there are a lot of different hunting techniques which have been applied to the pursuit of the various deer species. For the most part, however, a common thread runs through all of them; the importance of moving cautiously through the deer woods, going very slowly and carefully without making a sound.

"Walk a step then stop and listen for 10 steps." This is one phrase I've run across many times during my reading about deer hunting. Others suggest sitting in one spot, staying as motionless as possible lest a deer that may be about to move into view be spooked. Never, do I ever remember reading about just walking rapidly through the deer woods in hopes of spotting and shooting a good buck. In other words, to hunt deer "correctly,"

The author has had considerable mule deer hunting success by hunting "on-the-move" as opposed to traditional "still" or "stand" hunting.

and Bust Mulies

For some, the mule deer is the elusive trophy of a lifetime. If you know the mulies habitat, habits and apply the author's techniques, that trophy can be yours.

by RICK JAMISON

All of the trophy mule deer racks seen here were taken by the author when he employed his "move-fast" tactics.

do not simply blunder through the forest — take each step, one at a time. In the opinion of many hunters, that is the only way to kill a buck, and that's that.

There is certainly nothing wrong with those hunting tactics. Many of the aforementioned techniques were written about by scribes who have probably hunted longer than myself. There's no doubt that thousands of deer are killed every year by hunters who, for the most part, employ the *move cautious,* or *sit-in-one-spot* tactics.

Habitat Makes the Difference

After having hunted deer a good many years myself now, I am convinced that the bulk of the "quiet approach" deer hunting methods are keyed to hunting whitetails, not mulies. Whitetails, in general, have a reputation for being smarter than mule deer. It's generally thought that if you can bag a whitetail you ought to be able to bag a mule deer. However, I'm not certain it's because mule deer are any dumber than whitetails. The answer probably lies in the fact that whitetail deer, as a whole, have been

more intensively hunted and exposed to humans for a much longer period of time. In addition whitetails have become accustomed to not only living in heavily hunted areas, but also in close proximity to man. They see man, in some instances, almost on a daily basis, and apparently know pretty much what he's up to once hunting season opens. Deer east of the Mississippi have gone through many generations of hunting seasons. Consequently, through natural selection, the species has had the "opportunity" — developed the ability — to adapt or wise up. In simple terms, the deer that expose themselves to hunters get shot. A good portion of a deer's habits are inherited. If a fawn matures in a herd that is more secretive, wary, or has developed traits that allow it to escape hunters during the hunting season, the fawn will probably pick up these traits and pass them along when it reaches breeding age. Simply put, deer that get shot, get hit by cars, or killed by dogs don't pass on any traits. Only the deer that survive live to produce more fawns. Consequently, those deer have become "people-wise," hence, they avoid hunters.

Mule deer, on the other hand, have traditionally inhabited the wide open spaces of the West where there is lots of country and fewer people. Therefore, unlike their eastern cousins, mule deer haven't had the "opportunity" to wise up through generations of intensive hunting pressure.

There are other differences between the two deer, some of which are the result of habitat. For example, there are much smaller tracts of timber in the East than are generally found in the West, with the eastern timber patches often interspersed with small fields or broken by well-traveled roads. Much of the countryside east of the Mississippi has been altered drastically by modern farming practices and other by-products of civilization. This may be one of the reasons that whitetails have developed the habit of bedding down in one spot (generally in thick cover), and then moving to another location for nighttime feeding — hence the terms "feeding area" and "bedding area."

Mule deer inhabit large tracts of forest or rangeland, browsing (for the most part) on wild, native types of vegetation rather than on domestic

Mule deer are known to migrate great distances, especially when they inhabit regions that vary drastically in altitudes. However, such is not always the case. Much western deer habitat is composed of rolling hills where the mulies don't migrate seasonally. However, they still change residence from one week to the next, and the hunter who moves fast has a better chance of locating a trophy.

This particular 4-point mule deer was taken by using Jamison's move-fast-and-bust-mulies technique.

crops. Mule deer can also make a meal anywhere they find low-growing shrubs. In other words, mule deer "feeding areas" and "bedding areas" are not as well defined as those of the whitetail. The two areas can be practically synonymous when it comes to mule deer, a point often overlooked by the average hunter.

There is yet another difference between the two cousins regarding their habits. Due partially to the habitat, the whitetail deer not only has specific feeding and bedding areas, but it also tends to inhabit a relatively

small section of real estate. As a result, it knows its home ground intimately.

Mule deer, by contrast, migrate great distances in some regions, from high country in the summer to lower country in winter. It is true in much of the West that mule deer do not make these elevational migrations if they live in lower country where there are rolling hills and no extremes in elevation. Even in sections such as this, however, mule deer apparently wander greater distances than do whitetails back East.

It all boils down to the fact that, when it comes to mule deer, you can't always predetermine where they'll be. The whitetail hunter generally has a specific section of real estate that he considers to be a deer hunting hotspot; and that hunter will most likely return to the same area (if he has been successful), year after year. This is not always the case with mule deer. Since they are apt to either migrate or move considerably, last year's hotspot might not be so "hot" next time around.

When I first began hunting mule deer, I applied whitetail hunting tactics. I remember taking good mule deer bucks 2 years in a row in the same spot in northern Arizona. After

bagging two good bucks within the first half day of the season for 2 years in a row, I thought I really had a hotspot and knew what the deer "pattern" was in that particular area. I returned to the same spot the third, fourth and fifth years — without success! During 2 of those latter 3 years, there were almost no deer to be found in that immediate vicinity. It took me 3 years to realize that I had been merely lucky in stumbling onto those deer which just happened to be in the area the first 2 years that I hunted it.

In contrast with this, I traveled to south central Pennsylvania several years ago for a whitetail hunt. Not knowing the area, I relied upon a friend to direct me to a particular valley that he said had always contained whitetails in good numbers as long as he could remember. Following his precise direction, I found the area, and within a half hour of daylight had shot a 10-point buck.

I grew up in eastern Kansas where whitetails inhabit wooded areas along creeks and river bottoms, moving to corn or alfalfa fields during the nighttime to feed. I recall one patch of timber and brush about 1-mile square that always contained a lot of whitetails. Another section of real estate not 5 miles from the first had timber

Mule deer, unlike whitetails, are known for changing residence. The hunter who moves fast and covers the off-road jeep trails will have a chance to spot signs before the hunt begins.

It pays to scout for deer sign *before* the season opens. If there's snow on the ground it's very easy to spot tracks. In the absence of snow, tracks can still be seen if the area is well populated with deer.

and brush very similar to the first, but contained few, if any, whitetails. After a nearly 10-year absence I returned to this same area and found that, just like before, the same spot held whitetails while the other didn't.

Again, pre-season scouting, when it comes to hunting *any* deer, is important. Unfortunately, the "weekend-before-you-hunt" scouting trip for mulies could be misleading. If mule deer are migrating, which they sometimes are during hunting season, the deer you spot on the weekend *may* be many miles away by next Wednesday.

As a practical matter, most hunters have only weekends or vacations free to hunt. If vacation time is used, it's usually taken *during* hunting season. *If* scouting is conducted, even if the hunter lives relatively close to his hunting area, it's generally done the weekend *before* the season opens and it's possible that the deer may have moved by opening day.

Finding Mulie Stragglers

Though week-old tracks and droppings can be encouraging to the unsuccessful deer hunter, they don't do much toward putting venison in the family freezer. The important thing is to find a set of tracks filled with a deer.

So how does a mule deer hunter up his chances of success when he isn't seeing deer? First of all, when it comes to migrating mule deer, they don't vacate an area all at once — there's still deer to be had if you play your cards right. Secondly, I am convinced that one of the best ways to find these elusive stragglers is to forget all the old *whitetail* hunting saws about creeping along in the forest. When it comes to mule deer hunting, cover a lot of ground in a hurry!

I've consistently taken mule deer in areas where the hunter success runs

less than 20 percent year after year. Not only have I filled deer tags but I've generally filled them with good-sized, mature, 4-pointers. It's been done not by pussy-footing around day after day but rather covering country, learning the terrain, and finding where the deer are (and aren't). I much prefer to walk very fast and cover a lot of ground until I either spot steaming-hot sign or deer. That is the time to slow down, pussy-foot around, and start looking closely.

One of the reasons that I have developed such a deer hunting habit is partially a result of my own physical and mental makeup — I just don't like sitting still when temperatures hover near the zero mark. Secondly, it's my nature that if I'm not seeing a buck *here,* he must be over *there.* Consequently, I want to get over *there* as soon as possible. Perhaps this all sounds like a cat chasing its tail but it has worked for me.

Frequently, one of the best ways to get into country where there is a lot of deer is simply by driving down the road and looking for them. A lot more miles can be covered with a vehicle than on foot. Don't get me wrong, I'm not suggesting road hunting — the vehicle is used only as a means for determining where the deer are prior to

(Left) Fresh rubs where bucks have polished their antlers are yet another sign that deer are around.

(Below) The hunter can scout for deer in advance of the season or, move fast and scout it during season. Fresh droppings like these are an indication your mulie may be nearby.

burning up a lot of shoe leather and nonproductive hunting time. If I find a likely-looking spot, but haven't been seeing deer, I'll generally hunt a short distance from the road in a small loop and take note of the sign while looking for deer. If I see promising sign, I'll hunt a little more thoroughly and pay particular attention to how fresh the sign is. If I'm still not seeing deer after spotting a good amount of sign, I'll try and figure out where the deer moved and then head in that direction.

When using such a fast-moving method you'll frequently jump deer without seeing them. That's okay, as long as you know that they *were there*.

(Above) Even the hunter who moves fast should stop occasionally to glass distant peaks or canyons. The hunter who moves fast can glass more area in a given length of time than the hunter who "still" hunts.

(Right) The sportsman who hunts by moving fast may have to take a shot rapidly. He should become intimately familiar with his rifle to be effective in the field. For example, a hunter should instinctively know where the safety is without having to think about it. When a big buck is jumped, the safety should be released by the time the rifle's butt hits the hunter's shoulder.

Note the size of the rack on the mulie buck standing to the left. It was jumped in a very large area of pushed over juniper trees. When jumped, it offered an excellent 150-yard standing shot.

Perhaps the indication of having jumped a mulie will be a freshly abandoned bed in the snow, or fresh droppings, or both. If the cover isn't too dense (frequently the case in mule deer country) you may even see your "straggler" and get a shot.

By moving fast, I'm talking about really striding out. However, if you can get to a piece of ground that has some elevation to it, you just might find yourself overlooking a good section of real estate. Stop, pull out the binoculars, and take note of what the country below and around you contains. If you don't find what you're looking for (in terms of either deer or sign), move to another area. Don't stay in one spot long unless you're convinced that the deer are there.

Some hunters who have heard about this technique have been concerned about blundering into deer and spooking them. This *will* happen if you're walking fast through the forest. Deer, however, will usually see you first, although I have frequently found that they aren't quite as alarmed by someone walking quickly as they are by someone who is being sneaky about the whole thing. Even if you do spook a deer and see nothing more than a hind end disappearing in the brush, or perhaps only hear it crash away, it's probably just one deer. A mulie usually won't go far. Your best bet is to simply stay put — right where you jumped your buck — for 10 or 15 minutes. When you go after your mulie straggler, go slowly and carefully and use the binoculars, even if it's dense forest. Those field glasses may help you spot that deer before it spots you.

As you can see, the traditional hunting methods haven't been completely thrown out the window,

(Right) It's a habit of some extremely large bucks to seek out unlikely areas such as the wide open flats, as seen here. Though there won't be many deer in this type of country, the hunter is generally only after one. Jamison has frequently jumped very large deer in such unlikely-looking habitat during the hunting season. A hunter who moves fast can cover such country more quickly, and there's little worry about the deer getting out of sight in the thick cover before the hunter can get a shot.

they're just being more efficiently applied.

If you just want to get a buck — any buck — you're probably better off hunting where the *bulk* of the deer are. Generally, there are a lot of younger bucks that will be found with does during hunting season. A high percentage of legal mule deer will be these younger bucks, and your chances of bagging one of these will be a whole lot better than bagging a big ol' mossy-horned buck.

However, if it's one of the mossy horns that you're looking for, you'll be looking for something a little different than you will be if you're just looking for any legal deer. I have frequently found that the biggest mule deer bucks will be located (during hunting season) in areas where there are very few deer. Because of the lack of competition for food, and the absence of heavy hunting pressure, these well-antlered mulie bucks have the opportunity to live through many more hunting seasons. For the sportsman who's after a large mule deer, the fast-moving, cover-a-lot-of-ground-in-a-hurry technique works ideally. There's often such a vast amount of country between such big deer that the hunter will be better off by moving fast until he spots sign that indi-

cates ol' mossy horns has been in the area. At that point it's time to slow down and start looking *carefully*.

The largest mule deer buck I have ever seen was in Northern Arizona in a region of flat juniper country. There was almost no grass and little browse available — there were mighty few deer in the area. However, I knew that the area had a reputation for producing big-racked bucks. I hunted hard and covered a lot of dry, dusty forest floor that revealed nothing in the way of tracks from other hunters. By the third day of the season I hadn't seen a deer, but I did manage to find a small waterhole far from any road. Upon approaching the "tank" I could see that there were mulie tracks

(Left) Moving fast to bust mulies requires a lot of offhand-shooting practice. Regardless of cover, the hunter may not have the opportunity to take advantage of a rest or even get himself into a sitting, kneeling, or prone position.

(Below) Jumped deer often mean parting shots that require a bullet that penetrates deeply, won't destroy an excessive amount of meat. Hunters who reload should take advantage of bullets like these shown here—they are designed especially for big game.

around its circumference. Looking closer, I found the tracks of a deer that were larger than any I had ever seen. Those tracks made it apparent that the deer was entering the area of the waterhole from the northeast. I then started to methodically and slowly move in the direction of those tracks.

After a half day of sneaking around in the junipers, I spotted the buck. I didn't know it was *the* buck or even *a* buck at first for all I could see was an eyeball and part of its face framed by a large juniper bush. As I crept up behind the juniper, the deer, which apparently had been bedded down, immediately stood up on the other side of the bush not 10 feet away — and froze. So did I. I strained to see pieces of antler through the juniper, but couldn't — just the eye. We eyeballed each other for long seconds when I decided to make a move. I rushed around the right side of the juniper in an effort to identify the deer and possibly get a shot before it disappeared. I moved as fast as I could but the deer was faster; I got a good look at the largest, most massive, widest rack I

have ever seen. Simultaneously, instinctively, my rifle was coming up, and then I was looking through the gun's optics. The big buck was in the top of the scope's field of view — the crosshairs weren't aligned — when it disappeared in the trees. Though I didn't get a shot, I got close; and, I'm convinced that had I not quickly covered a lot of ground I would never have spotted the sign that eventually brought me to the biggest trophy mule deer I'd ever seen.

Another advantage to moving fast comes after the deer season has been under way for awhile. Deer frequently move as a result of hunting pressure and can often be found where there were none before the season opened. By covering a lot of ground, possibly in unlikely spots, the hunter is more likely to get shooting action than if he continues to stalk the thickets slowly and carefully, not covering much ground.

A little pre-season preparation can increase the fast-moving hunter's odds. Some pre-season exercise in the form of jogging doesn't hurt although

physical conditioning isn't absolutely necessary for this type of hunting. The hunt doesn't have to be strenuous. You can stroll along at a comfortable pace but one that allows you to get over the next ridge in the not too distant future. Besides physical conditioning, the fast-moving hunter should consider some practice at offhand shooting. He should also practice getting a well-placed shot off quickly. The sportsman who hunts "on the move" will frequently not have a chance to look for a natural rest for shooting. He may not even have a chance to get into a sitting position or kneeling position. He may be walking along and look up to see a deer just standing there only a few yards away, ready to bolt at even an instant's hesitation from the shooter.

With a little practice, quick accurate shots are not difficult. And with proper bullet selection, very little meat will be wasted — even when a north-bound deer is shot in the south end. If your pussy-footing around hasn't blessed you with a big deer, move faster and bust a buck. ●

A Western Dream Vacation

Is It For You?

by JIM ZUMBO

The mule deer is the No. 1 choice of hunters who head west for big game. It's racks like these that entice Eastern hunters to head west.

MORE THAN 20 years ago I sat in an upstate New York tavern and stared at a mule deer rack hanging on the wall. I didn't know what a mule deer looked like in the wild, because I'd never been West. I resolved to change that situation, and I did shortly after. I moved to the Rockies, and hunted everywhere I could.

Most sportsmen can't simply move West as I did, and many will never enjoy hunting in the wide open landscape. It's natural to be apprehensive and unsure of a place you've never been to, especially a hunting trip for strange animals.

If you've longed for a western hunt, consider doing it now. Prices are getting higher, and you're getting older. Furthermore, big game herds have never looked better for most species. Now is the time to do it.

Let's look at basics when planning your hunt. First, of course, you must determine the animals you want to pursue. Though the West offers sheep, goats, moose, whitetails, lions, and bears, among others, the "Big Three" are mule deer, elk, and antelope. I'm referring to the Rocky Mountain mule deer, which is the largest of the seven recognized subspecies, and the Rocky Mountain elk which grows much larger antlers than the Roosevelt elk, an animal that lives exclusively along the West Coast.

Once you've decided on the quarry, you need to determine your capability of having a successful hunt. Do you want to try it with a couple buddies, or do you want to hire an outfitter? Your decision depends on the amount of time you have, the money you want to spend, and your ability to find shootable animals. Let's take each species and examine the possibilities.

Antelope

Antelope are by far the easiest to hunt. They live in open areas and are highly visible. Vehicle access is usually good, and much of their domain is land administered by the Bureau of Land Management, a federal agency which offers public hunting on hundreds of millions of western acres.

In prime antelope country you can expect to see several hundred animals in a day, many of them decent bucks. If you're intent on a good representative buck, a do-it-yourself hunt on public land is a nice option. But if you're after a trophy class buck that measures 15 inches or better, you might do better by teaming up with an outfitter who has access to private land where hunting is restricted.

Wyoming is by far the top antelope

Western terrain is often an uphill/downhill proposition requiring (in many cases) a team effort and the right equipment to get downed game back to the car—which may be miles away.

For those who're blessed with a healthy body and a desire to hunt hard, backpacking for elk can be an experience of a lifetime.

This muley buck was taken by the author in Colorado, a state that is also known for its superb elk herd.

state. In 1982, the Wyoming Game and Fish Department offered 102,000 antelope tags, which is more antelope than in the rest of the West combined. A lottery draw is required for antelope with an application deadline of March 15 annually, but each year several thousand licenses are left over and offered on a first-come, first-serve basis. Antelope tags in other states are more difficult to obtain. Montana and Colorado are the next best choices in terms of large antelope populations.

Most antelope hunting seasons are in September. Be prepared for hot weather, though a storm can drop rain and even snow in much antelope range. The big problem with heat is cooling the antelope carcass once it's down. The animal must be skinned immediately, and the meat refrigerated. If possible, take the carcass to a local processing plant, or bone the meat and place it in a large cooler. An average buck antelope will yield between 35 to 40 pounds of trimmed, boned meat.

In many Wyoming antelope units you can take one or two extra animals, but they must be antlerless. At no other time in modern history have there been more antelope in the West. If you've always wanted a pronghorn, make your plans now.

Mule Deer

Mule deer are on the middle scale between antelope and elk. The big consideration, of course, is the kind of muley you're looking for. Do you want a decent buck, or are you interested in a trophy-class deer?

Every Rocky Mountain state has mule deer hunting, so you have plenty of choices. According to Boone and Crockett record book statistics, Colorado is by far the biggest producer of trophy bucks. If you want a truly big buck, either sign on with a reputable outfitter in a good area or do some homework and make a hunt by yourself. Prepare to hunt hard, however, because trophy bucks earn those outsize antlers by avoiding hunters for 5 or 6 years. They'll be as wary as any whitetail you've ever hunted.

There are some 90 national forests in the West. Excluding some on the West Coast, all offer good public hunting for mule deer. Many BLM lands have good mule deer habitat as well. If you're thinking of a hunt on your own, you'll have no problem finding a place to hunt. Your biggest concern will be getting away from other hunters. You might be surprised to learn that western deer country can be crowded with hunters, especially near roads. Of course, you might welcome other hunters to help move deer around, but if you're after a buster muley you won't want any competition. Then too, a western dream hunt shouldn't be a competitive event. You'll no doubt want to enjoy the gorgeous country as well as experience a good hunt.

Many hunters drive to the Rockies and tow a tent trailer or camp trailer, or some set up tents on public land. Others base in a motel close to the hunting area and drive to and from deer country every day. If you're intending to do this hunt yourself, you should have a sturdy hunting vehicle. Much of your hunting will be in mountain areas where you'll leave paved roads far behind. A 4WD is a wise choice if you have one. Sudden storms can leave you stranded. Worse yet, you might not be able to penetrate prime deer country with a lesser rig. In much mule deer habitat, you might have to drive several dozen miles just to reach deer country. Let's say, for example, that you've determined the best hunting on a particular mountain at 8500 feet elevation. If you leave the pavement at 5500 feet, you might need to drive winding, rugged roads to get where you want to go. A bad spot in the road a dozen miles or so from the good hunting spot could prevent you from reaching it. Although paved roads cross good deer country in many places, you'll have to work harder to get away from other hunters if your vehicle won't allow you access off the pavement.

Should you hire an outfitter? This depends on your motives. If you want the comfort of a warm tent, a horseback ride into the high country, a guide, great food, and superb camara-

derie, then by all means sign up with a reputable outfitter. Most will offer the niceties I just described. However, there are some outfitters who are crooks, pure and simple, just as there are dishonest people in every segment of life. If you don't know any outfitters, or don't have friends who can

recommend one, check magazine ads or write to several outfitter's associations for a list. Check past references, but do it by phone. You'll learn much more by chatting with a past client than in a letter. When you book with an outfitter, sign a contract or at least make sure you understand ev-

This hunter is scouting a high country basin for elk. It's Western scenery like this (Montana, in this instance) that makes for a memorable hunting experience.

In the author's opinion, Rocky Mountain elk are the toughest trophies of the big three.

Here an outfitter looks for elk with a spotting scope. Outfitters are often the best way to go for a Western hunt.

erything he offers for the fee he's asking. Most outfitters will ask you to sign an agreement and will require a deposit when you book the hunt. One way of insuring a good outfitter is to book with an agent such as Jack Atcheson of Butte, Montana. Atcheson and others like him deal only with outfitters who are reputable.

If you aren't in top physical condition, you can still enjoy a mule deer hunt, despite what you've read about hunting hard in high elevations. You might forfeit the chance for a big buck in some places, but if you work at it logically you could tag a nice deer. One option is to hire an outfitter who uses horses for most of his hunting. Many guides hunt from horseback or use horses to climb high into deer country. When there, the clients are placed on stands and the guide makes drives. Another possibility is to drive as high as you can and contour a ridgetop without doing much climbing. Bucks often bed just under a ridge, so you'll have a good chance of jumping one. Another option is to have a companion drive you up a mountain early in the morning. Put a daypack on and walk leisurely down the mountain, hunting as you go. Don't let a physical ailment prevent you from hunting, but by all means use good judgment. If you question your ability at all, have a good physical before you go, and don't overdo it. In the event you find yourself following an energetic young guide who walks or climbs too fast, don't be a hero and try to keep up. You might cause a problem for yourself. Tell the guide you can't keep up; if he persists, speak to the outfitter. If you want more details about mule deer hunting, write for my new 358-page hardcover book, *Hunting America's Mule Deer*, Ashley Valley Publishing Company.

Elk

Elk are the toughies of the Big Three. Jack Atcheson, is one of the most avid elk hunters I know. He's hunted around the world for big game, and rates the elk as the hardest animal to hunt. I agree. Elk live in the most miserable, rugged country they can find. Heavy timber is their bailiwick, as far from roads and people as they can get.

If your mind is set on a dream elk hunt, strongly consider hiring an outfitter. Though you'll find elk on much the same public land as mule deer, you're dealing with a different critter.

Finding a good bull elk takes some doing. They'll be hiding in thick forests during the daylight hours, and feed just a few minutes after dawn and before sundown. It takes more than luck to catch them in meadows as they feed, so the only choice is to locate them in the trees. You'll need plenty of time as well as savvy to center a bull in your scope.

To add to the problem, elk often require a marathon hike or climbing bout to get where they live. The big animals will continually seek out undisturbed places where they aren't bothered by hunters. In a lot of the West, that means a horseback trip or an extensive walk.

You can make an elk trip on your own in states where elk are numerous, and you'll have a decent chance of seeing animals if you work at it. Colorado is the top elk state, with an annual harvest of about 30,000. Many of those elk are young bulls, cows and calves, however. You'll have your work cut out for you if you expect to see a mature bull, even at a distance. If you're after a trophy, try Montana or Wyoming. Those states produce many more big bulls. Plan as much time as you can for your elk hunt — at least 10 days. It might take half that time alone to simply locate a herd.

If you're successful, the biggest problem you'll face is getting that downed elk out of the woods. A big bull will weigh about 800 pounds. Typically, you'll drop an elk on a steep hillside, and the road will be somewhere above you. That's when you wonder why you squeezed the trigger in the first place.

Elk—tough to hunt, tough to pack out. A good-sized bull will weigh in the neighborhood of 800 pounds.

This Midwest hunter bagged a huge Utah mulie. Note the truly beautiful rack.

An outfitter, of course, will take care of getting your elk out for you. He'll probably quarter it and haul it out on a pair of horses. However you elect to hunt this big animal, give it some serious thought as to your hunting preferences and objectives. You can do the elk hunt on your own or with a guide, but it will be a tough proposition no matter which way you try it.

Planning the Hunt Yourself

An important aspect of going on a hunt without an outfitter is obvious — where do you go? How do you begin looking for a good hunting area? The first thing to do is write to the state you're interested in and ask for a copy of their hunter success breakdown for herd units if they have one. Compare the best units and look them up on a state map. Then determine the extent of public land in the vicinity. National forests are usually marked on road maps, but you might need to write to the Bureau of Land Management for their maps. There are several guidebooks to public lands on the market; perhaps your library has a copy.

If you read outdoor books and magazines, you'll probably have a good idea of some of the best spots from articles you've read. Keep those in mind, and don't be afraid to ask public agencies in the area for more information. Even Chambers of Commerce are eager to help.

Another important necessity of planning a hunt is to obtain the proper permits. Some of the best western states have limited tags available on a lottery or first-come basis. Montana, for example, sells 17,000 elk tags to nonresidents on a first-come basis. Each year the licenses sell out more quickly than the year before. Idaho offers 9500 elk licenses and 10,500 deer licenses on a similar basis. Wyoming requires a lottery draw for *all* nonresident tags, including deer, antelope, elk, and the rest of the big game species. Application deadlines are extremely early — February 1 for elk, and March 15 for other big game.

Don't tarry once you've made up your mind to go. Get the information early so you won't miss a deadline or fail to get in on a first-come tag.

When you put it all together and finally make it West, sit down on a rock, breathe the sweet crisp air of the Rockies, and enjoy the magnificent scenery. Your dream hunt has arrived. And who knows, you might never be the same until you do it again — and again. The West has a way of doing that to you. ●

Murray Burnham of Burnham Brothers Game Calls is standing next to a trophy mule deer. Note the atypical nature of the rack.

Dove Hunting Tips & Techniques

by LANCE CORNELL

THE MOURNING DOVE is, perhaps, the most respected game bird in America in terms of speed, aerial maneuverability, and difficulty in hitting. More than one hunter has lamented the fact that it took a box of shells or more to collect a limit of the little gray birds. To be sure, it takes some doing to hit doves with any degree of consistency, though there are ways to improve the odds. The most important aspect, however, is finding enough doves to shoot at. In some areas that's no problem; in others it is.

Doves are legal game in all but

"No other shooting sport quite matches up to the demands of dove hunting.
Master it and you can shoot about anything else that flies."

about a dozen states. In several states, doves are numerous enough to allow a hunting season, but public sentiment runs high against making them game birds. Regardless, documented biological data proves that hunting simply allows a harvest of surplus birds and doesn't pose a threat to dove populations.

Most dove seasons open September 1 each year and close on varying dates, depending on the state. Longer seasons are generally the rule in southern states. Except for extremely southern locations where whitewings dwell, mourning doves are the primary species. They're the most ubiqui-

Sunflower fields like this one have always proven to be dove hunting hot spots. In cover like this it's important to mark each downed dove carefully as the "finding" can be tough, especially without a dog.

In the more arid parts of the country, dove hunters stake out water holes at dusk and dawn for best results. (**Editor's Note:** Even off-road trail ruts filled with a catch of recent rain can provide a bonanza of dove shooting in the more arid climes.)

tous game bird in the U.S., and live in each of the lower 48 states.

Shooting Techniques

Hunting techniques vary, but a few basics apply everywhere. Technically, the term "hunting" isn't quite appropriate. It's more a shooting activity, since little hunting is done.

Pass shooting is by far the most popular tactic. Doves are shot as they fly overhead, usually around feeding areas but also in the vicinity of waterholes.

Doves are fond of agricultural crops. Fields of wheat, barley, millet, oats and other grains are commonly visited by doves. In parts of the South, literally thousands of birds can work a single field.

Pass-shooting, no matter where it's done, requires two essentials: a good shooting location and reasonably acceptable shooting skills. The first requirement is most important. If you don't have doves zinging by, you won't have a chance of hitting them.

When I'm hunting a strange place with the intent of pass-shooting, I try to figure a strategy that will place as many birds within shotgun range as possible. The best way is to quietly observe a feeding area to determine the pattern the birds are using. Doves often settle into a standard routine and fly the same routes. More than once

I've stood idly along a field while another shooter was getting all the action a hundred yards away. Until I understood that doves had distinct, daily flight patterns, I wasn't putting many birds in my game pocket. But by figuring where and when they were most apt to fly, I was able to greatly increase my shooting opportunities.

In early morning, doves leave their nighttime roosts and head for feeding areas. During hot weather, they might stop for a drink of water, but that's not always the case. If you can find a direct path from roost to field, you're in for great shooting.

Finding a roost isn't always easy, but if you're determined, you can watch the behavior of the birds in the late afternoon. Doves tend to be gregarious when roosting and like to bed down with many of their brethren. I've found roosts where upwards of a thousand birds were present. One place was a small thicket of red pine in a hardwood forest. I found the roost while on my way out of the woods from a squirrel hunt. The next day I positioned myself between the pines and a wheat field and had unbelievable action as literally hundreds of birds flew overhead.

Once doves leave their roosts, they might be somewhat unpredictable as to their flight pattern, but they still

stick to a routine. Birds often loaf during feeding periods, generally in a place where they have good visibility. A tall, dead tree at the edge of a grain field is a likely candidate as a dove attractor. Doves will rest between feeds, on those limbs, surveying the tablefare. You can take advantage of such a place by positioning yourself close to the tree and shooting at incoming doves, or you can take up a place directly under the tree. The latter has a disadvantage because it's downright tough to draw a bead on a fluttering dove about to perch on a branch. It sounds easy unless you've tried it. Furthermore, birds often come in swiftly and sit before you can get a shot. When that happens, you're stuck under the tree with a dove sitting over your head. When you move, the bird will invariably flush, but too often a tree branch will block your view or the bird will take off in an unexpected direction.

Utility wires strung between poles bordering grainfields are a prime perching spot for doves, but there is one obvious reason why you shouldn't shoot at doves on or near those wires. Your shot might cause damage to the wires or insulators, but there's no reason why you can't take a station *near* the wires and shoot at incoming doves, providing the direction of your shots is away from powerlines. Each

Dogs and doves are a natural, especially when shooting over water holes. The dove season is also the *first* game bird season in most areas of the country. It serves nicely when it comes to peeling the summer fat off your favorite hunting dog.

A full limit of plump doves like these can make for some of the finest game bird eating you'll ever experience.

year I hunt along a grain field paralleled by power lines. Doves sit on the wires by the dozens. Once I counted more than 150 birds perched side by side between two poles on a single line. My usual strategy is to sit next to an irrigation pipe in camo garb about 50 yards from the lines. Doves coming into the utility lines behind me are easy pickings.

During normal flight, a dove slips along at a rather steady pace and isn't a difficult target if the proper lead is taken. But if you spook the bird as you raise your gun to your shoulder, the result is a remarkable maneuver envied by fighter pilots. The bird changes course abruptly and often makes a transition from a consistent flight to a short, jerky gyration that will almost certainly draw your shot pattern to a place where the bird was but isn't when the lead gets there.

To avoid the difficult aerial antics, try to stay hidden. Don't wear bright clothing, and don't take up a position where you stick out like a sore thumb. Try to spot birds long before they come in range so you can ease your gun up and get on them without being spotted.

Doves will fly by in singles, doubles, or large groups. Because doves change formation rapidly (and often) it's easy to make a premature move when several birds are within range.

The dove's slate-gray coloration seems to blend into darn near any foliage. As a result, the use of a dog will improve your chances of finding every bird you knock down.

Portable camouflage blinds are favored by many shooters. Also note the camo shirt and hat worn by the hunter.

Large, lone trees on the edges of grain fields serve as roosting points for feeding doves. In this instance the shooter stationed himself near the tree in the background and had instant success.

Directly above the shooter is "one that didn't get away." The shooter positioned this blind on the edge of a water hole, not far from a grain field — a perfect dove shooting combination.

Just as you prepare to lead a particular bird, another might look better. To avoid this problem, pick an incoming bird out of the flock and stay with it. If you drop it, continue your swing on the next best.

A word of caution when shooting at more than one bird: By all means mark where the first dove drops before trying for a second, especially if you're in a brushy area. Doves, because of their slate grey coloration, are tough to find, unless you have a dog. I've lost downed doves in places where it seemed impossible to find darned near anything. In most cases I find the birds, but only after a lot of searching which costs good shooting time.

Doves have a late afternoon pattern that makes them vulnerable. About an hour or so before sundown, they take a drink before heading to roost. Though birds actually may drink on and off during the day, late in the day finds them thirsty. If you can find their favorite watering hole, you're in for perhaps the fastest shooting of all.

I have a favorite hidden waterhole in the Utah desert that never fails at sundown. Birds come in from miles around to drink. By positioning myself in the dense greasewood bushes near the waterhole, I pick the birds I want to shoot at. Since I'm well hid-

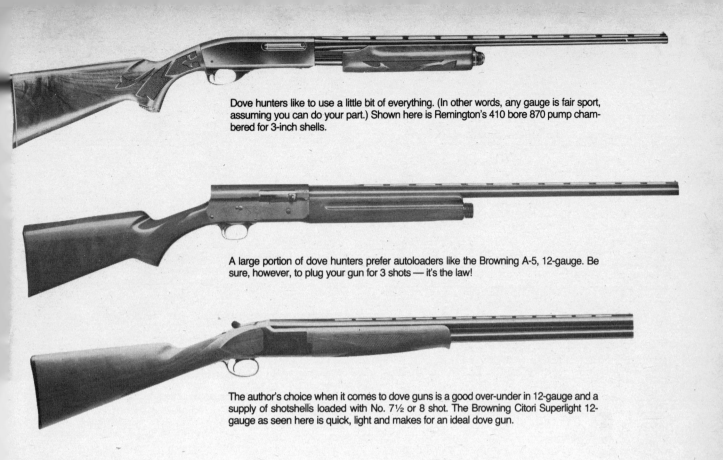

Dove hunters like to use a little bit of everything. (In other words, any gauge is fair sport, assuming you can do your part.) Shown here is Remington's 410 bore 870 pump chambered for 3-inch shells.

A large portion of dove hunters prefer autoloaders like the Browning A-5, 12-gauge. Be sure, however, to plug your gun for 3 shots — it's the law!

The author's choice when it comes to dove guns is a good over-under in 12-gauge and a supply of shotshells loaded with No. 7½ or 8 shot. The Browning Citori Superlight 12-gauge as seen here is quick, light and makes for an ideal dove gun.

den and directly adjacent to the main flight path, it's nothing to kill 10 birds with as many shots. I seldom run a string of 10, though, because I generally miss the second bird when trying for a double. When the first bird folds, the others swerve and veer as only doves can do.

A few years back while hunting deer in Texas, I watched dozens of doves swarm to a particular waterhole in the afternoon. When I claimed my buck, I traded rifle for shotgun and had a fine dove shoot several evenings in a row. Although there were other watering spots in the area, the one I shot over seemed to attract most of the birds.

Doves are frustrating when they are flying to water as they will often veer off a short way and perch on a tree limb, power pole, or light on the ground in full view. It seems they defy you to stalk them, and when you do, they never allow you to approach within shotgun range. This is standard behavior for doves—they're nervous birds and seldom sit still when danger threatens, even from a distance.

This behavior also makes it difficult to flush doves when they're feeding. This technique is as close to actually "hunting" doves as any other, but it's often the most futile. When a bird

takes to the air, it often flits about, never assuming straight flight. I find this kind of shooting the hardest of all. When you shoot at the first bird, several others usually take off at the same time. From then on, the remaining birds in the field will be alerted and will probably spook out of good range.

Find Those Birds!

One of the toughest parts of dove shooting is finding all you drop. I never hunt without my black Lab, unless I'm shooting in an area that's relatively free of brush and weeds, such as stubble fields and desert areas with sparse vegetation. My shooting usually improves when my dog sits alongside because I don't have to concentrate on where the last bird fell. The dog does it for me. Besides retrieving dead birds, a dog is valuable for chasing down and catching cripples.

Now and then I'll shoot doves along a river or next to a large waterhole. My Lab is invaluable then, because I'm not terribly fond of swimming. It's also great training for dogs, especially since dove season is the first game bird season in most places, and dogs are fat and lazy from the hot summer. You can work with your dog as much

as you want with training aids, but a good dove shoot complete with the smell of gunpowder and freshly killed birds does much to get a dog into the swing of the seasons to come.

I would be remiss if I didn't mention my favorite way of shooting doves. Show me a wild sunflower patch and I'll plunk down alongside them with shotgun in hand. In fact, I've gone so far as to buy a yellow hat and a green shirt so I'd look like an oversize sunflower. Doves feed in the sunflowers extensively, and always seem to be present wherever these plants grow.

Shot Size, Choke and Gauge

Shot size is seldom a talking point in dove hunting circles. Most shooters use 7½ or 8 shot. Being small birds, doves often escape nice patterns of larger shot. You'll want all the pellets you can get. And this means 7½ or 8 shot.

Choke varies with the preference of the shooter and the circumstances of the shoot. If you're trying to bust high-flying birds in a pass-shooting situation, you might want a full-choke, but you'll have to be good to score consistently. I prefer a modified choke and take my chances.

Choice of guns is up to the shooter. I've seen everything from 410's to 10-gauge Mags alongside in the dove fields. I'd recommend you shoot whatever you feel comfortable with. You probably won't be doing a lot of walking while shooting doves, so weight isn't much of a problem. I like an over-under 12-gauge, simply because I'm used to it. Since doves are regulated by federal laws, it's illegal to have a gun with a capacity of more than three shells in the chamber and magazine combined. Be absolutely sure your gun is properly plugged if it has a capacity greater than three shells.

Cleaning and Cooking

When the shoot is over, your next step is to clean the birds and prepare them for the kitchen.

When I first started dove hunting, I dutifully plucked every bird and carefully kept its little carcass intact, even the legs. It took a few years and a bit of friendly teasing from buddies to do it another way. Simply twist each wing off, press down with your thumb under the breastplate, and pull the breast free from the rest of the body. You'll have 95 percent of the meat, and you'll have the job done in a quarter of the time. Every now and then, though, when no one is looking, I'll pluck a bunch of birds and admire my handiwork. Then I'll stuff them and cook them like Cornish game hens.

Although doves feed extensively on grain, their meat is dark, and their flavor is gamy. Some folks like the flavor as is, others don't and doctor it a

Plucking doves can be laborious; however, some hunters prefer it to simply removing the breast — the source of 90 percent of the meat on a dove.

bit. I belong to the latter group. All of us are entitled to our own opinions, so I'll mention a tip or two that I use to make them more palatable to my tastes. First I soak the birds in milk for 6 to 8 hours before I cook them. Then I brown them in bacon grease, put them in a casserole with a whole diced onion, diced celery sticks, my choice of appropriate poultry spices, a can of mushrooms, and a can or two of cream of chicken soup. Simmer until the meat falls off the bones.

If you like their natural flavor, toss them on a barbeque grill, baste frequently with butter, add a little salt and pepper, and have at it.

One way or the other, you'll find a way to like these birds on the table. But enjoying their culinary qualities is only half the fun. The other is being in the outdoors with plenty of birds flying and plenty of shotgun shells in your pockets. No other shooting sport quite matches up to the demands of dove hunting. Master it and you can shoot about anything else that flies. That's a fact. ●

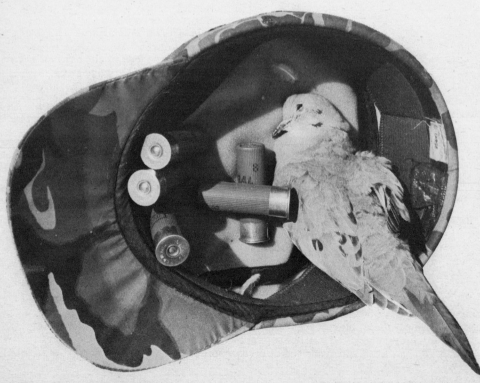

A hatful of fun is one way to describe what's seen here. More often than not it takes the 5 shotshells shown just to bag a single dove!

LIGHTWEIGHT hunting rifles are in vogue. Again. Eighty-odd years ago, short, light saddle guns like Winchester's Model 94 and Marlin's Model 93 were doing a land-office business. Such sizzling new cartridges as the 30-30 and the 25-35 were heating up discussions in the hot-stove league. The long, heavy, black powder boomers were being relegated to the back of the bus. Fans of the hunt were discovering the pleasures of a rifle so light one could carry it all day with scant fatigue; so short, one could stoop under a log without knocking off the front sight. Alas, not for long.

We had a war in Europe, and the doughboys returned singing the praises of the Springfield. Before long, nimrods were taking to the field bearing bolt-action sporters with 9-pound hefts and barrels as long as a Chrysler. Shot some game with 'em, too.

The years fled. We had another war; this time the returning soldiers touted the Garand. The day of the popular semi-auto had begun. Hunting rifles grew ever more cumbersome, ever more complicated. The little lever-action carbines were still around, still in use, still dropping assorted fauna as efficiently as they ever did, but the romance was waning.

The '50s saw an increased interest in scope sights. Marlin, Savage, and Winchester did a fair job of adapting their bread-and-butter guns to the use of glassware, although their stocking specifications continued to favor iron sight users. The '60s ushered in the Magnum era. Hunters of the scrawniest swamp deer went into a trance, came out frothing for a *magnum*. Readers of the firearms periodicals knew they needed at least 24 inches of barrel to realize true magnum ballistics; 26 inches was even better.

When the '70s dawned, nearly everyone was tromping the woods armed with scope-sighted, long-barreled, overweight, bolt-action or semi-automatic sporting rifles, frequently in calibers better suited to derailing a train then knocking over a nice buck. By the end of the decade, some of these ole boys were getting a little long in the tooth. Maybe a bit smarter, too. Why, they wanted to know, did they have to tote ordnance heavy enough to give a gorilla a hernia, powerful enough to smush a polar bear? The answer, of course, was they they didn't.

LIGHTWEIGHT RIFLES ARE BACK!

Short actions, slim-lined stocks and abbreviated barrels all add up to weight that doesn't have to be carried.

by CLAY HARVEY

In the author's opinion the new Winchester Model 70 Featherweight is the most attractive "production" rifle ever turned out in the U.S. The 100-yard accuracy ran from 1¾ inches to about 2½ inches, at the bench.

In 1980, Winchester broke the ice and resurrected their Model 70 Featherweight. Two years later, Ruger parried with the Model 77 International. Early in 1983, Remington entered their Model Seven into the fray. All of a sudden, it seemed, there were three terrific new *hunting* guns — light, short, and handsome. (Well, at least two of them were short. The Featherweight was of normal length for a non-magnum Model 70.)

Now, these rifles were not exactly the first to test the current of public acceptance. In the mid-'60s, Remington had introduced a nifty little bolt gun, the Model 600. It spawned the Model 660, was closeted for a while, reappeared some time later in a less-attractive permutation to be vended through the discount houses as the Mohawk. While I'm certain Remington made a dollar or two on the 600 line, it failed to become a classic success story by a long shot.

The tried-and-true lever guns were still in evidence, as light and as short as ever. In most cases, the stock design was still less than ideal for scope use, and in some instances the calibers available were hardly what one could refer to as all-around. Progress had abandoned the levers.

The only truly compact semi-autos were chambered for short-range or varmint cartridges. Remington and Browning autoloaders were both girthsome and weighty, as was the Remington Model 760 pump.

Single-shots, such as the Ruger Number One and the Browning 78, while adequate in available calibers and suitable for scope mounting, were a bit on the heavy side when scoped, slung, and loaded. (I don't believe *any* single-shot makes an ideal all-situation hunting rifle, anyway.)

Which brings us to the present. Let's establish some criteria, delete all modern sporters that don't measure up, and see what we have left. We'll start with an arbitrary weight ceiling of 6¾ pounds. (We have to cut it off somewhere, and a rifle that starts out at 6¼ pounds bare will end up weighing nearly 8 pounds field-ready.) We should insist on a range capability of 300 yards, which includes bullet drop, retained energy sufficient for game up to elk in size, and accuracy adequate for the smaller species of big game at that distance. The rifle should be reasonably priced and readily available from the average gun shop, not a high-ticket imported item that one reads about but never sees. Finally, the rifle must be stocked properly for glass sights.

What do we have? By my reckoning, just three guns: the Remington Model Seven, the Ruger International, and the Model 70 Featherweight. Let's look at them individually.

Remington Model Seven

The Model Seven is the new kid in town. Rumors have been floating that it's simply a modernizaiton of the old Model 600, *sans* nylon rib, dogleg bolt handle, and space-gun sight, but with the same light weight, short barrel, and laudable accuracy. The rumors are only partially true. The Model Seven does have a short (18½-inch) barrel; it is accurate; it tips the scales at 6¼ pounds as it comes from the box; it is bereft of the strange styling quirks of the 600 series. But it's far from an upscale version of the earlier rifle. The M7 has more in common with the Model 700: cut-checkered walnut stock, hinged floorplate (on the M7, it's steel), nicely contoured bolt knob, swivel studs, bolt release, trigger, and sights.

Stocking on the new gun is perfect for the use of scope sights. The length of pull is 13½ inches, drop at heel 1-inch, drop at comb ⅝-inch. Finish is low-gloss satin, similar to that of the M700 Classic. There is a solid rubber recoil pad. The fore-end sports an unusual Schnabel treatment at its tip. It's a handsome rifle.

The safety — located to the right of the bolt shroud — does not lock the bolt closed. This is said to be a safety feature; the user can cycle live rounds through the action more safely than if the rifle safety were "off." Interesting postulate. (If you do work the action with live ammo, be sure to point the muzzle in a safe direction just in case. No safety mechanism is 100 percent foolproof.)

Okay, so we have a neat little rifle here, short of limb, narrow of beam, impeccably dressed. How does it stack up when push comes to shove? My sample M7, chambered for the 7mm-08 Remington cartridge, weighed 7 pounds, 12 ounces scoped with a Leupold Vari-X III 1.5-5x variable, fully loaded, with a ⅞-inch carrying sling installed. Functioning was bobble-free. Bolt articulation was slick, due in part to the redesigned follower.

At the range, factory 140-grain Remington stuff grouped into 2¼ inches for a half-dozen five-shot strings. Handloads printed 1¾ inches for the most part, with one load averaging 1.69 inches. The load: 115-grain Speer HP, 46.0 grains of IMR 4064 and CCI 200 primers.

Note the Model 70's ribbon-pattern (cut) checkering. It's downright attractive.

The author's Winchester Featherweight came complete with hooded-ramp front and dovetail (adjustable) rear sight.

Rick Jamison has tested an identical M7. He likes to average five, three-shot groups instead of a string of five-shotters, as many writers do. Rick's M7 printed just under an inch with 44.0 grains of Winchester 760 behind the 140-grain Sierra Spitzer. He tried four other handloads that would group 1½ inches or better. His factory ammo did about the same as mine, 2.3 inches.

And so we illustrate that the new Model Seven is functional, as light as the factory catalog claims, and is amply accurate for any big game hunting, including long-range shooting at sheep and antelope. The available calibers are 222 Remington, 243 Winchester, 6mm Remington, 7mm-08, and 308 Winchester. The list is short but complete; a cartridge from that list will cover any type of hunting you should envision short of extremely long-range elk hunting and the big bears.

And what must one yield for such handiness and versatility? A little velocity, maybe 150 fps. That's all. The accuracy and reliability are intact. Remington did their homework.

Ruger Model 77 International

When I first saw the photo of the prototype Ruger International, in

Gun Digest's 1982 edition, I felt like cutting a backflip. Oh, goody, I thought, and ran to check the bank book. No need; I wasn't to see one of the new Rugers in person for more than a year. By then the fire had been

banked, my ardor had lost its urgency.

Don't misunderstand; the rifle was just as I expected, except for the deletion of the butter-knife bolt handle that graced the prototype. I have always had a weakness for Mannlicherstyled stocks, a predeliction for short, compact actions, a fondness for classic lines in a buttstock. All these were there. As frosting there were the handsome Ruger sighting systems (both iron and scope rings), cut checkering in a neat bordered pattern, a stylish stirrup-shaped front sling swivel, a thin rubber buttpad, and the snappy and convenient tang safety button. Then there were the subtleties: a steel forend cap, flutes in the front sight base, superb wood-to-metal fit.

Naturally, the International had the same engineering features as the standard M77 rifles. There were the Mauser-type side-spring extractor, the patented slant-screw bedding system, the satin finished stock, designed to reduce felt recoil, and the superbly adjustable trigger. The Ruger M77 was always a crackerjack rifle.

So why the lost enthusiasm? I dunno. Perhaps the long wait. Maybe the fact that the little gun was so near perfect the bulky trigger guard and floorplate offended my sensibilities more than was warranted. No matter. The gun's here now, and it's a very fine piece; all is forgiven.

The little rifle scales just ½-ounce

SPECIFICATIONS

	Remington Model Seven	Ruger M77 International	Winchester M70 Featherweight
Length (overall)	37½ inches	38⅜ inches	42½ inches
Barrel Length	18½ inches	18½ inches	22 inches
Weight	6¼ pounds	6¼ pounds	6¾ pounds
Stock	American Walnut	American Walnut	American Walnut
Length of Pull	13½ inches	13⅝ inches	13½ inches
Sights	Adjustable iron sights	Adjustable iron sights	Iron sights available
Safety	Two-position, does not lock bolt	Tang, two-position, locks bolt	Three-position, provision for locking bolt
Magazine Capacity	Four	Five	Five
Finish	Satin wood, high-gloss blue metal	Satin wood, high-gloss blue metal	Satin wood, high-gloss blue metal
Features	Rubber butt pad, sling swivel studs, hinged steel floorplate, steel trigger guard	Rubber butt pad, sling swivels, hinged floorplate, steel forend cap, steel scope rings	Rubber butt pad, sling swivel studs, hinged steel floorplate,
Cost	$449.95	$480	$481

The Winchester Model 70 Featherweight is in the middle with a Ruger No. 1 on the left and a Ruger Model 77 International on the right. The Model 70 Featherweight has a 22-inch barrel while the Ruger 77 International's barrel is even more abbreviated at 18½ inches.

over 6¼ pounds unscoped, almost exactly the same as the Remington M7. Length of pull is ⅛-inch longer, which I'm not too happy about; I'm not the tallest guy on my block. Otherwise, stock dimensions are about the same as those on the M7, maybe just a smidgen less drop at the heel and a tad less curve to the pistol grip. The Ruger is ¼-inch narrower through the middle at the action area, making it more comfortable to carry by your side.

Functionally, there have been no problems. The International feeds and ejects on schedule. The trigger pull is good; it has some creep, but not much. In fact, this Ruger's trigger is a little superior to the Remington's.

My sample International will group five shots under 2 inches all day with Hornady Frontier 165-grain factory-loaded 308 ammo. Since I've had the rifle such a short time, I've run no handloads through it. I'm guessing it'll print into 1½ inches with a load it

likes. For now, I'll have to call my test rifle a 2-inch gun.

Let me note that Layne Simpson tested an identical rifle, wrote it up in the May-June, 1983, issue of *Rifle*. Layne's International averaged 1.36 inches for several three-shot strings with the 150-grain Sierra and 45.0 grains of Norma 202. Using 200-grain Winchester Silvertip factory loads, his rifle did even better, 1.22 inches for six three-shot groups. Obviously Ruger has the knack for bedding a full-stocked rifle.

Currently, the M77 International is available in 243 and 308 only. I've been told by Ruger that it is soon to be chambered for the 7mm-08 Remington. There is even a rumor going around that Ruger might fabricate a small batch of 250-3000's. We'll see.

I have also heard about another air-weight Ruger M77. The word is that it will have a slim 20-inch barrel and a stock about like that of the standard M77 except for a few minor weight-

saving details. Said to weigh a scant 6¼ pounds, the new gun is obviously aimed at the Winchester Featherweight. Which we'll now examine.

Winchester Model 70 Featherweight

Right up front, let's establish my lack of objectivity; I am enamored of the Model 70 Featherweight. I think it's the most handsome bolt-action rifle ever cobbled up by a factory. Maybe it's the checkering, so crisp and aesthetically pleasing. Or the deft sweep of the bolt, the exquisite shroud, the trim length of barrel. Perhaps it's the forend treatment, schnabeled and slim. Whatever it is, the Featherweight's got it.

It weighs ½-pound more than the other two guns and has a barrel 3½ inches longer. The resulting increase in overall length is closer to 5 inches because the M70 has a long action, just right for the 270 Winchester or 30-06. Aside from the added length and heft, the Featherweight runs in the same crowd as its competitors. It has satin-finished furniture, high-gloss bluing, a hinged floorplate, cut checkering, a straight "classic" buttstock with rubber pad, a slender forend, sling swivel studs, and it can be had with iron sights. The list of available calibers is more complete. Aside from the two mentioned above, there are the 243, 257 Roberts, 7x57 Mauser, and the 308.

There are other advantages. The M70 has a three-position safety, so you can have your donut and eat it too. There's "on," for when you want to shoot, "off," for when you don't, and "in between," for when you want to cycle loaded ammunition through the action without endangering the neighborhood. There's an anti-bind bolt device that makes for a smooth action. And there's the famous Model 70 trigger than never seems to go haywire.

The sample gun is a 7x57. It works just fine, no miscues in the feeding/extraction systems. Accuracy is about like the others, between 1¾ and 2½ inches at 100 yards with factory loads. No time for handloads yet, and my deadline is upon me. (Gun companies are nearly always slow; editors are always in a hurry.)

Rick Jamison tested a 270 Featherweight last year. It printed 1.3 inches with 150-grain Remington factory ammo, for three three-shot groups. His best load was 58.0 grains of Winchester 785 under the 150-grain Hornady Spire Point, averaging 1.15 inches for six strings. Ed Matunas wrote in *Rifle* Number 87 that his

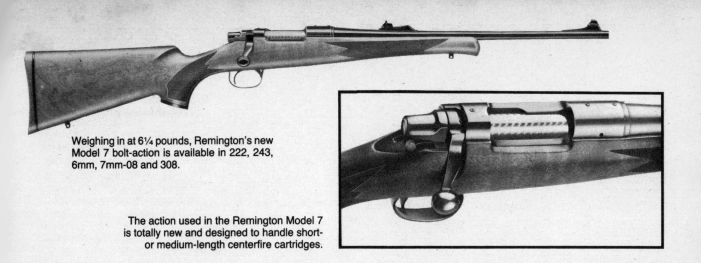

Weighing in at 6¼ pounds, Remington's new Model 7 bolt-action is available in 222, 243, 6mm, 7mm-08 and 308.

The action used in the Remington Model 7 is totally new and designed to handle short- or medium-length centerfire cartridges.

Featherweight, in 30-06, grouped 1.30 inches with 110-grain factory ammo, under 1½ inches with several others.

Conclusions

It is obvious from my testing and that of other reliable sources that cutting weight in a rifle does not hamper *intrinsic accuracy*. Nor does shortening the barrel. Whether the decrease in weight affects *field accuracy* depends on the shooter. (I can shoot any of these rifles 100 percent as well from offhand or sitting as I can other rifles I've worked with.) Additionally, a light compact rifle that mounts swiftly and swings easily is a demonstrable asset when jump-shooting game in the woods.

The advantages of light weight when carrying a rifle for many hours, particularly in mountainous terrain, can scarely be over-emphasized. In brushy country, the shorter the barrel the better. When I was elk hunting in Idaho a few years ago, I humped hill and wooded dale with a 24-inch barreled full-size rifle encumbering my person. What I would have given for a Model Seven or Ruger International at the time!

If I had to choose among the three rifles tested here, it would necessitate thoughtful scrutiny. For hunting in the thickets, I'd opt for either of the short-tubed models. Ditto for mountain hunting of sheep or goats, although I'd not feel hampered enough by the Featherweight to argue the point. If I were after elk or moose spe-cifically, I'd want a Featherweight 30-06 stuffed with 200-grain Nosler handloads, feeling more comfortable with the extra velocity and energy provided by the longer barrel. For open-country hunting, say for pronghorn or Barren Ground caribou, I'd again want the added speed and flatness of trajectory provided by the Model 70's longer tube.

But all the foregoing is conjecture, based on "what-ifs." Who knows when I'll make it out West for sheep, or elk, or even pronghorns? But come fall, God willing, I know where I'll be. Deep in whitetail cover, pussy-footing along, toting a short-barreled bolt-action rifle. It won't weigh me down, and it won't snag the greenery. We'll get along just fine. ●

For those who have a certain love for full-stocked rifles, the new Ruger 77 International will have a lot of appeal. Simply put, it's beautiful. The 77 International is currently available in 243 or 308, with speculation that the rifle *may* be chambered for 7mm-08, or, possibly, a small batch in 250-3000.

USRACO's new Model 70 Featherweight is available in 30-06, 308, 270, 7x57mm, 257 Roberts and 243. It weighs in at just under 7 pounds.

Indian hunting practices were tied to religion and magic as this photograph of Indian rock art, or petroglyphs, attest. (Kate Dowdy photo)

the historic whitetail

by DAN FLORES

To the Indian tribes, to the white settlers and finally to modern hunters, the whitetail deer has meant many things. Flores has captured the heart, soul and the mystery of this magnificent animal.

WHEN EUROPEAN man came to the New World, the North American environment, according to Hall and Kelson's two-volume *The Mammals Of North America*, had shaped 17 races of *Dama virginiana* — the whitetail deer — north of the Rio Grande, and another 13 subspecies in Mexico and Central America. In what would become the United States there were four types of whitetails specially evolved to Coastal Plains, and another five which evolved in geographic isolation on the Sea Islands, a chain off the coasts of South Carolina, Georgia and Florida. There were two major woodland types (including the original *Dama virginiana virginiana*) east of the Mississippi, a transition subspecies in the Central Prairies, and two major Great Plains races. *Dama virginiana ochroura* inhabited the Northern Rockies and Cascades, and the *D. v. couesi*, the Sonoran whitetail, occupied the seguaro deserts of the Southwest. Only on the Colorado Plateau and in the California/Great Basin area did the browsing, brush-loving whitetail fully give way to the more dryland-adapted mule deer *(Dama hemionus)*.

It was in the Eastern woodlands, however, that the whitetail was the dominant ungulate. Naturally shaped by and for forest land, its suitable habitat in the more open country of the West was confined to riparian settings and oak-clad canyons. But from the Atlantic seaboard to where the trees thinned into the bluestem grass prairies and oak groves of the post-oak savannah*, the whitetail in its eastern variations far outnumbered the woodland bison and elk herds.

---

*The post oak savannah is the transition zone in the United States where forest thins out to patches of oak woods with interspersed prairies. This zone runs from the Illinois/Indiana region south through western Missouri, down through eastern Oklahoma on into the southeastern portion of Texas.

Original abundance? In his classic, *The Ecology of North America*, pioneer American ecologist Victor Shelford estimated the average figure to have been 400 animals per 10 square miles in the Eastern forests, with possibly even heavier populations in the prairie-woodland edge west of the Mississippi!

Contrary to popular conception, such amazing figures were not based upon the conditions of a "virgin" continent. Most modern ecologists and historians of environment argue that the term "virgin" has not had an applicability to North America for many thousands of years. Instead, the great abundance of whitetail deer in early America was the direct result of Indian land-use practices, which were designed to perpetuate the continent as a vast hunting ground. Armed with the technology of fire, Indian peoples throughout the whitetail's range annually set understory fires which promoted tender new browse and so nourished whitetail populations. Their abandoned fields, originally cleared with fire and quick to re-forest, less directly served the same end.

The prairie tribes always favored bison over deer, but from the lands of the Micmacs, Narragansets, and Iroquois in the north woods, to the Cherokee highlands and the Seminole swamps of the South, westward to the Caddoan lands on the edge of the bluestem prairies on the western edge of the post oak savannah, the whitetail deer was the most important of all wild animals. Then, as now, it was a difficult creature to hunt successfully. We know, from the early chroniclers such as Mark Catesby and John Lawson, that a variety of methods were employed. Stand-hunting at salt licks, stalking under deerskin camouflage, even snares and "torch-hunting" at night were widespread Indian tactics. That deer were still not easy to take, even with the Indian's highly-developed woodcraft, is indicated by the fact that a deer-dependent people such as the Caddos made 10 deer kills a requisite for joining a war party.

The uncertainty of hunting deer was also reflected in the religious precepts of eastern North American Indians. Universally animists, they regarded deer as beings like themselves, who were under the control of an animal "master" or "keeper." Successful hunting depended upon incantations or perhaps a magical representation of the hunt on rock or cave walls, along with the strict observance of numerous taboos lest the "keeper" not allow its charges to be killed. There thus existed a spiritual contract between Indian and deer: in return for the sacrifice of its life in order to keep the Indian well-fed and healthy, the deer expected the hunter to kill only what he could use, and he should neither waste the products of its flesh nor show disrespect to its spirit (by neglecting to appreciate its death, or bury its remains, for example). Coupled with his land-use approach and hunter/gatherer population levels, this sort of relationship between Indian hunter and deer insured an abundant and perpetual supply of whitetails, kept healthy and culled of weak or sick individuals by Indians as well as other natural predators.

The almost simultaneous arrival in the New World of English, French, and Spanish settlers soon changed this millenia-old equilibrium. In the European world, wildlife — and most land — had been the exclusive property of rulers and aristocrats. Common folk who "poached" the King's deer risked serious punishment, even death. But in the wilds of game-rich North America these restrictions could not be enforced. Thus the "Virginia Deere" became, along with the wild turkey, the paramount wild food resource of Europeans from Spanish Florida to the Laurentian Highlands of eastern Canada. *Everyone* hunted deer, which were at first exceedingly abundant around the cleared village and old field Indian sites where the Europeans liked to locate their towns.

As with most New World resources, however, wild whitetails soon became commodities in the market economy of mercantilism. Deerskins were worth money to the Europeans, and

Petroglyphs like these are representative of those often found in the southwest portion of the U.S. They are indicative of the relationship between early man and this magnificent animal.

soon hundreds of thousands of animals were being slaughtered as a fur resource, their hides shipped to Bristol, England or La Rochelle, France, for conversion into a pliable and inexpensive leather. Particularly in the South, where the beaver and otter pelts were too thin to bring good prices, the deerskin trade was the cornerstone of the European fur trade. To accomplish it they enlisted the eastern Indians, who probably killed most of the whitetails sacrificed to the trade. With the Indian's faith in the old spiritual order shattered by the decimation of whole villages by European diseases, causes misunderstood, and fascinated with the iron/industrial products of European technology (easily procured with furs), the Indian proved a willing accomplice.

The magnitude of this ecological disaster may be sensed by noting only a handful of the abundant statistics. In 1706-07, the Carolinas shipped out 121,000 deerskins to English merchants; by 1730 the annual shipment from South Carolina alone exceeded a quarter-million whitetail hides! Tiny Natchitoches, founded by the French on the Red River frontier in present Louisiana, shipped out 36,000 deer-

This nice young buck has paused for a moment in his post-oak savannah habitat. Ecologists believe original whitetail density in this region may have exceeded 400 animals per 10 square miles.

Frederick Remington's "A Good Day's Hunting in the Adirondacks" *(Harper's Weekly,* January 16, 1892), appeared at a time when market hunting had made New York State's Adirondack Mountains one of the last strongholds of whitetail deer in the East.

Pioneers and wilderness traders regularly subsisted on the whitetail during their forays, as attested by this anonymous drawing appearing in the *Crayon Miscellany* in 1896. (Note whitetail at the bottom of the drawing.)

skins a year for most of the 18th century. As late as 1805, a lone Indian, hunting for the trade in east Texas, was credited with 400 whitetails from a single fall hunt — for which he received $200 credit in merchandise which had probably cost the manufacturer $30 to produce.

Market hunters, whether Indian or white, clearly exerted a fierce pressure before which even the adaptable and prolific whitetail withered. It was a trend accelerated by the rapid conversion of forestland to farm and plantation lands, and by the competition for forage from imported European stock which was often allowed to run feral in the woods. Even during the Colonial Period this disappearance of whitetails was already being noted with some alarm. According to James Trefethen's *An American Crusade for Wildlife,* Portsmouth, in the colony of Rhode Island, was the first American town to regulate New World hunting when in 1646 it announced a closed season on deer, " . . . from the first of May till the first of November; and if any shall shoot a deere within that time he shall forfeit five pounds." By 1720, most of the English colonies had adopted similar measures. Unfortunately, there were no provisions made

---

*A local official charged with enforcement of the deer law.

for the enforcement of these laws. When Massachusetts attempted to do so by appointing two "deer reeves*" and establishing a stiff fine of 10 pounds in 1739, it found the rural populace hostile and most of its deer already gone. By the time of the American Revolution, only pockets of whitetails remained in any of the colonies of the Atlantic Coast.

The rapid push westward continually brought Euro-Americans into untapped hunting grounds still maintained by the interior Indians. The early 19th century American government explorations into the West give us a good idea of the role of whitetails in the middle of the continent. The Lewis and Clark party, for example, made fare of a dozen black bears and some 70 whitetails between the mouth of the Missouri and the Kansas River, within what is now the state of Missouri. Similar experiences were recorded by Jefferson's Freeman and Custis exploration of the Red River in 1806, the naturalist Custis noting that the "Cervus virginianus" was "plenty" in the woodlands of the Southwest. Wilderness trading expeditions also depended heavily upon the whitetail. Anthony Glass's expedition, a 10-man party of traders from Natchez which journeyed into the Comanche country of west Texas in 1808, subsisted well on 16 "very fat deer" until they reached the buffalo grounds of the Blackland Prairies. The prairie tribes, Glass noted, were so geared to bison that, "Deer not being hunted are very plenty about their Villages and tame like Domestic animals."

Unfortunately, the pattern of exploitation established in the Carolinas and elsewhere was repeated each time the frontier line looped into an area still harboring its original herd of whitetails. By the time of the Civil War, three-quarters of the whitetail's range in the United States had already been broken up by settlements. Unlike those of the Indian, however, American land-use patterns were in no way committed to perpetuating the continent as a habitat for wild game. Farmers joined market hunters as threats to the whitetail's continued dominance in the wake of the frontier. Their cutting down of the great forests and rapid introduction of domestic stock to wood and pasture were as erosive and lethal as the market hunter's snare.

In a nation so wedded to *laissez-faire* as was 19th century America, government protection of wildlife was widely-regarded as an encroachment

The use of traditional arms such as bows and muzzleloaders is a recent and much-welcomed trend among modern whitetail hunters.

One of the oldest and most exciting woodland signs on the North American continent is the splayed hoof/dewclaw imprint of a heavy whitetail buck.

on personal freedoms. Thus the task of saving the whitetail from virtual obliteration fell to private sportsmen's clubs composed of upper-class urban dwellers from the East. The New York Sportsmen's Club, founded in 1844, was the prototype for others, many of which became potent lobbying forces. Although market hunters were their initial targets, the clubs soon came to realize that wildlife protection was beyond the ken of private action. They could police their own members, but not society at large.

At mid-century almost all of the eastern states had retained their colonial laws pertaining to closed seasons on deer, but these were ineffectual, and deer herds were left only in the isolated swamps and the mountainous country along the Allegheny/Adirondack/Appalachian cordillera.

Since the rural counties exempted themselves from the laws, or ignored them, and since no funds were appropriated for enforcement anyway, mid-century wildlife laws only regulated the sportsmen's groups which were willing to take them seriously. Market hunting was yet perfectly legal, and since there were no restrictions at all on the way wildlife could be taken, even "sports" thought nothing of shooting deer at night, or (pursued by hounds) in the water. One of Winslow Homer's best-known oils is of the latter scene, about which the British gunmaker, W.W. Greener, wrote: "Deer are often shot within 10 feet of the boat, and it is said that in some instances, the boatman has hold of the deer's tail before the hunter fired."

Maine, long a favorite hunting ground for eastern sportsmen, established the precedent for state control of hunting. Focusing its attention on whitetails, the state first appropriated funds for paid game wardens in 1852. In 1873 it enacted the first season bag limit for whitetails (three), and 7 years later combined its game department with the state fishery commission — the first centralized bureau of its sort in the country. These Maine laws became models for most other states. Regionally, the Northeast and Midwest had deer laws and at least some skeleton staff by the 1890s. The Southwest and West were

somewhat behind, while local-option-oriented Texas lagged by a decade. Financed by general treasury money with low salaries and much corruption and turnover, the early state bureaus were yet " . . . feeble organizations with miniscule appropriations and little power," according to Trefethen.

Initial federal involvement in wildlife work came indirectly, with the establishment of the beginnings of the national forest system in 1891, and the "multiple use" principle for them, embodied in the Pettigrew amendment of 1897. But the first national forests were all in the West, and thus impacted only western whitetails, whose numbers were not yet in danger. The U.S. Division of Biological Survey (established 1896) emerged to promote the Wildlife Refuge idea which would so flourish during the Teddy Roosevelt Presidency, while the Lacey Act of 1900 involved the federal government in the war on market hunting. Meanwhile, the adoption by states such as Pennsylvania and North Carolina of the "hunting license" insured reliable funds for game-law enforcement, and the introduction of restocking programs from the small breeding populations that remained.

In response to this attention, the whitetail deer, which had become locally extinct in many parts of the woodlands, soon began to demonstrate one of its innate characteristics as a species. It rebounded and adapted itself to the new farmland and pastoral patchwork of its former range. Ground fires were no longer a component of the woodland ecology, as the Indians had been removed, but as farmers allowed worn-out 18th and 19th century fields to revegetate, the "old field" pattern of the Indians was perpetuated, producing much prime edgeland habitat. The 1910 passage of the Weeks Act, which brought national forests to the East, guaranteed vital "core" whitetail habitats.

Aside from fire, only one component of the original equation was missing, and for years it went overlooked. But it was a vital component, the one which "balanced" the equation in the old natural order. Among the old predators, the Indian was not the only one which was gone. A great, continent-wide war on predators had been declared virtually from the moment the Old Worlders had arrived. With assistance from both state and federal governments, this had resulted by the early 20th century in the much-celebrated extirpation of wolves and cougars in the Eastern forests. Game bureaus were amazed at how quickly their restocking programs yielded fruit, and congratulated themselves without realizing the reasons for those exploding deer populations.

The most telling example of the consequences of such practices is probably the famous story of the mule deer population of the Kaibab Plateau of Arizona. It is so well-known that it warrants only mention here. But augmented by a second, lesser-publicized example provided by the Pennsylvania whitetail woods during the same period, Kaibab did set several astute observers to formulating the principles of modern ecological game management for deer.

When Pennsylvania first initiated its program of deer-law enforcement, refuges, and restocking in 1897, the annual take of whitetail deer was fewer than 500 animals per year. Overexploitation by both commercial interests, poachers and sport hunters had taken its toll. But the state poured money and men into the quest to resurrect the whitetail, and the deer responded. In dramatic fashion Pennsylvania proved that through such measures, deer herds could be brought back. By 1913 Pennsylvania hunters were taking 1,000 animals in a bucks-only season designed to harvest only the surplus males of this polygamous species. By 1920 the take had risen to 5,000, and by 1928 to 14,374. Yet smiles were fading, for Pennsylvania now wrestled with a new, totally unexpected problem. Their natural predators gone from the woods, the deer herds refused to stop growing. By the mid-'20s they had overeaten their range and the health of the herds plummeted. Widespread parasite infestations and undersized animals became common; then, in 1925, the first of several great die-offs began as first fawns and then does started to starve. This whitetail version of Kaibab was ultimately resolved with a bitterly-contested series of antlerless-only deer seasons between 1928 and 1938. (It was then that the herd stabilized at around half-a-million animals — a little less than the population that exists today. In order to perpetuate the carrying-capacity of the land, about 15-25 percent of Pennsylvania's deer population, today, must be taken by licensed hunters.)

Trial-and-error experimentation such as this, viewed over the long term, was essentially an attempt to help the whitetail adjust to a continent where man-made rules rather than natural

cybernetic values now held sway. With some initial help from man, deer had been able to rebuild and even to thrive, but they could not check their populations except by starving themselves and ruining the land in the process. Now it was that Aldo Leopold and others recognized the role of predators in the equation. But modern land-use brought together farmers and ranchers, with their vulnerable stock herds to consider, to oppose any reintroduction of natural predators.

The logical solution was also the most obvious one — to fashion human hunting of deer as a carefully-regulated substitute for natural predation. Healthy whitetail herds in balance with the land could be perpetuated with money from licenses and (after passage of the Pittman-Robertson act), from ammunition and arms sales. Those funds were used for wildlife enhancement (and the deer *used* by Americans), in a pattern as old as that of the ancient Indians, as venison, for buckskin, and for the wildland experience crucial in both the people and their historical experience as a nation. These were the conclusions drawn by Leopold, first published in his "American Game Policy" of 1930 and later in textbook form in his important *Game Management* (1933). After WW II every state established management principles based on these policies. As Leopold himself pointed out so frequently, and lyrically, it was the experience with American deer herds which laid the foundations for scientific and ecological game management in the United States.

The contemporary period has witnessed many changes in details and aspects of whitetail deer management, but the basic principles established by Leopold have only been modified, not replaced. Modern whitetail hunters are an essential tool of this management — a policy not without its critics, but one which undeniably works well within the constraints of American land-use. Certainly, the future of game and game management will not be without problems. The land/human population ratio continues to worsen, and with public hunting lands suffering increasing hunter pressure, the leasing of private land for hunting privileges has grown. So, too, have the prices of such leases — to the point where, in states such as Texas, deer are such a "cash crop" that management has suffered, and many ordinary people are being priced out of hunting.

Too, deer hunters (as evidenced a few years ago by New Jersey's great swamp deer debate as well as by common non-hunter perceptions) have experienced some difficulty with public image. The recent trend among many modern hunters towards the use of historic arms such as bows and muzzle-loading rifles for deer hunting should go far toward eradicating the image of deer hunters as insensitive slobs wedded to salt licks and electric feeders as necessary technology for their sport. Perhaps the continuing use of these traditional arms, along with a self-conscious cultivation of the primal hunter/gatherer's respect for, and identification with, the whitetail, are the keys to widespread acknowledgement of deer hunting as not just a necessary management tool, but as an activity as natural and authentic as "the Indian way" itself. ●

Bibliography

Cutright, Paul. *Lewis and Clark: Pioneering Naturalists*. Urbana: University of Illinois Press, 1969.

Flader, Susan. *Thinking Like A Mountain: Aldo Leopold and the Development of Ecological Attitudes Towards Deer and Wolves*. Madison: University of Wisconsin Press, 1980.

Flores, Dan. *Jefferson & Southwestern Exploration: The Accounts of Freeman & Custis of the Red River Expedition of 1806*. Norman: University of Oklahoma Press, 1983.

Journal of an Indian Trader: Anthony Glass and the Southwestern Trader's Frontier, 1790-1810. College Station: Texas A&M University Press, pending.

Hall, Raymond E., and Keith Kelson. *The Mammals Of North America*. Two volumes. New York: The Ronald Press, 1959.

Martin, Calvin. *Keepers of the Game: Indian-Animal Relations and the Fur Trade*. Berkeley: University of California Press, 1979.

Pyne, Stephen. *Fire In America: A Cultural History of Wildland and Rural Fire*. Princeton: Princeton University Press, 1982.

Reiger, John. *American Sportsmen and the Rise of Conservation* New York: Winchester Press, 1979.

Shelford, Victor. *The Ecology of North America*. Urbana: University of Illinois Press, 1963.

Trefethen, James. *An American Crusade for Wildlife*. New York: Winchester Press, second edition, 1975.

HILL'S SIDE

Some Things Never Change

by GENE HILL

I'D BE WILLING to bet, since you're a hunter, that your favorite necktie has ducks or pheasants or quail or some kind of big game head on it. And that you've got a print or two hanging in your house or office that's some kind of hunting scene. Further — that your favorite shotgun or rifle, or both, has some kind of relevant engraving on it, or you wish it had. Same with the glasses you use to hold your favorite version of spirits. Most of you are members of D.U., or the Wild Turkey Federation or one devoted to preserving more quail, or wild sheep or deer.

In one corner of my own office is an old spear and in another is a 375 H&H Magnum — with the usual variety of similar odds and ends scattered out in between. It's an odd obsession, this deep and tight hold that we and our animals have on each other, and it's as old as anything we know about the history of man. The walls of the ancient cave dwellers were covered with drawings of mammoths, saber-toothed tigers, deer, antelope and men hunting them. In fact, all of the hunting peoples down to the relatively modern American Indian, found the presence of animals, real or in art form, somewhat of a philosophical and emotional necessity.

There isn't any essential difference between your prints and a cave drawing or the engraving on the floorplate of your 30-06 and the scrimshaw on an ivory or flint spear point, or your cocktail glass and a pre-historic gourd or horn covered with rude antler-like scratchings.

I don't know for sure why we do this, but it's surely an interesting thing to speculate on. I suspect that the ancients felt their art encouraged bravery; knowing that someone before you has speared or hamstrung a lion or elephant is reassurance that such a thing is at least possible. No doubt some of the artwork was intended as a lesson or to commemorate an event. But, I suspect that most were close to our own reasons; a form of honor, a display of affection and some attempt to understand the independence and freedom that animals in the wild have always represented.

Some of the more primitive things I've done have always held some strangely strong appeal beyond the simple act of capture — if and when that actually happened. Using a fish spear is one of them; me with my flashlight, and some time-lost relative with a burning torch, staring into the mystery of water, leaning on exactly the same instinct. Setting a trap for a mink or a muskrat is another where the basics, if not the tools, haven't changed much over the past millenium.

I seem to find more and more hunters who are feeling the same way. Look at the incredible numbers of primitive-weapon hunters — the flintlock and cap-and-ball riflemen and shotgunners. The painted-face bow hunters and the handful of "Indians" who have taken to trying to run down a deer and end the hunt with a stroke of a sheath knife.

One way or another we are tied, each in our own fashion, about as tightly to our game as ever.

Those of us who still hunt with the latest models of hardware find variations according to our personal ideal as well. There are a growing number of deer hunters who are purely trophy hunters — hunters who will go from season to season without taking a shot until they find that particular animal that will, in their estimation, justify the chase. Others will take the first halfway decent head that comes by and some, with more than half an eye on the freezer, are delighted with a chance at some tender yearling.

Some live for the essence of the stalk — a particular animal under particular circumstances. Most take whatever comes along and is legal. Some are still hunters who like the odds and the mood of staying put in one place, while some can't stand still for a minute and others must have the convivialty and excitement of the old-fashioned gang drive.

The way we hunt is, of course, tied to the reason why we hunt. Some of us hunt to enter into things, others to get away from them. Some are lugging battered 30-30s that would look at home propping open a cabin door, others swear by the wildcat calibers that are the brainchildren of fear-naught technicians; all separated by a couple of million plain-vanilla 30-06s and 270s.

But we're all brothers under the skin; what we carry in our hands may vary a bit; what we carry in our heads and heart hasn't changed too much. The high road and the low road will both come out at the hunting camp — and the evening stories and the morning hopes will differ only in language from the plans and dreams that most surely once lived in a cave where on the walls some ancient artist scratched a set of horns — and no doubt debated whether or not to add an inch or two here, and a point or so there. Some things never change!

Most of us have a trophy or two on a wall somewhere or a set of antlers stuck on a shelf. Some of my non-hunting visitors seem to feel that this is a little barbaric or some sort of ego display. My hunting friends know better. First off, my "trophies" are of such mediocre proportions that anyone with any ego about such things certainly wouldn't put them out on display. I would admit to this being the wall of my "cave," and admit here that my moose horns will forever recall a near-dark evening in northern Ontario and a cold and thrilling stalk by canoe; a deep friendship made with an Indian for whom I have the greatest respect and admiration . . . and a week away from the world in the wilderness with the night sounds of the north country stirring through my ancient dreams. A small deer antler — just one, to remind me of an 11-year-old who was admitted to the society of men he deeply admired and a father who told him that he was a hunter and let him prove it. Our trophies are not there so much for the impression they might make on another as much as they are there for ourselves. . . . like the engraving on our favorite rifle or the print of canvasbacks swinging through a sleet storm.

Each of us honors our "hunts" in our own way, knowing that these experiences enrich us and that without them there would be a restlessness and feeling of being incomplete. We may not need them to survive in the physical sense or for food, but spiritually they are essential. I believe that hunting is a link in a brotherhood: it gives us a bond with each other, it is part of our deep involvement and understanding of animals — and the wilderness and the part of us that belongs there.

You and I and the game need each other; without one the other would lose a definition and meaning and purpose. As long as we are here, the wild things will be honored for what they really are: a symbol of our real evolution.

It was the hunter that evolved the rifle from the spear. It was the hunter that made art from rude etchings on stone walls. It was the hunter that formed civilization by letting others be dependent on him so that they might be free to do other things.

The songs that we hear carried on the wind are in different voices. But the meaning is clear to the one listening in the wilderness. It is about life at its most basic. It is about being strong and wise and successful. It is telling us who we are and why we are there. We learn again that without us there would have been no need for fire. . . . there would be no need for anything. ●

Loads & Reloads '84

by ED MATUNAS

THESE PAGES will be a recurring feature in each issue of the GUN DIGEST HUNTING ANNUAL. In part they will deal with new developments in hunting ammunition, reloading components, tools and related items. Listed will be those items that are of noteworthy benefit to the hunter. But simply being *new* will not be grounds to insure that a product or idea finds its way into these pages. No gimmicks, me-too products or ho-hum items will be discussed. Only ammunition and related products deserving of special attention will receive benefit of discussion. If you find it listed here, it's because we believe the item to be practical, well-performing and suitable to the needs of the hunter.

Perhaps more importantly, this department will also be used to bring to your attention, tips, reloading knowhow, bargains and top flight items which you may have simply overlooked. Often old items, methods and procedures are indeed just as newsworthy as some of the fine new products introduced annually. When we run across an old-line product, method or procedure that hasn't been given much current press, we will include it here.

Finally, you will find in each edition charts of extraordinarily fine performing factory and reloaded rifle ammunition. The tables will list those loads that, during the course of the previous year, established themselves as being capable of high levels of performance. Accuracy in hunting firearms and the capacity for taking the appropriate size game will be the criteria for inclusion in these tables. Loads will be deleted from or added to the list each year based on the performance of the particular ammunition tested during the year.

To qualify for a listing in either chart, a specific load must provide good uniform bullet expansion at both 50 and 250 yards without incurring any bullet failures (such as core

/jacket separations). Factory ammunition must provide an average accuracy of 2 inches or less at 100 yards in at least five separate test rifles. The listed group average will always be from a predetermined rifle. For a handload to qualify, its accuracy must average no greater than 1½ inches at 100 yards. For factory ammunition the lot number of the tested ammunition will be listed except when more than one lot has qualified.

The lack of a listing in our charts does not mean a specific load is not up to a given task. It may mean only that it has not been tested. It could, of course, also mean that when tested it performed at a level less than hoped for with respect to accuracy and/or expansion. Again, only the best loads will make these pages each year! For our first efforts 13 factory loads have been listed and 15 handloads are shown. Naturally other loads can get the job done. Our selections, however, represent our nominations for the best hunting loads of the year.

To begin, let's discuss factory ammunition and the new cartridges or loads which are noteworthy.

357 Remington Maximum

This new cartridge has been designed to work in conjunction with an elongated cylinder model of the Ruger Blackhawk. The energy level of the new 357 Remington Maximum is such that it will undoubtedly appeal to many handgun hunters. It is ideal-

ly suited for varmints but will also prove capable of taking deer-sized game, in my opinion, to about 50 yards, perhaps a bit further.

This new cartridge features a case that is, for all practical purposes, a lengthened 357 Magnum. How much? By about ⅓-inch. Currently this cartridge is offered only with a 158-grain short-jacket hollow point bullet. Its trajectory is much flatter than any other similar handgun load thus long range hits will be easier to make.

The new 357 Remington Maximum (left, next to 38 Spl.) is a flat shooting, high energy handgun cartridge that's well suited to a number of hunting applications. In full factory dress, this cartridge launches a 158-grain JHP slug at just under 1900 fps.

TABLE I

Caliber	Bullet Wgt. in grs.	Barrel Length	Velocity (ft/s) at:			Energy (ft/lbs) at:		
			Muz.	50 yds.	100 yds.	Muz.	50 yds.	100 yds.
38 SPl.+P	158 LHP	4"	890	855	823	278	257	238
357 Mag.	158 JHP	4"	1235	1104	1015	535	428	362
357 Max.	**158 JHP**	**10½"**	**1825**	**1588**	**1381**	**1169**	**885**	**669**
41 Mag.	210 JHP	4"	1300	1162	1062	788	630	526
44 Mag.	240 JHP	4"	1180	1081	1010	742	623	544
44 Mag.	240 Lead	4"	1350	1186	1069	972	750	609

TABLE II Mid-Range Trajectory			
Caliber	Bullet Wgt. in grs.	50 yards	100 yards
38 Special +P	158 LHP	1.4"	6.0"
357 Magnum	158 JHP	0.8"	3.5"
357 Maximum	**158 JHP**	**0.4"**	**1.7"**
41 Magnum	210 JHP	0.7"	3.2"
44 Magnum	240 JHP	0.9"	3.7"
44 Magnum	240 Lead	0.7"	3.1"

TABLE III Federal's Super Slug Ballistics					
Gauge & Type	Wgt. in grs.	Muzzle Velocity	(fps) 50 yds.	Muzzle Energy	(fpe) 50 yds.
10, 3½" Mag.	1¾	1280	1080	2785	1980
12, 2¾" Mag.	1¼	1490	1240	2695	1865
12, 2¾"	1	1580	1310	2425	1665
16, 2¾"	⅘	1600	1175	1990	1070
20, 2¾"	¾	1600	1270	1865	1175
410, 2½"	⅕	1830	1335	650	345

It is difficult to compare the new 357 Remington Maximum to other cartridges as its advertised ballistics are based on a 10½-inch barrel as opposed to the standard 4-inch barrel length used in establishing most revolver ballistics. However, the accompanying Tables I and II will help you to realize that the 357 Maximum is indeed a potent cartridge.

For varmint shooting the 357 Remington Maximum can be sighted in to put the point of impact 2 inches high at 50 yards and it will then be only 2 inches low at about 125 yards. For the qualified handgun hunter, varmints to 125 yards will be within a workable hunting range. This new round is in the class of the 22 Jet and 221 Fireball with respect to trajectory. For the deer hunter, the 357 Maximum is suitable to about 50 yards, perhaps a bit more. Why? There's an old adage that states a bullet must have 800-1000 foot-pounds of energy when it hits a deer. I agree. It's that simple.

10-gauge and 12-gauge Magnum Shotgun Slugs

For years big game hunters have been able to purchase shotgun slugs in 12-, 16- and 20-gauge. Not long ago Federal filled in two blank slots with very effective slugs. Federal now offers a 10-gauge 3½-inch Magnum slug and also one in 12-gauge 2¾-inch Magnum. The 10-gauge slug weighs 1¾-ounces and the 12-gauge offering weighs 1¼ ounces, a full ¼-ounce heavier than standard slugs. These two heavyweight slugs add a consid-

erable amount of punch over the previous offerings. Table III shows the 10-gauge slug producing 360 foot-pounds more energy than the standard 1-ounce 12-gauge offering, a noticeable increase indeed. Recoil with both the 10- and 12-gauge Magnum slug loads is indeed heavy, but most shooters will be able to handle the increased level of recoil without undue difficulty.

As with all currently offered shotgun slugs, the Federal line includes a Hollow Point configuration for all gauges. These loads, like any other slug load, can be used in any barrel regardless of choke. Cylinder, Skeet and improved-cylinder chokes will however usually provide better accuracy than modified, improved-modified or full chokes.

Federal's new 1¼-ounce 12-gauge slug is a fine candidate for accuracy trials in any shotgun which does not perform well with standard 1-ounce slugs.

307 Winchester and 356 Winchester

A great many deer hunters prefer short, lightweight lever-action carbines for their hunting. While such rifles are indeed handy in heavy cover they have been handicapped by the relatively modest level of ballistics obtained with the cartridges used in such rifles. Calibers such as the 25-35 Winchester, 30-30 Winchester, 32 Winchester Special, 35 Remington and even the newer 375 Winchester fall a bit short of the requirements for

anchoring deer when the ranges are anything but relatively short. To correct this, the folks at Olin have developed two new powerhouse lever-action carbine rounds—the 307 and 356 Winchester. These new rimmed cartridges eliminate the complaint of in-

The new 307 Winchester cartridge is available from the factory with either 180- or 150-grain bullets. The 150-grain loading leaves the muzzle at over 2800 fps. While the 180-grain load provides 1000 fps at 300 yards. Excellent deer fodder, indeed.

As of this writing, both Marlin and Winchester will be offering lever-action rifles/carbines for the new 307 and 356 Winchester cartridges. Shown here is the 356 Winchester as loaded with a 250-grain bullet. The muzzle velocity is just under 2200 fps.

sufficient energy at the longer ranges. In fact, the new rounds come very close to the ballistic levels produced by such potent rounds as the 308 and 358 Winchester cartridges.

The 307 Winchester is most efficient when the 180-grain bullet is selected, but the lighter 150-grain bullet is also a potent load. The 356 Winchester is offered in either a 200- or 250-grain bullet. Depending upon the bullet weight or caliber chosen, either of these two rounds have sufficient energy levels to make the taking of deer at 300 yards possible. The limiting factor will of course be accuracy rather than bullet energy. At this writing both U.S. Repeating Arms and Marlin offer lever-action

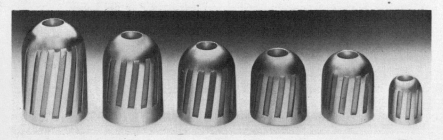

Federal hollow point shotgun slugs are available (from left to right) in: 10 gauge (3½-inch shell) 1¾-ounce slug; 12 gauge (Magnum) 1¼-ounce; 12 gauge 1-ounce; 16 gauge ⅘-ounce; 20 gauge ¾-ounce; and .410 bore ⅕-ounce.

TABLE IV

Caliber	Bullet Wgt. in grs.	Velocity in ft/s at (yds):				Energy in ft/lbs at (yds):				Trajecotry data (in.) at (Yds.)				
		Muzzle	100	200	300	Muzzle	100	200	300	100	150	200	250	300
30-30 Win.	150	2390	2018	1684	1398	1903	1357	945	651	+2.0	+0.5	−3.7	−10.8	−21.8
30-30 Win.	170	2200	1895	1619	1381	1828	1356	990	721	+2.0	⊕	−4.0	−13.0	−25.1
307 Win.	150	2764	2325	1928	1578	2545	1801	1238	830	+2.0	+1.2	−1.6	− 6.7	−14.7
307 Win.	180	2506	2175	1870	1596	2511	1891	1398	1018	+2.0	+0.8	−3.6	− 8.3	−17.1
308 Win.	150	2820	2488	2179	1893	2649	2062	1582	1194	+2.0	+1.4	−0.8	− 4.8	−11.0
32 Win.Spl.	170	2250	1870	1537	1267	1912	1320	892	606	+2.0	⊕	−5.1	−13.8	−27.1
35 Rem.	200	2020	1646	1335	1114	1813	1204	792	551	+2.0	−1.1	−8.1	−20.1	−37.9
356 Win.	200	2455	2109	1793	1513	2677	1976	1428	1017	+2.0	+0.6	−3.0	− 9.4	−18.9
356 Win.	250	2162	1914	1684	1478	2595	2034	1575	1213	+2.0	⊕	−4.7	−12.4	23.7
358 Win.	200	2490	2171	1876	1610	2754	2094	1563	1151	+2.0	+0.8	−2.6	− 8.4	−17.1
375 Win.	200	2200	1841	1526	1268	2150	1506	1034	714	+2.0	−0.1	−5.4	−14.4	−27.7
375 Win.	250	1900	1647	1424	1239	2005	1506	1126	852	+2.0	−1.1	−8.1	−20.1	−37.9
444 Marlin	240	2350	1815	1377	1087	2944	1756	1011	630	+2.0	−0.1	−5.8	−16.1	32.4

carbines for the 307 and 356 Winchester. My experience has shown the Marlins to be capable of a greater level of accuracy.

Deer hunters purchasing a new lever-action carbine would be wise to consider only one of these new cartridges as they do in effect actually make all lesser calibers normally used in such rifles obsolete. A comparison of external ballistics of the new cartridges is shown in Table IV. All of the listed ballistics are for a 24-inch barrel length. In that the rifles for these new cartridges are normally supplied with 20-inch barrels, actual velocities and energies will be somewhat lower than shown in the table. Of course, this same reasoning applies to the other calibers shown in the table.

If one accepts the fact that it takes about 1000 pounds of energy to cleanly kill deer it becomes apparent that the 30-30, 32 Winchester Special and the 35 Remington are not, in fact, suitable for 200-yard shooting. But the 307 Winchester with the 180-grain bullet and the 356 Winchester with either the 200- or 250-grain bullet have 1000 foot pounds of energy or more at 300 yards.

Marlin carbines equipped with a good 4x scope should be able to obtain accuracy sufficient for 225- to 250-yard shooting. At shorter ranges the extra energy will help insure quicker and cleaner kills on quartering or go-

ing away shots where the bullet must penetrate a long way before it reaches the vital organs of a deer.

All trajectories in Table IV are based on a common sighting-in with the bullet 2 inches high at 100 yards. This allows for easy comparison of trajectories.

257 Roberts +P

Winchester has beefed up two factory loadings of the 257 Roberts and is calling the resulting loads 257 Roberts +P. The old 100-grain Silvertip load has been elevated 100 ft/s to 3000 ft/s. The 117-grain Power Point bullet now travels at 2780 ft/s, a 130 ft/s increase over the standard loads.

Both +P and standard loads are shown in Winchster's current catalog but I would anticipate the standard

Winchester's new +P loads for the 257 Roberts will send a 100-grain Silvertip out the muzzle at 3000 fps—a clear 100 fps increase over standard factory loads. Winchester has also announced a 257 Roberts +P load using a 117-grain SP bullet which provides 2780 fps at the muzzle.

loads will become obsolete when current inventories are exhausted. While the increased velocity levels are no great feat for a handloader, any increase in the level of performance of the 257 factory rounds is certainly welcomed.

The added velocity will help flatten the trajectory of both 257 Roberts loads and will make the cartridge better suited for light big game such as pronghorn antelope and whitetail deer. Both loads shot very well in several Ruger 77's during my testing. Table V allows for quick comparison of the new and old loadings. The new loads will make this cartridge effective to about 250 yards when used on the appropriate sized game.

Handgun Ammunition Bargain

CCI's Blazer ammunition is for most hunters and shooters an overlooked bargain. Many hunters do not reload their own ammunition and usually discard their fired cases. In doing so they throw away the most costly part of their ammo—the brass case.

Blazer ammunition eliminates the use of a brass case and replaces it with a less costly aluminum cartridge case thus saving the manufacturer and the consumer a substantial amount of money. Blazer ammo also uses a Berdan-type primer which further reduces the manufacturing costs. The net result is that CCI's Blazer ammu-

TABLE V
Comparison Ballistics of 257 Roberts +P and 257 Roberts

Cartridge	Bullet Wt. in Grs.	Type	Barrel Length In.	Velocity in ft/s at (yds)						Energy in Ft/lbs at (yds)					
				Muzzle	100	200	300	400	500	Muzzle	100	200	300	400	500
257 Roberts +P	100	ST	24	3000	2633	2295	1982	1697	1447	1999	1540	1170	873	640	465
257 Roberts	100	ST	24	2900	2541	2210	1904	1627	1387	1868	1434	1085	805	588	427
257 Roberts +P	117	PP(SP)	24	2780	2411	2071	1761	1488	1263	2008	1511	1115	806	575	415
257 Roberts	117	PP(SP)	24	2650	2291	1961	1663	1404	1199	1825	1364	999	719	512	374

Omark's CCI Blazer ammo is quite a bargain and will save the non-reloader about 35 percent on the cost of regular ammo. How? The Blazer offering features non-reloadable, aluminum cases.

Blazer ammunition is plenty accurate. This shooter was able to keep all of his shots inside a 2-inch circle at 25 yards.

nition sells for about 35 percent less than comparable ammunition.

While it cannot be reloaded, this ammunition will fit the needs of a great many shooters. It is available only in handgun calibers with a number of these loads ideally suited to handgun hunting. Accuracy is satisfactory and no drawbacks exist with the aluminum cases for the non-reloader.

Blazer is available in a wide range of 38 Special, 38 Special +P, 357 Magnum, and several automatic pistol cartridge loads. This ammunition represents a real bargain for the non-reloading hunter.

Positive Expanding Handgun Bullets

If you load handgun cartridges for hunting, you are probably aware of the difficulty in obtaining handgun bullets that will provide positive expansion. Many bullets will give satisfactory results if their velocities remain above 1100 fps. However

terminal velocities with handguns are frequently well below such levels.

Sierra Bullets, Inc., has introduced a bullet style that will provide good expansion when velocities drop even to the 800 fps mark. This bullet may expand at lesser velocities, but I have not yet run tests below 800 fps. The new bullets incorporate a series of six notches at the mouth of the jacket, on the bullet nose. These jacket cuts look a lot like the notches on the Winchester Silvertip pistol bullets. Sierra calls these bullets "Power Jacket." Mike Bussard of Sierra has indicated that this new jacket construction will eventually be applied to all handgun bullets which are of the expanding type.

These bullets work well. With the proper loads, I have obtained positive expansion with 110-grain bullets fired from a 2-inch barreled 38 Special.

Overlooked Game Bullets

Nosler Partition bullets have long enjoyed a fine reputation as being a

premium quality bullet for big game hunting. While the pricing of this product has traditionally been double that of conventional bullets, most experienced hunters/handloaders have been (and continue to be) willing to pay the price.

Nosler's line of Solid Base bullets has gained a solid reputation for accuracy. The 6mm, 75-grain Spitzer bullet shown here is ideal for the varmint hunter who needs accuracy and expansion in the same package.

Sierra's new "Power Jacket" handgun bullets are designed to expand at velocities as low as 800 fps. The special "expansion notches" can be seen extending downward from the meplat (or just below the lead in the case of the soft points) in the nearby photo.

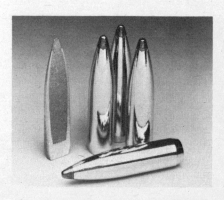

Among the newcomers to the Nosler Solid Base hunting bullet lineup are these new 7mm, 162-grain projectiles. They should serve well in the 7mm Remington Magnum, especially when it comes to the hunting applications this cartridge was designed for.

However, that firm also offers a superb line of conventional projectiles which are called Nosler Solid Base bullets. These bullets have not achieved the level of popularity they deserve perhaps because many reloaders do not realize that they cost no more than other conventional brands. The accuracy of these projectiles in many rifles is amazing. When in its infancy this line of bullets was somewhat limited. However, over the years it has been expanded to include bullets from the 45-grain 22 Hornet through heavy 30 caliber projectiles.

I recently tried some of the new 45-grain 22 Hornet bullets in a Kimber rifle and was pleased indeed with the superb accuracy (1.08-inches average). Expansion proved more than adequate for crows and woodchucks.

The Nosler 165-grain Solid Base 30-caliber Spitzer is one of the most accurate hunting bullets I have ever used in a 30-06 cartridge. And the Nosler Solid Base line includes a good number of other top performing bullets. Don't overlook them when testing loads.

38 Special / 357 Magnum Shotshells

Most hunters would never think of their 38 or 357 serving double duty as a small shotgun. Yet loads for this purpose are available from CCI. Granted they won't turn your handgun into a 410 bore shotgun but they are effective for specific purposes at short ranges.

Loaded with ¼-ounce of No. 9 shot these shells will drive approximately 135 pellets with sufficient force and pattern to take small game to about 15 yards. After a day of unsuccessful deer hunting, the ability to take a roosting partridge from a pine tree, without having to worry about where a solid bullet may come to rest, can certainly add a lot to a camp dinner.

When it comes to eliminating camp vermin or dispatching small game at short range, CCI's shotshell loads for the 38 Special/357 Magnum are perfect.

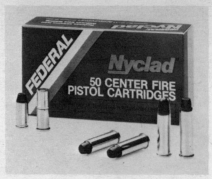

Federal's new line of Nyclad 38 Special ammo includes a 125-grain, semi-wadcutter hollow point that will provide positive expansion, even out of a 2-inch barrel, while maintaining a modest pressure level. Given these modest pressures, the load will be suitable for use in small, alloy-framed revolvers.

The elimination of poisonous snakes or rodents from around your camp is also a task easily accomplished with these loads. I have even killed a few rabbits for the stew pot at about 10 or 12 paces with these rounds.

Limitations should apply. Obviously squirrels are difficult to kill, and I would not recommend a load as light as these handgun shotshells for such purposes. But when used with discretion they are effective. You should pattern your gun by firing at a large sheet of paper from several distances. I suggest you try several shots at 5, 10 and 15 yards to determine the maximum range for effective patterns from your revolver.

38 Special Non + P Ammo and Expansion

Many hunters like to carry small frame, lightweight 38 Special revolvers as second guns when hunting with a long gun. However, such handguns have usually proved of very limited value even for the finishing shot on a mortally wounded and downed big game animal.

At the base of this performance level has been the total lack of expansion normally associated with standard pressure 38 Special ammo. The higher pressure +P loads will often provide expansion, but such loads are not normally recommended for small frame or alloy frame revolvers. And some shooters just prefer not to shoot heavier loads even in revolvers capable of handling the extra pressure.

Federal Cartridge Corporation has introduced a new load that will eliminate the problem. This load is one of the 38 Special Nyclad loads that Federal recently announced. Nyclad ammunition features lead bullets with a nylon coating that eliminates much if not all of the bore fouling smoke and airborne lead particles normally associated with lead ammunition. In this new product line Federal offers a 125-grain semi-wadcutter hollow point load that will provide positive expansion even when fired from a 2-inch barrel. And pressures are low enough to permit use of this load in small frame and alloy frame revolvers.

In my tests, velocity from my 2-inch barreled S&W Chief Special was well over 800 fps and the corresponding muzzle energy was almost 200 foot pounds. Expansion was extraordinary and very uniform. This new Special load is, in my opinion, the best factory 38 Special load available using standard pressures.

Accuracy was quite satisfactory even in a short-barreled revolver. This ammo, when fired through a 4-inch barrel grouped in a 4¼-inch circle at 50 yards from the standing position using a 2-hand hold. With a 6-inch barrel I was able to do even better. This load is certainly accurate enough for small game and potent enough to finish downed big game when required, and where legal.

A New Shotshell

Estate Cartridge Co. is a new ammunition manufacturer located in Texas. Their ammunition line is devoted exclusively to shotshells. Its merit is extremely uniform velocities. I have conducted tests on limited samples and I am very impressed.

The Estate Cartridge Company is a new shotshell loading firm headquartered in Conroe, Texas. At this point, Estate is confining its activities to shotshells, exclusively; and, early testing of samples has shown some positive results.

This mixed bag of quail, chukar partridge and pheasant demands the use of 1¼ ounces of 7½ shot. When it comes to pheasant alone, however, the author's recommendation differs drastically.

preserve in Millbrook, NY, three shooters bagged 72 birds in a full day's shooting. The number of birds involved allowed each shooter to test some pet theories on shot charge weights and shot sizes. Suffice to say that during the long morning when quail, chukar partridge, and pheasant provided a great variety of targets at varying ranges, Winchester's Upland 12-gauge 1¼ No. 7½ load proved the uncontested champ. Lighter loads failed to consistently put down the birds when the ranges were long or when the target was a big pheasant in

Estate Cartridge Company is mentioned here because they have indicated that they intend to market a number of unique hunting loads. At this writing I have received only very limited target load samples and these were used successfully while hunting the local woodcock population. If Estate Cartridge follows through in their promises, we will be reporting on them further in the next issue of the GUN DIGEST HUNTING ANNUAL.

Tips For Shot Sizes In The Uplands

At a recent shoot hosted by Winchester at the Sandanona Hunting

These flighted mallards were all taken at ranges running from 45 to 55 yards with Winchester Super X Double X shotshells loaded with No. 4 copper-plated shot and grex plastic filler.

During the mid-1960s, the author not only hunted pheasants, he raised them. As a result, he did a lot more pheasant hunting than the average guy. He concluded that a 12-gauge loading of 1½ ounces of No. 4 shot was, indeed, *the* pheasant getter of all time.

high gear. Smaller and larger size shot also proved less effective when one considered all three species of birds. For a mixed bag a 12-gauge standard velocity load proved the ideal selection if it contained 1¼ ounces of No. 7½ shot.

However, our afternoon shoot consisted of tower released pheasants and mallards. Shot sizes from No. 7½ to 2 were tried in shot charge weights from 1-ounce to 1½ ounces. Here the uncontested superior load, again based on the number of birds killed cleanly, proved to be 1½ ounces of No. 4 shot in the Double X loading. The Double X Winchester shell makes use of copper plated shot and pellet protecting grex filler.

The success of the No. 4 shot loads in the 1½-ounce charge weight came as no surprise. I have long been a supporter of 1½ ounces of No. 4s for pheasant whenever there were no smaller birds mixed into the day's bag. This load will stop pheasant easily at 50 yards without a notable loss of cripples. And for ducks such a load is ideal.

While others swapped loads back and forth on the tower released birds, I started with the 1½-ounce Super X Double X No. 4s and never had a bird get past my station. Nearly all were one shot kills. In fact I knocked down a number of flying cripples that had been hit with lesser loads by the other shooters. The ranges were long, often 45 to 55 yards, but the heavy loads of No. 4s proved more than up to the task.

I've been using this type of load since the mid-1960s when I raised 500 to 1000 pheasants each year. The hunting and shooting of these birds by myself, friends and guests proved beyond a doubt that 1½ ounces of No. 4s were indeed the best pheasant medicine. The worst possible load selection proved at that time to be light 20-gauge (⅞- and 1-ounce) charges of No. 7½s. The number of cripples with these loads were very high indeed. As shot sizes and charge weights were increased, the results became better and better until the optimum load of 1½ ounces of No. 4s was reached.

When the day's bag is a mixed one, 7½s are the best choice. Simply restrict your shooting to 35 yards or less when the target turns out to be a pheasant.

For those who may wonder about such things, I used a Winchester Model 12, 12-gauge gun with the Winchoke at the Sandanons shoot. I used Skeet and improved cylinder tubes in my barrels for the morning field shooting. Modified and improved-modified tubes were used for the tower shoot in the afternoon. Only on two birds did I wish I had a full-choke tube screwed into the gun. The choice of tubes proved perfect for all my other shots during the day and I tallied approximately 30 birds with very few misses.

RCBS Introduces Two New Reloading Tools

RCBS is without doubt the undisputed giant in metallic cartridge reloading tools, dies and equipment. Their recently introduced RCBS A4 "Big Max" Press enhances this image of a giant. This press is big, heavy and very strong. It includes an automatic shell holder that functions with most cartridges and a giant spade-type handle. With its positive primer catching bottle and bullet swagging capabilities, this press is up to any possible reloading task.

Priming is accomplished either at the die station or on a remote priming tool. Because this tool is so massive, I suggest using a remote priming tool

If you're looking for the beefiest metallic loading press made, look no further; the one you want is the A4 "Big Max" by RCBS. Here's the kicker: It'll handle everything from the 25 ACP on up to 50 BMG. (That's enough!)

in order to best feel your primers seating. Far from being inexpensive (it sells for about $200) this tool is, however, without question the sturdiest reloading tool that I have ever encountered. It will undoubtedly serve you, your grandchildren and perhaps their grandchildren before it begins to give up the ghost. For those who care to know, it will resize anything from a 25 ACP on up to 50 BMG (that's "Browning Machine Gun").

On the other end of the scale, RCBS has also introduced their new Reloader Special 2 reloading press. This is a lightweight, low-end price tool,

but it features a compound leverage system, a working primer catcher and sufficient strength to perform all the reloading tasks most of us would ever expect a press to handle. Its offset O-frame construction offers plenty of working room and more than adequate strength. This is a beginner's tool that will serve equally as well when you are a pro. It could well prove to be the only press you will ever need. The RS-2 surely qualifies as a best buy (about $71.50) and will prove in the long run to be a real bargain.

When using a full-sized reloading press, you lose much of the "feel" that's needed to correctly seat primers. The author suggests the use of a separate priming tool (like this RCBS unit) for best results.

When it comes to a one-stop, do-it-all, economically-priced reloading press, the new RCBS RS-2 is a beauty. It's small, but its rugged construction and offset O-frame will handle just about any loading chore you've got.

New, Huntington Compact Press — It's Portable and Practical

Through the years a number of portable reloading tools have been available. Such items as the Lyman 310 Tong Tool proved very popular and practical. Other tools disappeared almost as quickly as they were introduced. Such failures have been numerous. Only relatively few have proved successful. But in almost every case these portable tools were deficient in some way or another.

Now there is a tool that is 100 percent portable, will allow cases to be full-length resized when properly lubricated, allows the use of your standard ⅞ x 14 thread dies, permits the use of standard shell holders and needs no fastening to table, bench, or other means of support. This new tool along with a set of dies, shell holder, a wood loading block, priming unit, 100 bullets, 100 primers, and sufficient powder to load 100 rounds can be packed into a box 10 x 4 x 4½ inches. The tool I'm talking about is the new Huntington Compact Press. It sells for $49.95 complete with small and large primer punch and with the addition of your favorite set of dies, and shell holder it can load ammunition almost anywhere.

Apartment dwellers who lack a loading bench, shooters who like to load at the range in order to facilitate load development, benchrest shooters and those who wish to pack a loading tool into their hunting camp or other remote area will all find that the Huntington Compact Press fits a definite need.

I loaded 60 rounds of 30-06 cases on a sample tool without a hitch. I also tested the tool by full-length resizing some 270, 7mm Remington Magnum and 222 Remington cases. All operations proceeded without a problem. You need only to remember to keep your fingers from between the tool handles and the main part of the tool when squeezing the handles through the last portion of the stroke.

Huntington suggests the use of a window type seating die to ease bullet seating. Seating with a regular bullet seating die is a bit nettlesome as both hands are required for squeezing the tool handles, leaving no way to hold the bullet on the case mouth as the case enters the die. This can be overcome by clamping the base plate of the tool to a table, closet shelf or what-have-you. In this way one hand will suffice to operate the tool while the bullet is being seated. As the bullet starts into the case the second

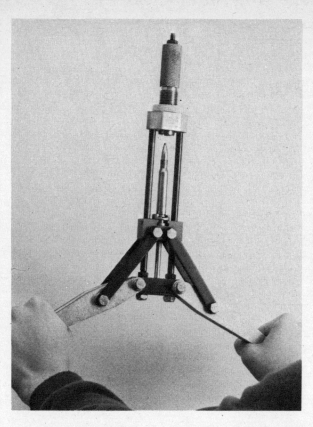

Compact portable reloading presses are perfectly suited for the hunter who wants to "take it all with him." The new Huntington Compact Press is truly portable and uses standard ⅞x14 dies and standard shell holders. It sells for $49.95, complete with small and large primer punch.

hand can then be used to assist the final seating operation.

Do not attempt to resize cases while the base plate is anchored to a support. Doing so will simply pull the base plate from its support or if it is firmly anchored you may damage it.

The use of an RCBS competition seating die or a die similar to the old Vickerman bullet seater will eliminate the need to clamp or screw down the base plate to some form of support.

This fine caribou was taken at more than 400 yards with a Winchester Model 70 Featherweight chambered for 30-06. The load was 60 grains of IMR 4350 and a Speer 150-grain Spitzer. (You'll find more info on this load in Table VI.)

RELOADS

Tables VI and VII respectively list the best reloads and the best factory loads that I have used during the previous year.

These charts will be updated annually to include new or delete old listings based on the performance of ammunition I have used during the preceding 12 months. As mentioned earlier only the very best hunting loads will be listed. The criteria for a listing will be:

1. The firing of 25 rounds in each of no fewer than five rifles in order to check accuracy.
2. Factory loads must produce an average group size of 2 inches or less for five consecutive 5-shot groups from each pre-determined rifle.
3. Handloads must produce an average group size of 1½ inches for five consecutive 5-shot groups in each pre-determined rifle.
4. The largest individual group size must not exceed 2½ inches for factory loads or 2 inches for reloads.

5. All bullets must prove their expansion capability either on game or in ordnance gelatin. Any single bullet failure (i.e. lack of expansion, fragmentation, or core/jacket separation) will disqualify a load from being listed.
6. Expansion will be tested at 50 and 250 yards. Certain loads which by their ballistic nature are unsuitable for hunting at 200 yards will be checked at shorter ranges for expansion. For example, the 22 Hornet is tested at 150 yards.
7. Reader input with regard to bullet failure in the field, when properly substantiated and accompanied by the recovered bullet, will disqualify a load from future listings unless the bullet manufacturer can prove the failure non-representative or corrects the problem.
8. Rimfire ammunition will be tested at 50 yards and the results of five, 10-shot groups will be reported. Rimfire ammunition must average 1¼ inches or less at this range to qualify for a list-

ing.
9. It is not my intention to attempt the impossible task of testing every load available each year. Rather I will report on those loads that prove up to the requirements during the course of my normal year's shooting.
10. Tests will be conducted at the request of ammunition or component manufacturers. However, in no way, will any waiver of my requirements be granted regardless of circumstane.

My requirements are tough to meet but that is the purpose of this selection. I intend to call to your attention only the outstanding ammunition. In every instance no rifle will weigh more than a total of 8½ pounds with sights, accessories and a full magazine when used in my testing. And as can be seen from the tables, lightweight hunting rifles will receive preference. I hope these selections will prove helpful to you in making your choice for hunting ammunition. Good shooting!

TABLE VI
Gun Digest Hunting Annual Picks This Year's Best Reloads

Caliber	Bullet Specifications Wgt. in grs.	Type	Powder Charge Brand	Charge wgt. in grs.	Velocity 10 feet in ft/s	Barrel Length	Primer	Case	100 yd. Avg. Five 5-shot grps.	Test Rifle	Test Scope	Suggested Application
22 Hornet	45	SP	Nosler	11.5 / IMR 4227	2650	22½"	Rem.	Rem.	1.442"	Kimber	4X Leupold	Varmint
222 Rem.	50	Spitzer	Sierra	20.0 / IMR 4198	2900	18½"	Rem.	Rem.	1.422"	Rem.Seven	4X Leupold	Varmint
243 Win.	70	SBSP	Nosler	47.0 / IMR 4350	3304	18½"	Win.	Win.	1.443"	Rem.Seven	4X Lyman AA	Varmint
243 Win.	100	Partition	Nosler	42.0 / IMR 4350	2864	18½"	Win.	Win.	1.443"	Rem. Seven	4X Lyman AA	Light big game
257 Roberts	100	HP	Speer	45.0 / IMR 4350	3000	22"	CCI	Win.	1.092"	Ruger 77	6X Lyman AA	Varmint
257 Roberts	120	Partition	Nosler	42.0 / IMR 4350	2850	22"	Win.	Win.	1.497"	Ruger 77	6X Lyman AA	Light big game
270 Win.	90	HP	Sierra	55.0 / IMR 4350	2935	22"	CCI	Win.	1.477"	Win.70 Fwgt.	4X Leupold	Varmint
270 Win.	90	HP	Sierra	60.0 / IMR 4350	3350	22"	Win.	Win.	0.997"	Rem.700 Class.	4X Leupold	Varmint
270 Win.	130	Spitzer	Speer	55.0 / IMR 4350	3000	22"	Win.	Norma	1.251"	Rem.700 Class.	4X Leupold	Big game
270 Win.	150	Spitzer	Speer	54.0 / IMR 4350	2866	22"	Win.	Rem.	1.105"	Rem.700 Class.	4X Leupold	Big game
7mm Rem.Mag.	145	Spitzer	Speer	63.0 / IMR 4350	3000	24"	Rem.	Rem.	1.500"	Rem.700 ADL	4X Leupold	Light big game
30-06 Spring.	110	HP	Sierra	61.0 / IMR 4350	3050	22"	Rem.	Rem.	1.113"	Win.70 Fwgt.	2 to 7X Red.	Varmint
30-06 Spring.	125	Spitzer	Sierra	61.0 / IMR 4350	2947	22"	Rem.	Rem.	1.124"	Win.70 Fwgt.	2 to 7X Red.	Varmint
30-06 Spring.	150	Spitzer	Speer	60.0 / IMR 4350	3018	22"	Rem.	Rem.	1.500"	Win.70 Fwgt.	2 to 7X Red.	Big game
30-06 Spring.	165	SBSP	Nosler	50.0 / IMR 4064	2662	22"	Rem.	Rem.	1.108"	Win.70 Fwgt.	2 to 7X Red.	Big game

Fwgt. = Featherweight Class. = Classic Red. = Redfield HP = Hollow Point SP = Soft Point SBSP = Solid Base Soft Point

TABLE VII

Loads and Reloads Picks This Year's Best Factory Loads

Caliber	Brand	Bullet Wgt. grs. and Type	Advertised MV. In ft/s	Lot No.	Actual Vel. 10 feet in ft/s	Barrel Length	100 yd.Avg. Five 5-shot grps.	Test Rifle	Test Scope	Suggested Application
22 L.R.	CCI	40 Comp. Green Tag	1138	M16M5	1076	22½"	0.999"[1]	Kimber 82	1.5 to 5x Leupold	Squirrel
22 L.R.	Win.	40 T22 Std. Vel.	1150	1SC81L	1126	22½"	1.056"[1]	Kimber 82	1.5 to 5x Leupold	Squirrel
22 L.R.	CCI	37 Mini Mag HP	1370	L16N11	1226	22½"	1.208"[1]	Kimber 82	1.5 to 5x Leupold	Varmint
22 Hornet	Win.	45 Pointed SP	2690	several	2575	22½"	1.922"	Kimber	4x Lyman AA	Varmint
222 Rem.	Rem.	50 Power Lokt HP	3140	several	2900	18½"	1.922"	Rem. Seven	4x Lyman AA	Varmint
243 Win.	Win.	100 Power Point	2960	86TK30	2665	18½"	2.000"	Rem. Seven	6x Lyman AA	Light big game
257 Roberts +P	Win.	100 Silvertip	3000	75UC41	2925	22"	1.957"	Ruger 77	6x Lyman AA	Light big game
270 Win.	Norma	130 Soft Point	3140	06912	3075	22"	1.497"	Rem. 700 Classic	4x Leupold	Big game
270 Win.	Win.	130 Power Point	3110	several	3025	22"	1.599"	Rem. 700 Classic	4x Leupold	Big game
7mm Rem.Mag.	Win.	175 Core Lokt PSP	2860	several	2800	24"	2.000"	Rem.700 ADL	4x Leupold	Big game
30-06 Spring.	Fed.	125 Spitzer	3140	1B-1104	3100	22"	1.103"	Win. 70 Fwgt.	2 to 7x Redfield	Varmint
30-06 Spring.	Rem.	150 Core Lokt PSP	2910	several	2875	22"	1.541"	Win. 70 Fwgt.	2 to 7x Redfield	Big game
30-06 Spring.	Rem.	220 Core Lokt SP	2410	several	2350	22"	1.122"	Win. 70 Fwgt.	2 to 7x Redfield	Very heavy big game

[1]Group size at 50 yards and is the measurement average of five 10-shot groups. Abbreviations: Rem. = Remington; Win. = Winchester; Mag. = Magnum; Spring. = Springfield; Fed. = Federal; L.R. = Long Rifle; Comp. = Competition; Std. Vel. = Standard Velocity; HP = Hollow Point; PSP = Pointed Soft Point; SP = Soft Point; Fwgt. = Featherweight.

new products '84

by Robert S.L. Anderson

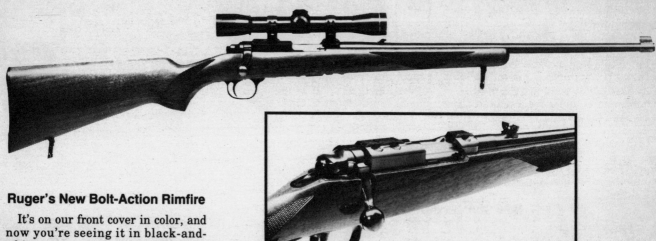

Ruger's New Bolt-Action Rimfire

It's on our front cover in color, and now you're seeing it in black-and-white.

To my eye, this is one of the most handsome 22-caliber, bolt-action rifles ever made in the U.S.A. Those of you who've owned (or own) Winchester 52 Sporters or Remington 40X Sporters will be standing in line for this one—it's that nice. The action is a totally new design by Bill Ruger and features mid-bolt lockup, the familiar rotary magazine, swivels, a 3-position safety that intercepts the striker, multiposition integral scope bases and more, much more.

As we go to press, the rifle is scheduled for delivery in late 1983, with a magnum rimfire version due out in early to mid-1984. Weighing in at 5 lbs. 13 oz., the new Ruger Bolt-Action 22 will sell for about $275. It's a bargain.

For more information write: Sturm, Ruger & Co., Inc., Southport, CT 06490 (Phone: 203-259-7843).

A&W Stock Repair and Refinishing

Seen nearby is a before-and-after example of A&W's stock refinishing. (In this instance the checkering was also recut.) The obvious quality speaks for itself.

A & W sent us the stock seen in the photo—one side refinished, one side not. After seeing the stock a local shooter sent his own Browning A-5 stocks (oil-soaked and 40 years old) to this outfit. The results were super, every bit as good as what you see here. A&W can work in oil (extra charge) or high gloss, the choice is yours. Here are their prices:

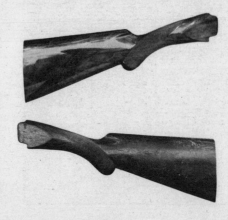

Refinish Average Shotgun or Rifle Stock.......................$45
Refinish Average Shotgun or Rifle Forearm....................$23
Refinish Average Full Rifle Stock..................$90
Fit Recoil Pad...............$25
Rechecker Average Stock $24
Rechecker Average Forearm . .$24

For more details, write: A&W Repair, 2930 Schneider Dr., Arnold, MO 63010 (Phone: 314-287-3725).

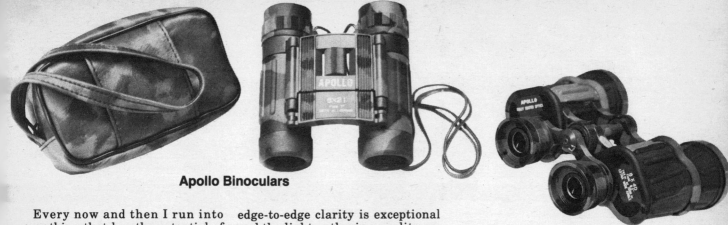

Apollo Binoculars

Every now and then I run into something that has the potential of qualifying for the "Best-Buy-of-the-Year" award.

About 2 days ago I was asked to stop by our local sporting goods store to "take a look at some super binoculars." I stopped, I looked, I was amazed at the price and the quality.

Apollo Optics, a division of the Senno Corporation, is offering camo-rubber armored 8x21 pocket-sized binoculars. They weigh in at 10½ ounces, come with a vinyl (camo) carrying case and nylon neck cord. The edge-to-edge clarity is exceptional and the light gathering quality superb. They sell for a suggested retail price of $134.95—our local store was selling them for $98.50!

Also seen nearby is a set of conventional 8x40 binoculars (also camo-rubber armored) that carry a suggested retail price of $99.95—our local shop was moving them for $74.50!

Considering the product excellence and prices, I think the Apollo line of optics will be around for a while.

For more information, write: Apollo Optics, E. 505 Third Ave., Spokane, WA 99220 (Phone: 800-541-5689).

Dan's Whetstones

When I attended this year's SHOT Show I ran across an outfit that was offering a nice line of Arkansas whetstones.

The story could easily end right here, because the proliferation of firms selling hard, soft and god-knows-what grade of Arkansas stones has been overwhelming in recent years. I started to walk right by the

New Shepherd Rifle Scope

This one is unique. All wrapped up in one beautifully built 4x9 variable are the following features: bullet drop compensation, range finding and a built-in collimating system that lets you know if the windage and/or elevation has been moved, and how to correct it.

There are even more features, and I could expand upon the characteristics of the features mentioned above. The problem is the amount of space. I will say, however, that the Shepherd product is *impressive*. I honestly believe that this scope will find an enthusiastic following in the months and years to come. It's the only scope I've ever seen that had a potentially higher I.Q. than the guy who stuck his eye behind one!

The Shepherd scope possesses system after system. It's beautiful. For price and more information, write: Shepherd Scope, Ltd., RR #1, P. O. Box 23, Waterloo, NE 68069 (Phone: 800-228-3527).

Dan's Whetstones booth when something caught my eye. Seen nearby is what stopped me in my tracks: sets of hard and soft *"Arkansas Sticks."*.

As you can see, this is a takeoff on the familiar ceramic-stick routine. The only difference is that the Arkansas Sticks are better because they're faster. They're made for hunters who *use* their knives. (They are not made for the beautiful folks who *must* have a sharp paring knife complete with Gucci sheath.) *This product works*.

Price is $10 for soft Arkansas and $16 for the black, hard Arkansas.

For more information write: Dan's Whetstones, Rt. 2, Box 619, Royal, AR 71968.

Zeiss 30x Spotting Scope

You won't find many 30x spotting scopes selling for a hefty $730. You also won't get the quality and engineering Zeiss is known for.

This spotting scope is truly for the hunter who wants the best-quality spotting scope that money can buy. What's amazing is the over-all length of 8.8 inches and a weight of 35.3 ounces. (If you're familiar with the subject of spotting scopes, you know that this one is extremely small and reasonable in weight.) The compact nature of the product is a result of mirror-lens technology.

Image quality, brightness and resolution are superb. The objective lens is a full 60mm. For more information write: Carl Zeiss, Inc., Consumer Optics Div., 1015 Commerce St., Petersburg, VA 23803.

Bausch & Lomb

Bausch & Lomb has wisely moved a pair of riflescopes into the Bushnell line of optics.

Like the rest of the B&L line, the new fixed 4x and 3x9 variable scopes possess superb resolution, brightness and edge-to-edge clarity. Both scopes feature a 40mm objective bell and a rather large ocular cell. I'm impressed with the general ruggedness of the 4x we received for testing.

If a good warranty puts you in a buying frame of mind, you better grab your wallet fast—these scopes carry a 25-year limited warranty! The 3x9 sells for about $340, while the straight 4x (seen nearby) goes for a nickel shy of $220.

For more information, write: Bushnell, 2828 E. Foothill Blvd., Pasadena, CA 91107 (Phone: 213-577-1500).

Remington Ammunition Recall

If you've bought any 12-gauge Remington slugs in the past 12 months, we ask you to read the following notice from Remington:

Remington Arms Co., Inc., has announced the recall of defective Remington 12-gauge rifled slug shotshells manufactured in the summer of 1982.

A small quantity of these shotshells were found to have been loaded with insufficient powder with the result that the slugs could lodge in barrels. Tests by Remington have shown that use of this ammunition can result in gun damage and could present a hazard to the shooter.

The 12-gauge, rifled slug, Remington Shotshells covered by the recall have the following markings on the package:

Product:	12-gauge rifled slugs
Index Number:	Remington SP12RS-5PK Slugger 12-gauge 2¾" 1 oz. HPRS 5 Hollow Point Rifled Slugs (on end flap)
Lot Number:	AT01H218 (on inside of end flap)

The company said it is informing wholesalers and dealers to withhold from sale all Remington 12-gauge rifled slug shotshells in their inventories which bear this lot number. Remington representatives will make arrangements for the return of these shotshells.

Consumers who have purchased Remington 12-gauge rifled slug shotshells in boxes so marked should return them to Remington for prompt, free replacement. They should be sent collect via United Parcel Service to:

Remington Arms Company, Inc., Attn.: R. H. Potter, 939 Barnum Ave., P.O. Box #1939, Bridgeport, CT 06601.

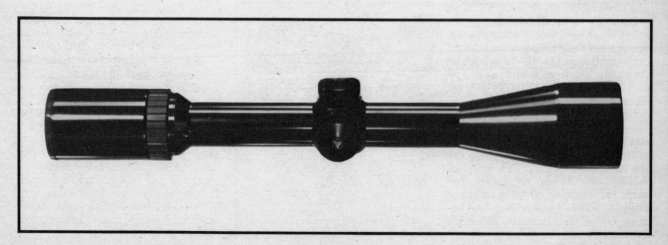

Buck Gun Oil

The folks at Buck Knives have long recognized that their product is used by shooters. Given this, it's not hard to see why they might want to extend their product line a bit.

Buck Gun Oil (with Teflon) cleans, preserves and lubricates. Frankly, I like the plastic packaging, complete with flip-up pour spout. Unlike most aerosols, you can direct the flow and amount of oil and not end up soaking everything in sight. Gun oils with a Teflon additive are also useful in the clean-up department. What I mean is that they generally make bore cleaning a snap, provided you gave the bore of your shotgun, rifle or pistol a *light* coating of that lubricant prior to shooting. In my experience this is especially evident in shotgun barrels.

The suggested retail price is $2.50 per each 3-ounce bottle. For more information write: Buck Knives, P. O. Box 1267, El Cajon, CA 92022 (phone: 714-449-1100).

Baker Jumbo Seat Climber and Pro Hunter Tree Stand

Archers and riflemen alike have come to recognize the Baker Tree Stand as one of the best things to ever happen to the sport of deer hunting.

Shown here is Baker's Jumbo Seat Climber and the Pro Hunter Tree Stand. The Jumbo Seat Climber is designed for trees up to 18 inches in diameter and can be folded flat for backpacking. The seat board weighs 8½ pounds and measures ¾x6x19½ inches, providing plenty of seating space. The Pro Hunter tree stand is sturdy, rugged and reliable—it weighs in at a portable 19 pounds.

The Jumbo Seat Climber sells for $54.95; the Pro Hunter Tree Stand sells for $142.95. For more information write Baker Manufacturing, 428 St. Augustine Rd., P. O. Box 1003, Valdosta, GA 31601 (phone: 912-244-0648).

Kimber's Super America Bolt Action Rifle

During the past five years, Kimber of Oregon has gained a reputation as a maker of some of the finest rimfire and small caliber centerfire rifles ever seen.

To my eye, the Kimber Model 82 Super America is truly beautiful. It's available in 22 LR, 22 WMR or 22 Hornet. The claro walnut stock is of classic design and carries full coverage checkering, Niedner buttplate and continental cheekpiece.

Standard on the Super America is a set of quick detachable scope mounts which were designed by the renowned custom riflemaker, the late Lenard Brownell. The front mount, as can be seen, is married to a stylish quarter rib.

Lest you think you think it's all "show," just talk to any hunter who has shot a Kimber. Groups of 1-inch at 100 yards are usually the norm, not the exception. Price: 22 LR, $950; 22 WMR, $969; 22 Hornet, $1055. For more information write: Kimber of Oregon, 9039 Jannsen Rd., Clackamas, OR 97015 (phone: 503-656-1704).

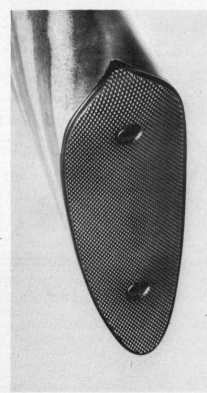

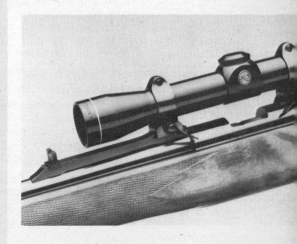

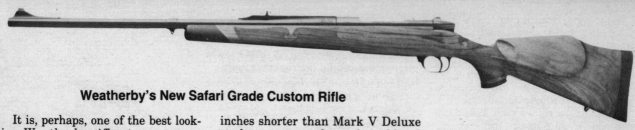

Weatherby's New Safari Grade Custom Rifle

It is, perhaps, one of the best look-ing Weatherby rifles to ever come down the pike. It's also functional, the kind of rifle that fairly screams *hunting*.

Each Safari Rifle features a custom, satin oil finished, French-European walnut stock with rounded ebony for-end tip and pistol grip cap; black pre-sentation recoil pad, with no spacers (at tip, grip or pad) and a checkering pattern that runs 24 lines to the inch. The forend is approximately 1½

inches shorter than Mark V Deluxe stock, to accommodate a barrel-band swivel.

The metal has been given a sub-dued deep-matte finish, and the ac-tion customized (hand honed and da-mascened bolt and follower, check-ered bolt knob and the floorplate en-graved — WEATHERBY SAFARI GRADE).

Each Safari Rifle is available in 300, 340, 378 or 460 Weatherby Mag-num. These rifles are hand craft-

ed and the delivery time on each is 8-10 months. The Safari Rifle is avail-able in either right- or left-hand configuration. Depending on caliber and action style (right or left hand), the prices range from $2203.50 to $2352.50. For more information write Tom Hall, Weatherby, Inc., 2781 Fire-stone Blvd., South Gate, CA 90280 (phone: 213-569-7186).

RCBS Loading Die Popularity

In recent years RCBS has been pro-viding the P.R. arm of the shooting/hunting fraternity with a break down of the past years most popular cali-bers, based on loading die sales.

Recognizing that many hunters handload their own ammo for maxi-mum performance, I felt that many of our readers would like to know where their own pet cartridge "fits in." Here's the top 30 in their order of pop-ularity:

1. 357 Mag/38 Spl	16. 45 Colt
2. 30-06	17. 41 Mag.
3. 44 Mag/44 Spl	18. 30 Carbine
4. 223 Rem.	19. 6mm Rem.
5. 30-30 WCF	20. 380 Auto
6. 45 ACP	21. 7x57
7. 270 Win.	22. 22 Hornet
8. 9mm Luger	23. 257 Roberts
9. 308 Win.	24. 45-70
10. 243 Win.	25. 35 Rem.
11. 7mm Rem. Mag.	26. 220 Swift
12. 22-250	27. 7mm Exp. Rem.
13. 222 Rem.	28. 8x57
14. 25-06	29. 7-08 Rem.
15. 300 Win. Mag.	30. 338 Win. Mag.

For a *free* catalog of RCBS, Speer, CCI and Outers products, write: Speer, P. O. Box 856, Lewiston, ID 83501 (phone: 208-746-2351).

Zeiss Shooting Glasses

Every optics maker in the U.S. sells shooting glasses. But none of those glasses carry the Zeiss trademark. In the opinion of many hunters, the name *Zeiss* stands alone when it comes to quality optics.

Two styles of Zeiss shooting glasses are offered—the Sportsman and the Competition, the former having nar-rower, general-purpose lenses. Each

variety comes with dull-finish alloy frames and is available in four lens colors: gray, green, vermillion and yellow (the latter being especially suited for shooting in low-light situa-tions).

Price: $59.95. For more information write: Carl Zeiss, Inc., Consumer Prod. Div., 1015 Commerce St., Pe-tersburg, VA 23803.

Pachmayr Announces New Hunting School

Hunting schools have become popular with shotgunners in recent years. However, none have carried the Pachmayr logo, nor had the instructional expertise of John Satterwhite, U.S. Olympic shotgun champ and three-time U.S. International Skeet champion.

I must admit, up front, that there is more than a casual degree of exclusivity in what's being offered. All instruction takes place, during a 2½ day (weekend) seminar, at the Coto de Caza resort in Orange County, California. (For those who may not be familiar with the name "Coto de Caza," it should be said that this resort is legendary with Westerners. In short, advertising hype doesn't even come close.)

Each seminar is limited to 15 students; and, Satterwhite will personally tutor each student on the fine points of shotgunning, i.e., Skeet, duck tower, quail walk and more. The price for the entire seminar is $650 per student.

After a brief conversation with Ms. Ashley Baker of Pachmayr, I came to the conclusion that there are even more details to relate; however, space is limited. I strongly suggest you call Ms. Baker, at Pachmayr (phone: 213-748-7271) for more details.

Flashette Bore-Illuminator

Checking the bore of your favorite hunting firearm *before* you head for the field is a safety precaution every hunter should adhere to.

As most of you know, a bore obstruction (in any firearm) can spell disaster, and, yes, limbs and lives have been lost. It will suffice to say the Flashette Bore-Illuminator makes bore inspection an easy chore. What I like about this unit is that you can easily use it, i.e., its physical design is well thought out, as you can see in the nearby photo. The Flashette operates on two AA-size batteries (not included) and the body of the illuminator is made of ABS acrylic—it's durable. Price: $4.95. For more information write: Flashette Company, 4725 S. Kolin Ave., Chicago, IL 60632 (phone: 312-927-1302).

DUX-Bak Water Repellent For Leather

Like a lot of hunters, I've been using silicone leather sprays for a long, long time. However, when it comes to buying this sort of product I've found it wise to shop around.

During one of my local shopping trips I happened to wander into a True Value hardware store that was selling the Dux-Bak brand of leather water repellent for $1.79; this the 10-ounce aerosol can. On the surface this might not strike a chord, however, the suggested retail price is normally $3. Considering the fact that many hunters will go through several cans of silicone spray in a single hunting season, the bargain price I stumbled across was a real find.

I would suggest you do your own shopping and see if you can come up with a price similar to what I encountered. The product is a good one; and, it contains neatsfoot oil which keeps leather from drying out and cracking. For more info write the Whittemore Polish Company, P. O. Box 92846, Milwaukee, WI 53202 (phone: 414-276-6190).

Federal "Spitfire" 22s

Having written up a test report on hyper-velocity rimfires for *Shooting Times,* some time back, I'm particularly happy to be reporting this new product from Federal.

Federal's Spitfires feature distinctive, 33-grain, truncated, semi-wadcutter hollow point bullets that exit a rifle's muzzle at about 1500 fps. This new round is, of course, in the same league as the Remington Yellow Jacket. Personally, I like the truncated bullet shape as it has a long history for reliable feeding in repeating firearms.

What about performance? When you start coupling a truncated, lightweight hollow point bullet with 1500 fps muzzle velocity, you end up with one hell of a rimfire. For squirrels and rabbits you'll have to pick your shots a bit more carefully, to avoid meat damage; but, if you connect, you won't lose your game.

For short range (under 100 yards) varminting, Spitfires should prove ideal with their 20 percent greater muzzle velocity and resulting good expansion. I might also add that I said the following in the *Shooting Times* article a few years ago—it's worth repeating here: The first company to come out with a Standard Velocity, solid point load utilizing this same bullet shape, will win the hearts and minds of target shooters everywhere. The truncated bullet shape, again, makes for reliable feeding in autoloaders and is *accurate.*

For the moment, though, run out and get some Spitfires. They're super! The suggested retail price per 50 rounds is $2.70. For more information write: Federal Cartridge, 2700 Foshay Tower, Minneapolis, MN 55402 (phone: 612-333-8255).

GDHA HUNTING LICENSE DIRECTORY '84

Introduction

It is the intention of these pages to supply you with basic information regarding license fees and other applicable fees incurred by the resident and non-resident hunter alike in each state or province. Because of the complex nature of the regulations from state to state, it is impossible to list all the pertinent data herein. Therefore, it is suggested that you write to the source(s) indicated for each jurisdiction that may be of interest to you.

Every attempt has been made to supply information that was correct and up-to-date at the time this was prepared. However, license fees, posted seasons and other information can and do change. Therefore, it is essential that you write for the most current regulations when giving consideration to hunting in a specific state or province.

We have attempted to list fees for small and big game (usually deer) wherever applicable. When the information was available we have included other big game fees.

Some states offer lowered fees or have different regulations for hunters under 16 or over 65 years of age. Additionally, general sportsman's licenses are available in some states and these may be less expensive than purchasing separate licenses for small game, big game, special permits and so forth.

Some states require the purchase of a small game or general hunting license before allowing the purchase of any specific big game license, tag or permit. Also, in most states, turkey is considered big game. In some areas a special turkey license is required while in others, such as Vermont, the turkey, deer and bear tags are all part of one big game license.

Some states have made licensing extremely easy to understand while the regulations of other states are complex indeed. You will need to review the specific regulations of the state or province of interest. It is not possible for these pages to list the regulations for each in detail. In at least one instance the state-issued information was over 50 pages long. Any attempt to oversimplify such lengthy details would lead only to confusion. For this reason the source or sources of information listed are perhaps the most valuable portion of this synopsis.

The non-resident will also find the listings of available big game helpful in obtaining information on hunting the animals that are of particular interest to him.

Finally, keep in mind that our comments are necessarily geared to the amount and type of information supplied by each state or province as a result of our questionnaire response. Some states and provinces, most notably Quebec, go to great lengths to supply information in detail about hunting. Others have a rather poor approach. In some cases it took quite a bit of coaxing to obtain even meager information. Obviously, skimpy information does not necessarily affect the quality of hunting one may expect to find. It will be up to you to insure that you obtain as much information as possible prior to your hunt.

Many states offer special archery and muzzle-loading licenses for big game in addition to the standard firearms licenses.

The states are grouped by geographic regions beginning in the Northeast and concluding in the West.

New England States

Maine

Current small game and big game licenses cost residents $10 each while non-residents pay $36 and $66 respectively. The license year runs from the beginning of January to the end of December.

There will be a price increase for 1984 licenses, but the amount has not as yet been determined at this writing. A pheasant stamp sells for $5.25. As with most states a number of combination or specialty licenses do exist. In addition to non-resident licenses there are also alien licenses (non-U.S. citizens). For more details contact the:

**Inland Fisheries & Wildlife
Licensing - 284 State Street
State House Station 41
Augusta, ME 04333**

Maine is a large state and non-residents unfamiliar with this state would do best to hunt the central coastal section for deer. This area is mostly farm and woodland cover with a high density of deer. Some excellent bear hunting can be had in the area surrounding the town of Patton (on Route 11). Over 37,000 deer were killed in Maine during the 1980 season giving one hunter, in slightly more than six, vension for the freezer.

New Hampshire

The residents of New Hampshire pay $11.25 for all hunting privileges plus $5 for a turkey permit and $10 for a pheasant stamp. Non-residents pay $31 for small game and $59 for big game privileges. The license year is January 1st to December 31st.

New Hampshire is considering the adoption of a state waterfowl stamp at $4 per year. For additional information contact:

**New Hampshire Fish & Game Dept.
34 Bridge St.
Concord, NH 03301**

New Hampshire splits the state into two separate hunting zones. An antlerless deer season may again be held in the southern zone.

Vermont

Residents pay $7 for an all-inclusive hunting license which includes small game, deer, bear and turkey. Non-residents spend $55 for the same license. A non-resident small-game-only license is available for $27. The license year runs from January 1st to December 31st.

1984 fees may be raised. A bill to do so is now being considered by the Vermont legislature. For detailed information write to:

**Information & Education Section
Vermont Fish & Game Dept.
Montpelier, VT 05602**

Antlerless deer permits are available to landowners only, including non-residents who do not post their land. Vermont offers some truly fine whitetail deer and turkey hunting. It also allows Sunday hunting, a relative rarity in New England.

It is not uncommon for 25,000 or more deer to be harvested annually in Vermont. The biggest deer are killed in the north but the greatest harvest occurs in the southern portion of the state.

Massachusetts

Residents pay $12.50 each for small and big game hunting licenses. The non-resident pays $23.50 and $48.50 for the same licenses. The license year is from January 1st to December 31st.

A Massachusetts waterfowl stamp sells for $1.25 while anterless deer, bear and wild turkey permits are an additional $5 each. Specific information can be obtained from the following:

**Massachusetts Div. of Fisheries &
  Wildlife
Leverett Saltonstall Building
Government Center
100 Cambridge St.
Boston, MA 02202**

or

**Division of Fisheries & Wildlife
Field Headquarters
Route 135
Westboro, MA 01581**

Massachusetts does not allow rifle hunting of deer — the legal means of harvesting is a shotgun. Buck-only are allowed to be taken, and there is no Sunday hunting. The western counties of Berkshire, Franklin, Hampden and Hampshire offer the best deer hunting.

Rhode Island

Residents pay $6.50 and $7.50 for small and big game licenses. Non-residents are charged $15.50 and $20 for the same privileges. License year runs from the first day of March to the last day of February. The small game license is a prerequisite for obtaining a big game license. For detailed information:

**Rhode Island Division of Fish & Wildlife
Group Center
Wakefield, RI 02879**

Licenses are issued by the:
**Rhode Island Division of Enforcement
83 Park St.
Providence, RI 02803**

Shotguns and bows are the only legal methods for deer hunting in this small state.

Connecticut

Residents pay $9 for the basic firearms hunting license while non-residents pay $27. Turkey permits are available at $10 each. Deer permits are also $10. Non-resident deer permits sell for $30 each.

Connecticut requires very early spring deadlines for most turkey and deer permits. Those hunters who fail to meet the required license-purchase deadlines are ineligible to hunt.

The license year runs from January 1 to December 31. For specific details write for a copy of the Abstract of Hunting, Trapping and Sport Fishing Laws and Regulations. The deer and turkey hunting field guide is part of this publication. Write to:

**Dept. of Environmental Protection
Wildlife Unit
State Office Building
Hartford, CT 06106**

A new regulation requring the use of pheasant tags has been enacted. The tags (10 of them) sell for $5. All deer, turkey and pheasant tags must be obtained directly from the Department of Environmental Protection.

Sunday hunting may become a reality for the 1984 deer season.

Mid-Atlantic States

New York

Residents pay $8.50 for a hunting (small game) license and $8.50 for a big game license. A non-resident pays $35.50 and $55.50 for the same rights. License year is October 1st to September 30th.

A number of combination or sportsman's licenses are available at a cost savings.

Deer, bear and turkey are available to the big game hunter. For specific information write to:

**N.Y. State Dept. of Environmental
  Conservation
50 Wolf Road
Albany, NY 12233**

New York offers a great number of informative booklets. Order the ones of interest to you. They include:
1. "Annual Big Game Guide"
2. "Deer Sections of New York State"
3. "Application Booklet for Deer Management Permit System" (antlerless deer permits)
4. "I Love N.Y. Small Game Hunting"
5. "I Love N.Y. Big Game Hunting"
6. "Guide to Outdoor Recreation in N.Y. State"
7. "Use of N.Y. State Public Forest Lands"

The densest deer populations occur in the southern tier, Catskill Mountains and the Taconic highlands.

Pennsylvania

Residents pay $8.25 for a combination big and small game license while non-residents spend $60.50 for the same privileges. The license year runs from September 1 to August 31.

Special archery licenses sell for $2.20 to residents and non-residents alike. Muzzle-loading permits are $3.25. Residents pay $5 for a bear tag and non-residents spend $15. Additional information can be obtained from:

Pennsylvania Game Commission
P.O. Box 1567
Harrisburg, PA 17105-1567

Antlerless deer permits are available within specific time-frames. It is not uncommon for the deer harvest in Pennsylvania to exceed 120,000 annually. The bear season has been restricted to a 1-day hunt in recent years.

New Jersey

A combination small and big game license costs residents $16.75 and non-residents $55.50. The license year is January 1st to December 31st.

A pheasant stamp is required on all wildlife management areas and sells for $15. A short term non-resident small game license is available. For more information contact:

New Jersey Div. of Fish, Game & Wildlife
363 Pennington Ave.
C.N. 400
Trenton, NJ 08625

The non-resident sportsman will find the northern half of New Jersey extremely difficult to hunt due to the overwhelming amount of posted land. The southern half of the state is also heavily posted by landowners. However, those landowners frequently respond positively to requests to hunt their land from responsible parties.

Delaware

Residents pay $5.20 for a basic hunting license while non-residents must ante up $40.25. The state waterfowl stamp sells for $5. Information can be obtained from:

Division of Fish and Wildlife
P.O. Box 1401
Dover, DE 19901

The best deer hunting in Delaware is in Kent and Sussex counties. A large amount of state land is available for hunting. In order of excellence these include the following areas: Norman G. Wilder; Little Creek; Milford Neck; Blackiston; Woodland Beach; Blackbird State Forest. Approximately 1700 deer are taken annually in Delaware.

Maryland

A resident pays $10 for a basic hunting license and an additional $5.50 for a deer tag. Non-residents pay $45 or the reciprocal rate charged by their home state for a small game license. The deer tag fee is also $5.50 for non-residents.

The license year runs from August 1st to July 31st. A state waterfowl stamp sells for $3. Licenses can be obtained from:

Division of Licensing and Consumer Services
580 Taylor Ave.
Annapolis, MD 21401

For general information write to:
Maryland Wildlife Administration
580 Taylor Ave.
Annapolis, Maryland 21401

Dorchester, Allegany, Worchester and Garret counties usually produce the greatest number of deer.

Sitka deer are also hunted in parts of Maryland. Over 550 sitka's were harvested in 1981 in Dorchester county.

West Virginia

Residents pay $8 for a hunting license. Non-residents pay $50 and are not allowed to take bear with firearms. A national forest stamp is applicable and costs $1.

Antlerless deer may be taken by residents possessing the required $8 stamp. Bear stamps are $4 and a boar permit, for residents only, sells for $5.

The license year is January 1 to December 31. An issuing fee of 50¢ is charged when purchasing licenses or stamps. For licenses write to:

Dept. of Natural Resources
Hunting & Fishing License Section
1800 Washington St. East
Charleston, WV 25305

For general information write to:
Dept. of Natural Resources
Division of Wildlife Resources
Room 812
1800 Washington St. East
Charleston, WV 25305

The best area for deer hunting is the northern half of the state. Over 50,000 deer are usually harvested each season.

——————Southeastern States——————

Virginia

Residents spend $7.50 each for big game or small game licenses. Non-residents pay $30 each for these same licenses. Also, a $2 National Forest stamp may be required. The license year runs from July 1 to June 30. For more information write to:

Commission Game & Inland Fisheries
P.O. Box 11104
Richmond, VA 23230

Virginia is divided into 13 different deer hunting areas and one should be sure to *carefully* review the annual game law summary before hunting. Antlerless deer are hunted to a rather large extent.

The best counties for deer hunting are perhaps Southhampton and York, but access to available land is severely limited. Public access to deer hunting is good in the George Washington and Jefferson National forests. The average annual harvest of deer is approximately 75,000.

North Carolina

Residents pay $4.50 for a county or $9.50 for a state small game license. Non-residents pay $31 for a season license. The license year is July 1 to June 30. The small game license is a prerequisite for obtaining a big game tag for which residents pay $4.50 and non-residents pay $18.50. An annual state game land license sells for $8.

In addition to deer there are bear, wild turkey and wild boar available to the big game hunter.

A resident may also obtain a Lifetime Sportsman's license for $300 or a Lifetime Hunting license for $150. For specific information contact:

North Carolina Wildlife Resources Comm.
512 North Salisbury St.
Archdale Building
Raleigh, NC 27611

For additional information:
Travel and Tourism Division
N.C. Dept. of Commerce
Raleigh, NC 27611

South Carolina

Residents pay $9.50 for a statewide hunting license or $3.50 for a county (of residence) license. A state duck stamp is $5.50 and a resident game management area permit is $10.25.

The non-resident pays $46.50 for his hunting license, $25.50 for a big game permit and $25.25 for a game management area permit.

The license year runs from July 1 to June 30. For specific details write to:

South Carolina Wildlife & Marine Resources
P.O. Box 167
Columbia, SC 29202

Short term non-resident licenses are available to the non-resident for either a 3- or 10-day period. Hunting seasons are set individually for each of the 11 different state game zones. The deer herd is large enough to permit a no-limit bag on antlered deer in some areas. Over 40,000 deer are taken each year in South Carolina.

Turkey hunting is also available to residents and non-residents alike.

Georgia

Residents pay $6.50 for a small game license and $5.50 for a deer permit. A nonresident pays $36 for either license with a reduced rate, short-period small game license being available.

A wildlife management area stamp at $10.25 is applicable. License year is January 1 to December 31. Additional information is available by writing to:

Dept. of Natural Resources
Game Management — Room 713
270 Washington St., S.W.
Atlanta, GA 30334

Georgia's three-deer-limit mandates that at least one deer taken must be antlerless. The best deer hunting areas are the lower Piedmont and the upper coastal plain. The deer harvest per season frequently exceeds 70,000. A number of Boone and Crockett records have been taken in Georgia. This state's fine deer hunting is attributable, in large extent, to very good deer herd management.

Florida

Residents pay $4.50 for a county general hunting license or $11.50 for a state-wide license. A non-resident pays $50.50 for hunting privileges. A short term license is available to non-residents.

A wildlife management area fee of $10 and a state duck stamp fee of $3.25 are applicable. The license year runs from July 1 to June 30. Specific details can be obtained from:

Florida Game & Fresh Water Fish Commission
620 South Meridian St.
Tallahassee, FL 32301

The best deer hunting in Florida is in the central northeast and northwest regions of the state. Antlerless deer hunting is available to landowners with more than 150 acres. Bear may be taken only in two northeast counties at the time of this writing.

──────South Central States──────

Kentucky

A statewide hunting license sells for $7.50 to residents and $40 to non-residents. Deer permits are $11.50 for residents and non-residents alike and turkey permits are $6.50. The basic hunting license is required in order to obtain deer and turkey permits.

Two deer permits may be purchased and filled. For specific details write to:

Kentucky Dept. of Fish & Wildlife Resources
Wildlife Division
1 Game Farm Road
Frankfort, KY 40601

Antlerless deer may be taken in certain counties during a brief season — usually only 1-day long. The best deer hunting occurs west of Interstate 75 to the Missouri state line. The annual harvest is usually about 16,000 deer.

Tennessee

Residents pay $10.50 each for small and big game licenses. Non-residents pay $30.50 and $70.50 respectively for the same hunting rights. A short term non-resident license is available at a reduced rate. The license year runs from March 1st to the last day of February.

A wildlife management area permit is required of all those using these areas. The permit is $8.50 for small game and $10.50 for big game.

Hunting licenses for big game are required for each type of weapon used, i.e., rifle, bow or muzzleloader. The licenses issuing agency is:

Tennessee Wildlife Resources Agency
P.O. Box 40747
Nashville, TN 37204

Additional information:
Ms. Paulette Hooper
Information Section
Tennessee Wildlife Resources Agency
P.O. Box 40747
Nashville, TN 37204

Alabama

Resident license fees for combination small and big game are $5 for county and $10 for statewide. A state waterfowl stamp sells for $5.

Non-resident fees can vary as reciprocal agreements have been made with Tennessee, Mississippi, Florida, Georgia and Louisianna. Residents of states not having a reciprocal agreement with Alabama will pay $175 for an all-game license. For specific information contact:

D & E Section
Dept. of Conservation & Water Resources
64 N. Union St.
Montgomery, AL 36130

Alabama's one-per-day limit on deer makes it possible for a hunter to enjoy deer hunting in a manner not generally available. Special antlerless deer seasons are also available.

Turkey hunting is permitted and this state offers some very fine hunting for a wide variety of game.

Mississippi

A resident will pay $6 for a small game license or $25 for a Sportsman's license. Non-residents pay $60 for an all-game license or $30 for a small game license. Other fees are

applicable and a state waterfowl stamp is $2. License year runs from July 1 to June 30.

Costs for non-resident licenses shown are minimum with actual fees equal to the minimum of the fees charged by the state of residence — in other words, fees are reciprocal or minimum base, whichever is higher. Details can be obtained from:

Mississippi Dept. of Wildlife Conservation
P.O. Box 451
Jackson, MS 39205

Over 200,000 deer were taken during a recent hunting season. Considering the size of Mississippi this number makes the state prime deer hunting country. A one-antlered-deer and one-antlerless-deer per day limit has not caused any decline in Mississippi's deer herd.

Arkansas

A resident small game license sells for $10.50 while the big game fee is $17.75. Non-residents pay $38.50 and $115 for the respective privileges. The license year begins July 1 and ends June 30.

A number of license variations do exist and turkey hunting is available. For specific details contact:

Arkansas Game & Fish Commission
#2 Natural Resources Dr.
Little Rock, AR 72205

The best areas for deer hunting appear to be the wildlife management areas, the national forest and the southern and western parts of the state. Harvests of 40,000 deer (or more) are not uncommon.

Louisianna

Residents pay $5 for the basic hunting license and another $5 for a big game hunting license which includes deer, turkey and bear. Non-residents pay $25 and $20 respectively for the same hunting rights. The license year runs from July 1 to June 30. For complete details write to:

Louisianna Dept. Wildlife and Fisheries
P.O. Box 15570
Baton Rouge, LA 70895

The chambers of commerce in the larger communities can often supply additional information on local hunting and accommodations.

The legal limit is one deer per day, offering a fine opportunity for the serious hunter to gain invaluable experience. Under certain conditions antlerless deer may be legal quarry. Seasons are broken down individually into six different areas. A copy of the Louisianna Hunting, Fishing and Motorboat Regulations will explain all the various laws in detail.

The best areas for public hunting are in the parishes of Clarborne, Bienville, De Soto, Red River, Natchitoches, Winn, Vernon and the southern portions of La Salle and Catahoula.

──────North Central States──────

Michigan
The resident will spend $7.25 for a small game license and $9.75 for deer hunting fees. This latter price tag can go to $28.25 if the resident wishes to hunt bear and turkey in addition to deer.

The non-resident pays $35.25 for a small game license and $75.25 to $195.75 for big game fees. The license year runs from April 1st to March 31st.

Public access stamp and the annual park permit add up to another $11 when applicable. For more details contact:

Michigan Dept. of Natural Resources
Information Service Center
Box 30028
Lansing, MI 48909

Additional information:
Michigan Travel Bureau
Box 30226
Lansing, MI 48909

Ohio
A small game license sells for $7.75 to residents and a deer and turkey license is $10.75. Non-residents pay $30.75 for the basic small game license and an additional $10.75 for a deer and turkey permit.

A wetlands habitat stamp is applicable at $5.75. The small game license is a prerequisite to obtaining big game tags. The license year is September 1 to August 31. For additional license information contact:

Ohio Division of Wildlife
Fountain Square
Columbus, OH 43224

For a copy of the Ohio regulations write:
Ohio Dept. of Natural Resources
Publications Sections
Fountain Square
Columbus, OH 43224

Antlerless deer permits are available to residents and non-residents on a reciprocal basis. Rifles are not legal for deer in Ohio. Shotguns and muzzle-loading rifles are permitted.

Indiana
Residents pay $6 and $10 respectively for small game and deer licenses. A resident turkey (big game) license may be purchased for $10. Non-residents pay $37 for small game licenses and a deer license is $75. Non-residents are not permitted to hunt turkey. License year runs from March 1 to the

last day of February.

A game bird habitat stamp is required at a cost of $3. For additional information contact:

Dept. of Natural Resources
Division of Fish & Wildlife
607 State Office Building
Indianapolis, IN 46204

Special antlerless deer hunts are held in specific areas. Consult the annual deer hunting guide for particulars. The total deer harvest is usually near 20,000 deer annually.

Illinois
The small game fee is $7.50 and deer tags are $15 for residents. The visitor will pay from $15.75 to $100.75 for small game privileges. Non-resident deer tag fees are reciprocal. If your home state does not allow non-resident big game hunting then you will pay a minimum license fee of $15 and an additional $15 for a permit to hunt the county your license is issued for. The license year runs from April 1st to March 31st. Information is available from:

Dept. of Conservation (License issuing)
Room 210
Lincoln Tower Plaza
524 So. 2nd St.
Springfield, IL 62706

Dept. of Conservation
Division of Fish & Wildlife
600 North Grand Ave. West
Springfield, IL 62706

Approximately 20,000 deer are taken annually in this state.

Wisconsin
An anticipated price increase will take effect in 1984. Current prices are $6.50 for resident small game and $11 for resident deer licenses. Non-residents pay $60.50 and $80.50 for the same privileges. License year is September 1 to August 31.

Short term licenses are available for the non-resident. For more specific information write to:

Wisconsin Dept. of Natural Resources
Box 7924
Madison, WI 53707

For additional hunting information:
Wisconsin Dept. of Natural Resources
Wildlife Management
Box 7921
Madison, WI 53707

Annual harvests of 160,000 or more deer are not uncommon in this state. Antlerless deer hunting is permitted in certain areas.

Poor landowner tolerance of hunters prevails in the southern and central portions of the state. Ask before you go! Burnett and

Polk counties in the north have a good deal of county forest land open to public hunting.

Minnesota
A small game resident license sells for $11 and a deer tag is $15. Non-residents pay $37 and $75 respectively. License year runs from March 1st to the end of February.

Bear tags by drawing are available to residents at $15 and to non-residents at $100. A state duck stamp is required for waterfowl ($3). A non-resident fee of $100 is charged for raccoon, fox, bobcat, lynx and coyote. For additional information write to:

Dept. of Natural Resources
License Center
625 North Robert St.
St. Paul, MN 55101

Approximately 45 percent of Minnesota's deer hunters fill their tags each year resulting in a harvest of over 75,000 deer. Antlerless deer permits are readily available.

Iowa
Small game fees are $6 and $35 for residents and non-residents respectively. Residents pay $15 for a deer or turkey permit. A state duck stamp sells for $5.

No non-resident big game hunting is allowed. Additionally, non-residents are required to purchase a pheasant or raccoon stamp as applicable. A wildlife habitat stamp is required for all hunters ($3). License year is January 1 to December 31.

Conservation Commission
Wallace State Office Building
Des Moines, IA 50319

Best areas for deer seem to be the southern sections of the state. About 20,000 to 21,000 deer are harvested annually.

Missouri
Resident small game licenses sell for $6 with deer and turkey tags going for $8 each. A non-resident pays $25.50 for small game and $50.50 each for deer and turkey tags.

A state waterfowl stamp is required at $3. License year is January 1st to December 31st. It should be noted that separate turkey licenses are required for the spring and fall. For additional information write to:

Missouri Dept. of Conservation
P.O. Box 180
Jefferson City, MO 65102

Information also available from:
Missouri Division of Tourism
308 East High St.
Jefferson City, MO 65101

Approximately 50,000 deer are harvested annually with most coming from game management areas, 4, 5, 10, 12 and 20.

Plains States

North Dakota

Residents pay $9 for small game and $19 for big game licenses. Residents can also obtain a furbearer license for $7. Non-residents will pay $53 for small game and $101 for big game licenses. License year runs from January 1st to December 31st. For specific information write to:

North Dakota Game & Fish Dept.
2121 Lovett Ave.
Bismark, ND 58505

South Dakota

Residents will spend $13 to hunt small game and from $6 to $250 for the various big game permits. Non-residents spend $2 for the general hunting license and from $10 to $75 each for the applicable non-resident fees. License year is from January 1 to December 31. The actual breakdown of non-resident fees currently in effect is as follows:

general hunting	$2
small game license	50
pheasant restoration stamp	5
deer	75
antelope (archery only)	75
waterfowl	50
turkey	10
predators	25

For specific information write to:
South Dakota Dept. of Game, Fish &
 Parks
Information & Education Office
445 E. Capitol
Pierre, SD 57501

For license applications write:
Licensing
Game, Fish & Parks
1429 East Sioux
Pierre, SD 57501

Nebraska

Nebraska charges residents $8.50 for a small game license, $20 for deer or antelope tags and $15 for a turkey permit. Non-residents pay $4 for a basic hunting license, $100 for antelope and deer tags and $35 for a turkey permit.

The license year runs from January 1st to December 31st. For specific details write to:

Nebraska Game & Parks Commission
P.O. Box 30370
Lincoln, NE 68503

Best areas for deer are the following wildlife management areas: Blue, Buffalo, Elkhorn, Frenchman, Keya Paha, Missouri and Pine Ridge. Both mule deer and whitetails are hunted in Nebraska.

Kansas

Residents pay $8 for a small game license and $25, $20 and $30 for deer, turkey and antelope permits.

While Kansas permits non-residents to hunt small game for $40, it does not allow them to hunt deer, turkey or antelope. The license year is January 1st to December 31st. For additional information contact:

Kansas Fish and Game Commission
Route 2 Box 54A
Pratt, KS 67124

Antlerless deer may be hunted by special permit. About 10,000 deer are harvested each year.

Southwestern States

Oklahoma

Residents will spend $7.50 for a hunting license and non-residents pay $50.75. Turkey tags sell for $5.75 for both groups of hunters. Deer tags are $10.75 and $100.75 for resident and non-resident respectively. The bonus deer tags sell for the same price. Elk tags are $10.75 and $150.75 for the resident and non-resident. A state stamp is required for waterfowl and sells for $4.

A short term non-resident small game license is available. Turkey and elk are also hunted in Oklahoma. Seasons are set by areas and a copy of the annual Oklahoma Hunting Regulations is a must. For this information write to:

Dept. of Wildlife Conservation
P.O. Box 53465
Oklahoma City, OK 73105

Approximately 14,000 deer are harvested annually.

Texas

Texas residents pay $5.25 for a small game or big game license. Non-residents pay $37.75 for a small game fee and $100.75 for a deer tag. The license year is September 1st to August 31st. For specific details write to:

Texas Parks & Wildlife Dept.
4200 Smith School Road
Austin, TX 78744

Antlerless deer permits are available to landowners. The best areas are Edwards Plateau and the southern portion of the state. Very little public land is available. As a result, Texas is a *poor* choice for the non-resident hunter who does *not* have access to private land.

Over 250,000 deer harvested annually.

New Mexico

New Mexico has just put new fees into effect. The resident now pays $18.50 for a deer license and a non-resident pays $145. For $21.50 the resident can obtain a general hunting license which includes small game and deer.

Turkey and bear tags cost the resident $10 while the non-resident must ante up $50 and $75 for these. Cougar, antelope, elk, bighorn sheep, barbary sheep, oryx, ibex, gazelle, javelina and buffalo licenses are also available with prices ranging from $10 to $100 depending upon species. The non-resident will spend from $50 to $500 for each of these tags. Additional deer tags are $3 for the resident and $50 for the non-resident.

The license year runs from April 1 to March 31. License information can be obtained by writing to:

New Mexico Dept. of Game & Fish
Villagra Building
Santa Fe, NM 87501

For other hunting information:
Byron R. Donaldson
Villagra Building
Santa Fe, NM 87501

Mountain States

Montana

Resident licenses range from $2 to $9 while non-resident costs range from $50 to $275 depending upon species being hunted. The license year is from May 1 to April 30.

An additional $2 conservation license is a prerequisite for all licenses. For specific information write:

Fish, Wildlife and Parks
1420 East Sixth
Helena, MT 59620

Big game species also available include elk and antelope. Over 85,000 deer are often taken annually.

Wyoming

Small game licenses sell for $5 to residents and $25 to non-residents. Big game fees vary with species but start with $15 for the resident and $100 for the non-resident. The license year is January 1st to December 31st.

An application fee of $5 is required per each big game species allocated to a limited quota.

Deer, elk, antelope, moose, bighorn sheep, mountain goat, mountain lion and turkey can be hunted in Wyoming. Most big game licenses are on a lottery basis.

For detailed information specify if you are a resident or non-resident and write to:

Wyoming Game & Fish Dept.
5400 Bishop Blvd.
Cheyenne, WY 82002

Approximately 60,000 deer are harvested each year.

Colorado

Residents are charged $5 for a small game license while non-residents pay $25. A resident pays $13 for a deer tag and non-residents pay $90. The license year runs from January 1 to December 31.

Elk, bear, antelope and mountain lion tags are available to the resident at $16, $10, $13 and $25 respectively. Non-residents spend $135, $50, $100, and $150 for the same tags.

There is a bill pending in the Colorado legislature which will, if passed, raise all the license fees effective January 1, 1984. For more information write:

**Division of Wildlife
Dept. of Natural Resources
6060 Broadway
Denver, CO 80216**

For additional information:
**Colorado Guides & Outfitters Assoc.
Box 78AA
Loma, CO 81524**

The best deer hunting areas are the Eagle area, Uncompaghre Plateau, sage brush country north and northwest of Craig, Grand Mesa, White River National Forest and the upper reaches of the Yampa River drainage (Oak Creek to headwaters).

Better than 50,000 deer are harvested during most seasons.

Idaho

Residents will spend $6.50 for a general game license. Deer tags are $6.50, elk are $12.50, mountain lion are $10.50, bear are $6.50 and turkey are $6.50. The license year runs January 1st to December 31st. Special additional fees apply to controlled hunts for deer, elk, moose, antelope, bighorn sheep and mountain goat.

Non-residents pay $75.50 for a game license and $50.50 for a deer tag. Non-resident elk tags are $150.50, mountain lion are $50.50, bear are $25.50 and turkey are $12.50. Additional fees are applied to controlled hunts. Quotas are applied to non-resident deer and elk tags.

The basic game license is a prerequisite to obtaining big game tags. For additional information write to:

**Idaho Dept. of Fish & Game
P.O. Box 25
Boise, ID 83707**

A total of more than 40,000 deer are taken annually. Idaho regulations are extensive, and you will need a copy of the annual big game regulations and a copy of the controlled hunt regulations to understand all of the opportunities.

Utah

Residents will pay $8 for a small game license and $10 for a big game license which includes a deer tag. Non-residents pay $30 and $120 for the same hunting privileges. The license year is January 1 to December 31. For details write:

**Bruce Anderson
Information Specialist
Utah Division of Wildlife Resources
1596 West North Temple
Salt Lake City, UT 84116**

Antlerless deer permit applications are accepted during July. The forests of northern Utah have been very productive during recent years. Over 75,000 deer have been taken in seasons past.

Arizona

The fee for a resident small game license is $9.50 and for deer it is $11. Total resident fees for all big game add up to $1032. It is, however, unlikely that one would be able to hunt all the big game available which includes: deer, javelina, bear, mountain lion, antelope, elk, bighorn sheep, turkey, buffalo, and bobcat. A small game (general hunting) license is required to obtain a big game tag.

Non-residents pay $55.50 for a small game license and $75.50 for a big game tag. Total cost of all non-resident big game tags is $1587.50. This includes everything except buffalo. Again, it is not practical to attempt to hunt all big game animals in a given season.

The license year runs from January 1 to December 31. For additional information contact:

**Arizona Game & Fish Dept
P.O. Box 9099
Phoenix, AZ 85023**

Non-residents will want to obtain a copy of the list of Arizona licensed guides.

Nevada

Residents pay $13 for a general hunting license. Reduced fee licenses are available for certain persons. A non-resident pays $75 for a general hunting license. A state duck stamp is $2 and a special swan tag is $5.

Antelope, bighorn sheep, deer, elk, mountian goat and mountain lion tags are available. Residents spend $9 for a deer tag while non-residents pay $75. For additional information write to:

**Nevada Dept. of Wildlife
P.O. Box 10678
Reno, NV 89520**

Washington

State residents pay $10.50 for small game and $10 for a deer tag. Non-residents pay $100 and $10 for the same privileges.

Elk, bear and turkey tags are available to

residents at $15, $10 and $10 respectively. A non-resident is charged $75 for an elk tag.

License year is January 1 to December 31. For additional information contact:

**James R. Carlin
Game License Supervisor
Dept. of Game
600 North Capitol Way
Olympia, WA 98504**

There is only a small amount of non-resident hunting in Washington and no licensed guides are available. About 60,000 deer are harvested annually during a good season along with 10,000 elk and 2,500 bear.

Oregon

Residents pay $8 for a basic license and $4 for a deer tag. Non-residents pay $75 for a basic hunting license and $50 for a deer tag. The license year runs from January 1st to December 31st.

Besides deer, licenses are available for bear and elk. Elk tags are sold for both Roosevelt and Rocky Mountain species. Deer tags are sold for both blacktail and mule deer. Residents pay $5 for a bear tag while non-residents must spend $75. Elk tags sell for $15 to residents and $105 to non-residents. Additional information can be obtained from:

**Oregon Dept. of Fish & Wildlife
P.O. Box 3503
Portland, OR 97208**

Best areas for mule deer seem to be the central and southeast portions of the state. The annual harvest of deer is frequently in excess of 100,000.

California

Residents pay $13.25 and non-residents pay $46.50 for the basic hunting license. A resident will spend $4 for the first deer tag and $10.75 for a second one. Resident bear tags are $5. Non-residents pay $33.25, $79.75 and $81.25 respectively for the same tags. The license year is July 1 to June 30. For specific information write:

**M.E. Foster
License Officer
Dept. of Fish & Game
License Section
1722 J St.
Sacramento, CA 95814**

In addition to deer and bear, antelope and feral pigs can be hunted. California is broken into more than two dozen specific hunting areas and the seasons and bag limits are set according to the specific area. The antelope hunting in specific areas is for residents only. Due to the great number of hunting areas a copy of the annual California Hunting Regulations is a must.

Alaska

Alaska is considered by many to be the last hunting paradise. License year is from January 1st to December 31st. Residents pay $12 for a hunting license. Those residents 60 years or older may not have to purchase a hunting license. Resident fees for musk oxen are from $25 to $500 depending upon the area to be hunted. Brown or grizzly bear tags are $25.

Non-residents pay $60 for a hunting license with the following tag fees:

black bear	$200
brown, grizzly bear	350
bison	350
caribou	300
deer	135
elk	250
mountain goat	250
moose	300
dall sheep	400
walrus	500
wolf	150
wolverine	150
musk ox	1,100

For more details write to:
Dept. of Fish & Game
P.O. Box 3-2000
Juneau, AK 99802

Hawaii

According to the information I received, residents pay $7.50 each for small and big game licenses. Non-resident fees are $15 each. The licensing year is July 1 to June 30. For more details write to:

Dept. of Land & Natural Resources
Div. of Conserv. and Resources
Enforcement
1151 Punchbowl St.
Honolulu, HI 96813

Axis deer and blacktails are the big game of Hawaii. However blacktails are hunted only on Kauai. Axis deer are hunted on both Molokai and Lanai. On Lanai, hunting is permitted on Sundays only. Most of the other hunting for deer is restricted to weekends. The annual harvest is small. For instance in 1981, 214 axis deer and 14 blacktail were taken. Hunting privileges are on a lottery system.

Canada

(License fees expressed in Canadian dollars)

Quebec

Residents pay $6.25 for a small game license, $20 for a caribou tag, $10 for a deer tag, $6.25 for a bear tag and $20 for a moose tag.

Non-resident Canadians pay $25.50 for small game, $175 for caribou, $50 for deer, $25.50 for bear and $125 for moose.

Alien non-residents (*U.S. Citizens*) pay slightly higher fees for certain tags. This in-cludes $250 for a caribou license, $75 for a deer tag and $200 for a moose tag. Anticosti Island deer tags are sold separately.

Quebec publishes an annual summary of regulations for hunting and a listing of Quebec Outfitters — Fish and Game. These are available from:

Gouvernement du Quebec
Ministere du Loisir de la Chasse et de
la Peche
Direction Generale de Frune
150 est., boul. Saint-Cyrille
Quebec, Quebec
Canada G1R 4Y1

Anticosti Island provides some very fine deer hunting and supplies over 40 percent of the annual 7,000 to 8,000 deer harvest.

New Brunswick

The resident fee for a small game license is $2 and non-residents pay $15. Resident deer and bear tags are $10 each. Non-residents pay $50 for a deer tag and $25 for a bear tag. *All non-residents are required to use a guide.* License year is January 1 to December 31. A game bird license is required for grouse. See the annual hunting summary for details. Information can be obtained by writing to:

Fish & Wildlife Branch D.N.R.
P.O. Box (C.P.) 6000
Fredericton, N.B.
Canada E3B 5H1

Antlerless deer may be hunted in New Brunswick. The farm country of the south and the St. John River valley as well as the Tobeque valley are the best hunting areas for deer. During a good season in excess of 20,000 deer are harvested in New Brunswick.

Nova Scotia

Residents spend $10 for a small game license and $15 for a big game license. Non-residents pay $35 and $75 respectively for the same privileges. The license year runs from April 1 to March 31. Specific information can be had from the:

Dept. of Lands & Forests
Box 698
Halifax, Nova Scotia
Canada B3J 2T9

or

Dept. of Tourism
Box 130
Halifax, Nova Scotia
Canada B3J 2M7

Approximately 35,000 deer are taken each year. Antlerless deer are hunted and the northeastern counties provide best hunting.

Ontario

Ontario residents pay $15 to hunt deer and non-residents pay $80. Moose fees are $20 (resident) and $200 (non-resident). Bear tags are $10 for residents and $25 for non-residents.

Small game licenses are $5 for natives and $35 for the visitor. A number of types of small game licenses are available, and the hunter may require more than one.

Export fees are charged for big game. For additional information contact:

Wildlife Branch
Whitney Block, Queen's Park
Toronto, Ontario
Canada M7A 1W3

Some antlerless deer hunting is permitted on a lottery basis. The best deer hunting is in the southern and central portions of the province.

Prince Edward Island

Resident hunting licenses sell for $6 and non-resident licenses for $25. There is no big game hunting on P.E.I. Pheasant, ruffed grouse, Hungarian partridge, snowshoe rabbit, fox and racoon make up the upland game list. A migratory bird season is also held and includes ducks, geese, snipe and woodcock. Additional information may be obtained by writing:

Dept. of Community Affairs
P.O. Box 2000
Charlottetown, P.E.I.
Canada C1A 7N8

Newfoundland (including Labrador)

There is no deer hunting in Newfoundland, but moose, caribou and black bear are hunted. Residents pay $25 for either a moose or caribou tag and $15 for a bear tag. Canadian non-residents pay $250 for a moose permit and $400 for a caribou license. These same non-resident Canadians pay $25 for a bear tag.

Non-residents aliens (*U.S. citizens*) will pay $350 for a moose permit, $600 for a caribou permit and $50 for a bear license.

Rabbit, ptarmigan and grouse licenses are $5 each and $10 each for non-residents. For additional information contact:

Wildlife Division
Bldg. 810, Pleasantville
St. Johns, Newfoundland
Canada A1A 1P9

Manitoba

Deer, black bear and moose are hunted in Manitoba. A resident pays $15, $16 and $10 respectively for licenses. A game bird license is $5 and a wildlife certificate is $3.

Canadian non-residents pay $35 for a game bird license, $80 for deer, $60 for moose, and $50 for black bear.

Alien non-resident *(U.S. citizens)* pay $60 for a game bird license, $100 for a deer permit, $250 for a moose permit and $100 for a bear license. For more information:

Dept. of Natural Resources
1495 St. James St.
Winnipeg, Manitoba
Canada R3H 0W9

and

Dept. of Economic Development &
Tourism
Travel Manitoba
Dept. 3041
Winnipeg, Manitoba
Canada R3C 0V8

Antlerless deer are hunted in Manitoba. Some caribou hunting is done by residents.

Saskatchewan

License types are game birds, pheasant, deer, moose, elk, caribou, bear and antlope. Not all species available to non-residents.

Deer fees are $15, $50 and $100 for residents, Canadian non-residents and alien non-residents *(U.S. citizens)* respectively. Moose fees are $20 for residents and $200 for others. Elk tags are $20 for residents. Woodland caribou fees are $20 for residents, $100 for Canadian non-residents and $200 for alien non-residents *(U.S. citizens)*. Black bear fees are $10, $50 and $100 respectively.

Most other big game licenses, available on a draw basis to residents only, are $20. Additional information may be obtained from:

Dept. of Tourism & Removable
Resources
3211 Albert St.
Regina, Saskatchewan
Canada S4S 5W6

A good number of antlerless deer are among the 40,000-plus deer harvested annually in this province.

Alberta

A wildlife certificate and resource development stamp must be purchased ($11) before obtaining any hunting licenses. License types are many and are cataloged in part as follows:

Additional information available from:
Energy & Natural Resources
Fish & Wildlife Division
8th Floor, South Tower
Petroleum Plaza
9915-108 St.
Edmonton, Alberta
Canada T5K 2C9

British Columbia

Resident fees include $17 for an all-game license plus fees as small as $8 for black bear to as much as $70 for grizzly bear. Canadian non-residents pay $17 for a basic all game license and non-resident aliens *(U.S. citizens)* are charged $93. Non-residents pay from $50 to $320 per big game tag depending upon the species being hunted. The license year runs from April 1 to March 31. Additional information may be obtained by writing:

Fish & Wildlife Branch
Ministry of Environment
Parliment Building
Victoria, B.C.
Canada V8V 1X4

Available species include whitetail deer, mule deer, mountain goat, grizzly and black bear, elk, caribou and moose. Approximately 30,000 deer are harvested annually in British Columbia.

Yukon Territory

Residents pay $5 for a small game license and $10 for a big game license. Non-residents pay $20 for a small game license. Canadian non-residents pay $75 for a big game license and alien non-residents *(U.S. citizens)* pay $150. The license year is April 1 to March 31.

Game hunted includes mountain sheep, moose, grizzly bear, caribou, mountain goat, black bear, wolf, wolverine and coyote. Additional information is available from:

Renewable Resources
Wildlife & Parks Services
Box 2703
Whitehorse, Yukon
Canada Y1A 2C6

		Resident	Non-resident	Alien
	Bear (black)	$10	$ 50	$100
	Bear (grizzly)	20	125	250
	Cougar	20	100	200
ALBERTA	Deer (3 types of licenses)	10	75	150
LICENSE TYPES	Elk (2 types of licenses)	10	100	200
	Moose (2 types of licenses)	10	100	200/100
	Sheep	20	125	250
	Wolf	—	75	100
	Game bird	5	25	50